ARTICLES
OF
FAITH

ARTICLES
OF
FAITH

JAMES E. TALMAGE

Cover painting, *The First Vision* by Gary L. Kapp.

Cover design copyrighted 2003 by Covenant Communications, Inc.

Originally published in 1924

Published by Covenant Communications, Inc.
American Fork, Utah

Printed in China
First Printing: November 2003

10 09 08 07 06 05 04 03   10 9 8 7 6 5 4 3 2 1

ISBN 1-59156-282-1

A STUDY OF THE

ARTICLES OF FAITH

BEING A CONSIDERATION OF THE PRINCIPAL DOCTRINES OF THE
CHURCH OF JESUS CHRIST OF LATTER-DAY SAINTS

BY

JAMES E. TALMAGE
ONE OF THE TWELVE APOSTLES OF THE CHURCH

REVISED AND IN PARTS REWRITTEN

ORIGINAL PUBLISHED BY THE CHURCH OF JESUS CHRIST OF LATTER-DAY SAINTS.
CONTENTS ARE FROM THE 1924 PRINTING.

TABLE OF
CONTENTS

BOOK-TITLES AND ABBREVIATIONS

Used in Footnotes and References

Books of the Holy Bible are designated by the usual contractions.

Books of the Book of Mormon are generally named without abbreviation.

"D&C" indicates the book of Doctrine and Covenants, the divisions of which are Sections and Verses.

"P.of G.P." indicates the Pearl of Great Price, the component books of which are named without abbreviation. In the specification of pages the double column editions are referred to.

"HC" refers to the six volume work, *History of The Church of Jesus Christ of Latter-day Saints,* published by the Church, Salt Lake City, Utah.

1

INTRODUCTORY

THE ARTICLES OF FAITH
OF THE CHURCH OF JESUS CHRIST OF LATTER-DAY SAINTS

1. We believe in God, the Eternal Father, and in His Son, Jesus Christ, and in the Holy Ghost.

2. We believe that men will be punished for their own sins, and not for Adam's transgression.

3. We believe that through the Atonement of Christ, all mankind may be saved, by obedience to the laws and ordinances of the Gospel.

4. We believe that the first principles and ordinances of the Gospel are: first, Faith in the Lord Jesus Christ; second, Repentance; third, Baptism by immersion for the remission of sins; fourth, Laying on of hands for the gift of the Holy Ghost.

5. We believe that a man must be called of God, by prophecy, and by the laying on of hands, by those who are in authority to preach the Gospel and administer in the ordinances thereof.

6. We believe in the same organization that existed in the Primitive Church, viz., apostles, prophets, pastors, teachers, evangelists, etc.

7. We believe in the gift of tongues, prophecy, revelation, visions, healing, interpretation of tongues, etc.

8. We believe the Bible to be the word of God as far as it is translated correctly; we also believe the Book of Mormon to be the word of God.

9. We believe all that God has revealed, all that He does now reveal, and we believe that He will yet reveal many great and important things pertaining to the Kingdom of God.

10. We believe in the literal gathering of Israel and in the restoration of the Ten Tribes; that Zion will be built upon this [the American] continent; that Christ will reign personally upon the earth; and, that the earth will be renewed and receive its paradisiacal glory.

11. We claim the privilege of worshiping Almighty God according to the dictates of our own conscience, and allow all men the same privilege, let them worship how, where, or what they may.

12. We believe in being subject to kings, presidents, rulers, and magistrates, in obeying, honoring, and sustaining the law.

13. We believe in being honest, true, chaste, benevolent, virtuous, and in doing good to all men; indeed, we may say that we follow the admonition of Paul—We believe all things, we hope all things, we have endured many things, and hope to be able to endure all things. If there is anything virtuous, lovely, or of good report or praiseworthy, we seek after these things.
—*Joseph Smith.*

Theology—The word "Theology" is of Greek origin; it comes to us from *Theos,* meaning God, and *logos*—a treatise, or discourse, signifying by derivation, therefore collated knowledge of Deity, or the science that teaches us of God, implying also the relation existing between Him and His creatures. The term is of ancient usage, and may be traced to pagan sources. Plato and Aristotle speak of theology as the doctrine of Deity and divine things.

It has been held by some that theological knowledge is not properly a subject for analytical and otherwise scientific treatment on the part of man; that inasmuch as a true conception of Deity, with which theology has primarily to deal, must necessarily be based upon divine revelation, we can but receive such knowledge as it is graciously given; and that to attempt critical investigation thereof by the fallible powers of human judgment would be to apply as a standard of measurement to the doings of God the utterly inadequate wisdom of man. Many truths are beyond the scope of unaided human reason, and theological facts have been declared to belong to that class. This is true only so far as the same classification is applicable to truths other than theological in the restricted application of the term; for all truth, being eternal, is superior to reason in the sense of being manifest to reason but not a creation of reason. Nevertheless, truths are to be estimated and compared by the exercise of reason.

Importance of Theological Study—In the short span of mortal existence it is impossible for man to explore with thoroughness any considerable part of the vast realm of knowledge. It becomes, therefore, the part of wisdom to direct our efforts to the investigation of the field that promises results of greatest worth. All truth is of value, above price indeed in its place; yet, with respect to their possible application some truths are of incomparably greater worth than others.

A knowledge of the principles of trade is essential to the success of the merchant; an acquaintance with the laws of navigation is demanded of the mariner; familiarity with the relation of soil and crops is indispensable to the farmer; an understanding of the principles of mathematics is necessary to the engineer and the astronomer; so too is a personal knowledge of God essential to the salvation of every human soul that has attained to powers of judgment and discretion. The value of theological knowledge, therefore, ought not to be underrated; it is doubtful if its importance can be overestimated.

Comprehensiveness of Theology—The ultimate boundaries of the science, if boundaries there be, are beyond the capacity of man to survey. Theology deals with Deity, the fountain of knowledge, the source of wisdom; with the proofs of the existence of a Supreme Being, and of other supernatural personalities; with the conditions under which, and the means by which, divine revelation is imparted; with the eternal principles governing the creation of worlds; with the laws of nature in all their varied manifestations. Primarily, theology is the science that deals with God and religion; it presents the facts of observed and revealed truth in orderly array, and indicates the means of their application in the duties of life. Theology then has to do with other facts than those that are specifically called spiritual; its domain is that of truth.

The industrial pursuits that benefit mankind, the arts that please and refine, the sciences that enlarge and exalt the mind—these are but fragments of the great though yet uncompleted volume of truth that has come to earth from a source of eternal and infinite supply. A complete survey of theology, therefore, would embrace all known truths. God has constituted Himself as the great teacher; by personal manifestations or through the ministrations of His appointed servants, He instructs His mortal children. To Adam He introduced the art of agriculture,[a] and demonstrated that of tailoring,[b] to Noah and Nephi He gave instructions in ship-building,[c] Lehi and Nephi were taught of Him in the arts of navigation;[d] and for their guidance on the water, as in their journeyings on land, He prepared for them the Liahona,[e] compass operated by an influence more effective for its purposes than that of terrestrial magnetism; furthermore, Moses received divine instructions in architecture.[f]

Theology and Religion, although related, are not identical. One may be deeply versed in theological lore, and yet be lacking in religious and even in moral character. If theology be theory then religion is practise; if theology be precept religion is example. Each should be the complement of the other; theological knowledge should strengthen religious faith and practise. As accepted by the Latter-day Saints, theology comprises the plan of the Gospel of Jesus Christ in its entirety. Theology as a science has to do with classified or collated knowledge respecting the relationship between God and man, primarily as it appeals to the intellect; while religion includes the application of that knowledge, or genuine belief, to the individual course of life.

The Articles of Faith—Beliefs and prescribed practises of most religious sects are usually set forth in formulated creeds. The Latter-day Saints announce no such creed as a complete code of faith; for they accept the principle of continuous revelation as an essential feature of their belief. Joseph Smith, the first divinely commissioned prophet and the first president of the Church of Jesus Christ in the latter-day, or current, dispensation, set forth as an epitome of the tenets of the

[a] Gen. 2:8; P.of G.P., Moses 3:15.
[b] Gen. 3:21; P.of G.P., Moses 4:27.
[c] Gen. 6:14; 1 Nephi 17:8, 18:1–4.
[d] 1 Nephi 18:12, 21.
[e] 1 Nephi 16:10, 16, 26-30; 18:12, 21; Alma 37:33.
[f] Ex. chaps. 25, 26, 27.

Church the thirteen avowals known as the "Articles of Faith of The Church of Jesus Christ of Latter-day Saints." These include fundamental and characteristic doctrines of the Gospel as taught by this Church; but they are not to be regarded as a complete exposition of belief, for, as stated in Article 9, "We believe all that God has revealed, all that He does now reveal, and we believe that He will yet reveal many great and important things pertaining to the Kingdom of God." From the time of their first promulgation, the Articles of Faith have been accepted by the people as an authoritative exposition; and on October 6, 1890, the Latter-day Saints, in general conference assembled, readopted the Articles as a guide in faith and conduct.[g] As these Articles of Faith present important doctrines of the Church in systematic order, they suggest themselves as a convenient outline for a study of the theology of The Church of Jesus Christ of Latter-day Saints.

The Standard Works of the Church constitute the written authority of the Church in doctrine. Nevertheless, the Church holds itself in readiness to receive additional light and knowledge "pertaining to the Kingdom of God" through divine revelation. We believe that God is as willing today as He ever has been to reveal His mind and will to man, and that He does so through His appointed servants—prophets, seers, and revelators—invested through ordination with the authority of the Holy Priesthood. We rely therefore on the teachings of the living oracles of God as of equal validity with the doctrines of the written word. The works adopted by the vote of the Church as authoritative guides in faith and doctrine are four: the *Bible,* the *Book of Mormon,* the *Doctrine and Covenants,* and the *Pearl of Great Price.*[h] Many books have been and are being published by officers and members of the Church, and such may be sanctioned by the people and the ecclesiastical authorities; but the four publications named are the regularly adopted "Standard Works of the Church." Of the doctrines treated in the authorized standards, the Articles of Faith may be regarded as a fair though but partial summary.

JOSEPH SMITH, THE PROPHET

Joseph Smith, whose name is appended to the Articles of Faith, is the prophet and revelator through whom was restored to earth the Gospel of Jesus Christ, in these the last days, the dispensation of the fulness of times, declared and predicted by prophets in earlier dispensations. The question of this man's divine commission is a challenging one to the world today. If his claims to a divine appointment be false, forming as they do the foundation of the Church in this the last dispensation, the superstructure cannot be stable; if, however, his avowed ordination under the hands of heavenly personages be a fact, one need search no farther for the cause of the phenomenal vitality and continuous development of the restored Church.

The circumstances of the divine dealings with Joseph Smith, the marvelous enlargement of the work instituted by this latter-day prophet, the fulfilment through his instrumentality of many of the momentous predictions of old, and his own prophetic utterances with their literal realizations, will yet be widely acknowledged as proof conclusive of the validity of his ministry.[i] The exalted claims maintained for him and his life's work, the fame that has made his name known for good or evil among most of the civilized nations of the earth, the stability of the religious and social systems that owe their origin as nineteenth century establishments to the ministrations of this man, give to him an individual importance demanding serious and impartial consideration.

[g] See Appendix 1:1.
[h] See Appendix 1:2.
[i] See Appendix 1:3.

His Parentage and Youth—Joseph Smith, the third son and fourth child in a family of ten, was born December 23, 1805, at Sharon, Windsor County, Vermont.[j] He was the son of Joseph and Lucy Mack Smith, a worthy couple, who though in poverty lived happily amid their home scenes of industry and frugality. When the boy Joseph was ten years old, the family left Vermont and settled in the State of New York, first at Palmyra and later at Manchester. At the place last named, the future prophet spent most of his boyhood days. In common with his brothers and sisters he had but little schooling; and for the simple rudiments of an education, which by earnest application he was able to gain, he was mostly indebted to his parents, who followed the rule of devoting a portion of their limited leisure to the teaching of the younger members of the household.

In their religious inclinations the family favored the Presbyterian church; indeed the mother and some of the children joined that sect; but Joseph, while at one time favorably impressed by the Methodists, kept himself free from all sectarian membership, being greatly perplexed over the strife and dissensions manifest among the churches of the time. He had a right to expect that in the Church of Christ there would be unity and harmony; yet he saw among the wrangling sects only confusion. When Joseph was in his fifteenth year the region of his home was visited by a storm of fierce religious excitement, which, beginning with the Methodists, soon became general among all the sects; there were revivals and protracted meetings, and discreditable exhibitions of sectarian rivalry were many and varied. These conditions added much to the distress of the young man earnestly seeking the truth.

His Search and the Result—Here is Joseph's own account of his course of action:

In the midst of this war of words and tumult of opinions, I often said to myself: What is to be done? Who of all these parties is right; or, are they all wrong together? If any one of them be right, which is it, and how shall I know it?

While I was laboring under the extreme difficulties caused by the contests of these parties of religionists, I was one day reading the Epistle of James, first chapter and fifth verse, which reads: *If any of you lack wisdom, let him ask of God, that giveth to all men liberally, and upbraideth not; and it shall be given him.*

Never did any passage of scripture come with more power to the heart of man than this did at this time to mine. It seemed to enter with great force into every feeling of my heart. I reflected on it again and again, knowing that if any person needed wisdom from God, I did; for how to act I did not know, and unless I could get more wisdom than I then had, I would never know; for the teachers of religion of the different sects understood the same passages of scripture so differently as to destroy all confidence in settling the question by an appeal to the Bible.

At length I came to the conclusion that I must either remain in darkness and confusion, or else I must do as James directs, that is, ask of God. I at length came to the determination to "ask of God," concluding that if he gave wisdom to them that lacked wisdom, and would give liberally, and not upbraid, I might venture.

So, in accordance with this, my determination to ask of God, I retired to the woods to make the attempt. It was on the morning of a beautiful, clear day, early in the spring of eighteen hundred and twenty. It was the first time in my life that I had made such an attempt, for amidst all my anxieties I had never as yet made the attempt to pray vocally.

After I had retired to the place where I had previously designed to go, having looked around me, and finding myself alone, I kneeled down and began to offer up the desires of my heart to God. I had scarcely done so, when immediately I was seized upon by some

[j] See Appendix 1:4.

power which entirely overcame me, and had such an astonishing influence over me as to bind my tongue so that I could not speak. Thick darkness gathered around me, and it seemed to me for a time as if I were doomed to sudden destruction.

But, exerting all my powers to call upon God to deliver me out of the power of this enemy which had seized upon me, and at the very moment when I was ready to sink into despair and abandon myself to destruction—not to an imaginary ruin, but to the power of some actual being from the unseen world, who had such marvelous power as I had never before felt in any being—just at this moment of great alarm, I saw a pillar of light exactly over my head, above the brightness of the sun, which descended gradually until it fell upon me.

It no sooner appeared than I found myself delivered from the enemy which held me bound. When the light rested upon me I saw two Personages, whose brightness and glory defy all description, standing above me in the air. One of them spake unto me, calling me by name, and said, pointing to the other—*This is My Beloved Son. Hear Him!*

My object in going to inquire of the Lord was to know which of all the sects was right, that I might know which to join. No sooner, therefore, did I get possession of myself, so as to be able to speak, than I asked the Personages who stood above me in the light, which of all the sects was right—and which I should join.

I was answered that I must join none of them, for they were all wrong; and the Personage who addressed me said that all their creeds were an abomination in his sight; that those professors were all corrupt; that: "they draw near to me with their lips, but their hearts are far from me; they teach for doctrines the commandments of men, having a form of godliness, but they deny the power thereof."[k]

Such knowledge as was communicated in this unprecedented revelation could not be held secret within the breast of the youth. He hesitated not to impart the glorious truth, first to the members of his family, who received his testimony with reverence, and then to the sectarian ministers who had labored so diligently to convert him to their respective creeds. To his surprise, these professed teachers of Christ treated his statements with the utmost contempt, declaring that the days of revelation from God had long since passed; and that the manifestation, if indeed he had received any such at all, was from Satan. Nevertheless, the ministers exerted themselves, with a unity of purpose strangely at variance with their former hostility toward one another, to ridicule the young man, and to denounce his simple though solemn affirmations. The neighborhood was aroused; bitter and vindictive persecution was waged against him and his family; and he was fired upon by a would-be assassin. Through it all he was preserved from bodily injury; and in spite of increasing opposition he remained faithfully steadfast to his testimony of the heavenly visitation.[l] In this condition of trial he continued without further direct manifestation by heavenly beings for three years, expecting but not receiving the additional light and added instructions for which he yearned. He was keenly sensitive of his own frailty and conscious of human weaknesses. He pleaded before the Lord, acknowledging his imperfections and supplicating help.

Angelic Visitations—On the night of September 21, 1823, while praying for forgiveness of sins and for guidance as to his future course, he was blessed with another heavenly manifestation. There appeared in his room a brilliant light, in the midst of which stood a personage clothed in white, and with a countenance of radiant purity. The heavenly visitant announced himself as

[k] P.of G.P., pp. 48, 49; *HC*, vol. 1, p. 4.
[l] See Appendix 1:5.

Moroni, a messenger sent from the presence of God; and he proceeded to instruct the youth as to some of the divine purposes in which his instrumentality would be of great import. The angel said that God had a work for Joseph to do, and that his name "should be had for good and evil among all nations, kindreds, and tongues, or that it should be both good and evil spoken of among all people. He said there was a book deposited, written upon gold plates, giving an account of the former inhabitants of this continent, and the source from whence they sprang. He also said that the fulness of the everlasting Gospel was contained in it, as delivered by the Savior to the ancient inhabitants; Also, that there were two stones in silver bows—and these stones, fastened to a breastplate, constituted what is called the Urim and Thummim—deposited with the plates; and the possession and use of these stones were what constituted 'seers' in ancient or former times; and that God had prepared them for the purpose of translating the book."

The visiting angel, Moroni, then repeated several prophecies which are recorded in the ancient scriptures; some of the quotations were given with variations from the readings in the Bible. Of the words of Malachi the following were given, presenting small but significant variations from the Biblical version: "For behold, the day cometh that shall burn as an oven, and all the proud, yea, and all that do wickedly shall burn as stubble; for they that come shall burn them, saith the Lord of Hosts, that it shall leave them neither root nor branch." Further: "Behold, I will reveal unto you the Priesthood, by the hand of Elijah the prophet, before the coming of the great and dreadful day of the Lord." He also quoted the next verse differently: "And he shall plant in the hearts of the children the promises made to the fathers, and the hearts of the children shall turn to their fathers. If it were not so, the whole earth would be utterly wasted at his coming."[m] Among other scriptures, Moroni cited the prophecies of Isaiah relating to the restoration of scattered Israel, and the promised reign of righteousness on earth,[n] saying that the predictions were about to be fulfilled; also the words of Peter to the Jews, concerning the prophet who Moses said would be raised up, explaining that the prophet referred to was Jesus Christ, and that the day was near at hand when all who rejected the words of the Savior would be cut off from among the people.[o]

Having delivered his message the angel departed, the light in the room seeming to condense about his person and disappearing with him. But during the night he returned twice, and at each visit repeated what he had said at the first, with admonitions to which were added warnings as to the temptations that would assail the youth in the fulfilment of his mission. On the following day Moroni appeared to Joseph again, reciting anew the instructions and cautions of the preceding night, and telling him to acquaint his father with all he had heard and seen. This the boy did, and the father promptly testified that the communications were from God.

Joseph then went to the hill described to him in the vision. He recognized the spot indicated by the angel, and with some labor laid bare a stone box containing the plates and other things spoken of by Moroni. The messenger again stood beside him, and forbade the removal of the contents at that time, saying that four years were to elapse before the plates would be committed to his care, and that it would be his duty to visit the spot at yearly intervals. On the occasion of each of these visits the angel instructed the young man more fully regarding the great work awaiting him.

It is not our present purpose to review in detail the life and ministry of Joseph Smith;[p] what has been said herein respecting the opening scenes of his divinely appointed mission is justified by

[m] See Mal., chap. 4.
[n] See Isa., chap. 11.
[o] See Acts 3:22, 23.
[p] See Appendix 1:6.

the great importance associated with the ushering in of the latter-day or new dispensation of divine providence through his instrumentality. The bringing forth of the plates from their resting-place of centuries, their translation by divine power, and the publication of the record as the Book of Mormon, will receive later attention. It is sufficient to say here that the ancient record has been translated; that the Book of Mormon has been given to the world; and that the volume is accepted as scripture by the Latter-day Saints.

Later Developments: the Martyrdom—In due time The Church of Jesus Christ of Latter-day Saints was established, the Holy Priesthood having been restored through the ordination of Joseph Smith by those who had held the keys of that authority in former dispensations. The organization of the Church as a body corporate was effected on the sixth day of April, A.D., 1830, at Fayette in the State of New York, and the names of but six persons are of record as those of active participants. True, by that time a few times six had identified themselves with the new and unprecedented movement; but as the laws of the State specified six as the required minimum in the incorporation of a religious society only that number formally took part in the legal procedure. And they, save one, were relatively unknown and may be called obscure. The name of Joseph Smith the Prophet had already been heard beyond his home district. He was a subject of rapidly spreading notoriety if not of enviable fame. The Book of Mormon, purporting to be a record of the aboriginal peoples of the western continent, particularly an account of the dealings of God with those peoples, in short the scriptures of what came afterward to be called the New World, had already been translated by him and published. It is in reference to the title-page of that book that the appellation "Mormon," first given in derision, as a nickname in fact, has become a popular designation of the Church and its individual members. From the small initial membership stated, the Church grew to include thousands during the lifetime of Joseph Smith; and the growth has continued with phenomenal rapidity and permanence until the present time. One by one the powers and authorities possessed by the Church of old were restored through the man who was ordained to be the first elder of the latter-day dispensation. With the development of the Church, persecution increased; and the effect of evil opposition reached a climax in the cruel martyrdom of the Prophet, and his brother Hyrum, then Patriarch to the Church, June 27, 1844. The incidents leading up to and culminating in the foul murder of these men at Carthage, Illinois, are matters of common history. Prophet and patriarch gave the sacred seal of their life's blood to the testimony of the truth, which they had valiantly maintained in the face of intolerant persecution for nearly a quarter of a century.[q]

Authenticity of Joseph Smith's Mission—The evidence of divine authority in the work established by Joseph Smith, and of the justification of the claims made by and for the man, may be summarized as follows:

1. Ancient prophecy has been fulfilled in the restoration of the Gospel and the reestablishment of the Church upon the earth through his instrumentality.
2. He received by direct ordination and appointment, at the hands of those who held the power in former dispensations, authority to minister in the various ordinances of the Holy Priesthood.
3. His possession of the power of true prophecy, and of other spiritual gifts, is shown by the results of his ministry.

[q] See Appendix 1:7.

4. The doctrines he proclaimed are true and scriptural.

Each of these classes of evidence will receive attention and find ample demonstration in the course of the present study; and no detailed consideration will be attempted at this stage of our investigation; though a few illustrations, briefly stated, will be cited.[r]

1. Fulfilment of Prophecy, wrought through the lifework of Joseph Smith, is abundantly attested. John the Revelator, from his prophetic vision of the latter-day dispensation, understood and predicted that the Gospel would be again sent from the heavens, and be restored to the earth through the direct ministration of an angel in the latter-days: "And I saw another angel fly in the midst of heaven, having the everlasting gospel to preach unto them that dwell on the earth, and to every nation, and kindred, and tongue, and people, Saying with a loud voice, Fear God, and give glory to him; for the hour of his judgment is come: and worship him that made heaven, and earth, and the sea, and the fountains of waters."[s] A partial fulfilment of this prediction appears in the coming of the angel Moroni to Joseph Smith, as already described, whereby the restoration of the Gospel was announced, and the speedy realization of other ancient prophecies was promised; and a record, described in part as containing "the fulness of the everlasting Gospel" as delivered by the Savior to the ancient inhabitants of the western continent was committed to his care for translation and publication amongst all nations, kindred, and tongues. A further fulfilment was realized in the personal visitations of resurrected beings, who had ministered as bearers of the Holy Priesthood during their time of mortality, this Priesthood comprising divine authority and appointment to preach the Gospel and administer the ordinances thereof. The remainder of John's fateful utterance, regarding the authorized call for repentance and the execution of God's judgment preparatory to the scenes of the last days, is now in process of rapid and literal fulfilment.

Malachi predicted the coming of Elijah especially commissioned with power to inaugurate the work of cooperation between the fathers and the children, and announced this mission as a necessary preliminary to "the great and dreadful day of the Lord."[t] The angel Moroni confirmed the truth and significance of this prediction in an emphatic reiteration as already set forth. Joseph Smith and his associate in the ministry, Oliver Cowdery, solemnly testify that they were visited by Elijah the prophet, in the Temple at Kirtland, Ohio, on the third day of April, 1836; on which occasion the ancient prophet declared to the prophet of the latter days that the day spoken of by Malachi had come: "Therefore," continued he, "the keys of this dispensation are committed into your hands; and by this ye may know that the great and dreadful day of the Lord is near, even at the doors."[u] The particular nature of the union of the fathers and the children, upon which Malachi, Moroni, and Elijah laid great stress, has been explained as comprising vicarious ordinances, including baptism for the dead who have passed from earth without a knowledge of the Gospel or opportunity of complying with its laws and ordinances. In the teaching and practise of this doctrine, The Church of Jesus Christ of Latter-day Saints stands alone amongst all the churches professing Christianity.

The ancient scriptures teem with prophecies concerning the restoration of Israel in the last days, and the gathering of the people from among the nations and from the lands into which they have been led or driven as a penalty for their waywardness.[v] In the predictions of olden times such promi-

[r] See Appendix 1:8.
[s] Rev. 14:6, 7; see Appendix 1:9.
[t] Mal. 4:5, 6.
[u] D&C 110:13–16.
[v] See chaps. 17, 18, herein.

nence and importance are attached to this work of gathering that, from the days of Israel's exodus, the last days have been characterized in sacred writ as distinctively a gathering dispensation. The return of the tribes after their long and wide dispersion is made a preliminary work to the establishment of the predicted reign of righteousness with Christ upon the earth as Lord and King; and its accomplishment is given as a sure precursor of the Millennium. Jerusalem is to be reestablished as the City of the Great King on the eastern hemisphere; and Zion, or the New Jerusalem, is to be built on the western continent; the Lost Tribes are to be brought from their place of exile in the north; and the curse is to be removed from Israel.

From the early days of Joseph Smith's ministry he taught the doctrine of the gathering as imposing a present duty upon the Church; and this phase of Latter-day Saint labor is one of its most characteristic features. Joseph Smith and Oliver Cowdery affirm that the commission for prosecuting this work was committed to the Church through them by Moses, who held authority as Israel's leader in the dispensation known specifically as the Mosaic. Their testimony is thus stated, in the description given of manifestations in the Kirtland Temple, April 3, 1836: "Moses appeared before us, and committed unto us the keys of the gathering of Israel from the four parts of the earth, and the leading of the ten tribes from the land of the north."[w] As to the earnestness with which this labor has been begun, and the fair progress already made therein, consider the hundreds of thousands belonging to the families of Israel already assembled in the valleys of the Rocky Mountains, about the Temples of the Lord now established; and hear the psalm of the hosts of Israel among the nations, chanted to the accompaniment of effective deeds: "Come, and let us go up to the mountain of the Lord, and to the house of the God of Jacob; and he will teach us of his ways, and we will walk in his paths: for the law shall go forth of Zion, and the word of the Lord from Jerusalem."[x]

The bringing forth of the Book of Mormon is held by the Latter-day Saints to be a direct fulfilment of prophecy.[y] In predicting the humiliation of Israel, to whom had been committed the power of the Priesthood in early days, Isaiah gave voice to the word of the Lord in this wise: "And thou shalt be brought down, and shalt speak out of the ground, and thy speech shall be low out of the dust, and thy voice shall be, as of one that hath a familiar spirit, out of the ground, and thy speech shall whisper out of the dust."[z] The Book of Mormon is verily the voice of a people brought low, speaking from the dust, for from the earth the book was literally taken. The record is the history of a small division of the house of Israel, a part of the family of Joseph indeed, who were led by a miraculous power to the western continent six centuries prior to the Christian era.

Of the record of Joseph and its coming forth as a parallel testimony to that of Judah, or the Bible in part, the Lord thus spake through the prophet Ezekiel: "Moreover, thou son of man, take thee one stick, and write upon it, For Judah, and for the children of Israel his companions: then take another stick, and write upon it, For Joseph, the stick of Ephraim, and for all the house of Israel his companions: And join them one to another into one stick; and they shall become one in thine hand. And when the children of thy people shall speak unto thee, saying, Wilt thou not shew us what thou meanest by these? Say unto them, Thus saith the Lord God; Behold, I will take the stick of Joseph, which is in the hand of Ephraim, and the tribes of Israel his fellows, and will put them with him, even with the stick of Judah, and make them one stick, and they shall be one in mine hand."[aa] The

[w] D&C 110:11.
[x] Mic. 4:2.
[y] See chaps. 14, 15 herein.
[z] Isa. 29:4; see also 2 Nephi 3:19.; 16–19
[aa] Ezek. 37:16–19.

succeeding verses declare that the gathering and restoration of Israel would immediately follow the united testimony of the records of Judah and Joseph. The two records are before the world, a unit in their testimony of the everlasting Gospel; and the work of gathering is in effective progress.

It is further evident from the scriptures that the dispensation of the Gospel in the latter days is to be one of restoration and restitution, truly a "dispensation of the fulness of times." Paul declares it to be the good pleasure of the Lord, "That in the dispensation of the fulness of times he might gather together in one all things in Christ, both which are in heaven, and which are on earth; even in him."[bb] This prediction finds a parallel in an utterance of the prophet Nephi: "Wherefore, all things which have been revealed unto the children of men shall at that day be revealed."[cc] And in accord with this is the teaching of Peter: "Repent ye therefore, and be converted, that your sins may be blotted out, when the times of refreshing shall come from the presence of the Lord; And he shall send Jesus Christ, which before was preached unto you: Whom the heaven must receive until the times of restitution of all things, which God hath spoken by the mouth of all his holy prophets since the world began."[dd]

Now comes Joseph Smith with the declaration that unto him has been given the authority to open up this, the dispensation of fulness, restitution, and restoration; and that through him the Church has been endowed with all the keys and powers of the Priesthood as held and exercised in earlier periods. Unto the Church "is the power of this priesthood given, for the last days and for the last time, in the which is the dispensation of the fulness of times. Which power you hold, in connection with all those who have received a dispensation at any time from the beginning of the creation."[ee] The actual possession of these combined and unified powers is sufficiently demonstrated by the comprehensive work of the Church in its present-day ministry.

2. Joseph Smith's Authority was conferred upon him by direct ministrations of heavenly beings, each of whom had once exercised the same power upon the earth. We have already seen how the angel Moroni, formerly a mortal prophet among the Nephites, transmitted to Joseph the appointment to bring forth the record which he, Moroni, had buried in the earth over fourteen hundred years before. We learn further, that on the 15th of May, 1829, the lesser or Aaronic Priesthood was conferred upon Joseph Smith and Oliver Cowdery under the hands of John the Baptist,[ff] who came in his immortalized state with that particular order of Priesthood, which comprises the keys of the ministrations of angels, the doctrine of repentance and of baptism for the remission of sins. This was the same John who, as the voice of one crying in the wilderness, had preached the same doctrine and administered the same ordinance in Judea, as the immediate forerunner of the Messiah. In delivering his message John the Baptist stated that he was acting under the direction of Peter, James, and John, apostles of the Lord, in whose hands reposed the keys of the higher or Melchizedek Priesthood, which in time would also be given. This promise was fulfilled a month or so later, when the apostles named visited in person Joseph Smith and Oliver Cowdery, ordaining them to the apostleship,[gg] which comprises all the offices of the higher order of Priesthood and which carries authority to minister in all the established ordinances of the Gospel.

Then, some time after the Church had been duly organized, commission for certain special functions was given, the appointing messenger in each case being the one whose right it was so to

---

bb Eph. 1:9, 10.
cc 2 Nephi 30:18.
dd Acts 3:19–21.
ee D&C 112:30–32.
ff D&C, sec. 13.
gg D&C 27:12.

officiate by virtue of the authority he had held in the days of his mortality. Thus, as has been seen, Moses conferred the authority to prosecute the work of gathering; and Elijah, who, not having tasted death, held a peculiar relation to both the living and the dead, delivered the appointment of vicarious ministry for the departed. To these divine commissions is added that given by Elias, who appeared to Joseph Smith and Oliver Cowdery and "committed the dispensation of the gospel of Abraham," saying as was said of the patriarch named and his descendants in olden times, that in them and in their seed should all succeeding generations be blessed.[hh]

It is evident, then, that the claims made by the Church with respect to its authority are complete and consistent as to the source of the powers professed and the channels through which such have been delivered again to earth. Scripture and revelation, both ancient and modern, support as an unalterable law the principle that no one can delegate to another an authority which the giver does not possess.

3. Joseph Smith was a true Prophet—In the days of ancient Israel an effective method of testing the claims of a professed prophet was prescribed. "When a prophet speaketh in the name of the Lord, if the thing follow not, nor come to pass, that is the thing which the Lord hath not spoken, but the prophet hath spoken it presumptuously: thou shalt not be afraid of him."[ii] Conversely, if the words of the prophet are verified by fulfilment there is at least proof presumptive of his divine calling. Of the many predictions uttered by Joseph Smith and already fulfilled or awaiting the set time of their realization, a few citations will suffice.

One of the earliest prophecies delivered through him, which, while not his independent utterance but that of the angel Moroni was nevertheless given to the world by Joseph Smith, had specific reference to the Book of Mormon, of which the angel said: "The knowledge that this record contains will go to every nation, and kindred, and tongue, and people, under the whole heaven."[jj] This declaration was made four years before the work of translation was begun, and fourteen years before the elders of the Church began their missionary labor in foreign lands. Since that time the Book of Mormon has been published in many languages and the work of its worldwide distribution is still in progress.

In August, 1842, while the Church was suffering persecution in Illinois, and when the western part of what is now the United States of America was but little known and so only as the territory of an alien nation, Joseph Smith prophesied "that the saints would continue to suffer much affliction, and would be driven to the Rocky Mountains," and that while many then professing allegiance to the Church would apostatize, and others, faithful to their testimony, would meet the martyr's fate, some would live to "assist in making settlements and build cities and see the saints become a mighty people in the midst of the Rocky Mountains."[kk] The literal fulfilment of this prediction, uttered in 1842, and it may be added, foreshadowed by an earlier prophecy in 1831,[ll] the one five, the other sixteen years before the migration of the Church to the west, is attested by the common history of the settlement and development of this once forbidding region. Even skeptics and pronounced opponents of the Church proclaim the miracle of the establishment of a great commonwealth in the valleys of the Rocky Mountains.

A remarkable prediction regarding national affairs was uttered by Joseph Smith, December 25, 1832; it was soon thereafter promulgated among the members of the Church and was preached by the elders, but did not appear in print until 1851.[mm] The revelation reads in part as follows: "Verily,

[hh] D&C 110:12.
[ii] Deut. 18:21, 22.
[jj] Times and Seasons, vol. 2, No. 13.
[kk] Millennial Star, vol. 19, p. 630; also HC, vol. 5, p. 85.
[ll] D&C 49:24, 25.
[mm] See P.of G.P., British edition of 1851, and Millennial Star, vol. 49, p. 396. The prophecy is now a part of the D&C, sec. 87.

thus saith the Lord concerning the wars that will shortly come to pass, beginning at the rebellion of South Carolina, which will eventually terminate in the death and misery of many souls; And the time will come that war will be poured out upon all nations, beginning at this place. For behold, the Southern States shall be divided against the Northern States, and the Southern States will call on other nations, even the nation of Great Britain * * * And it shall come to pass, after many days, slaves shall rise up against their masters, who shall be marshaled and disciplined for war."

Every student of United States history is acquainted with the facts establishing a complete fulfilment of this astounding prophecy. In 1861, more than twenty-eight years after the foregoing prediction was recorded, and ten years after its publication in England, the Civil War broke out, beginning in South Carolina. The ghastly records of that fratricidal strife sadly support the prediction concerning "the death and misery of many souls," though this constituted but a partial fulfilment. It is known that slaves deserted the South and were marshaled in the armies of the North, and that the Confederate States solicited aid of Great Britain. While no open alliance between the Southern States and the English government was effected, British influence gave indirect assistance and substantial encouragement to the South, and this in such a way as to produce serious international complications. Vessels were built and equipped at British ports in the interests of the Confederacy; and the results of this violation of the laws of neutrality cost Great Britain fifteen and a half millions of dollars, which sum was awarded the United States at the Geneva arbitration in settlement of the Alabama claims. The Confederacy appointed commissioners to Great Britain and France; these appointees were forcibly taken by United States officers from the British steamer on which they had embarked. This act, which the United States government had to admit as overt, threatened for a time to precipitate a war between this nation and Great Britain.

A careful study of the Revelation and Prophecy on War, given, as stated, through the Prophet Joseph Smith, December 25, 1832, makes plain that the conflict between North and South in America was to be, as now we know it to have been, but the beginning of a new era of strife and bloodshed. The Lord's words were definite in predicting wars "beginning at the rebellion of South Carolina"; and declared further: "And the time will come that war will be poured out upon all nations, beginning at this place." The great World War, 1914–1918, embroiled, directly or indirectly, every nation of the earth; and recovery from the effects of that stupendous conflict is beyond the horizon of human vision. Nations have been dismembered or destroyed; thrones have fallen; kingly crowns have lost all value beyond the market price of their gold and jewels; and, withal, new units of government have been created, and nations have sprung into existence, literally born in a day. The very elements are in anger, and what we call natural phenomena are surpassing in destructive fury all records made by man; and verily the end is not reached. The word of the Lord through His prophet, Joseph Smith, has never been revoked: "And thus, with the sword and by bloodshed the inhabitants of the earth shall mourn; and with famine, and plague, and earthquake, and the thunder of heaven, and the fierce and vivid lightning also, shall the inhabitants of the earth be made to feel the wrath, and indignation, and chastening hand of an Almighty God, until the consumption decreed hath made a full end of all nations."[nn]

The revelation cited, as given through Joseph Smith, contained other predictions, some of which are yet awaiting fulfilment. The evidence presented is sufficient to prove that Joseph Smith is prominent among men by reason of his instrumentality in fulfilling prophecies uttered by the

[nn] D&C 87:6.

Lord's representatives in former times, and that his own place as a prophet is abundantly vindicated. But the endowment of prophecy so richly bestowed upon this Elias of the last days, and so freely yet unerringly exercised by him, is but one of the many spiritual gifts by which he, in common with a host of others who have received the Priesthood through him, was distinguished. The scriptures declare that certain signs shall attend the Church of Christ, among them the gifts of tongues, healing, immunity from threatening death and the power to control evil spirits.[oo] The exercise of these powers, resulting in what are ordinarily termed miracles, is by no means an infallible proof of divine authority; for some true prophets have wrought no such wonders, so far as records show, and men have been known to work miracles at the instigation of evil spirits.[pp] Nevertheless, the possession of the power implied by the working of miracles is an essential characteristic of the Church; and when such acts are wrought in the accomplishment of holy purposes they serve as confirmatory evidence of divine authority. Therefore we may expect to find, as find we do in the ministry of Joseph Smith and in that of the Church in general, the attested record of miracles, comprising manifestations of all the promised gifts of the Spirit.[qq]

4. **The Doctrines Taught by Joseph Smith,** and by the Church today, are true and scriptural. To sustain this statement we must examine the principal teachings of the Church in separate order.

[oo] Mark 16:16–18; Luke 10: 19, etc.; D&C 84:65–72.
[pp] Ex.7:11, 22; 8:7, 18; Rev. 13:13-15; 16:13, 14.
[qq] See chap.12 herein.

2

GOD AND THE HOLY TRINITY

ARTICLE 1

E BELIEVE in God, the Eternal Father, and in His Son, Jesus Christ, and in the Holy Ghost.

The Existence of God—Since faith in God constitutes the foundation of religious belief and practise, and as a knowledge of the attributes and character of Deity is essential to an intelligent exercise of faith in Him, this subject claims first place in our study of the doctrines of the Church.

The existence of God is scarcely a question for rational dispute; nor does it call for proof by the feeble demonstrations of man's logic, for the fact is admitted by the human family practically without question, and the consciousness of subjection to a supreme power is an inborn attribute of mankind. The early scriptures are not devoted to a primary demonstration of God's existence, nor to attacks on the sophistries of atheism; and from this fact we may infer that the errors of doubt developed in some later period. The universal assent of mankind to the existence of God is at least strongly corroborative. There is a filial passion within human nature that flames toward heaven. Every nation, every tribe, every individual, yearns for some object of reverence. It is natural for man to worship; his soul is unsatisfied until he finds a deity. When men through transgression fell into darkness concerning the true and living God, they established for themselves other deities, and so arose the abominations of idolatry. And yet, even the most revolting of these practises testify to the existence of a God by demonstrating man's hereditary passion for worship.

The evidence upon which mankind rest their conviction regarding the existence of a Supreme Being,[a] may be classified for convenience of consideration under the three following heads:

1. The evidence of history and tradition.
2. The evidence furnished by the exercise of human reason.
3. The conclusive evidence of direct revelation from God.

1. History and Tradition—History as written by man, and authentic tradition as transmitted from generation to generation prior to the date of any written record now extant, give evidence of the actuality of Deity and of close and personal dealings between God and man in the early epochs of human existence. One of the most ancient records known, the Holy Bible, names God as the Creator of all things,[b] and moreover, declares that He revealed Himself to our first earthly parents and to many other holy personages in the early days of the world. Adam and Eve heard His voice[c] in the garden, and even after their transgression they continued to call upon God and to sacrifice to Him. It is plain, therefore, that they carried with them from the Garden a personal knowledge of God. After their expulsion they heard "the voice of the Lord from the way toward the Garden of Eden," though they saw Him not; and He gave unto them commandments, which they obeyed. Then came to Adam an angel, and the Holy Ghost inspired the man and bare record of the Father and the Son.[d]

Cain and Abel learned of God from the teachings of their parents, as well as from personal ministrations. After the acceptance of Abel's offering and the rejection of that of Cain, followed by Cain's crime of fratricide, the Lord talked with Cain, and Cain answered the Lord.[e] Cain must, therefore, have taken a personal knowledge of God from Eden into the land where he went to dwell.[f] Adam lived to be nine hundred and thirty years old and many children were born unto him. Them he instructed in the fear of God, and many of them received direct ministrations. Of Adam's descendants, Seth, Enos, Cainan, Mahalaleel, Jared, Enoch, Methuselah, and Lamech the father of Noah, each representing a distinct generation, were all living during Adam's lifetime. Noah was born but a hundred and twenty-six years after the time of Adam's death, and moreover lived nearly six hundred years with his father Lamech, by whom he was doubtless instructed in the traditions concerning God's personal manifestations, which Lamech had learned from the lips of Adam. Through Noah and his family a knowledge of God by direct tradition was carried beyond the flood; and, moreover, Noah held direct communication with God,[g] and lived to instruct ten generations of his descendants. Then followed Abraham, who also enjoyed personal communion with God,[h] and after him Isaac, and Jacob or Israel, among whose descendants the Lord wrought great wonders through the instrumentality of Moses. Thus, had there been no written records, tradition would have preserved and transmitted a knowledge of God.

a See Appendix 2:1.
b See Gen., chap. 1; see also P.of G.P., Moses, chap. 2; Abraham, chap. 4.
c See Gen. 3:8; see also P.of G.P., Moses 4:14.
d See P.of G.P., Moses 5:6–9.
e See Gen. 4:9–16; see also P.of G.P., Moses 5:22–26, 34–40.
f See Gen. 4:16; see also P.of G.P., Moses 5:41.
g See Gen. 6:13; 7:1–4; 8:15–17; 9:1–17.
h See Gen., chap. 12; see also P.of G.P., Abraham 1:16–19; 2:6–11, 19, 22–24; 3:3–10, 12–21, 23.

But even if accounts of the earliest of man's personal communion with God had become dimmed with time, and therefore weakened in effect, they could but give place to other traditions founded upon later manifestations of the divine personality. Unto Moses the Lord made Himself known, not alone from behind the curtain of fire and the screen of clouds,[i] but by face to face communion, whereby the man beheld even "the similitude" of his God.[j] This account of direct communion between Moses and God, in part of which the people were permitted to share[k] so far as their faith and purity permitted, has been preserved by Israel through all generations. And from Israel the traditions of God's existence have spread throughout the world; so that we find traces of this ancient knowledge even in the perverted mythologies of heathen nations.

2. Human Reason, operating upon observations of nature, strongly declares the existence of God. The mind, already imbued with the historical truths of the divine existence and its close relationship with man, will find confirmatory evidence in nature on every side; and even to him who rejects the testimony of the past, and assumes to set up his own judgment as superior to the common belief of ages, the multifarious evidences of design in nature appeal. The observer is impressed by the manifest order and system in creation; he notes the regular succession of day and night providing alternate periods of work and rest for man, animals, and plants; the sequence of the seasons, each with its longer periods of activity and recuperation; the mutual dependence of animals and plants; the circulation of water from sea to cloud, from cloud to earth again, with beneficent effect. As man proceeds to the closer examination of things he finds that by study and scientific investigation these proofs are multiplied many fold. He may learn of the laws by which the earth and its associated worlds are governed in their orbits; by which satellites are held subordinate to planets, and planets to suns; he may behold the marvels of vegetable and animal anatomy, and the surpassing mechanism of his own body; and with such appeals to his reason increasing at every step, his wonder as to who ordained all this gives place to adoration for the Creator whose presence and power are thus so forcefully proclaimed; and the observer becomes a worshiper.

Everywhere in nature is the evidence of cause and effect; on every side is the demonstration of means adapted to end. But such adaptations, says a thoughtful writer, "indicate contrivance for a given purpose, and contrivance is the evidence of intelligence, and intelligence is the attribute of mind, and the intelligent mind that built the stupendous universe is God." To admit the existence of a designer in the evidence of design, to say there must be a contriver in a world of intelligent contrivance, to believe in an adapter when man's life is directly dependent upon the most perfect adaptations conceivable, is but to accept self-evident truths. The burden of proof as to the non-existence of God rests upon him who questions the solemn truth that God lives. "Every house is builded by some man; but he that built all things is God."[l] Plain as is the truth so expressed, there are among men a few who profess to doubt the evidence of reason and to deny the author of their own being. Strange, is it not, that here and there one, who finds in the contrivance exhibited by the ant in building her house, in the architecture of the honey-comb, and in the myriad instances of orderly instinct among the least of living things, a proof of intelligence from which man may learn and be wise, will yet question the operation of intelligence in the creation of worlds and in the constitution of the universe?[m]

i See Ex. 3:4; 19:18; Num. 12:5.
j See Num. 12:8; see also P.of G.P., Moses 1:1, 2, 11, 31.
k See Ex. 19:9, 11, 17–20.
l Heb. 3:4.
m See Appendix 2:4.

Man's consciousness tells him of his own existence; his observation proves the existence of others of his kind and of uncounted orders of organized beings. From this we conclude that something must have existed always, for had there been a time of no existence, a period of nothingness, existence could never have begun, for from nothing, nothing can be derived. The eternal existence of something, then, is a fact beyond dispute; and the question requiring answer is, what is that eternal something—that existence which is without beginning and without end? Matter and energy are eternal realities; but matter of itself is neither vital nor active, nor is force of itself intelligent; yet vitality and activity are characteristic of living things, and the effects of intelligence are universally present. Nature is not God; and to mistake the one for the other is to call the edifice the architect, the fabric the designer, the marble the sculptor, and the thing the power that made it. The system of nature is the manifestation of an order that argues a directing intelligence; and that intelligence is of an eternal character, coeval with existence itself. Nature herself is a declaration of a superior Being, whose will and purpose she exhibits in her varied aspects. Beyond and above nature stands nature's God.

While existence is eternal, and therefore to being there never was a beginning, never shall be an end, in a relative sense each stage of organization must have had a beginning, and to every phase of existence as manifested in each of the countless orders of created things, there was a first, as there will be a last; though every ending or consummation in nature is but another beginning. Thus, man's ingenuity has invented theories to illustrate, if not to explain, a possible sequence of events by which the earth has been brought from a state of chaos to its present habitable condition; but by these hypotheses this globe was once a barren sphere, on which none of the innumerable forms of life that now tenant it could have existed. The theorist therefore must admit a beginning to life on the earth, and such a beginning is explicable only on the assumption of some creative act, spontaneous generation, or a contribution from outside the earth. If he admit the introduction of life upon the earth from some other and older sphere, he does but extend the limits of his inquiry as to the beginning of life; for to explain the origin of a rose-bush in our own garden by saying that it was transplanted as an offshoot from a rose-tree growing elsewhere, is no answer to the question concerning the origin of roses. Science of necessity assumes a beginning to vital phenomena on this planet, and admits a finite duration of the earth in its current course of progressive change; and as with the earth so with the heavenly bodies in general. The eternity of existence, then, is no more positive as an indication of an eternal Ruler than is the endless sequence of change, each stage of which has both beginning and end. The origination of created things, the beginning of an organized universe, is utterly inexplicable on any assumption of spontaneous change in matter, or of fortuitous and accidental operation of its properties.

Human reason, so liable to err in dealing with subjects of lesser import, may not of itself lead its possessor to a convincing knowledge of God; yet its exercise will aid him in his search, strengthening and confirming his inherited instinct toward his Maker.[n] "The fool hath said in his heart, There is no God."[o] In this passage as in scriptural usage elsewhere, the fool[p] is a wicked man, one who has forfeited his wisdom by wrongdoing, bringing darkness over his mind in place of light, and ignorance instead of knowledge. By such a course, the mind becomes depraved and incapable of appreciating the finer arguments in nature. A wilful sinner grows deaf to the voice of both intuition and reason in holy things, and loses the privilege of communing with his Creator, thus forfeiting the strongest means of attaining a personal knowledge of God.

n See Appendix 2:5.
o Ps. 14:1.
p See Ps. 107:17; Prov. 1:7; 10:21; 14:9.

3. Revelation gives to man his surest knowledge of God. Scriptural instances of the Lord, specifically Jehovah, manifesting Himself to His prophets in olden as in later times are abundant. We have already noted, as the foundation of many traditions relating to the existence and personality of God, His revelations of Himself to Adam and other antediluvian patriarchs; then to Noah, Abraham, Isaac, Jacob, and Moses. An example briefly mentioned in Genesis is that of Enoch, the father of Methuselah; of him we read that he walked with God;[q] and furthermore that the Lord manifested Himself with particular plainness to this righteous prophet,[r] revealing unto him the course of events until the time of Christ's appointed ministry in the flesh, the plan of salvation through the sacrifice of the Only Begotten Son, and the scenes that were to follow until the final judgment.

Of Moses we read that he heard the voice of God, who spoke to him from the midst of the burning bush in Mount Horeb, saying: "I am the God of thy father, the God of Abraham, the God of Isaac, and the God of Jacob. And Moses hid his face; for he was afraid to look upon God."[s] Unto Moses and assembled Israel God appeared in a cloud, with the terrifying accompaniment of thunders and lightnings, on Sinai: "Thus thou shalt say unto the children of Israel, Ye have seen that I have talked with you from heaven."[t] Of a later manifestation we are told: "Then went up Moses, and Aaron, Nadab, and Abihu, and seventy of the elders of Israel: And they saw the God of Israel: and there was under his feet as it were a paved work of a sapphire stone, and as it were the body of heaven in his clearness."[u]

On through the time of Joshua and the Judges and during the period of kingly rule, the Lord declared His presence and His power to Israel. Isaiah saw the Lord enthroned in the midst of a glorious company, and cried out, "Woe is me! for I am undone; because I am a man of unclean lips, and I dwell in the midst of a people of unclean lips: for mine eyes have seen the King, the Lord of hosts."[v]

At a subsequent period, when Christ emerged from the waters of baptism, the voice of the Father was heard declaring: "This is my beloved Son, in whom I am well pleased;"[w] and on the occasion of our Lord's transfiguration, the same voice repeated this solemn and glorious acknowledgment.[x] While Stephen was suffering martyrdom at the hands of his cruel and bigoted countrymen, the heavens were opened, and he "saw the glory of God, and Jesus standing on the right hand of God."[y]

The Book of Mormon is replete with instances of communication between God and His people, mostly through vision and by the ministration of angels, but also through direct manifestation of the divine presence. Thus, we read of a colony of people leaving the Tower of Babel and journeying to the western hemisphere, under the leadership of one who is known in the record as the brother of Jared. In preparing for the ocean voyage, the man prayed that the Lord would touch with His finger, and thereby make luminous, certain stones, so that the voyagers might have light in the ships. In answer to this petition, the Lord stretched forth His hand and touched the stones, revealing His finger, which the man was surprised to see resembled the finger of a human being. Then the

q See Gen. 5: 18–24; see also Heb. 11:5; Jude 14.
r See P.of G.P., Moses, chaps. 6, 7.
s Ex.3:6.
t Ex. 20: 18-22.
u Ex. 24:9, 10.
v Isa.6:1-5.
w Matt.3:16, 17; Mark 1:11.
x See Matt. 17: 1–5; see also Luke 9:35.
y Acts 7:54-60.

Lord, pleased with the man's faith, made Himself visible, and demonstrated to the brother of Jared that man was formed literally after the image of the Creator.[z] To the Nephites who inhabited the western continent, Christ revealed Himself after His resurrection and ascension. To these sheep of the western fold, He testified of His commission received from the Father, showed the wounds in His hands, feet, and side, and ministered unto the believing multitudes in many ways.[aa]

In the present dispensation, God has revealed Himself to His people. By faith and sincerity of purpose Joseph Smith, while yet a youth, won for himself a manifestation of God's presence, being privileged to behold both the Eternal Father and Jesus Christ the Son. His testimony of the existence of God is not dependent upon tradition or studied deduction; he declares to the world that both the Father and Christ the Son live, for he has beheld their persons, and has heard their voices. In addition to the manifestation cited, Joseph Smith and his fellow servant, Sidney Rigdon, state that on February 16, 1832, they saw the Son of God, and conversed with Him in heavenly vision. In describing this manifestation they say: "And while we meditated upon these things, the Lord touched the eyes of our understandings and they were opened, and the glory of the Lord shone round about. And we beheld the glory of the Son, on the right hand of the Father, and received of his fulness; And saw the holy angels, and them who are sanctified before his throne, worshiping God, and the Lamb, who worship him forever and ever. And now, after the many testimonies which have been given of him, this is the testimony, last of all, which we give of him: That he lives! For we saw him, even on the right hand of God; and we heard the voice bearing record that he is the Only Begotten of the Father—That by him, and through him, and of him, the worlds are and were created, and the inhabitants thereof are begotten sons and daughters unto God."[bb]

Again, on April 3, 1836, in the Temple at Kirtland, Ohio, the Lord manifested Himself to Joseph Smith and Oliver Cowdery, who say of the occasion: "We saw the Lord standing upon the breastwork of the pulpit, before us; and under his feet was a paved work of pure gold in color like amber. His eyes were as a flame of fire; the hair of his head was white like the pure snow; his countenance shone above the brightness of the sun; and his voice was as the sound of the rushing of great waters, even the voice of Jehovah, saying: I am the first and the last; I am he who liveth, I am he who was slain; I am your advocate with the Father."[cc]

The Godhead: The Trinity—Three personages composing the great presiding council of the universe have revealed themselves to man: (1) God the Eternal Father; (2) His Son, Jesus Christ; and (3) the Holy Ghost. That these three are separate individuals, physically distinct from each other, is demonstrated by the accepted records of divine dealings with man. On the occasion of the Savior's baptism, John recognized the sign of the Holy Ghost; he saw before him in a tabernacle of flesh the Christ, unto whom he had administered the holy ordinance; and he heard the voice of the Father.[dd] The three personages of the Godhead were present, manifesting themselves each in a different way, and each distinct from the others. Later the Savior promised His disciples that the Comforter,[ee] who is the Holy Ghost, should be sent unto them by His Father; here again are the three members of the Godhead separately defined. Stephen, at the time of his martyrdom, was blessed with the power of heavenly vision, and he saw Jesus standing on the right hand of

z Ether, chap. 3.
aa 3 Nephi, chaps. 11–28.
bb D&C 76:19–24.
cc D&C 110:2–4.
dd See Matt. 3:16, 17; see also Mark 1:9-11; Luke 3:21, 22.
ee See John 14:26; 15:26.

God.[ff] Joseph Smith, while calling upon the Lord in fervent prayer, saw the Father and the Son, standing in the midst of light that shamed the brightness of the sun; and one of these declared of the other, "This is My Beloved Son. Hear Him!" Each of the members of the Trinity is called God,[gg] together they constitute the Godhead.

Unity of the Godhead—The Godhead is a type of unity in the attributes, powers, and purposes of its members. Jesus, while on earth[hh] and in manifesting Himself to His Nephite servants,[ii] repeatedly testified of the unity existing between Himself and the Father, and between them both and the Holy Ghost. This cannot rationally be construed to mean that the Father, the Son, and the Holy Ghost are one in substance and in person, nor that the names represent the same individual under different aspects. A single reference to prove the error of any such view may suffice: Immediately before His betrayal, Christ prayed for His disciples, the Twelve, and other converts, that they should be preserved in unity,[jj] "that they all may be one" as the Father and the Son are one. We cannot assume that Christ prayed that His followers lose their individuality and become one person, even if a change so directly opposed to nature were possible. Christ desired that all should be united in heart, spirit, and purpose; for such is the unity between His Father and Himself, and between them and the Holy Ghost.

This unity is a type of completeness; the mind of any one member of the Trinity is the mind of the others; seeing as each of them does with the eye of perfection, they see and understand alike. Under any given conditions each would act in the same way, guided by the same principles of unerring justice and equity. The one-ness of the Godhead, to which the scriptures so abundantly testify, implies no mystical union of substance, nor any unnatural and therefore impossible blending of personality. Father, Son, and Holy Ghost are as distinct in their persons and individualities as are any three personages in mortality. Yet their unity of purpose and operation is such as to make their edicts one, and their will the will of God. Even in bodily appearance the Father and the Son are alike; therefore said Christ when importuned by Philip to show to him and others the Father: "Have I been so long time with you, and yet hast thou not known me, Philip? He that hath seen me hath seen the Father; and how sayest thou then, Shew us the Father? Believest thou not that I am in the Father, and the Father in me? The words that I speak unto you I speak not of myself: but the Father that dwelleth in me, he doeth the works. Believe me that I am in the Father, and the Father in me."[kk]

Personality of Each Member of the Godhead—From the evidence already presented, it is clear that the Father is a personal being, possessing a definite form, with bodily parts and spiritual passions. Jesus Christ, who was with the Father[ll] in spirit before coming to dwell in the flesh, and through whom the worlds were made,[mm] lived among men as a man, with all the physical characteristics of a human being; after His resurrection He appeared in the same form;[nn] in that form He ascended into heaven;[oo] and in that form He has manifested Himself to the Nephites,

---

ff See Acts 7:55, 56.

gg See 1 Cor. 8:6; John 1:1-14; Matt. 4:10; 1 Tim. 3:16; 1 John 5:7; Mosiah 15:1, 2.

hh See John 10:30, 38; 17:11, 22.

ii See 3 Nephi 11:27, 36; 28:10; see also Alma 11:44; Mormon 7:7.

jj See John 17:11-21.

kk John 14:9-11; see also Heb. 1:3.

ll See John 17:5.

mm See John 1:3; Heb. 1:2; Eph. 3:9; Col. 1:16.

nn See John 20:14, 15, 19, 20, 26, 27; 21:1-14; Matt. 28:9; Luke 24:15-31, 36–44.

oo See Acts 1:9–11.

and to modern prophets. We are assured that Christ was in the express image of His Father,[pp] after which image man also has been created.[qq] Therefore we know that both the Father and the Son are in form and stature perfect men; each of them possesses a tangible body, infinitely pure and perfect and attended by transcendent glory, nevertheless a body of flesh and bones.[rr]

The Holy Ghost, called also Spirit, and Spirit of the Lord,[ss] Spirit of God,[tt] Comforter,[uu] and Spirit of Truth,[vv] is not tabernacled in a body of flesh and bones, but is a personage of spirit;[ww] yet we know that the Spirit has manifested Himself in the form of a man.[xx] Through the ministrations of the Spirit the Father and the Son may operate in their dealings with mankind;[yy] through Him knowledge is communicated,[zz] and by Him the purposes of the Godhead are achieved.[aaa] The Holy Ghost is the witness of the Father and the Son,[bbb] declaring to man their attributes, bearing record of the other personages of the Godhead.[ccc]

Some of the Divine Attributes—*God is Omnipresent*—There is no part of creation, however remote, into which God cannot penetrate; through the medium of the Spirit the Godhead is in direct communication with all things at all times. It has been said, therefore, that God is everywhere present; but this does not mean that the actual person of any one member of the Godhead can be physically present in more than one place at one time. The senses of each of the Trinity are of infinite power; His mind is of unlimited capacity; His powers of transferring Himself from place to place are infinite; plainly, however, His person cannot be in more than one place at any one time. Admitting the personality of God, we are compelled to accept the fact of His materiality; indeed, an "immaterial being," under which meaningless name some have sought to designate the condition of God, cannot exist, for the very expression is a contradiction in terms. If God possesses a form, that form is of necessity of definite proportions and therefore of limited extension in space. It is impossible for Him to occupy at one time more than one space of such limits; and it is not surprising, therefore, to learn from the scriptures that He moves from place to place. Thus we read in connection with the account of the Tower of Babel, "And the Lord [i.e., Jehovah, the Son] came down to see the city and the tower."[ddd] Again, God appeared to Abraham, and having declared Himself to be "the Almighty God," He talked with the patriarch, and established a covenant with him; then we read "And he left off talking with him, and God went up from Abraham."[eee]

God is Omniscient—By Him matter has been organized and energy directed. He is therefore the Creator of all things that are created; and "Known unto God are all his works from the

pp See Heb. 1:3; Col. 1:15; 2 Cor. 4:4.
qq See Gen. 1:26, 27; James 3:8, 9.
rr See D&C 130:22.
ss See 1 Nephi 4:6; 11:112; Mosiah 13:5; Mark 1:10; John 1:32; Acts 2:4; 8:29; 10:19; Rom. 8:10, 26; 1 Thess. 5:19.
tt See Matt. 3:16; 12:28; 1 Nephi 13:12, 13.
uu See John 14:16, 26; 16:7.
vv See John 15:26; 16:13.
ww See D&C 130:22.
xx See 1 Nephi 11:11.
yy See Neh. 9:30; Isa. 42:1; Acts 10:19; Alma 12:3; D&C 105:36; 97:1.
zz See John 16:13; 1 Nephi 10:19; D&C 35:13; 50:10.
aaa See Gen. 1:2; Job 26:13; Ps. 104:30; D&C 29:31.
bbb See John 15:26; Acts 5:32; 20:23; 1 Cor. 2:11; 12:3; 3 Nephi 11:32.
ccc See chap. 8 herein.
ddd Gen. 11:5.
eee Gen. 17:1, 22.

beginning of the world."[fff] His power and His wisdom are alike incomprehensible to man, for they are infinite. Being Himself eternal and perfect, His knowledge cannot be otherwise than infinite. To comprehend Himself, an infinite Being, He must possess an infinite mind. Through the agency of angels and ministering servants He is in continuous communication with all parts of creation, and may personally visit as He may determine.

God is Omnipotent—He is properly called the Almighty. Man can discern proofs of the divine omnipotence on every side, in the forces that control the elements of earth and guide the orbs of heaven in their prescribed courses. Whatever His wisdom indicates as necessary to be done God can and will do. The means through which He operates may not be of infinite capacity in themselves, but they are directed by an infinite power. A rational conception of His omnipotence is power to do all that He may will to do.

God is kind, benevolent, and loving—tender, considerate, and longsuffering, bearing patiently with the frailties of His children. He is just and merciful in judgment,[ggg] yet combining with these gentler qualities firmness in avenging wrongs.[hhh] He is jealous[iii] of His own power and the reverence paid to Him; that is to say, He is zealous for the principles of truth and purity, which are nowhere exemplified in a higher degree than in His personal attributes. This Being is the author of our existence, Him we are permitted to approach as Father.[jjj] Our faith will increase in Him as we learn of Him.

Idolatry and Atheism—From the abundant evidence of the existence of Deity, the idea of which is so generally held by the human family, there seems to be little ground on which man may rationally assert and maintain a disbelief in God; and, in view of the many proofs of the benignant nature of the divine attributes, there ought to be little tendency to turn aside after false and unworthy objects of worship. Yet the history of the race shows that theism, which is the doctrine of belief in and acceptance of God, is opposed by many varieties of atheism;[kkk] and that man is prone to belie his claim as a creature of reason, and to offer his worship at idolatrous shrines. Atheism is probably a development of later times, while idolatry asserted itself as one of the early sins of the race. Even at the time of Israel's exodus from Egypt, God deemed it proper to command by statute, "Thou shalt have no other gods before me";[lll] yet even while He wrote those words on the stony tablets, His people were defiling themselves before the golden calf they had fashioned after the pattern of an Egyptian idol.

Man possesses an instinct for worship; he craves and will find some object of adoration. When he fell into the darkness of persistent transgression, and forgot the author of his being and the God of his fathers, he sought for other deities. Some came to regard the sun as the type of the supreme, and before that luminary they prostrated themselves in supplication. Others selected for adoration earthly phenomena; they marveled over the mystery of fire, and worshiped the flame. Some saw, or thought they saw, the emblem of the pure and the good in water, and they rendered their devotions by running streams. Others, awed into reverence by the grandeur of towering mountains, repaired to these natural temples and worshiped the altar instead of Him by whose power it had been raised. Another class, more strongly imbued with a reverence for the emblematic, sought to create for themselves artificial

---

[fff] Acts 15:18; see also P.of G.P., Moses 1:6, 35, 37; 1 Nephi 9:6.

[ggg] See Deut. 4:31; 2 Chr. 30:9; Ex. 20:6; 34:6; Neh. 9:17, 31; Ps. 116:5; 103:8; 86:15; Jer. 32:18.

[hhh] See Ex. 20:5; Deut. 7:21; 10:17; Ps. 7:11.

[iii] Ex. 20:5, 34:14; Deut. 4:24; 6:14, 15; Josh. 24:19, 20.

[jjj] See Appendix 2:11.

[kkk] See Appendix 2:6.

[lll] Ex. 20:3.

objects of adoration. They made images by hewing uncouth figures from tree trunks, and chiseling strange forms in stone, and to these they bowed.[mmm]

Idolatrous practises in some of their phases came to be associated with rites of horrible cruelties, as in the custom of sacrificing children to Moloch, and, among the Hindoos, to the Ganges; as also in the slaughter of human beings under Druidical tyranny. The gods that human-kind have set up for themselves are heartless, pitiless, cruel.[nnn]

Atheism is the denial of the existence of God; in a milder form it may consist in ignoring Deity. But the professed atheist, in common with his believing fellow mortals, is subject to man's universal passion for worship; though he refuses to acknowledge the true and living God, he consciously or unconsciously deifies some law, some principle, some attribute of the human soul, or perchance some material creation; and to this he turns, to seek a semblance of the comfort that the believer finds in rich abundance through prayer addressed to his Father and God. I doubt the existence of a thorough atheist—one who with the sincerity of a settled conviction denies in his heart the existence of an intelligent and supreme power.

The idea of God is an inherent characteristic of the human soul. The philosopher recognizes the necessity of such in his theories of being. He may shrink from the open acknowledgment of a personal Deity, yet he assumes the existence of a governing power, of a great unknown, of the unknowable, the illimitable, the unconscious. Oh, man of learning though not of wisdom, why reject the privileges extended to you by the omnipotent, omniscient Being to whom you owe your life, yet whose name you will not acknowledge? No mortal can approach Him while contemplating His perfections and might with aught but awe and reverence; regarding Him only as Creator and God, we are abashed in thought of Him; but He has given us the right to approach Him as His children, and to call upon Him by the name of Father. Even the atheist feels, in the more solemn moments of his life, a yearning of the soul toward a spiritual Parent, as naturally as his human affections turn toward the father who gave him mortal life. The atheism of today is but a species of paganism after all.

Sectarian View of the Godhead—The consistent, simple, and authentic doctrine respecting the character and attributes of God, such as was taught by Christ and the apostles, gave way as revelation ceased and as the darkness incident to the absence of divine authority fell upon the world, after the apostles and the Priesthood had been driven from the earth; and in its place appeared numerous theories and dogmas of men, many of which are utterly incomprehensible in their inconsistency and mysticism.

In the year 325, the Council of Nice was convened by the emperor Constantine, who sought through this body to secure a declaration of Christian belief that would be received as authoritative, and be the means of arresting the increasing dissension incident to the prevalent disagreement regarding the nature of the Godhead and other theological subjects. The Council condemned some of the theories then current, including that of Arius, which asserted that the Son was created by the Father, and therefore could not be coeternal with the Father. The Council promulgated what is known as the Nicene Creed; and this was followed in time by the Athanasian Creed over which, however, controversy has arisen as to authorship.[ooo] The creed follows: "We worship one God in Trinity, and Trinity in Unity, neither confounding the persons, nor dividing the substance. For there is one person of the Father, another of the Son, and another of the Holy Ghost. But the Godhead

[mmm] See Appendix 2:7.
[nnn] See Appendix 2:8, 10.
[ooo] See the author's *The Great Apostasy,* chap. 7.

of the Father, Son, and Holy Ghost, is all one; the glory equal, the majesty coeternal. Such as the Father is, such is the Son, and such is the Holy Ghost. The Father uncreate, the Son uncreate, and the Holy Ghost uncreate. The Father incomprehensible, the Son incomprehensible, and the Holy Ghost incomprehensible. The Father eternal, the Son eternal, and the Holy Ghost eternal. And yet there are not three eternals, but one eternal. As also there are not three incomprehensibles, nor three uncreated; but one uncreated, and one incomprehensible. So likewise the Father is Almighty, the Son Almighty, and the Holy Ghost Almighty; and yet there are not three Almighties, but one Almighty. So the Father is God, the Son is God and the Holy Ghost is God, and yet there are not three Gods but one God." It would be difficult to conceive of a greater number of inconsistencies and contradictions expressed in words as few.

The Church of England teaches the present orthodox view of God as follows: "There is but one living and true God, everlasting, without body, parts, or passions; of infinite power, wisdom, and goodness." The immateriality of God as asserted in these declarations of sectarian faith is entirely at variance with the scriptures, and absolutely contradicted by the revelations of God's person and attributes, as shown by the citations already made.

We affirm that to deny the materiality of God's person is to deny God; for a thing without parts has no whole, and an immaterial body cannot exist.[PPP] The Church of Jesus Christ of Latter-day Saints proclaims against the incomprehensible God, devoid of "body, parts, or passions," as a thing impossible of existence, and asserts its belief in and allegiance to the true and living God of scripture and revelation.

REFERENCES [*]

God is a Personage—Note that distinction is not always indicated here between the Eternal Father or Elohim, and the Son who is Jehovah or Jesus Christ. In the Authorized or King James Version of the Old Testament, JEHOVAH is rendered LORD, printed in capitals, while LORD GOD indicates the personalities of Elohim and Jehovah, or both the Father and the Son. See *Jesus the Christ* chap. 4.

Man in the image of God—Gen. 1:26, 27; 5:1.

In the image of God made he man—hence the heinousness of murder—Gen. 9:6.

Men made after similitude of God—James 3:9.

Christ, who is the image of God—2 Cor. 4:4, Col. 1:15, Philip. 2:6.

The Son is in the express image of the Father's person—Heb. 1:3.

Jesus said: He that seeth me seeth him that sent me—John 12:45.

Jesus said to Philip: He that hath seen me hath seen the Father—John 14:9.

Christ who was to come in the flesh should be in the image after which man was created in the beginning, the image of God—Mosiah 7:27.

Man created after the image of God—Alma 18:34.

Jesus Christ, before embodiment in flesh, showed himself to the brother of Jared, saying: Seest thou that ye are created after mine own image?—Ether 3:15.

[PPP] See Appendix 2:9.

[*] In the "References" following the several chapters, but a few of the scriptural passages relating to the subject are assembled. The passages are frequently condensed and therefore are not presented as full or otherwise exact quotations, the purpose being to indicate only the subject of each citation. The sequence is that of convenience in study, related scriptures being brought together in some instances. When the need of subject relationship is not strong, the citations are arranged in the order of the Standard Works—1, Bible; 2, Book of Mormon; 3, Doctrine and Covenants (D&C); and 4, Pearl of Great Price (P.of G.P.).

Mankind created after God's own image and likeness—D&C 20:18.

The Father and the Son each has a body of flesh and bones as tangible as man's—D&C 130:22.

Man in the image of the Father and of the Only Begotten—Moses 2:27.

Moses in the similitude of the Only Begotten—Moses 1:6.

God created man in the image of his own body—Moses 6:9.

Male and female organized in the image of the Gods—Abraham 4:27.

The Lord spake unto Moses face to face as a man speaketh unto his friend—Ex. 33:11; see also Num. 12:8; Deut. 34:10.

Moses, Aaron, and others with seventy elders saw the God of Israel—Ex. 24:10.

Moses saw God face to face and talked with him—Moses 1:2, 11.

Joseph Smith beheld the Father and the Son—P. of G.P. p. 49.

Joseph Smith and Sidney Rigdon saw the Lord on the right hand of God—D&C 76:23.

Joseph Smith and Oliver Cowdery saw the Lord in the Kirtland Temple—D&C 110:2.

God is a Being of Parts and Passions

The Lord spake to Moses *face* to *face*—see above. And *mouth* to *mouth*—Num. 12:8; see also Moses chaps. 1–5.

The voice of the Lord heard, by Adam and Eve—Gen. 3:8; by Cain—Gen. 4:9; By Moses, Aaron and Miriam—Num. 12:4; by the Israelites as a body—Deut. 5:22.

I the Lord thy God am a *jealous* God—Ex. 20:5.

The Lord, whose name is *Jealous*, is a jealous God—Ex. 34:14. see also Deut. 4:24; Josh. 24:19.

The Lord is a *jealous* God; his *anger* may be kindled—Deut. 6:15.

The Lord's *anger* was hot against Israel—Jud. 2:14; 3:8; see also 2 Kings 13:3; Isa. 30:27.

The Lord provoked to *anger*—Jer. 7:19, 20; see also 1 Kings 22:53.

The *wrath* of God is against unrighteousness—Rom. 1:18; see also Rev. 15:1, 7; D&C 1:9.

I beheld that the *wrath* of God was poured out—1 Nephi 14:15.

These are things that I *hate*, saith the Lord—Zech. 8:17.

Tender *mercies* of the Lord over men—1 Nephi 1:20.

Mercies of the Father unto Gentiles—3 Nephi 16:9.

The Lord shows *mercy*—Ex. 20:6.

The Lord proclaimed as *merciful, gracious, longsuffering*, abundant in *goodness* and *truth—forgiving* yet *just* in dealing with the guilty—Ex. 34:6, 7.

The Lord thy God is a *merciful* God—Deut. 4:31; see also 7:9.

God *ready to pardon, gracious, merciful, slow to anger, of great kindness*—Neh. 9:17; See also Ps. 116:5; Jas. 5:11.

He is full of *mercy, justice, grace, truth, peace*—D&C 84:102.

The Lord *loved* Israel—Deut. 7:8; see also 10:15, 18; Ps. 69:16; Hos. 11:1.

The Father himself *loveth* you—John 16:27; see also 1 John 3:1.

God is *love*—1 John 4:8–11, 16, 19.

Encircled eternally by the Lord's *love*—2 Nephi 1:15.

The *wisdom* of God, his *mercy* and *grace*—2 Nephi 9:8.

Goodness of God, *wisdom, patience*, etc.—Mosiah 4:6.

Is anything too hard for the Lord?—Gen. 18:14.

His judgments unsearchable, his ways past finding out—Rom. 11:33.

The Lord God of gods, he knoweth—Josh. 22:22.

The Lord by wisdom hath founded the earth—Prov. 3:19.

Known unto him are all his works—Acts 15:18; see also Ps. 139; Prov. 5:21.

The glory of God is intelligence—D&C 93:36.

All things done in the wisdom of him who knoweth all things—2 Nephi 2:24.

With God all things are possible—Matt. 19:26; see also Job 42:2; Jer. 32:17.

The Lord governs and comprehends all things—D&C 88:40, 41.

The Holy Trinity—Three Personages

The Father, the Son, and the Holy Ghost individually specified—Luke 3:22; see also Matt. 3:16, 17; John 1:32, 33; 15:26; Acts 2:33; 1 Peter 1:2.

Baptism to be administered in the names of the Three—Matt. 28:19; 3 Nephi 11:25; D&C 20:73.

The Father and the Son and the Holy Ghost—3 Nephi 11:27, 36.

The Holy Ghost beareth record of the Father and the Son—3 Nephi 28:11; D&C 20:27.

Father, Son, and Holy Ghost—D&C 20:28.

Commission to baptize in the name of the Father, Son, and Holy Ghost—D&C 68:8.

Idolatry

Thou shalt have no other gods before me; worshiping of idols forbidden—Ex. 20:3–5; Deut. 5:7–9.

Idolatry amongst Ephraim, and the penalty—Hos. 13:1–4.

Israelites worship the golden calf—Ex., chap. 32; see also Acts 7:40, 41.

Wo unto those that worship idols—2 Nephi 9:37.

Nephites guilty of idolatry—Helaman 6:31.

Human sacrifices to idols by Lamanites—Mormon 4:14.

Abraham's forefathers were idolaters—Abraham 1:5–7.

Egyptian idolaters; Abraham an intended victim—Abraham 1:8–18.

Idolatry in the world today—D&C 1:16.

Let there be no idolatry nor wickedness practised—D&C 52:39.

3

TRANSGRESSION AND THE FALL

ARTICLE 2

E BELIEVE that men will be punished for their own sins, and not for Adam's transgression.

TRANSGRESSION AND ITS RESULTS

Man's Free Agency—The Church teaches as a strictly scriptural doctrine, that man has inherited among the inalienable rights conferred upon him by his divine Father, freedom to choose the good or the evil in life, to obey or disobey the Lord's commandments, as he may elect. This right cannot be guarded with more jealous care than is bestowed upon it by God Himself; for in all His dealings with man He has left the mortal creature free to choose and to act, without compulsion or restraint beyond the influences of paternal counsel and direction.[a] True, He has given commandments and has established statutes, with promises of blessings for compliance and penalties for infraction; but in the choice of these, men are untrammeled. In this respect, man is no less free than are the angels except as he has fettered himself with the bonds of sin and forfeited his power of will and force of soul. The individual has as full a measure of capability to violate the laws of health, the requirements of nature, and the commandments of God in matters both temporal and spiritual, as he has to obey all such; in the one case he brings upon himself the penalties that belong to the broken law; as in the other he inherits the specific blessings and the added freedom that attend a law-abiding life. Obedience to law is the habit of the free

[a] See Appendix 3:1.

man; the transgressor fears the law, for he brings upon himself deprivation and restraint, not because of the law, which would have protected him in his freedom, but because of his antagonism to law.

The predominant attribute of justice, recognized as part of the divine nature, forbids the thought that man should receive promises of reward for righteousness, and threats of punishment for evil deeds, if he possessed no power of independent action. It is no more a part of God's plan to compel men to work righteousness than it is His purpose to permit evil powers to force His children into sin. In the days of Eden, the first man had placed before him commandment and law,[b] with an explanation of the penalty to follow violation of that law. No law could have been given him in righteousness had he not been free to act for himself. "Nevertheless, thou mayest choose for thyself, for it is given unto thee; but remember that I forbid it"[c] said the Lord God to Adam. Concerning His dealings with the first patriarch of the race, God has declared in this day: "Behold, I gave unto him that he should be an agent unto himself."[d]

When the brothers Cain and Abel offered their sacrifices, the elder one became angry because his offering was rejected. Then the Lord reasoned with Cain, and endeavored to teach him that he must expect results of his actions to follow in kind, good or evil: "If thou doest well, shalt thou not be accepted? And if thou doest not well, sin lieth at the door."[e]

A knowledge of good and evil is essential to the advancement that God has made possible for His children to achieve; and this knowledge can be best gained by actual experience, with the contrasts of good and its opposite plainly discernible. Therefore has man been placed upon earth subject to the influence of good and wicked powers, with a knowledge of the conditions surrounding him, and the heaven-born right to choose for himself. The words of the prophet Lehi are explicit: "Wherefore, the Lord God gave unto man that he should act for himself. Wherefore, man could not act for himself save it should be that he was enticed by the one or the other. * * * Wherefore, men are free according to the flesh; and all things are given them which are expedient unto man. And they are free to choose liberty and eternal life, through the great mediation of all men, or to choose captivity and death, according to the captivity and power of the devil; for he seeketh that all men might be miserable like unto himself."[f]

Another of the Nephite prophets, in speaking of those who had died, said they had gone "that they might reap their rewards according to their works, whether they were good or whether they were bad, to reap eternal happiness or eternal misery, according to the spirit which they listed to obey, whether it be a good spirit or a bad one. For every man receiveth wages of him whom he listeth to obey, and this according to the words of the spirit of prophecy."[g]

Samuel, a converted Lamanite upon whom the spirit of the prophets had fallen, admonished his fellows in this wise: "And now remember, remember, my brethren, that whosoever perisheth, perisheth unto himself; and whosoever doeth iniquity, doeth it unto himself; for behold, ye are free; ye are permitted to act for yourselves; for behold, God hath given unto you a knowledge and he hath made you free. He hath given unto you that ye might know good from evil, and he hath given unto you that ye might choose life or death."[h]

---

[b] See Gen. 1:27–29; 2:15–17; P.of G.P., Moses 2:27–29; 3:15–17.

[c] P.of G.P., Moses 3:17.

[d] D&C 29:35.

[e] Gen. 4:7.

[f] 2 Nephi 2:16, 27; see also 2 Nephi 10:23; Alma 12:31; 29:4, 5; 30:9.

[g] Alma 3:26, 27.

[h] Helaman 14:30, 31.

When the plans for creating and peopling the earth were under discussion in heaven, Lucifer sought to destroy the free agency of man by obtaining power to force the human family to do his will, promising the Father that by such means he would redeem all mankind so that not one of them should be lost.[i] This proposition was rejected, while the original purpose of the Father—to use persuasive influences of wholesome precept and sacrificing example with the inhabitants of the earth, then to leave them free to choose for themselves—was agreed upon; and the one to be known as the Only Begotten Son was chosen as the chief instrument in carrying the purpose into effect.

Man's Accountability for his individual acts is as complete as is his agency to elect for himself.[j] The ultimate result of good deeds is happiness, the consequence of evil is misery; these follow in every man's life by inviolable laws. There is a plan of judgment[k] divinely foreordained, by which every man will be called to answer for his deeds; and not for deeds alone but for his words also and even for the thoughts of his heart. "But I say unto you, That every idle word that men shall speak, they shall give account thereof in the day of judgment."[l] These are the words of the Savior Himself. "And let none of you imagine evil in your hearts against his neighbor, and love no false oath: for all these are things that I hate, saith the Lord."[m] John the Revelator was permitted to learn in vision something of the scenes connected with the last judgment; he wrote: "And I saw the dead, small and great, stand before God; and the books were opened: and another book was opened, which is the book of life: and the dead were judged out of those things which were written in the books, according to their works. And the sea gave up the dead which were in it; and death and hell delivered up the dead which were in them: and they were judged every man according to their works."[n]

The execution of judgment is not always made to follow the acts of men immediately; good deeds may not be at once rewarded, nor evil be peremptorily punished; and this is according to divine wisdom, for were it otherwise the test of individual character and the trial of human faith, for which purposes this mortal probation was primarily ordained, would be greatly lessened; as the certainty of immediate pleasure or pain would largely determine human acts to secure the one and avoid the other. Judgment, therefore, is postponed, that every one may prove himself, the good man increasing in righteousness, and the evil-doer having opportunity for repentance and reparation. On rare occasions, speedy judgment of a temporal nature has been executed, the physical results of worldly blessing for good,[o] and calamity for evil deeds[p] following swiftly upon the acts. Whether such retribution entirely satisfies the claims of justice, or a further visitation of judgment is to take place beyond this life matters not. Such acts are exceptional in the divine administration.

It is the prerogative of Jesus Christ[q] to judge mankind, and He will do it as His own purposes, which are the purposes of His Father, may be best served. John records the words of Christ: "For the Father judgeth no man, but hath committed all judgment unto the Son: That all men should honor the Son even as they honor the Father."[r] And Peter, while expounding the Gospel to the devout Gentile, Cornelius, declared concerning Jesus Christ, that "it is he which was

[i] See P.of G.P., Moses 4:1; see also P.of G.P., Abraham 3:27, 28; and *Jesus the Christ*, chap. 2.

[j] See Appendix 3:4.

[k] See Matt. 10:15; 11:22; 2 Peter 2:9; 3:7; 1 John 4:17.

[l] Matt. 12:36.

[m] Zech. 8:17.

[n] Rev. 20:12, 13.

[o] See Job 42:10–17.

[p] See Num. 12:1, 2, 10–15; 15:32-36; chap.16; 21:4–6; 1 Sam. 6:19; 2 Sam. 6:6, 7; Acts 5:1–11.

[q] See John 5:22–27; see also Acts 10:42; 17:31; Rom. 2:16; 2 Cor. 5:10; 2 Tim. 4:1, 8; D&C 133:2.

[r] John 5:22, 23.

ordained of God to be the Judge of quick and dead."[s] Of the fate of the wicked reserved for the judgment-day many prophets have borne record;[t] and the presiding Judge of that awful tribunal has given in His own words descriptions[u] so vivid and forceful as to leave no shadow of doubt that every living soul shall be called to acknowledge his record, and to accept the results of his acts. The Lord's words and those of His prophets are unequivocal—that He is no respecter of persons,[v] and that any species of favor foreign to justice is unknown to Him. This judgment none but the unrepentant wicked need fear; to the righteous it is to be a time of triumph.[w]

Sin—What is the nature of sin? To this question the Apostle John replies: "Sin is the transgression of the law."[x] In the original language of the Biblical records, many words occur for which our single term sin is used, all, however, conveying the common idea of opposition to the divine will.[y] As God is the embodiment of perfection, such opposition is rebellion against the principles of advancement and adherence to the practises that lead to degradation. Sin is any condition, whether omission of things required or in commission of acts forbidden, that tends to prevent or hinder the development of the human soul. As a righteous course leads to eternal life, so sin tends toward the darkness of the second death. Sin was introduced to the world by Satan;[z] yet it is by divine permission that mankind are brought in contact with sin, the contrast between evil and good thus being learned by experience.

According to the technical definition of sin it consists in the violation of law, and in this strict sense sin may be committed inadvertently or in ignorance. It is plain, however, from the scriptural doctrine of human responsibility and the unerring justice of God, that in his transgressions as in his righteous deeds man will be judged according to his ability to comprehend and obey law. To him who has never been made acquainted with a higher law the requirements of that law do not apply in their fulness. For sins committed without knowledge—that is, for laws violated in ignorance—a propitiation has been provided in the atonement wrought through the sacrifice of the Savior; and sinners of this class do not stand condemned, but shall be given opportunity yet to learn and to accept or reject the principles of the Gospel.

Jacob taught this doctrine: "Where there is no law given there is no punishment; and where there is no punishment there is no condemnation; and where there is no condemnation the mercies of the Holy One of Israel have claim upon them, because of the atonement; for they are delivered by the power of him. For the atonement satisfieth the demands of his justice upon all those who have not the law given to them, that they are delivered from that awful monster, death and hell and the devil, and the lake of fire and brimstone which is endless torment; and they are restored to that God who gave them breath, which is the Holy One of Israel." And then, in contrast, the prophet adds: "But wo unto him that has the law given, yea, that has all the commandments of God, like unto us, and that transgresseth them, and that wasteth the days of his probation, for awful is his state!"[aa] This is in strict agreement with the teachings of Paul to the Romans, "For as many as have sinned without law shall also perish without law: and as many as

[s] Acts 10:42.
[t] See Dan. 7:9–12; see also 2 Thess. 1:7, 8; 3 Nephi 26:35; D&C 76:31–49, 103–106.
[u] See Matt. 25:31–46; D&C, 1:9–12.
[v] See Acts 10:34, 35; see also Rom. 2:11; Eph. 6:9; Col. 3:25.
[w] See 2 Tm. 4:8.
[x] 1 John 3:4.
[y] See Appendix 3:2.
[z] See P.of G.P., Moses 4:4; see also Gen., chap. 3.
[aa] 2 Nephi 9:25–27.

have sinned in the law shall be judged by the law."[bb] And the word of modern scripture is to the same effect, for we are told, through recent revelation to the Church, that among those who are to receive the blessings of redemption are "they who died without law."[cc] These will include the heathen nations, whose redemption is promised with the added declaration that "they that knew no law shall have part in the first resurrection."[dd]

Punishment for Sin—As rewards for righteous deeds are proportionate to deserving acts, so the punishment prescribed for sin is made adequate to the offense.[ee] But, be it remembered, both rewards and punishments are natural consequences. Punishment is inflicted upon the sinner for disciplinary and reformatory purposes and in accordance with justice. There is nothing of vindictiveness or of desire to cause suffering manifest in the divine nature; on the contrary, our Father is cognizant of every pang, and permits such to afflict for beneficent purposes only. God's mercy is declared in the retributive pains that He allows, as in the blessings of peace that issue from Him. It is scarcely profitable to speculate as to the exact nature of the spiritual suffering imposed as punishment for sin. Comparison with physical pain,[ff] such as the tortures of fire in a sulphurous lake, serve to show that the human mind is incapable of comprehending the extent of these penalties. The sufferings entailed by the fate of condemnation are more to be feared than are any possible inflictions of physical torture; the mind, the spirit, the whole soul is doomed to suffer, and the torment is known by none in the flesh.

Consider the word of the Lord regarding those whose sin is the unpardonable one, whose transgression has carried them beyond the present horizon of possible redemption; those who have sunk so low in their wickedness as to have lost the power and even the desire to attempt reformation.[gg] Sons of Perdition they are called. These are they who, having learned the power of God afterward renounce it; those who sin wilfully in the light of knowledge; those who open their hearts to the Holy Spirit and then put the Lord to a mockery and a shame by denying it; and those who commit murder wherein they shed innocent blood;[hh] these are they of whom the Savior has declared that it would be better for them had they never been born.[ii] These are to share the punishment of the devil and his angels—punishment so terrible that the knowledge is withheld from all except those who are consigned to this doom, though a temporary view of the picture is permitted to some.[jj] These sinners are the only ones over whom the second death hath power: "Yea, verily, the only ones who shall not be redeemed in the due time of the Lord."[kk]

The Duration of punishment—As to the duration of punishment, we may take assurance that it will be graded according to the sin; and that the conception of every sentence for misdeeds being interminable is false.[ll] Great as is the effect of this life upon the hereafter, and certain as is the responsibility of opportunities lost for repentance, God holds the power to pardon beyond the grave. Yet the scriptures speak of eternal and endless punishment. Any punishment ordained of God is eternal, for

---

bb Rom. 2:12; see also Acts 17:30, 31.

cc D&C 76:72.

dd D&C 45:54.

ee See D&C 76:82-85; 82:21; 104:9; 63:17; 2 Nephi 1:13; 9:27; 28:23.

ff See D&C 76:36, 44; see also Jacob 6:10; Alma 12:16, 17; 3 Nephi 27:11, 12.

gg See D&C 76:26, 32, 43; John 17:12; 2 Thess. 2:3.

hh See D&C 132:27.

ii See D&C 76:32; see also Matt. 26:24; Mark 14:21.

jj See D&C 76:45–48.

kk D&C 76:38, 39.

ll See D&C 19:6-12; 76:36, 44.

He is eternal.[mm] His is a system of endless punishment, for it will always exist as a place or condition prepared for disobedient spirits; yet the infliction of the penalty will have an end in every case of acceptable repentance and reparation. And repentance is not impossible in the spirit world.[nn] However, as seen, there are some sins so great that their consequent punishments are not made known to man;[oo] these extreme penalties are reserved for the sons of Perdition.

The false doctrine that the punishment to be visited upon erring souls is endless, that every sentence for sin is of interminable duration, must be regarded as one of the most pernicious results of misapprehension of scripture. It is but a dogma of unauthorized and erring sectaries, at once unscriptural, unreasonable, and revolting to one who loves mercy and honors justice. True, the scriptures speak of everlasting burnings, eternal damnation, and the vengeance of eternal fire,[pp] as characteristics of the judgment provided for the wicked; yet in no instance is there justification for the inference that the individual sinner will have to suffer the wrath of offended justice forever and ever. The punishment in any case is sufficiently severe without the added and supreme horror of unending continuation. Justice must have her due; but when "the uttermost farthing" is paid, the prison doors shall open and the captive be free. But the prison remains, and the law prescribing punishment for offenses is not to be repealed.

So general were the ill effects of the commonly accepted doctrine, unscriptural and untrue though it was, regarding the endless torment awaiting every sinner, that even before the Church had been formally organized in the present dispensation, the Lord gave a revelation through the Prophet Joseph Smith touching this matter, in which we read: "And surely every man must repent or suffer; for I, God, am endless. Wherefore, I revoke not the judgments which I shall pass, but woes shall go forth, weeping, wailing and gnashing of teeth, yea, to those who are found on my left hand. Nevertheless, it is not written that there shall be no end to this torment, but it is written *endless torment*. Again, it is written *eternal damnation*. * * * For behold, I am endless, and the punishment which is given from my hand is endless punishment, for Endless is my name. Wherefore, Eternal punishment is God's punishment. Endless punishment is God's punishment."[qq]

Satan—We have had occasion to refer frequently to the author of evil among men. This is Satan,[rr] the adversary or opponent of the Lord, the chief of evil spirits, called also the Devil,[ss] Beelzebub,[tt] or the Prince of Devils, Perdition,[uu] and Belial.[vv] The figurative appellations dragon and serpent are applied to Satan when reference is made to his fall.[ww] We learn from the revealed word[xx] that Satan was once an angel of light, then known as Lucifer, a Son of the Morning; but his selfish ambition led him to aspire to the glory and power of the Father, to secure which he made the pernicious proposition to redeem the human family by compulsion; and, failing in this purpose, he headed an open rebellion against the Father and the Son, drawing a third of the hosts of heaven into his impious league.[yy] These rebellious spirits were expelled from heaven, and have

[mm] See D&C 19:1–12.
[nn] See 1 Peter 3:18–20; 4:6; D&C 76:73.
[oo] See D&C 76:45.
[pp] See Matt. 18:8; 25:41, 46; 2 Thess. 1:9; Mark 3:29; Jude 7.
[qq] Revelation, given March, 1830; D&C 19:4–12.
[rr] See Job 1:6–22; 2:1–7; Zech. 3:1, 2.
[ss] See Matt. 4:5, 8, 11; see also 1 Peter 5:8.
[tt] See Matt. 12:24.
[uu] See D&C 76:26.
[vv] See 2 Cor. 6:15.
[ww] See Rev. 12:9; 20:2.
[xx] See D&C 76:25–27; see also Isa. 14:12.
[yy] See D&C 29:36, 37; see also P.of G.P., Moses 4:37; Abraham 3:27, 28; *Jesus the Christ*, pp. 8, 9; Dan. 8:10; Rev. 12:4.

since followed the impulses of their wicked natures by seeking to lead human souls into their own condition of darkness. They are the devil and his angels. The right of free agency, maintained and vindicated by the war in heaven, prevents the possibility of compulsion being employed in this fiendish work of degradation; but the powers of these malignant spirits to tempt and persuade are used to the utmost. Satan tempted Eve to transgress the law of God;[zz] it was he who imparted the secret of murder for gain to the fratricide, Cain.[aaa]

Satan exerts a mastery over the spirits that have been corrupted by his practises; he is the foremost of the angels who were thrust down, and the instigator of the ruin of those who fall in this life; he seeks to molest and hinder mankind in good efforts, by tempting to sin; or it may be by imposing sickness,[bbb] or possibly death. Yet in all these malignant doings, he can go no farther than the transgressions of the victim may enable him, or the wisdom of God may permit; and at any time he may be checked by the superior power. Indeed, even the operations of his utmost malice may be turned to the accomplishment of divine purposes. The scriptures prove to us that the days of Satan's power are numbered;[ccc] his doom has been pronounced, and in the Lord's own time he will be completely overcome. He is to be bound during the millennial reign,[ddd] and after that thousand years of peace he will be loosed for a little season; then his defeat will be made complete, and his power over the children of God will be destroyed.

THE FALL

Our First parents in Eden[eee]—The crowning scene of the great drama of creation was the forming of man in the image of his spiritual Father, God.[fff] For the reception of the first man the Creator had especially prepared a choice region of earth, and had embellished it with natural beauties to gladden the heart of its possessor. "The Lord God planted a garden eastward in Eden;[ggg] and there he put the man whom he had formed."[hhh] Soon after man's advent upon the earth the Lord created a companion or help meet for him, declaring that it was not good that man should be alone.[iii] Thus, male and female, Adam and his wife Eve were placed in the garden. They had been given dominion "over the fish of the sea, and over the fowl of the air, and over every living thing that moveth upon the earth."[jjj] With this great power were associated certain commandments, the first of which in point of importance was that they "be fruitful, and multiply, and replenish the earth, and subdue it"; then, that they refrain from eating or even touching the fruit of a certain tree, the tree of knowledge of good and evil, which grew in the midst of the garden; though of all other fruits they were at liberty to freely partake. The words of God concerning this command and the penalty for its violation are: "And I, the Lord God, commanded the man, saying: Of every tree of the garden thou mayest freely eat, But of the tree of the knowledge of good and evil, thou shalt not eat of it; nevertheless, thou mayest choose for thyself, for it is given unto thee; but remember that I forbid it, for in the day thou eatest thereof thou shalt surely die."[kkk]

[zz] See Gen. 3:4, 5; see also P.of G.P., Moses 4:6–11.
[aaa] See P.of G.P., Moses 5:29–33.
[bbb] See Luke 13:16; see also Job, chap. 1.
[ccc] See John 12:31; 16:11.
[ddd] See Rev. 20:1–10.
[eee] Read Gen., chaps. 2, 3; see also P.of G.P., Moses 3:4; Abraham 5:7–21.
[fff] See Gen. 1:26, 27; see also P.of G.P., Moses 2:26, 27.
[ggg] See Appendix 3:3.
[hhh] Gen. 2:8, 9.
[iii] See Gen. 2:18; see also P.of G.P., Moses 3:18, 21–24.
[jjj] Gen. 1:28; see also P.of G.P., Moses 2:28; Abraham 4:28.
[kkk] P.of G.P., Moses 3:16, 17; see also Gen. 2:16, 17.

The Temptation to disobey this injunction soon came. Satan presented himself before Eve in the garden, and, speaking by the mouth of the serpent, questioned her about the commandments that God had given respecting the tree of knowledge of good and evil. Eve answered that they were forbidden even to touch the fruit of that tree, under penalty of death. Satan then sought to beguile the woman, contradicting the Lord's statement and declaring that death would not follow a violation of the divine injunction; but that, on the other hand, by doing that which the Lord had forbidden she and her husband would become like unto the gods, knowing good and evil for themselves. The woman was captivated by these representations; and, being eager to possess the advantages pictured by Satan, she disobeyed the command of the Lord, and partook of the fruit forbidden. She feared no evil, for she knew it not. Then, telling Adam what she had done, she urged him to eat of the fruit also.

Adam found himself in a position that made it impossible for him to obey both of the specific commandments given by the Lord. He and his wife had been commanded to multiply and replenish the earth. Adam had not yet fallen to the state of mortality, but Eve already had; and in such dissimilar conditions the two could not remain together, and therefore could not fulfil the divine requirement as to procreation. On the other hand, Adam would be disobeying another commandment by yielding to Eve's request. He deliberately and wisely decided to stand by the first and greater commandment; and, therefore, with understanding of the nature of his act, he also partook of the fruit that grew on the tree of knowledge. The fact that Adam acted understandingly in this matter is affirmed by scripture. Paul, in writing to Timothy, explained that "Adam was not deceived, but the woman being deceived was in the transgression."[lll] The prophet Lehi, in expounding the scriptures to his sons, declared: "Adam fell that men might be; and men are that they might have joy."[mmm]

The Tree of Life—There was another tree of special virtues in Eden; its fruit assured life to those who ate of it. While Adam and Eve lived in innocence, immune to death, this tree had not been forbidden them. Now that they had transgressed, however, now that the divine decree had issued fixing death as their lot, it was necessary that the fruit of the tree of life be no longer within their reach. They were, therefore, expelled from the garden, and cherubim with a flaming sword guarded the way, that man might not return in an unregenerate state. By transgression our first parents acquired a knowledge, which in their condition of pristine innocence they had not possessed—the experimental knowledge of good and evil. The result of their fall could have been of none but ill effect had they been immediately brought to a condition of immortality, without repentance, without atonement. In the despair following their realization of the great change that had come upon them, and in the light of the knowledge they had gained at such cost as to the virtues of the tree of life, it would have been natural for them to seek the seeming advantage of an immediate escape by partaking of the immortalizing food. In mercy they were prevented from so doing.

The words of the Creator are unmistakable as to the necessity of banishing Adam and Eve from Eden: "And the Lord God said, Behold, the man is become as one of us, to know good and evil: and now, lest he put forth his hand, and take also of the tree of life, and eat, and live forever: Therefore the Lord God sent him forth from the garden of Eden, to till the ground from whence he was taken. So he drove out the man; and he placed at the east of the garden of Eden Cherubims, and a flaming sword which turned every way, to keep the way of the tree of life."[nnn]

[lll] 1 Tim. 2:14.
[mmm] 2 Nephi 2:25.
[nnn] Gen. 3:22–24; see also P.of G.P., Moses 4:31.

Alma, the Nephite prophet, comprehended the result that would have followed had Adam and his wife eaten of the tree of life; he thus explained the matter: "Now, we see that the man had become as God, knowing good and evil; and lest he should put forth his hand, and take also of the tree of life, and eat and live forever, the Lord God placed cherubim and the flaming sword, that he should not partake of the fruit—And thus we see, that there was a time granted unto man to repent, yea, a probationary time, a time to repent and serve God. For behold, if Adam had put forth his hand immediately, and partaken of the tree of life, he would have lived forever, according to the word of God, having no space for repentance; yea, and also the word of God would have been void, and the great plan of salvation would have been frustrated."[ooo]

The Immediate Result of the Fall was the substitution of mortality, with all its attendant frailties, for the vigor of the primeval deathless state. Adam felt directly the effects of transgression in finding a barren and dreary earth, with a relatively sterile soil, instead of the beauty and fruitfulness of Eden. In place of pleasing and useful plants, thorns and thistles sprang up; and the man had to labor arduously, under the conditions of physical fatigue and suffering, to cultivate the soil that he might obtain necessary food. Upon Eve fell the penalty of bodily infirmity; pains and sorrows, which since have been regarded as the natural lot of womankind, came upon her, and she was made subject to her husband's authority. Having lost their sense of former innocence they became ashamed of their nakedness, and the Lord made for them garments of skins. Upon both the man and the woman was visited the penalty of spiritual death; for in that very day they were banished from Eden and cast out from the presence of the Lord. The serpent, having served the purposes of Satan, was made a subject of divine displeasure, being doomed to crawl forever in the dust, and to suffer from the enmity which it was decreed should be placed in the hearts of Eve's children.

Atonement provided for—God did not leave His now mortal children without hope. He gave other commandments to Adam, requiring him to offer sacrifices in the name of the Only Begotten Son, and promising redemption unto him and all his descendants who would comply with the conditions prescribed. The opportunity of winning the victor's reward by overcoming evil was explained to our parents, and they rejoiced. Adam said: "Blessed be the name of God, for because of my transgression my eyes are opened, and in this life I shall have joy, and again in the flesh I shall see God." Eve was glad and declared: "Were it not for our transgression we never should have had seed, and never should have known good and evil, and the joy of our redemption, and the eternal life which God giveth unto all the obedient."[ppp]

The Fall came not by Chance—It would be unreasonable to suppose that the transgression of Eve and Adam came as a surprise to the Creator. By His infinite foreknowledge, God knew what would be the result of Satan's temptation to Eve, and what Adam would do under the resulting conditions. Further, it is evident that the fall was foreseen to be a means whereby man could be brought into direct experience with both good and evil, so that of his own agency he might elect the one or the other, and thus be prepared by the experiences of a mortal probation for the exaltation provided in the beneficent plan of his creation: *"For behold, this is my work and my glory—to bring to pass the immortality and eternal life of man"*[qqq] spake the Lord unto Moses. It was the purpose of God to place within the reach of the spirits begotten by Him in the heavens the means of individual effort, and the opportunity of winning not merely redemption from death but also salvation and even exaltation, with the powers of eternal progression and increase. Hence it was necessary that the spiritual offspring

[ooo] Alma 42:3-5.
[ppp] P.of G.P., Moses 5:10, 11; see also Appendix 3:6, 7, 8.
[qqq] P.of G.P., Moses 1:39.

of God should leave the scenes of their primeval childhood and enter the school of mortal experience, meeting, contending with, and overcoming evil, according to their several degrees of faith and strength. Adam and Eve could never have been the parents of a mortal posterity had they not themselves become mortal; mortality was an essential element in the divine plan respecting the earth and its appointed inhabitants; and, as a means of introducing mortality, the Lord placed before the progenitors of the race a law, knowing what would follow.

Eve was fulfilling the foreseen purposes of God by the part she took in the great drama of the fall; yet she did not partake of the forbidden fruit with that object in view, but with intent to act contrary to the divine command, being deceived by the sophistries of Satan, who also, for that matter, furthered the purposes of the Creator by tempting Eve; yet his design was to thwart the Lord's plan. We are definitely told that "he knew not the mind of God, wherefore he sought to destroy the world."[rrr] Yet his diabolical effort, far from being the initiatory step toward destruction, contributed to the plan of man's eternal progression. Adam's part in the great event was essentially different from that of his wife; he was not deceived; on the contrary he deliberately decided to do as Eve desired, that he might carry out the purposes of his Maker with respect to the race of men, whose first patriarch he was ordained to be.

Even the transgressions of men may be turned to the accomplishment of high purposes. The sacrificial death of Christ was ordained from before the foundation of the world, yet Judas who betrayed, and the Jews who brought about the crucifixion of the Son of God, are none the less guilty of the awful crime.

It has become a common practise with mankind to heap reproaches upon the progenitors of the family, and to picture the supposedly blessed state in which we would be living but for the fall; whereas our first parents are entitled to our deepest gratitude for their legacy to posterity—the means of winning title to glory, exaltation, and eternal lives. But for the opportunity thus given, the spirits of God's offspring would have remained forever in a state of innocent childhood, sinless through no effort of their own; negatively saved, not from sin, but from the opportunity of meeting sin; incapable of winning the honors of victory because prevented from taking part in the conflict. As it is, they are heirs to the birthright of Adam's descendants—mortality, with its immeasurable possibilities and its God-given freedom of action. From Father Adam we have inherited all the ills to which flesh is heir; but such are necessarily incident to a knowledge of good and evil, by the proper use of which knowledge man may become even as the Gods.[sss]

REFERENCES

Free Agency
The Lord God gave Adam commandment and prescribed the penalty for disobedience—Gen. 2:16, 17.

Thou shalt not eat of it, nevertheless, thou mayest choose for thyself, for it is given unto thee—Moses 3:17.

And we will prove them herewith, to see if they will do all things whatsoever the Lord their God shall command them—Abraham 3:25.

If thou doest well, shalt thou not be accepted?—Gen. 4:7.

[rrr] P. of G.P., Moses 4:6.
[sss] See Appendix 3:5.

Behold, I set before you this day a blessing and a curse—Deut. 11:26; see also 30:15.

If thou shalt hearken diligently unto the voice of the Lord thy God—Deut. 28:1; see also 1 Kings 3:14.

Choose you this day whom ye will serve—Josh. 24:15.

How long halt ye between two opinions?—1 Kings 18:21.

Death may be chosen rather than life—Jer. 8:3.

The Lord gave unto man to act for himself—2 Nephi 2:16.

Men free to choose the way of everlasting death, or the way of eternal life—2 Nephi 10:23.

Wo upon him who listeth to obey the evil spirit—Mosiah 2:33.

To reap eternal happiness or eternal misery according to the spirit they listed to obey—Alma 3:26, 27.

Men in a state to act according to their wills and pleasures, to do evil or good—Alma 12:31.

Even those called from the foundation of the world were left to choose evil or good—Alma 13:3.

God granteth to men according to their desire, and allotteth to them according to their wills—Alma 29:4.

Man's privilege to serve God—Alma 30:9.

Ye are free, ye are permitted to act for yourselves—Helaman 14:30.

Adam was an agent unto himself—D&C 29:35.

A third part of the hosts of heaven were turned to evil through their agency—D&C 29:36.

Temptation necessary to test men's agency—D&C 29:39.

Power in men whereas they are agents unto themselves—D&C 58:28; see also 104:17.

Satan sought to destroy agency of men—Moses 4:3.

Given to men to know good and evil and thus be agents unto themselves—Moses 6:56.

Needs be that there be opposition in all things—2 Nephi 2:11, 15.

Man's Accountability—the Judgment

Sin is the transgression of the law—1 John 3:4; also 5:17.

For all these things God will bring thee into judgment—Eccl. 11:9; also 12:14.

The Lord to punish for iniquity—Isa. 26:21.

According to their deeds will he repay—Isa. 59:18.

Everyone shall die for his own iniquity—Jer. 31:30.

With what judgment ye judge ye shall be judged—Matt. 7:2.

He shall reward every man according to his works—Matt. 16:27.

Day appointed for judgment of the world—Acts 17:31.

Whatsoever a man soweth, that shall he also reap—Gal. 6:7; see also D&C 6:33.

I come quickly; and my reward is with me, to give every man according as his work shall be—Rev. 22:12.

Requisite with justice of God that men be judged according to their works—Alma 41:3; also verse 4.

The reward of their hands shall be upon them—2 Nephi 13:11.

To be judged of their works whether good or evil—3 Nephi 26:4; also verse 5.

Which words shall judge them at the last day—2 Nephi 25:18.

All shall rise from the dead and be judged—Alma 11:41.

To stand before God to be judged of their works—1 Nephi 15:33; also Alma 5:15 and 11:41.

Judging every man according to his works—D&C 19:3.

Every man accountable for his own sins—D&C 101:78.

The Lord shall come, his recompense with him, and shall reward every man—D&C 56:19.

The righteous and the wicked shall be separated—D&C 29:27.

To reward every man according as his work shall be—D&C 101:65.

They who keep their first estate shall be added upon—Abraham 3:26.

Satan

The great dragon was cast out into the earth, called also that old serpent, the Devil, and Satan, which deceiveth the whole world—Rev. 12:9; see also Luke 10:18.

Lucifer, son of the morning, his wicked ambition and fate—Isa. 14:12 and succeeding verses; see also D&C 76:25–28.

Called also Perdition; and those who sin beyond redemption are called sons of Perdition—D&C 76:26, 32, 43.

Tempted Eve and brought about the fall—Gen. chap. 3; Moses chap. 4; D&C 29:40.

A sinner from the beginning—1 John 3:8; Moses 4:1–4.

The father of lies; a liar from the beginning—John 8:44; D&C 93:25, 37; 2 Nephi 2:18.

Tempted Cain and taught him murder—Moses 5:16–24.

Came with others who presented themselves before the Lord—Job 1:6–12.

Tempted Christ—Matt. 4:1–11.

Tempted Judas Iscariot to betray Christ—John 13:2.

To be restrained during the Millennium—Rev. 20:1–3.

His doom decreed—Rev. 20:7–10; see also Matt. 25:41.

Fallen from heaven and miserable he sought the misery of mankind—2 Nephi 2:18, 27.

He that committeth sin is of the devil—1 John 3:8.

Resist the devil and he will flee from you—Jas. 4:7.

Adversary, the devil, as a roaring lion seeking whom he may devour—1 Peter 5:8.

Led according to will and captivity of the devil—2 Nephi 1:18.

That which is evil cometh of the devil—Moroni 7:12.

Satan desireth to have you—3 Nephi 18:18.

Devil shall have power over his own dominion—D&C 1:35.

Stirs up to contention over doctrine—D&C 10:63; see also 3 Nephi 11:28, 29.

Devil will rage in hearts of men and stir them up to anger; and pacify others, leading them gently—2 Nephi 28:19–23.

The Fall

Temptation of Adam and Eve—Gen. chap. 3; Moses chap. 4; D&C 29:40; see also 2 Cor. 11:3.

By one man sin entered the world—Rom. 5:12, 18.

Fall brought upon mankind spiritual death as well as temporal—Alma 42:9.

Lehi's discourse on the fall and its consequences—2 Nephi 2:14–27.

By Adam's fall mankind became a fallen people—Alma 12:20–24; see also Helaman 14:16.

Adam fell that men might be and men are that they might have joy—2 Nephi 2:25.

The resurrection comes by reason of the fall—2 Nephi 9:6.

Christ's blood atoneth for those who have fallen by the transgression of Adam—Mosiah 3:11.

Every spirit of man innocent in the beginning—D&C 93:38.

Adam rejoiced in the blessings following his transgression—Moses 5:10, 11.

Because that Adam fell, we are; and by his fall came death—Moses 6:48.

For as in Adam all die, even so in Christ shall all be made alive—1 Cor. 15:21, 22; see also Rom. 5:11–19.

4

THE ATONEMENT AND SALVATION

ARTICLE 3

WE BELIEVE that through the Atonement of Christ, all mankind may be saved, by obedience to the laws and ordinances of the Gospel.

THE ATONEMENT

The Atonement of Christ is taught as a leading doctrine by all sects professing Christianity. The expression is so common a one, and the essential point of its signification is so generally admitted, that definitions may appear to be superfluous; nevertheless, there is a peculiar importance attached to the use of the word "atonement" in a theological sense. The doctrine of the atonement comprises proof of the divinity of Christ's earthly ministry, and the vicarious nature of His death as a foreordained and voluntary sacrifice, intended for and efficacious as a propitiation for the sins of mankind, thus becoming the means whereby salvation may be secured.

The New Testament, which is properly regarded as the scripture of Christ's mission among men, is imbued throughout with the doctrine of salvation through the work of atonement wrought by the Savior; and yet the word, atonement, occurs but once in the record; and in that single instance, according to the opinion of most Biblical authorities, it is misused. The instance referred to is found in the words of Paul addressed to the saints at Rome: "But we also joy in God through our Lord Jesus Christ, by whom we have now received the atonement."[a] The marginal rendering gives,

a Rom. 5:11.

instead of atonement, "reconciliation," and of this word a related form is used in the preceding verse. A consistent translation, giving a full agreement between the English and the Greek, would make the verse quoted, and that immediately preceding it, read in this way: For if, when we were enemies, we were reconciled to God by the death of his Son, much more, being reconciled, we shall be saved by his life. And not only so, but we also joy in God through our Lord Jesus Christ, by whom we have now received the reconciliation.[b] The term "atonement" occurs repeatedly in the Old Testament, with marked frequency in three of the books of the Pentateuch, Exodus, Leviticus, and Numbers; and the sense in which it is employed is that of a sacrifice of propitiation, usually associated with the death of an acceptable victim, whereby reconciliation was to be effected between God and men.

The structure of the word in its present form is suggestive of the true meaning; it is literally *at-one-ment,* "denoting reconciliation, or the bringing into agreement of those who have been estranged."[c] And such is the significance of the saving sacrifice of the Redeemer, whereby He expiated the transgression of the fall, through which death came into the world, and provided ready and efficient means for man's attainment of immortality through reconciliation with God.

Nature of the Atonement—The atonement wrought by Jesus Christ is a necessary sequel of the transgression of Adam; and, as the infinite foreknowledge of God made clear to Him the one even before Adam was placed upon the earth, so the Father's mercy prepared a Savior for mankind before the world was framed. Through the fall Adam and Eve have entailed the conditions of mortality upon their descendants; therefore all beings born of earthly parents are subject to bodily death. The sentence of banishment from the presence of God was in the nature of a spiritual death; and that penalty, which was visited upon our first parents in the day of their transgression, has likewise followed as the common heritage of humanity. As this penalty came into the world through an individual act, it would be manifestly unjust to cause all to eternally suffer here from without means of deliverance. Therefore was the promised sacrifice of Jesus Christ ordained as a propitiation for broken law, whereby Justice could be fully satisfied, and Mercy be left free to exercise her beneficent influence over the souls of mankind.[d] All the details of the glorious plan, by which the salvation of the human family is assured, may not lie within the understanding of man; but man has learned, even from his futile attempts to fathom the primary causes of the phenomena of nature, that his powers of comprehension are limited; and he will admit, that to deny an effect because of his inability to elucidate its cause would be to forfeit his claims as an observing and reasoning being.

Simple as is the plan of redemption in its general features, it is confessedly a mystery in detail to the finite mind. President John Taylor has written in this wise: "In some mysterious, incomprehensible way, Jesus assumed the responsibility which naturally would have devolved upon Adam; but which could only be accomplished through the mediation of Himself, and by taking upon Himself their sorrows, assuming their responsibilities, and bearing their transgressions or sins. In a manner to us incomprehensible and inexplicable, He bore the weight of the sins of the whole world, not only of Adam, but of his posterity; and in doing that, opened the kingdom of heaven, not only to all believers and all who obeyed the law of God, but to more than one-half of the human family who die before they come to years of maturity, as well as to the heathen,

[b] Rom. 5:10, 11; see Revised Version.
[c] Standard Dictionary, under *propitiation.*
[d] See Appendix 4:1.

who, having died without law, will through His mediation be resurrected without law, and be judged without law, and thus participate, according to their capacity, works, and worth, in the blessings of His atonement."[e]

However incomplete may be our comprehension of the scheme of redemption through Christ's vicarious sacrifice in all its parts, we cannot reject it without becoming infidel; for it stands as the fundamental doctrine of all scripture, the very essence of the spirit of prophecy and revelation, the most prominent of all the declarations of God unto man.

The Atonement a Vicarious Sacrifice—It is to many a matter of surpassing wonder that the voluntary sacrifice of a single being could be made to operate as a means of ransom for the rest of mankind. In this, as in other things, the scriptures are explicable by the spirit of scriptural interpretation. The sacred writings of ancient times, the inspired utterances of latter-day prophets, the traditions of mankind, the rites of sacrifice, and even the sacrileges of heathen idolatries, all involve the idea of vicarious atonement. God has never refused to accept an offering made by one who is authorized on behalf of those who are in any way incapable of doing the required service themselves. The scapegoat[f] and the altar victim[g] of ancient Israel, if offered with repentance and contrition, were accepted by the Lord in mitigation of the sins of the people. It is interesting to note that while the ceremonies of sacrifice formed so large and so essential a part of the Mosaic requirements, these rites long antedated the establishment of Israel as a distinct people; for, as already shown, altar sacrifice was rendered by Adam. The symbolism of the immolating of animals as a prototype of the great sacrifice to follow on Calvary was thus instituted with the beginning of human history.

The many kinds of sacrifice prescribed by the Mosaic law are classifiable as bloody and bloodless. Offerings of the first order only, involving the infliction of death, were acceptable in propitiation or atonement for sin, and the victim had to be clean, healthy, and without spot or blemish. So for the great sacrifice, the effects of which were to be infinite, only an innocent subject could be accepted. It was Christ's right to become the Savior as the only sinless being on earth, and as the Only Begotten of the Father, and above all as the one ordained in the heavens to be the Redeemer of mankind; and though the exercise of this right involved a sacrifice, the extent of which man cannot comprehend, yet Christ made that sacrifice willingly and voluntarily. To the last He had the means of terminating the tortures of His persecutors, by the exercise of His inherent powers.[h] In some way, though that way may be inexplicable to us, Christ took upon Himself the burdensome onus of the sins of mankind. The means may be to our finite minds a mystery, yet the results are our salvation.

Something of the Savior's agony as He groaned under this load of guilt, which to Him, as a type of purity, must have been in itself bitter in the extreme, He has told us in this day: "For behold, I, God, have suffered these things for all, that they might not suffer if they would repent; But if they would not repent they must suffer even as I; Which suffering caused myself, even God, the greatest of all, to tremble because of pain, and to bleed at every pore, and to suffer both body and spirit—and would that I might not drink the bitter cup, and shrink—Nevertheless, glory be to the Father, and I partook and finished my preparations unto the children of men."[i] Further

[e] John Taylor, *Mediation and Atonement,* pp. 148, 149; see also Appendix 4:5.
[f] See Lev. 16:20–22.
[g] See Lev., chap. 4.
[h] See Matt. 26:53, 54; John 10:17, 18.
[i] D&C 19:16–19; see *Jesus the Christ,* pp. 610–614.

instances of the validity of vicarious service are found in the rites of baptism for the dead[j] as taught in apostolic and modern times, and in the institution of other temple ordinances[k] in the current dispensation.

Christ's Sacrifice was Voluntary and Love-inspired—We have noted in passing that Christ gave His life willingly and voluntarily for the redemption of mankind. He had offered Himself, in the primeval council in heaven, as the subject of the atoning sacrifice made necessary by the foreseen transgression of the first man; and the free agency shown and exercised in this, the early stage of His saving mission, was retained to the very last of the agonizing fulfilment of the accepted plan. Though He lived on earth a man in every particular that concerns us in our regard for Him as an example of godliness in humanity, yet it is to be remembered that, though born of a mortal mother, he was begotten in the flesh by an immortal Father; and so combined within His being the capacity to die, and the power to hold death indefinitely in abeyance. He gave up His life; it was not taken from Him against His will. Note the significance of His own declaration: "Therefore doth my Father love me, because I lay down my life, that I might take it again. No man taketh it from me, but I lay it down of myself. I have power to lay it down, and I have power to take it again."[l] On another occasion Jesus testified of Himself in this way: "For as the Father hath life in himself, so hath he given to the Son to have life in himself; And hath given him authority to execute judgment also, because he is the Son of Man."[m] Amidst the tragic scenes of the betrayal, when one who had been a professed follower and friend gave Him with a traitorous kiss to His persecutors, and when Peter, with a rashness prompted by personal zeal, drew and used the sword in His defense, the Master said: "Thinkest thou that I cannot now pray to my Father, and he shall presently give me more than twelve legions of angels? But how then shall the scriptures be fulfilled, that thus it must be?"[n] And on to the bitter end, marked by the expiring though triumphant cry "It is finished," the incarnated God held in subjection within Himself the power to thwart His torturers had He so willed.

The motive inspiring and sustaining Him through all the scenes of His mission, from the time of His primeval ordination to the moment of victorious consummation on the cross, was twofold: first, the desire to do His Father's will in accomplishing the redemption of mankind; second, His love for humanity, of whose welfare and destiny He had assumed charge. Far from cherishing the least feeling of vindictiveness against those who put Him to death, He entertained for them compassion to the last. Hear Him in the hour of extreme agony, praying aloud: "Father, forgive them; for they know not what they do."[o] Not less is the Father's love, as shown by His accepting the Son's offer and permitting Him whom He delighted to call His Beloved to suffer as only a God could suffer: "For God so loved the world, that he gave his only begotten Son, that whosoever believeth in him should not perish, but have everlasting life. For God sent not his Son into the world to condemn the world, but that the world through him might be saved."[p] Further, we hear the teaching of the apostle, whom the Savior loved so well: "In this was manifested the love of God toward us, because that God sent his only begotten Son into the world, that we might live through him."[q]

[j] See 1 Cor. 15:29; see also chap. 7 herein.
[k] See D&C 127:4–9; sec. 128.
[l] John 10:17, 18; *see Jesus the Christ,* pp. 22, 23, 81, 418.
[m] John 5:26, 27.
[n] Matt. 26:53, 54.
[o] Luke 23:34.
[p] John 3:16, 17.
[q] 1 John 4:9; see also *Jesus the Christ,* chaps. 2, 3.

The Atonement Foreordained and Foretold—As already shown, the plan of the Father to open a way for the redemption of mankind, then to leave all men free to exercise their agency, was adopted by the council in heaven to the rejection of Lucifer's plan of compulsion. Even at that remote period Christ was thus ordained as a mediator for all mankind; in fact, "a covenant was entered into between Him and His Father, in which He agreed to atone for the sins of the world, and He thus, as stated, became the 'Lamb slain from before the foundation of the world.'"[r] Prophets who lived centuries before the time of Christ's birth testified of Him and of the great work He had been ordained to perform. These men of God had been permitted to behold in prophetic vision many of the scenes incident to the Savior's earthly mission, and they solemnly bore record of the manifestations. The testimony of Christ is the spirit of prophecy, and without it no person can rightly claim the distinction of being a prophet of God. Adam's despair incident to the fall was changed to joy when, through revelation, he learned of the plan of redemption to be wrought by the Son of God in the flesh.[s] Righteous Enoch taught the same truths, which had been declared to him from the heavens.[t] This testimony was borne by Moses,[u] Job,[v] David,[w] Zechariah,[x] Isaiah,[y] and Micah.[z] The same declaration was made by John the Baptist[aa] who was characterized by the Lord as more than a prophet.

Should there be doubt as to the application of such prophecies, we have the conclusive testimony of Christ that they refer to Himself. On that memorable day, immediately following His resurrection, while walking incognito with two disciples on the road to Emmaus, He taught them the scriptures that had been written concerning the Son of God: "Beginning at Moses and all the prophets, he expounded unto them in all the scriptures the things concerning himself."[bb] A few hours after this event the Lord appeared to the eleven at Jerusalem. He operated upon their minds "that they might understand the scriptures; and said unto them: Thus it is written, and thus it behoved Christ to suffer,"[cc] in this way testifying that He was fulfilling a previously ordained plan. Peter, one of the Savior's most intimate earthly associates, refers to Him as "a lamb without blemish and without spot: Who verily was foreordained before the foundation of the world."[dd] In his epistle to the Romans, Paul characterizes Christ as the one "Whom God hath set forth to be a propitiation through faith in his blood, to declare his righteousness for the remission of sins that are past."[ee] These are but a few of the Biblical evidences of Christ's foreordination; both Old and New Testament[ff] writings abound in proofs of the Messiah's appointed work.

Book of Mormon prophets are characterized by the directness of their testimonies concerning the Messiah. Because of his faith the brother of Jared was permitted to behold the Savior, twenty-two

---

[r] John Taylor, in *Mediation and Atonement,* p. 97; see also Appendix 4:4.

[s] See P.of G.P., Moses 5:9–11; see also Appendix 4:6.

[t] See P.of G.P., Moses 6:51–68.

[u] See Deut. 18:15, 17–19.

[v] See Job 19:25–27.

[w] See Ps. 2.

[x] See Zech. 9:9; 12:10; 13:6.

[y] See Isa. 7:14; 9:6, 7.

[z] See Micah 5:2.

[aa] See Matt. 3:11.

[bb] See Luke 24:27.

[cc] Luke 24:45, 46; see *Jesus the Christ,* pp. 685-690.

[dd] 1 Peter 1:19, 20.

[ee] Rom. 3:25.

[ff] See Rom. 16:25, 26; Eph. 3:9–11; Col. 1:24–26; 2 Tim. 1:8–10; Titus 1:2, 3; Rev. 13:8.

centuries prior to the meridian of time, and to be shown that man was created after the image of the Lord, at the same time being taught of the Father's purpose that the Son take upon Himself flesh and dwell upon the earth.[gg] Note the personal declaration of the foreordained Redeemer to this prophet: "Behold, I am he who was prepared from the foundation of the world to redeem my people. Behold, I am Jesus Christ. I am the Father and the Son. In me shall all mankind have light, and that eternally, even they who shall believe on my name; and they shall become my sons and my daughters."[hh]

Nephi records the prophecy of his father Lehi concerning the future appearing of the Son in the flesh, His baptism, death, and resurrection; and this prophetic utterance specifies the exact date of the Savior's birth—six hundred years after the time of Lehi's exodus from Jerusalem. The mission of John the Baptist is described and even the place of baptism is designated.[ii] Shortly after the time of Lehi's vision, Nephi was shown by the Spirit the same things, as also many others, some of which he has written but the greater part of which he was forbidden to write, as another, the Apostle John, had been ordained to set them forth in a book which should form part of the Bible. But, from the partial account of his vision we learn that he saw, in Nazareth, Mary the Virgin, first alone and shortly afterward with a child in her arms; and that the demonstrator of the vision informed him that the infant was the Lamb of God, the Son of the Eternal Father. Then Nephi beheld the Son ministering among the children of men, proclaiming the word, healing the sick, and working many other wondrous miracles; he saw John, the prophet of the wilderness, going before Him; he beheld the Savior baptized of John, and the Holy Ghost descending upon Him with the visible sign of the dove. Then he saw and prophesied that twelve apostles would follow the Savior in His ministry; that the Son would be taken and judged of men and finally be slain. Piercing the future even beyond the time of the crucifixion, Nephi beheld the strife of the world against the apostles of the Lamb and the final triumph of God's cause.[jj]

Jacob, brother of Nephi, prophesied to his brethren that Christ would appear in the flesh among the Jews, and that He would be scourged and crucified.[kk] King Benjamin lifted his voice in support of the same testimony, and preached unto his people the righteous condescension of God.[ll] So also declared Abinadi,[mm] Alma,[nn] Amulek,[oo] and Samuel the Lamanite prophet.[pp] The literal fulfilment of these prophecies furnishes proof of their truth. The signs and wonders indicative of Christ's birth[qq] and death were all realized;[rr] and after His death and ascension the Savior manifested Himself among the Nephites while the Father proclaimed Him to the multitude.[ss]

The ancient scriptures, then, are plain in declaring that Christ came upon the earth to do a work previously allotted. He lived, suffered and died, in accordance with a plan that had been framed in righteousness even before the world was, for the redemption of the children of Adam. Equally important and explicit is the word of latter-day revelation through which the Son has declared Himself as Alpha and Omega, the beginning and the end, man's Advocate with the

[gg] See Ether 3:13, 14; see also 13:10, 11.
[hh] Ether 3:14; read also 8-16; see Appendix 2:11.
[ii] See 1 Nephi 10:3–11.
[jj] See 1 Nephi 11:14–35; see also 2 Nephi 2:3–21; 25:20–27; 26:24.
[kk] See 2 Nephi 6:8–10; 9:5, 6.
[ll] See Mosiah 3:5–27; 4:1-8.
[mm] See Mosiah 15:6–9; chap. 16.
[nn] See Alma 7:9–14.
[oo] See Alma 11:36–44.
[pp] See Helaman 14:2–8.
[qq] See Helaman 14:2–5, 20–27.
[rr] See 3 Nephi 1:5–21; 8:3–25.
[ss] See 3 Nephi 11:1–17; see also *Jesus the Christ*, chap. 39.

Father, the universal Redeemer.[tt] Consider a single citation from the many revelations concerning Christ given in the present dispensation: "Listen to the voice of the Lord your God, even Alpha and Omega, the beginning and the end, whose course is one eternal round, the same today as yesterday, and forever. I am Jesus Christ, the Son of God, who was crucified for the sins of the world, even as many as will believe on my name, that they may become the sons of God, even one in me as I am one in the Father, as the Father is one in me, that we may be one."[uu]

The Extent of the Atonement is universal, applying alike to all descendants of Adam. Even the unbeliever, the heathen, and the child who dies before reaching the years of discretion, all are redeemed by the Savior's self-sacrifice from the individual consequences of the fall.[vv] It is proved by scripture that the resurrection of the body is one of the victories achieved by Christ through His atoning sacrifice. He Himself proclaimed the eternal truth: "I am the resurrection, and the life";[ww] and He was the first of all men to rise from the grave to immortality—"the firstfruits of them that slept."[xx] The scriptures leave no room for doubt concerning the fact that the resurrection will be universal. The Savior announced to His apostles the beginning of this work of deliverance from the tomb; hear His words: "Marvel not at this: for the hour is coming, in the which all that are in the graves shall hear his voice, And shall come forth; they that have done good, unto the resurrection of life; and they that have done evil, unto the resurrection of damnation"[yy] or, as the latter part of the declaration has been rendered through inspiration in the present day, "They who have done good in the resurrection of the just, and they who have done evil in the resurrection of the unjust."[zz]

Paul preached the doctrine of a universal resurrection: "That there shall be a resurrection of the dead, both of the just and unjust."[aaa] On another occasion he wrote: "For as in Adam all die, even so in Christ shall all be made alive."[bbb] John the Revelator testifies of his vision concerning futurity: "And I saw the dead, small and great, stand before God; * * * And the sea gave up the dead which were in it; and death and hell delivered up the dead which were in them."[ccc] Thus it is plain that the effect of the atonement, so far as it applies to the victory over temporal or bodily death, includes the entire race. It is equally clear that the release from spiritual death, or banishment from the presence of God, is offered to all; so that if any man lose salvation such loss will be due to himself, and in no way be the inescapable effect of Adam's transgression. That the gift of redemption through Christ is free to all men was specifically taught by the apostles of old. Thus Paul says: "Therefore as by the offence of one judgment came upon all men to condemnation; even so by the righteousness of one the free gift came upon all men unto justification of life."[ddd] And further: "For there is one God, and one mediator between God and men, the man Christ Jesus; Who gave himself a ransom for all."[eee] John spoke of the Redeemer's sacrifice, saying: "And he is the propitiation for our sins; and not for ours only, but also for the sins of the whole world."[fff]

[tt] See D&C 6:21; 14:9; 18:10–12; 19:1, 2, 24; 21:9; 29:1; 34:1–3; 35:1, 2; 38:1–5; 39:1–3; 45:3–5; 46:13, 14; 76:1–4, 12–14, 19–24, 68, 69; 93:1–17, 38.
[uu] D&C 35:1, 2.
[vv] See Appendix 4:2.
[ww] John 11:25.
[xx] 1 Cor. 15:20; see Acts 26:23.
[yy] John 5:28, 29.
[zz] D&C 76:17.
[aaa] Acts 24:15.
[bbb] 1 Cor. 15:22.
[ccc] Rev. 20:12, 13.
[ddd] Rom. 5:18.
[eee] 1 Tim. 2:5, 6.
[fff] 1 John 2:2.

The same truths were taught among the Nephites. Benjamin, the righteous king, preached of "the atonement which was prepared from the foundation of the world for all mankind, which ever were since the fall of Adam, or who are, or who ever shall be, even unto the end of the world."[ggg] In revelation of the present day we read of Christ's having come into the world, to suffer and to die: "That through him all might be saved whom the Father had put into his power and made by him."[hhh]

But besides this universal application of the atonement, whereby all men are redeemed from the effects of Adam's transgression both with respect to the death of the body and inherited sin, there is application of the same great sacrifice as a means of propitiation for individual sins through the faith and good works of the sinner. This twofold effect of the atonement is implied in the article of our faith now under consideration. The first effect is to secure to all mankind alike, exemption from the penalty of the fall, thus providing a plan of *General Salvation.* The second effect is to open a way for *Individual Salvation* whereby mankind may secure remission of personal sins. As these sins are the result of individual acts it is just that forgiveness for them should be conditioned on individual compliance with prescribed requirements—"obedience to the laws and ordinances of the Gospel."

The General Effect of the Atonement, so far as it applies to all who have arrived at years of accountability and judgment, has been demonstrated by the scriptures already quoted. Its application to children may properly receive attention. The Church of Jesus Christ of Latter-day Saints teaches as a doctrine founded on reason, justice, and scripture, that all children are innocent in the sight of God, and that, until they reach an age of personal responsibility, baptism is neither requisite nor proper in their behalf; that, in short, they are saved through the atonement of Christ. To a degree, children are born heirs to the good or evil natures of their parents; the effects of heredity are admitted. Good and evil tendencies, blessings and curses, are transmitted from generation to generation. Through this divinely-appointed order, the justice of which is plain in the revealed light of knowledge concerning the antemortal state of the spirits of mankind, the children of Adam are natural heirs to the ills of mortality; but through Christ's atonement they are all redeemed from the curse of this fallen state. The debt, which comes to them as a legacy, is paid for them and thus are they left free. Children who die before reaching the state of accountability for their acts are innocent in the eyes of God, even though they be the offspring of transgressors. We read in the Book of Mormon: "Little children cannot repent; wherefore, it is awful wickedness to deny the pure mercies of God unto them, for they are all alive in him because of his mercy. * * * For behold that all little children are alive in Christ, and also all they that are without the law. For the power of redemption cometh on all them that have no law."[iii]

The prophet Mormon, writing to his son Moroni, expressed in the following manner his conviction of the innocence of children: "Listen to the words of Christ, your Redeemer, your Lord and your God. Behold, I came into the world not to call the righteous but sinners to repentance; the whole need no physician, but they that are sick; wherefore, little children are whole, for they are not capable of committing sin; wherefore the curse of Adam is taken from them in me, that it hath no power over them. * * * Behold I say unto you that this thing shall ye teach—repentance and baptism unto those who are accountable and capable of committing sin; yea, teach parents that they must repent and be baptized, and humble themselves as their little children, and they shall all be saved with their little children. And their little children need no repentance, neither baptism.

ggg Mosiah 4:7.
hhh D&C 76:42.
iii Moroni 8:19–22.

Behold, baptism is unto repentance to the fulfilling the commandments unto the remission of sins. But little children are alive in Christ, even from the foundation of the world."[jjj]

In a revelation through the Prophet Joseph Smith in this dispensation, the Lord has said: "But behold, I say unto you, that little children are redeemed from the foundation of the world through mine Only Begotten; Wherefore, they cannot sin, for power is not given unto Satan to tempt little children, until they begin to become accountable before me."[kkk] President John Taylor, after citing instances of Christ's affection for little children, and proofs of the innocent condition in which they are regarded in heaven, says: "Without Adam's transgression those children could not have existed; through the atonement they are placed in a state of salvation without any act of their own. These would embrace, according to the opinion of statisticians, more than one- half of the human family who can attribute their salvation only to the mediation and atonement of the Savior."[lll]

The Individual Effect of the Atonement makes it possible for any and every soul to obtain absolution from the effect of personal sins, through the mediation of Christ; but such saving intercession is to be invoked by individual effort as manifested through faith, repentance, and continued works of righteousness. The laws under which individual salvation is obtainable have been prescribed by Christ, whose right it is to say how the blessings made possible by His own sacrifice shall be administered. All men are in need of the Savior's mediation, for all are transgressors. So taught the apostles of old: "For all have sinned, and come short of the glory of God."[mmm] And again: "If we say that we have no sin, we deceive ourselves, and the truth is not in us."[nnn] That the blessing of redemption from individual sins, while open for all to attain, is nevertheless conditioned on individual effort, is as plainly declared as is the truth of unconditional redemption from death as an effect of the fall. There is a judgment ordained for all, and all will be judged "according to their works." The free agency of man enables him to choose or reject, to follow the path of life or the road that leads to destruction; therefore it is but just that he be held to answer for the exercise of his power of choice and that he meet the results of his acts.

Hence the justice of the scriptural doctrine that salvation comes to the individual only through obedience. "He became the author of eternal salvation unto all them that obey him"[ooo] is said of the Christ. And further: God "will render to every man according to his deeds: To them who by patient continuance in well doing seek for glory and honor and immortality, eternal life: But unto them that are contentious, and do not obey the truth, but obey unrighteousness, indignation and wrath, Tribulation and anguish, upon every soul of man that doeth evil, of the Jew first, and also of the Gentile; But glory, honor, and peace, to every man that worketh good, to the Jew first, and also to the Gentile: For there is no respect of persons with God."[ppp] To these may be added the words of the risen Lord, "He that believeth and is baptized shall be saved; but he that believeth not shall be damned."[qqq]

Consider further the prophecy that King Benjamin proclaimed to the Nephite multitude: Christ's blood "atoneth for the sins of those who have fallen by the transgression of Adam, who have died not knowing the will of God concerning them, or who have ignorantly sinned. But wo,

---

[jjj] Moroni 8:8–12.
[kkk] D&C 29:46, 47.
[lll] *Mediation and Atonement,* p. 148; see also Appendix 4:3.
[mmm] Rom. 3:23.
[nnn] 1 John 1:8.
[ooo] Heb. 5:9.
[ppp] Rom. 2:6–11.
[qqq] Mark 16:16.

wo unto him who knoweth that he rebelleth against God! For salvation cometh to none such except it be through repentance and faith on the Lord Jesus Christ."[rrr]

But why multiply scriptural citations when the whole tenor of sacred writ supports the doctrine? Without Christ no man can be saved, and the salvation provided at the cost of Christ's sufferings and bodily death is offered upon certain clearly defined conditions only; and these are summarized under "obedience to the laws and ordinances of the Gospel."

Salvation and Exaltation—Some degree of salvation will come to all who have not forfeited their right to it; exaltation is given to those only who by righteous effort have won a claim to God's merciful liberality by which it is bestowed. Of the saved, not all will be exalted to the higher glories; rewards will not be bestowed in violation of justice; punishments will not be meted out to the ignoring of mercy. No one can be admitted to any order of glory, in short, no soul can be saved until justice has been satisfied for violated law. Our belief in the universal application of the atonement implies no supposition that all mankind will be saved with like endowments of glory and power. In the kingdom of God there are numerous degrees or gradations provided for those who are worthy of them; in the house of our Father there are many mansions, into which only those who are prepared are admitted. The false assumption, based upon sectarian dogma, that in the hereafter there shall be but two places, states, or conditions for the souls of mankind—heaven and hell, with the same glory in all parts of the one and the same terrors throughout the other—is untenable in the light of divine revelation. Through the direct word of the Lord we learn of varied kingdoms or glories.

Degrees of Glory—The revelations of God have defined the following principal kingdoms or degrees of glory, as prepared through Christ for the children of men.

1. *The Celestial Glory*[sss]—There are some who have striven to obey all the divine commandments, who have accepted the testimony of Christ, obeyed "the laws and ordinances of the Gospel," and received the Holy Spirit; these are they who have overcome evil by godly works and who are therefore entitled to the highest glory; these belong to the Church of the Firstborn, unto whom the Father has given all things; they are made kings and priests of the Most High, after the order of Melchizedek; they possess celestial bodies, "whose glory is that of the sun, even the glory of God, the highest of all, whose glory the sun of the firmament is written of as being typical"; they are admitted to the glorified company, crowned with exaltation in the celestial kingdom.

2. *The Terrestrial Glory*[ttt]—We read of others who receive glory of a secondary order, differing from the highest as "the moon differs from the sun in the firmament." These are they who, though honorable, failed to comply with the requirements for exaltation, were blinded by the craftiness of men and unable to receive and obey the higher laws of God. They proved "not valiant in the testimony of Jesus," and therefore are not entitled to the fulness of glory.

3. *The Telestial Glory*[uuu]—There is another grade, differing from the higher orders as the stars differ from the brighter orbs of the firmament; this is for those who received not the testimony of Christ, but who nevertheless, did not deny the Holy Spirit; who have led lives exempting them from the heaviest punishment, yet whose redemption will be delayed until the last resurrection. In the telestial world there are innumerable degrees comparable to the varying light

[rrr] Mosiah 3:11, 12.
[sss] See D&C 76:50–70, 92–96.
[ttt] See D&C 76:71–80, 87, 91, 97.
[uuu] See D&C 76:81–86; 88–0, 98–106, 109–112.

of the stars.[vvv] Yet all who receive of any one of these orders of glory are at last saved, and upon them Satan will finally have no claim. Even the telestial glory "surpasses all understanding; And no man knows it except him to whom God has revealed it."[www] Then there are those who have lost all claim upon the immediate mercy of God, whose deeds have numbered them with Perdition and his angels.[xxx]

REFERENCES

The Atonement Wrought by Jesus Christ

Sacrificial death of Christ prefigured by altar sacrifices under the Law of Moses. For it is the blood that maketh an atonement for the soul—Lev. 17:11.

For sins of the people, sacrifice by shedding of blood of animals before the Lord—Lev., chap. 4; see also 5:5–10.

Adam required to offer firstlings of the flocks, in similitude of the sacrifice of the Only Begotten—P. of G.P. 5:5–8; see also verse 20.

A virgin to bear a son and call his name Immanuel—Isa. 7:14; see also Matt. 1:21–23.

Prediction of the Savior's life and work—Isa. 53:3–12.

Mine Only Begotten is and shall be the Savior—Moses 1:6.

Plan of salvation unto all men through the blood of mine Only Begotten—Moses 6:62.

Only Begotten Son prepared before foundation of the world—Moses 5:57.

The Son of God hath atoned for original guilt—Moses 6:54.

Must be cleansed by blood, even that of the Only Begotten—Moses 6:59.

Jesus Christ who gave himself a ransom for all—Matt. 20:28; see also 1 Tim. 2:5, 6.

The Lamb of God which taketh away the sins of the world—John 1:29.

I lay down my life for the sheep—John 10:15.

My blood, shed for many for remission of sins—Matt. 26:28; see also Luke 22:19; John 6:51.

I lay down my life that I might take it again—John 10:17; see also verses 11 and 15.

The Son of Man lifted up that men may have eternal life—John 3:14, 15; see also 8:28; 12:32.

Christ exalted to be a Prince and a Savior to give repentance and remission of sins—Acts 5:31.

Christ must needs have suffered—Acts 17:3; see the Lord's words—Luke 24:26, 46.

Christ died for us; we shall be saved from wrath through him—Rom. 5:8, 9.

Christ died and rose and revived, Lord of dead and living—Rom. 14:9.

Christ came into the world to save sinners—1 Tim. 1:15; a ransom for all—2:6; the Savior of all men—4:10; hath abolished death—2 Tim. 1:10.

To make reconciliation for the sins of the people—Heb. 2:17; the author of eternal salvation—5:9; the mediator of the New Testament—9:15.

Who bare our sins in his own body—1 Pet. 2:24; hath suffered for us in the flesh—4:1.

Worthy is the Lamb that was slain—Rev. 5:12.

Lehi prophesies concerning the Messiah to come—1 Nephi 10:4–17; Nephi's vision of the Messiah—chap. 11.

Messiah to come to redeem men from the fall—2 Nephi 2:26.

---

vvv See D&C 76:81–86, 98.
www D&C 76:89, 90.
xxx See chap. 3 herein under "Punishment for Sin," and chap. 22 under "Sons of Perdition."

Jacob teaches that the atonement is infinite—2 Nephi chap. 9.

From death by the resurrection, from everlasting death by the power of the atonement—2 Nephi 10:25.

None other way nor name given under heaven whereby man can be saved—2 Nephi 31:21; see also Helaman 5:9–12; D&C 18:23–25.

Be reconciled to him through the atonement of Christ—Jacob 4:11.

Come unto Christ and partake of his salvation—Omni 26.

Law of Moses availeth nothing except through the atonement—Mosiah 3:15; Law of Moses fulfilled by Christ, by whom the law had been given—3 Nephi 12:17; 15:2–6.

They have eternal life through Christ who has broken the bands of death—Mosiah 15:23; also verses 24–28.

No redemption save through death and sufferings of Christ and the atonement—Alma 21:9; see also Helaman 5:9–11; 14:16, 17.

Expedient that an atonement be made—Alma 34:9–16.

Mercy cometh because of the atonement—Alma 42:23.

The Lord not to redeem men in their sins but from their sins—Helaman 5:10.

I have come to bring redemption unto the world—3 Nephi 9:21; see also D&C 49:5.

I have glorified the Father in taking upon me the sins of the world—3 Nephi 11:11.

Because of Jesus Christ came the redemption of man—Mormon 9:12, 13. He hath brought to pass the redemption of the world—7:7.

He that saith little children need baptism denieth the mercies of Christ and setteth at naught the atonement—Moroni 8:20.

The Lord suffered pain of all men, and death, that they might come unto him—D&C 18:11. Jesus Christ the only name given by which men may be saved—verses 23–25. I, God, have suffered these things for all, that they might not suffer if they would repent—19:16; see also P. of G.P. 6:52.

Salvation provided for all men in all ages—D&C 20:23–29.

Your Redeemer, whose arm of mercy hath atoned for your sins—D&C 29:1. Little children redeemed—verses 46, 47.

Only Begotten Son sent into the world for redemption of the world—D&C 49:5.

I, the Lord, who was crucified for sins of the world—D&C 53:2; also 54:1; 76:41.

The Lord is God, and beside him there is no Savior—D&C 76:1; see verses 39–42.

Through redemption comes the resurrection—D&C 88:14–17.

Through redemption from the fall men became again innocent—D&C 93:38.

Mine Only Begotten is and shall be the Savior—Moses 1:6; see also verse 39.

A similitude of the sacrifice of the Only Begotten—Moses 5:7.

Thou mayest be redeemed, and all mankind, even as many as will—Moses 5:9.

Salvation

Prophetic call to salvation—Isa. 55:17; see also Luke 3:36.

Obtainable through Christ—Isa. 61:10; see also Luke 19:10; 24:46, 47; John 3:14, 17; Acts 4:12; 13:38; Rom. 5:15-21; D&C 18:23; Moses 5:15; see references above under *Atonement.*

A reconciliation with God effected through Jesus Christ—2 Cor. 5:18, 19; see also Col. 1:19–23.

Endure to the end to be saved—Matt. 24:13; see also 10:22; Heb. 3:14; D&C 53:7.

Conditioned on obedience—Matt. 28:19, 20; Mark 1:4; 16:16.

To be worked out with fear and trembling—Philip. 2:12.

The engrafted word, which is able to save your souls—Jas. 1:21.

Salvation to come through overcoming Satan—Rev. 12:10.

Salvation is free—2 Nephi 2:4; see also 26:24; to be declared to every nation—Mosiah 15:28; Matt. 24:14. See references under *Free Agency,* following Chap. 3 herein.

Possible to procrastinate day of salvation until too late—Helaman 13:38.

Righteous to reap salvation of their souls—Alma 9:28.

No gift greater than salvation—D&C 6:13; see also 11:7.

Conditions of salvation set forth—D&C 49:5.

Impossible to be saved in ignorance—D&C 131:6.

Salvation without exaltation—D&C 132:17.

Salvation graded; exaltation higher—John 14:2; 1 Cor. 15:40–42; D&C, sec. 76; 132:19–21.

Revelation to Adam as to conditions of salvation—Moses 5:9–15.

5

FAITH AND REPENTANCE

ARTICLE 4

E BELIEVE that the first principles and ordinances of the Gospel are: first, Faith in the Lord Jesus Christ; second, Repentance; * * *

FAITH

Nature of Faith—The predominating sense in which the term faith is used throughout the scriptures is that of full confidence and trust in the being, purposes, and words of God. Such trust, if implicit, will remove all doubt concerning things accomplished or promised of God, even though such things be not apparent to or explicable by the ordinary senses of mortality; hence arises the definition of faith given by Paul: "Now faith is the substance [i.e., confidence, or assurance] of things hoped for, the evidence [i.e., the demonstration or proof] of things not seen."[a] It is plain that such a feeling of trust may exist in different persons in varying degrees; indeed, faith may manifest itself from the incipient state which is little more than feeble belief, scarcely free from hesitation and fear, to the strength of abiding confidence that sets doubt and sophistry at defiance.

Belief, Faith, and Knowledge—The terms faith and belief are sometimes regarded as synonyms; nevertheless each of them has a specific meaning in our language, although in earlier usage there was little distinction between them, and therefore the words are used interchangeably in many scriptural passages. Belief, in one of

[a] Heb. 11:1.

its accepted senses, may consist in a merely intellectual assent, while faith implies such confidence and conviction as will impel to action. Dictionary authority justifies us in drawing a distinction between the two, according to present usage in English; and this authority defines belief as a mental assent to the truth or actuality of anything, excluding, however, the moral element of responsibility through such assent, which responsibility is included by faith. Belief is in a sense passive, an agreement or acceptance only; faith is active and positive, embracing such reliance and confidence as will lead to works. Faith in Christ comprises belief in Him, combined with trust in Him. One cannot have faith without belief; yet he may believe and still lack faith. Faith is vivified, vitalized, living belief.

Certainly there is great difference in degree, even if no essential distinction in kind be admitted between the two. As shall be presently demonstrated, faith in the Godhead is requisite to salvation; it is indeed a saving power, leading its possessor in the paths of godliness, whereas mere belief in the existence and attributes of Deity is no such power. Mark the words of James,[b] in his general epistle to the saints wherein he chided his brethren for certain empty professions. In substance he said: You take pride and satisfaction in declaring your belief in God; you boast of being distinguished from the idolaters and the heathen because you accept one God; you do well to so profess, and so believe; but, remember, others do likewise; even the devils believe; and so firmly that they tremble at thought of the fate which that belief makes plain to them. Satan and his followers believe in Christ; and their belief amounts to knowledge as to who He is, and as to what constitutes His part, past, present, and to come, in the divine plan of human existence and salvation. Call to mind the case of the man possessed by evil spirits in the land of the Gadarenes, a man so grievously tormented as to be a terror to all who came near him. He could be neither tamed nor bound; people were afraid to approach him; yet when he saw Christ, he ran to Him and worshiped, and the wicked spirit within him begged for mercy at the hands of that Righteous One, addressing Him as "Jesus, thou Son of the most high God."[c] Again, an unclean spirit in the synagogue at Jerusalem implored Christ not to use His power, crying in fear and agony: "I know thee, who thou art, the Holy One of God."[d] Christ was once followed by a multitude made up of people from Idumæa and Jerusalem, from Tyre and Sidon; among them were many who were possessed of evil spirits, and these, when they saw Him, fell down in the attitude of worship, exclaiming: "Thou art the Son of God."[e] Was there ever mortal believer who confessed more unreservedly a knowledge of God and His Son Jesus Christ than did these servants of Satan? Satan knows God and Christ; remembers, perchance, somewhat concerning the position which he himself once occupied as a Son of the Morning;[f] yet with all such knowledge he is Satan still. Neither belief nor its superior, actual knowledge, is efficient to save; for neither of these is faith. If belief be a product of the mind, faith is of the heart; belief is founded on reason, faith largely on intuition.

We frequently hear it said that faith is imperfect knowledge; that the first disappears as the second takes its place; that now we walk by faith but some day we shall walk by the sure light of knowledge. In a sense this is true; yet it must be remembered that knowledge may be as dead and unproductive in good works as is faithless belief. Those confessions of the devils, that Christ was the Son of God, were based on knowledge; yet the great truth, which they knew, did not change their evil

[b] See James 2:19; Appendix 5:1.
[c] Mark 5:1–18; also Matt. 8:28–34.
[d] Mark 1:24.
[e] Mark 3:8–11; see *Jesus the Christ,* pp. 181, 310–312.
[f] See D&C 76:25–27.

natures. How different was their acknowledgment of the Savior from that of Peter, who, to the Master's question "Whom say ye that I am?" replied in practically the words used by the unclean spirits before cited: "Thou art the Christ, the Son of the living God."[g] Peter's faith had already shown its vitalizing power; it had caused him to forsake much that had been dear, to follow his Lord through persecution and suffering, and to put away worldliness with its fascinations for the sacrificing godliness which his faith made so desirable. His knowledge of God as the Father, and of the Son as the Redeemer, was perhaps no greater than that of the unclean spirits; but while to them that knowledge was but an added cause of condemnation to him it was a means of salvation.

The mere possession of knowledge gives no assurance of benefit therefrom. It is said that during an epidemic of cholera in a great city, a scientific man proved to his own satisfaction, by chemical and microscopic tests, that the water supply was infected, and that through it contagion was being spread. He proclaimed the fact throughout the city, and warned all against the use of unboiled water. Many of the people, although incapable of comprehending his methods of investigation, far less of repeating such for themselves, had faith in his warning words, followed his instructions, and escaped the death to which their careless and unbelieving fellows succumbed. Their faith was a saving one. To the man himself, the truth by which so many lives had been spared was a matter of knowledge. He had actually perceived, under the microscope, proof of the existence of death-dealing germs in the water; he had demonstrated their virulence; he knew of what he spoke. Nevertheless, in a moment of forgetfulness he drank of the unsterilized water, and soon thereafter died, a victim to the plague. His knowledge did not save him, convincing though it was; yet others, whose reliance was only that of confidence or faith in the truth that he declared, escaped the threatening destruction. He had knowledge; but, was he wise? Knowledge is to wisdom what belief is to faith, one an abstract principle, the other a living application. Not possession merely, but the proper use of knowledge constitutes wisdom.

Foundation of Faith—Primarily, and in a theological sense, we are considering faith as a living, inspiring confidence in God, and an acceptance of His will as our law, and of His words as our guide, in life. Faith in God is possible only as we come to know that He exists, and moreover, that He is a Being of worthy character and attributes.

Upon such knowledge of God's existence, the worthiness of His character, and the perfection of His attributes, is man's faith in Him established. Faith in God then cannot be exercised in the absence of all knowledge of Him; yet even the benighted heathen show some of the fruits of faith, for they have at least the inborn conviction that arises from man's natural intuition as to the existence of a supreme power. In every human soul, even in that of the savage, there is some basis for faith, however limited and imperfect the darkness of heredity or of wilful sin may have made it. The heathen's faith may be weak and imperfect, for his ability to recognize the evidence upon which belief in God depends may be small. While the first promptings of faith toward God may be the result of natural intuition, the later development will be largely the result of unprejudiced and prayerful investigation and search for truth.

From trustworthy evidence, rightly interpreted, true faith will spring; from false evidence, only distorted and misplaced faith can arise. Our conclusions concerning any question under test will be governed largely by the number and credibility of witnesses, or the weight of evidence as we investigate for ourselves. However improbable a declaration may appear to us, if the truth of it be affirmed by witnesses in whom we have confidence we are led to admit the statement, at least

[g] Matt. 16:15, 16; see also Mark 8:29; Luke 9:20.

provisionally, as true. If many credible witnesses testify, and moreover, if collateral evidence appear, we may consider the statement as proved. Nevertheless we would still be incompetent to affirm the truth of it on our personal knowledge until we had seen and heard for ourselves, until in fact each of us had become a competent witness through personal observation. To illustrate: Relatively few of the citizens of this country have visited the seat of government; the masses know nothing by actual observation of the capitol, the executive mansion and other buildings of national interest and importance; very few have personally met the President of the United States who resides there. How does any one of the multitude who have not seen for themselves know of the city of Washington, of the capitol, and of the president? Through the testimony of others. He may have among his acquaintances many who have been in Washington and whose statements he accepts as true; assuredly he has heard or read of those who do know for themselves. Then he learns of laws being framed there, and of edicts issuing from the nation's headquarters; his studies in school, his use of maps and books, and many other incidents add to the evidence, which soon becomes decisive. His inferences multiply, and develop into a positive conviction. He acquires faith in the existence of a center of national government and regard for the laws which emanate therefrom.

Let us take another illustration: Astronomers tell us that the earth is of a kind with certain of the stars; that it is one of a family of planets which revolve about the sun in concentric orbits; and that some of those planets are many times the size of our globe. We may not be skilled in astronomical methods of observation and calculation, and may therefore be unable to test the truth of these statements for ourselves; but we find such a mass of evidence resulting from the united testimony of those in whose skill as scientific workers we have confidence that the conclusions are accepted by us as proved.

So too concerning the existence, authority, and attributes of God, the testimonies of many holy men in ancient and modern times—prophets whose credibility is established by the fulfilment of their predictions—have come to us in united declaration of the solemn truths, and nature furnishes corroborative testimony on every side. To reject without disproving such evidence is to ignore the most approved methods of investigation and research known to man. The development of faith from evidence is illustrated in the scenes of a certain Pentecostal celebration, on which occasion thousands of Jews, imbued with a preconceived prejudice that Jesus was an impostor, heard the apostles' testimony and witnessed the attendant signs; three thousand of them were convinced of the truth and became followers of the Son of God, their prejudice giving place to belief, and their belief developing into faith with its accompanying works.[h] The foundation of faith in God, then, is a sincere belief in or knowledge of Him as sustained by evidence and testimony.

Faith a Principle of Power—In its broad sense, faith—the assurance of things for which we hope, and the evidence of things not discernible through our senses—is the motive principle that impels men to resolve and to act. Without its exercise, we would make no exertion the results of which are future; without faith that he may gather in the autumn, man would not plant in the spring; neither would he essay to build, did he not have confidence that he would finish the structure and enjoy its use; had the student no faith in the possibility of successfully following his studies he would not enter upon his courses. Faith thus becomes to us the foundation of hope, from which spring our aspirations, ambitions, and confidences for the future. Remove man's faith in the possibility of any desired success, and you rob him of the incentive to strive. He would not

[h] See Acts, chap 2.

stretch forth his hand to seize did he not believe in the possibility of securing that for which he reaches. This principle becomes therefore the impelling force by which men struggle for excellence, ofttimes enduring vicissitudes and suffering that they may achieve their purposes. Faith is the secret of ambition, the soul of heroism, the motive power of effort.

The exercise of faith is pleasing unto God, and thereby His interposition may be secured. It was through faith that the Israelites in their exodus from Egypt followed their leader into the bed of the sea; and through the protecting agencies of God, which that faith drew forth, they were saved, while the Egyptians met destruction in attempting to follow.[i] With full confidence in the instructions and promises of God, Joshua and his intrepid followers laid siege to Jericho; and the walls of that city of sin fell before the faith of the besiegers without the use of battering rams or other engines of war.[j] By the same power Joshua gained the assistance of the luminaries of heaven in his work of victory over the Amorites.[k] Paul cites[l] us also to the instances of Gideon,[m] Barak,[n] Samson,[o] Jephthah,[p] David,[q] Samuel,[r] and the prophets, "who, through faith, subdued kingdoms, wrought righteousness, obtained promises, stopped the mouths of lions, quenched the violence of fire, escaped the edge of the sword, out of weakness were made strong." It was through faith that Alma and Amulek were delivered from captivity, while the prison walls were demolished.[s] Through faith, Nephi and Lehi,[t] sons of Helaman, were protected from their Lamanite foes by fire, in the midst of which they were preserved unscorched; and a yet greater work was wrought in the hearts of their persecutors, for these became enlightened, and repentant. Through the operation of faith even the waves of the sea may be subdued;[u] trees are subject to the voice of him who commands by faith;[v] mountains may be removed for the accomplishment of righteous purposes;[w] the sick may be healed;[x] evil spirits may be cast out,[y] and the dead raised to life.[z] All things are wrought through faith.[aa]

But, it may be argued that faith of itself is not a source of power; that its effect is due to an external interposition of divine aid, which faith merely invokes; and the skeptic may add that an omniscient God, if loving and kind, would act independently and give without waiting to be invoked through faith or prayer. A sufficient answer is found in the abundant proof furnished by scripture, that the Almighty operates in accordance with law, and that arbitrary and capricious action is foreign to His nature. Howsoever the laws of heaven may have been formulated, the application of their beneficent provisions to humanity is dependent on the faith and obedience of the mortal subjects.

[i] See Ex. 14:22–29; Heb. 11:29.

[j] See Josh. 6:20; Heb. 11:30.

[k] See Josh. 10:12.

[l] See Heb. 11:32–34.

[m] See Judges 6:11.

[n] See Judges 4:6.

[o] See Judges 13:24.

[p] See Judges 11:1; 12:7.

[q] See 1 Sam. 16:1, 13; 17:45.

[r] See 1 Sam. 1:20; 12:20.

[s] See Alma 14:26–29; see also Ether 12:13.

[t] See Helaman 5:20–52; see also Ether 12:14.

[u] See Matt. 8:23–27; see also Mark 4:36–41; Luke 8:22–25; Matt. 14:24–32; Mark 6:47–51; John 6:16–21.

[v] See Matt. 21:17–22; see also Mark 11:12–14, 20–24; Luke 17:6; Jacob 4:6.

[w] See Matt. 17:20; 21:21; see also Mark 11:23, 24; Ether 12:30; Jacob 4:6.

[x] See Luke 13:11–13; 14:2–4; 17:11–19; 22:50, 51; see also Matt. 8:2, 3, 5–13, 14, 15, 16, etc.

[y] See Matt. 8:28–32; 17:18; see also Mark 1:23–26, etc.

[z] See Luke 7:11–16; see also John 11:43–45; 1 Kings 17:17–24; 3 Nephi 7:19; 19:4; 26:15.

[aa] See Matt. 17:20; see also Mark 9:23; Eph. 6:16; 1 John 5:4; D&C 35:8–11, etc.

Consider the defeat of Israel by the men of Ai; a law of righteousness had been violated, and things that were accursed had been introduced into the camp of the covenant people; this transgression interposed resistance to the current of divine help, and until the people had sanctified themselves the power was not renewed unto them.[bb] Furthermore, Christ was influenced and to some extent controlled in His miracles among men by the faith or lack of faith of the people. The common benediction, "Thy faith hath made thee whole," with which He announced the healing interposition, is evidence of the fact. Then we learn that on a certain occasion in His own country He could do no mighty work, being restrained by the unbelief of the people.[cc]

A Condition of Effective Faith—A condition essential to the exercise of a living, growing, sustaining faith in Deity is the consciousness on man's part that he is at least endeavoring to live in accordance with the laws of God as he has learned them. A knowledge that he is wilfully and wantonly sinning against the truth will deprive him of sincerity in prayer and faith and estrange him from his Father. He must feel that the trend of his life's course is acceptable, that with due allowance for mortal weakness and human frailty he is in some measure approved of the Lord; otherwise he is restrained from supplicating the throne of grace with confidence. The consciousness of earnest effort toward godly conduct is a power of itself, strengthening its possessor in sacrifice and under persecution, and sustaining him in all good works. It was this knowledge of assured communion with God that enabled the saints of olden time to endure as they did, though their sufferings were extreme. Of them we read that some "were tortured, not accepting deliverance; that they might obtain a better resurrection: And others had trial of cruel mockings and scourgings, yea, moreover of bonds and imprisonment: They were stoned, they were sawn asunder, were tempted, were slain with the sword: they wandered about in sheepskins and goatskins; being destitute, afflicted, tormented; Of whom the world was not worthy:) they wandered in deserts, and in mountains, and in dens and caves of the earth."[dd] As in former days so in the present, the saints have been sustained through all their sufferings by the sure knowledge of divine approval; and the faith of righteous men has ever grown through a consciousness of their sincere and devoted endeavor.

Faith Essential to Salvation—Inasmuch as salvation is attainable only through the mediation and atonement of Christ, and since this is made applicable to individual sin in the measure of obedience to the laws of righteousness, faith in Jesus Christ is indispensable to salvation. But no one can effectively believe in Jesus Christ and at the same time doubt the existence of either the Father or the Holy Ghost; therefore faith in the entire Godhead is essential to salvation. Paul declares that without faith it is impossible to please God, "for he that cometh to God must believe that he is, and that he is a rewarder of them that diligently seek him."[ee] The scriptures abound in assurances of salvation to those who exercise faith in God, and obey the requirements which that faith makes plain. Christ's words on the matter are conclusive: "He that believeth and is baptized shall be saved; but he that believeth not shall be damned."[ff] And again: "He that believeth on the Son hath everlasting life; and he that believeth not the Son shall not see life, but the wrath of God abideth on him."[gg] Similar doctrines did His apostles teach after His death throughout all the days

bb See Joshua, chaps 7, 8.
cc See Matt. 13:58; Mark 6:5, 6.
dd Heb. 11:35–38.
ee Heb. 11:6.
ff Mark 16:16.
gg John 3:36; see also John 3:15; 4:42; 5:24; 11:25; Gal. 2:20; 1 Nephi 10:6, 17; 2 Nephi 25:25; 26:8; Enos 1:8; Mosiah 3:17; Helaman 5:9; 3 Nephi 27:19; D&C 45:8.

of their ministry.[hh] A natural result of implicit faith in the Godhead will be a growing confidence in the scriptures as containing the word of God, and in the words and works of His authorized servants who speak as His living oracles.

Faith a Gift of God—Though within the reach of all who diligently strive to gain it, faith is nevertheless a divine gift.[ii] As is fitting for so priceless a pearl, it is given to those only who show by their sincerity that they are worthy of it, and who give promise of abiding by its dictates. Although faith is called the first principle of the Gospel of Christ, though it be in fact the foundation of religious life, yet even faith is preceded by sincerity of disposition and humility of soul, whereby the word of God may make an impression upon the heart.[jj] No compulsion is used in bringing men to a knowledge of God; yet, as fast as we open our hearts to the influences of righteousness, the faith that leads to life eternal will be given us of our Father.

Faith and Works—Faith in a passive sense, that is, as mere belief in the more superficial sense of the term, is inefficient as a means of salvation. This truth was clearly set forth both by Christ and the apostles, and the vigor with which it was declared may be an indication of the early development of a most pernicious doctrine—that of justification by belief alone. The Savor taught that works were essential to the validity of profession and the efficacy of faith. Mark his words: "Not every one that saith unto me, Lord, Lord, shall enter into the kingdom of heaven; but he that doeth the will of my Father which is in heaven."[kk] "He that hath my commandments, and keepeth them, he it is that loveth me: and he that loveth me shall be loved of my Father, and I will love him, and will manifest myself to him."[ll] The exposition by James is particularly explicit: "What doth it profit, my brethren, though a man say he hath faith, and have not works? Can faith save him? If a brother or sister be naked, and destitute of daily food, And one of you say unto them, Depart in peace, be ye warmed and filled; notwithstanding ye give them not those things which are needful to the body; what doth it profit? Even so faith, if it hath not works, is dead, being alone. Yea, a man may say, Thou hast faith, and I have works: shew me thy faith without thy works, and I will shew thee my faith by my works."[mm] And to this may be added the words of John: "And hereby we do know that we know him, if we keep his commandments. He that saith, I know him, and keepeth not his commandments, is a liar, and the truth is not in him. But whoso keepeth his word, in him verily is the love of God perfected: hereby know we that we are in him."[nn]

To these teachings may be added many inspired utterances from Nephite scriptures[oo] and from modern revelation,[pp] all affirming the necessity of works, and denying the saving efficacy of passive belief. Yet in spite of the plain word of God, dogmas of men have been promulgated to the effect that by faith alone may salvation be attained, and that a wordy profession of belief shall open the doors of heaven to the sinner.[qq] The scriptures cited and man's inherent sense of justice furnish a sufficient refutation of these false assertions.[rr]

---

hh See Acts 2:38; 10:42; 16:31; Rom. 10:9; Heb. 3:19; 11:6; 1 Pet. 1:9; 1 John 3:23; 5:14.
ii See Matt. 16:17; John 6:44, 65; Eph. 2:8; 1 Cor. 12:9; Rom. 12:3; Moroni 10:11.
jj See Rom. 10:17.
kk Matt.7:21.
ll John 14:21.
mm James 2:14–18.
nn 1 John 2:3–5.
oo See 1 Nephi 15:33; 2 Nephi 29:11; Mosiah 5:15; Alma 7:27; 9:28; 37:32-34; 41:3–5.
pp See D&C throughout.
qq See Appendix 5:2, 3; also *Vitality of Mormonism,* article "Knowing and Doing," p. 282.
rr See *Vitality of Mormonism,* article "Obedience Is Heaven's First Law," p. 75.

REPENTANCE

Nature of Repentance—The term repentance is used in the scriptures with several different meanings, but, as representing the duty required of all who would obtain forgiveness for transgression it indicates a godly sorrow for sin, producing a reformation of life,[ss] and embodies (1) a conviction of guilt; (2) a desire to be relieved from the hurtful effects of sin; and (3) an earnest determination to forsake sin and to accomplish good. Repentance is a result of contrition of soul, which springs from a deep sense of humility, and this in turn is dependent upon the exercise of an abiding faith in God. Repentance therefore properly ranks as the second principle of the Gospel, closely associated with and immediately following faith. As soon as one has come to recognize the existence and authority of God, he feels a respect for divine laws, and a conviction of his own unworthiness. His wish to please the Father, whom he has so long ignored, will impel him to forsake sin; and this impulse will acquire added strength from the sinner's natural and commendable desire to make reparation, if possible, and so avert the dire results of his own waywardness. With the zeal inspired by fresh conviction, he will crave an opportunity of showing by good works the sincerity of his newly developed faith; and he will regard the remission of his sins as the most desirable of blessings. Then he will learn that this gift of mercy is granted on certain specific conditions.[tt] The first step toward the blessed state of forgiveness consists in the sinner confessing his sins; the second, in his forgiving others who have sinned against him; and the third in his showing his acceptance of Christ's atoning sacrifice by complying with the divine requirements.

1. Confession of Sins is essential, for without it repentance is incomplete. John tells us: "If we say that we have no sin, we deceive ourselves, and the truth is not in us. If we confess our sins, he is faithful and just to forgive us our sins, and to cleanse us from all unrighteousness."[uu] We read also: "He that covereth his sins shall not prosper: but whoso confesseth and forsaketh them shall have mercy."[vv] And unto the saints in this dispensation the Lord has said: "Verily I say unto you, I, the Lord, forgive sins unto those who confess their sins before me and ask forgiveness, who have not sinned unto death."[ww] And that this act of confession is included in repentance is shown by the Lord's words: "By this ye may know if a man repenteth of his sins—behold, he will confess them and forsake them."[xx]

2. The Sinner Must be Willing to Forgive Others, if he hopes to obtain forgiveness. A man's repentance is but superficial if his heart be not softened to the degree of tolerance for the weaknesses of his fellows. In teaching His hearers how to pray, the Savior instructed them to supplicate the Father: "Forgive us our debts, as we forgive our debtors."[yy] He gave them no assurance of forgiveness if in their hearts they forgave not one another: "For," said He, "if ye forgive men their trespasses, your heavenly Father will also forgive you; But if ye forgive not men their trespasses, neither will your Father forgive your trespasses."[zz] Forgiveness between man and man, to be acceptable before the Lord, must be unbounded. In answering Peter's question: "Lord, how oft shall my brother sin against me, and I forgive him—till seven times?" the Master replied: "I say not unto thee, Until seven times: but, Until seventy times seven"; clearly intending to teach

---

[ss] See Alma 36:6–21.
[tt] See Appendix 5:4.
[uu] 1 John 1:8, 9; see also Ps. 32:5; 38:18; Mosiah 26:29, 30.
[vv] Prov. 28:13.
[ww] D&C 64:7.
[xx] D&C 58:43.
[yy] Matt. 6:12; see also Luke 11:4.
[zz] Matt. 6:14, 15; 3 Nephi 13:14, 15.

that man must ever be ready to forgive. On another occasion He taught the disciples, saying: "If thy brother trespass against thee, rebuke him; and if he repent, forgive him. And if he trespass against thee seven times in a day, and seven times in a day turn again to thee, saying, I repent, thou shalt forgive him."[aaa]

Illustrating further the divine purpose to mete unto men the measure they mete unto their fellows[bbb] the Savior put forth a parable of a king to whom one of his subjects owed a large sum of money, ten thousand talents; but when the debtor humbled himself and pleaded for mercy, the compassionate heart of the king was moved and he forgave his servant the debt. But the same servant, going out from the presence of the king, met a fellow servant who was indebted to him in a small sum, and, forgetting the mercy so recently shown unto himself, he seized his fellow servant and cast him into prison till he would pay the debt. Then the king, hearing of this, sent for the wicked servant, and, denouncing him for his lack of gratitude and consideration, handed him over to the tormenters.[ccc] The Lord has not promised to listen to petitions nor accept offerings from one who has bitterness in his heart toward others: "First be reconciled to thy brother, and then come and offer thy gift."[ddd] In His revealed word to the saints in this day, the Lord has placed particular stress upon this necessary condition: "Wherefore, I say unto you, that ye ought to forgive one another; for he that forgiveth not his brother his trespasses standeth condemned before the Lord; for there remaineth in him the greater sin";[eee] and to remove all doubt as to the proper subjects for human forgiveness, it is added: "I, the Lord, will forgive whom I will forgive, but of you it is required to forgive all men."

3. Confidence in Christ's Atoning Sacrifice constitutes the third essential condition in obtaining remission of sins. The name of Jesus Christ is the only name under heaven whereby men may be saved;[fff] and we are taught to offer our petitions to the Father in the name of the Son. Adam received this instruction from the mouth of an angel,[ggg] and the Savior personally instructed the Nephites to the same effect.[hhh] But no person can truthfully profess faith in Christ and refuse to obey His commandments; therefore obedience is essential to remission of sin; and the truly repentant sinner will eagerly seek to learn what is required of him.

Repentance, to be worthy of its name, must comprise something more than a mere self-acknowledgment of error; it does not consist in lamentations and wordy confessions, but in the heartfelt recognition of guilt, which carries with it a horror for sin and a resolute determination to make amends for the past and to do better in the future. If such a conviction be genuine it is marked by that godly sorrow which, as Paul has said, "worketh repentance to salvation, not to be repented of; but the sorrow of the world worketh death."[iii] Apostle Orson Pratt has wisely said: "It would be of no use for a sinner to confess his sins to God unless he were determined to forsake them; it would be of no benefit to him to feel sorry that he had done wrong unless he intended to do wrong no more; it would be folly for him to confess before God that he had injured his fellow man unless he were determined to do all in his power to make restitution. Repentance,

[aaa] Matt. 18:22, 23; Luke 17:3, 4.
[bbb] See Matt. 7:2; Mark 4:24; Luke 6:38.
[ccc] See Matt. 18:23-35; see *Jesus the Christ*, pp. 392–395.
[ddd] Matt. 5:23, 24; 3 Nephi 12:23, 24.
[eee] D&C 64:9, 10.
[fff] See P.of G.P., Moses 6:52.
[ggg] See P.of G.P., Moses 5:6–8.
[hhh] See 3 Nephi 27:5–7.
[iii] 2 Cor.7:10.

then, is not only a confession of sins, with a sorrowful, contrite heart, but a fixed, settled purpose to refrain from every evil way.

Repentance Essential to Salvation—This evidence of sincerity, this beginning of a better life, is required of every candidate for salvation. In the obtaining of divine mercy, repentance is as indispensable as faith; it must be as extensive as sin. Where can we find a sinless mortal? Sagely did the preacher of old declare: "There is not a just man upon earth, that doeth good, and sinneth not."[jjj] Who, therefore, has no need of forgiveness, or who is exempt from the requirements of repentance? God has promised forgiveness unto those who truly repent; it is unto such that the advantages of individual salvation, through the atonement of Christ, are extended. Isaiah thus admonishes to repentance, with assuring promises of forgiveness: "Seek ye the Lord while he may be found, call ye upon him while he is near: Let the wicked forsake his way, and the unrighteous man his thoughts: and let him return unto the Lord, and he will have mercy upon him; and to our God, for he will abundantly pardon."[kkk]

The burden of inspired teachers in every age has been the call to repentance. To this effect was heard the voice of John crying in the wilderness, "Repent ye: for the kingdom of heaven is at hand."[lll] And the Savior followed with "Repent ye, and believe the gospel"[mmm] and, "Except ye repent, ye shall all likewise perish."[nnn] So too proclaimed the apostles of old, that God "commandeth all men everywhere to repent."[ooo] And in the present dispensation has come the word: "We know that all men must repent and believe on the name of Jesus Christ and worship the Father in his name, and endure in faith on his name to the end, or they cannot be saved in the kingdom of God."[ppp]

Repentance a Gift from God—Repentance is a means of pardon and is therefore one of God's great gifts to man. It is not to be had for the careless asking; it may not be found upon the highway; nevertheless it is given with boundless liberality unto those who have brought forth works that warrant its bestowal.[qqq] That is to say, all who prepare themselves for repentance will be led by the humbling and softening influence of the Holy Spirit to the actual possession of this great gift. When Peter was charged by his fellow worshipers with a breach of law in that he had associated with Gentiles, he told his hearers of the divine manifestations he had so recently received; they believed and declared: "Then hath God also to the Gentiles granted repentance unto life."[rrr] Paul also, in writing to the Romans, teaches that repentance comes through the goodness of God.[sss]

Repentance Not Always Possible—The gift of repentance is extended to men as they humble themselves before the Lord; it is the testimony of the Spirit in their hearts. If they hearken not unto the monitor it will leave them, for the Spirit of God strives not ever with man.[ttt] Repentance becomes more difficult as sin is more wilful; it is by humility and contrition of the heart that sinners may increase their faith in God, and so obtain from Him the gift of repentance. As the time of repentance is procrastinated, the ability to repent grows weaker; neglect of opportunity in holy things develops inability. In giving commandment to Joseph Smith in the early days of the present

jjj Eccl. 7:20; see also Rom. 3:10; 1 John 1:8.
kkk Isa. 55:6, 7; see also 2 Nephi 9:24; Alma 5:31–36, 49–56; 9:12; D&C 1:32, 33; 19:4; 20:29; 29:44; 133:16.
lll Matt. 3:2.
mmm Mark 1:15.
nnn Luke 13:3.
ooo Acts 17:30.
ppp D&C 20:29.
qqq See Matt. 3:7, 8; Acts 26:20.
rrr Acts 11:18.
sss See Rom. 2:4; see also 2 Tim. 2:25.
ttt See Gen. 6:3; D&C 1:33.

Church, the Lord said: "For I the Lord cannot look upon sin with the least degree of allowance; Nevertheless, he that repents and does the commandments of the Lord shall be forgiven; And he that repents not, from him shall be taken even the light which he has received; for my Spirit shall not always strive with man, saith the Lord of Hosts."[uuu]

Repentance Here and Hereafter—Alma, a Nephite prophet, described the period of earthly existence as a probationary state, granted unto man for repentance;[vvv] yet we learn from the scriptures that repentance may be obtained, under certain conditions, beyond the veil of mortality. Between the times of His death and resurrection, Christ "preached unto the spirits in prison; Which sometime were disobedient, when once the longsuffering of God waited in the days of Noah";[www] these the Son visited, and unto them He preached the Gospel, "that they might be judged according to men in the flesh; Who received not the testimony of Jesus in the flesh, but afterwards received it."[xxx]

No soul is justified in postponing his efforts to repent because of this assurance of longsuffering and mercy. We know not fully on what terms repentance will be obtainable in the hereafter; but to suppose that the soul who has wilfully rejected the opportunity of repentance in this life will find it easy to repent there is contrary to reason. To procrastinate the day of repentance is to deliberately place ourselves in the power of the adversary. Thus Amulek taught and admonished the multitude of old: "For behold, this life is the time for men to prepare to meet God; * * * therefore, I beseech of you that ye do not procrastinate the day of your repentance until the end; * * * Ye cannot say, when ye are brought to that awful crisis, that I will repent, that I will return to my God. Nay, ye cannot say this; for that same spirit which doth possess your bodies at the time that ye go out of this life, that same spirit will have power to possess your body in that eternal world. For behold, if ye have procrastinated the day of your repentance even until death, behold, ye have become subjected to the spirit of the devil, and he doth seal you his."[yyy]

REFERENCES

Faith—In considering the passages cited here the student should bear in mind that in English versions the terms "faith," "belief" and "knowledge," with their verbs and adjectives, are frequently used with one or nearly the same meaning.

Believe in the Lord, your God, so shall ye be established—2 Chr. 20:20.

That ye may know and believe me—Isa. 43:10.

The just shall live by his faith—Hab. 2:4; see also Rom. 1:17; Gal. 3:11; Heb. 10:38.

Abraham believed in the Lord and he accounted it to him for righteousness—Gen. 15:6; see also Rom. 4:3; Gal. 3:6. Because of his faith Abraham was called the Friend of God—James 2:23; see also Isa. 41:8. When called to go he went, not knowing whither—Gen. 12:1–4; Heb. 11:8.

O ye of little faith—Matt. 6:30; 8:26. How is it that ye have no faith?—Mark 4:40. Where is your faith?—Luke 8:25.

He did not many mighty works there because of their unbelief—Matt. 13:58; Mark 6:5, 6; see also 3 Nephi 19:35; Ether 12:12.

[uuu] D&C 1:31–33; see also Alma 45:16; and Appendix 5:5.
[vvv] See Alma 12:24; 34:32; 42:4.
[www] 1 Peter 3:19, 20.
[xxx] D&C 76:73, 74; 1 Pet. 4:6; see *Jesus the Christ*, chap. 36.
[yyy] Alma 34:32–35.

Lord, I believe; help thou mine unbelief—Mark 9:24.

Healings wrought by Jesus Christ through faith: Thy faith hath made thee whole—Matt. 9:22; Mark 5:34; Luke 8:48; see also Mark 10:52; Luke 7:50. According to your faith be it unto you—Matt. 9:29. Because of faith the Lord said: Man, thy sins are forgiven thee—Luke 5:20; see also Luke 7:47.

Daughter of Jairus raised from the dead; Jesus said: Fear not: believe only, and she shall be made whole—Luke 8:50.

Those who believed on Christ were given power to become sons of God—John 1:12; see also Moroni 7:26; Moses 7:1.

If ye believe not that I am he ye shall die in your sins—John 8:24. He that believeth on me, the works that I do shall he do also—John 14:12. Believe that Jesus is the Christ, the Son of God—John 20:31. He that believeth not shall be damned—Mark 16:16.

When the Son of Man cometh, shall he find faith on the earth?—Luke 18:8.

Whosoever believeth in him should not perish—John 3:16; see also 5:24.

Life eternal, to know God and the Savior—John 17:3.

Ask and it shall be given you, etc.—Luke 11:9; see also Enos 15; D&C 66:9.

Purifying the hearts of the Gentiles by faith—Acts 15:9.

Faith cometh by hearing, and hearing by the word of God—Rom. 10:17.

Whatsoever is not of faith is sin—Rom. 14:23.

We walk by faith, not by sight—2 Cor. 5:7.

I live by the faith of the Son of God—Gal. 2:20.

Salvation through faith which is in Jesus Christ—2 Tim. 3:15.

I have kept the faith—2 Tim. 4:7.

Faith more than sight; evidence of things not seen; mighty works wrought through faith—Heb. chap. 11; see also Ether chaps. 3 and 12; 4 Nephi 5.

Let him ask in faith, nothing wavering—Jas. 1:6. By works was faith made perfect—2:22. Prayer of faith shall save the sick—5:15.

Without faith, impossible to please God—Heb. 11:6; see also D&C 63:11.

Faith a gift from God: Flesh and blood hath not revealed it unto thee, but my Father—Matt. 16:17. No man can come to Christ except the Father draw him—John 6:44, 65. If any man will do the will of God he shall know for himself—John 7:17. According as God has dealt to every man the measure of faith—Rom. 12:3. To some is given faith, by the Spirit of God—1 Cor. 12:8. Saved by grace through faith, the gift of God—Eph. 2:8.

Faith essential to salvation: He that believeth and is baptized shall be saved; but he that believeth not shall be damned—Mark 16:16; see also Ether 4:18; 3 Nephi 11:33, 34, 35; D&C 68:9; Moses 5:15.

Unbeliever is condemned because he hath not believed in the name of the Only Begotten Son of God—John 3:18. Receiving the end of your faith, even the salvation of your souls—1 Peter 1:9. But be ye doers of the word, and not hearers only, deceiving your own selves—Jas. 1:22. No one can be saved without faith in Jesus Christ—Moroni 7:38; see also D&C 20:29.

Power of the Holy Ghost received through faith in the Son of God—1 Nephi 10:17.

Having perfect faith in the Holy One of Israel—2 Nephi 9:23.

By the word of Christ, with unshaken faith in him—2 Nephi 31:19.

Remission of sins brought about through faith—Mosiah 4:3.

Faith is not to have a perfect knowledge of things—Alma, 32:21, 26, 40.

Strong exhortation to faith and repentance—Alma, chap. 13.

Look upon the Son of God with faith, and have eternal life—Helaman 8:15.

Remission of sins by endurance of faith to the end—Moroni 3:3; 8:3.

Faith in its relation to hope and charity—Moroni, chap. 7.

By faith they did lay hold upon every good thing—Moroni 7:25.

God is merciful unto all who believe in his name—Alma 32:22; 34:15; Mormon 7:5.

That salvation may come to the children of men through faith in his name—Mosiah 3:9.

It is he that cometh to take away the sins of the world—Alma 5:48; 11:40; 12:15; 19:36; 22:13; Helaman 14:2.

Holy Spirit deals with men according to their faith—Jarom 4.

All things you shall receive by faith—D&C 26:2. Without faith you can do nothing—8:10; 18:19. According to your faith shall it be done unto you—8:11; 10:47; 11:17; 52:20.

Faith cometh not by signs, but signs follow—D&C 63:9; 68:10; 85:65; compare 63:12.

He that hath faith to be healed shall be—D&C 42:48–52.

Minds darkened because of unbelief—D&C 84:54.

The faithful shall overcome and be preserved—D&C 61:9, 10; 63:47; 75:16; 79:3.

Repentance

All mankind have need of repentance. If we confess our sins God is just to forgive—1 John 1:8, 9; see also Rom. 3:10; Eccl. 7:20.

Return unto the Lord for he will abundantly pardon—Isa. 55:7.

Who turneth away from his wickedness shall save his soul alive—Ezek. 18:27.

Proclaimed by John the Baptist: Repent ye—Matt. 3:2, 8; Mark 1:4; Luke 3:3.

Preached by Jesus Christ: Repent: for the kingdom of heaven is at hand—Matt. 4:17; see also Mark 1:15; 2:17. Christ came to call sinners to repentance—Luke 5:32. Joy in heaven over the sinner that repenteth—Luke 15:7, 10. Repentance and remission of sins preached in his name—Luke 24:47. Penalty following nonrepentance—Rev. 2:5, 16; compare 3:19. Wo unto the inhabitants of the whole earth except they shall repent—3 Nephi 9:2. How oft will I gather you if ye will repent—10:6. Whosoever repenteth and is baptized shall be saved—23:5.

Preached by the Apostles: They preached that men should repent—Mark 6:12. Repent, and be baptized every one of you—Acts 2:38; see also 3:19; 8:22. God commandeth all men to repent—Acts 17:30. Rejoicing over those who sorrowed to repentance—2 Cor. 7:9, 10. The Gentiles were granted repentance—Acts 11:18.

Blessing to him who brings a soul to repentance—Jas. 5:20; see also D&C 18:15, 16.

The Lord desirous that all come to repentance—2 Peter 3:9.

Way prepared for all men if they repent—1 Nephi 10:18.

To be well with Gentiles if they repent; whoso repenteth not must perish—1 Nephi 14:5.

Repentant Gentiles to become covenant people; nonrepentant Jews to be cast off—2 Nephi 30:2; 3 Nephi 16:13.

All nations to dwell safely in the Holy One of Israel if they will repent—1 Nephi 22:28.

Days of men mercifully prolonged for repentance—2 Nephi 2:21. Space granted that men might repent; a probationary state, a time to prepare to meet God—Alma 12:24; 34:32.

People of God to persuade all men to repentance—2 Nephi 26:27.

A curse upon the land, and destruction of the people if they would not repent—Jacob 3:3.

Believe that ye must repent—Mosiah 4:10.

Repentance preached by Alma at Mormon—Mosiah 18:7, 20.

Words of the Spirit: Except ye repent ye can in no wise inherit the kingdom of heaven—Alma 5:51; see also 7:14.

Do not procrastinate the day of your repentance—Alma 34:32–35.

To the repentant and faithful it is given to know the mysteries of God—Alma 26:22.

O that I were an angel, to cry repentance unto every people—Alma 29:1, 2.

Lord has power to redeem men from their sins because of repentance—Helaman 5:11. O repent ye, why will ye die?—7:17.

Would that I could persuade all ye ends of the earth to repent—Mormon 3:22.

Repentance is unto them who are under condemnation and the curse of a broken law—Moroni 8:24.

Chastened that they might repent—D&C 1:27.

Light to depart from him who repents not; Spirit of the Lord will not always strive with man—D&C 1:33; see also Moses 8:17.

Every man must repent or suffer—D&C 19:4, 15.

All men must repent, believe, worship God, and endure, or they cannot be saved—D&C 20:29.

Call upon the nations to repent—D&C 43:20.

May know if a man repenteth of his sins, he will confess and forsake them—D&C 58:43.

Their sorrow shall be great unless they repent speedily—D&C 136:35.

No one to be received into the Church unless he be capable of repentance—D&C 20:71.

The thing of most worth to you will be to declare repentance—D&C 16:6; see also 18:15, 16.

Adam and his immediate posterity were commanded to repent—Moses 5:8, 14, 15.

Adam called upon his sons to repent—Moses 6:1. They called upon all men to repent—6:23; see verses 50, 57.

Enoch called the people to repent—Moses 7:12.

If men do not repent, I will send in the floods upon them—Moses 8:17; see verses 20, 24, 25.

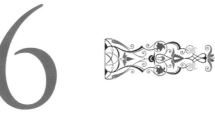

6

BAPTISM

ARTICLE 4

W E BELIEVE that the first principles and ordinances of the Gospel are:* * * third, Baptism by immersion for the remission of sins; * * *

Nature of Baptism—In the theology of The Church of Jesus Christ of Latter-day Saints, water baptism ranks as the third principle and the first essential ordinance of the Gospel. Baptism is the gateway leading into the fold of Christ, the portal to the Church, the established rite of naturalization in the kingdom of God. The candidate for admission into the Church, having obtained and professed faith in the Lord Jesus Christ and having sincerely repented of his sins, is properly required to give evidence of this spiritual sanctification by some outward ordinance, prescribed by authority as the sign or symbol of his new profession. The initiatory ordinance is baptism by water, to be followed by the higher baptism of the Holy Spirit; and, as a result of this act of obedience, remission of sins is granted.

Simple indeed are the means thus ordained for admission into the fold; they are within the reach of the poorest and weakest, as also of the rich and powerful. What symbol more expressive of a cleansing from sin could be given than that of baptism in water? Baptism is made a sign of the covenant entered into between the repentant sinner and his God, that thereafter he will seek to observe the divine commands. Concerning this fact, Alma the prophet thus admonished and instructed the people of Gideon: "Yea, I say unto you, come and fear not, and lay aside every sin, which easily doth beset you, which doth bind you down to destruction, yea, come and go forth, and show unto your God that ye are willing to repent of your sins and enter into a covenant with him to keep his commandments, and witness it unto him this day by going into the waters of baptism."[a]

The humbled sinner, convicted of his transgression through faith and repentance, will hail most joyfully any means of cleansing himself from pollution, now so repulsive in his eyes. All such will cry out as did the stricken multitude at Pentecost, "What shall we do?" Unto such comes the answering voice of the Spirit, through the medium of scripture or by the mouths of the Lord's appointed servants: "Repent, and be baptized every one of you in the name of Jesus Christ for the remission of sins."[b] Springing forth as a result of contrition of soul, baptism has been very appropriately called the first fruits of repentance.[c]

The Establishment of Baptism dates from the time of the earliest history of the race. When the Lord manifested Himself to Adam after the expulsion from the Garden of Eden, He promised the patriarch of the race: "If thou wilt turn unto me, and hearken unto my voice, and believe, and repent of all thy transgressions, and be baptized, even in water, in the name of mine Only Begotten Son, who is full of grace and truth, which is Jesus Christ, the only name which shall be given under heaven, whereby salvation shall come unto the children of men, ye shall receive the gift of the Holy Ghost, asking all things in his name, and whatsoever ye shall ask, it shall be given you. * * * And it came to pass, when the Lord had spoken with Adam, our father, that Adam cried unto the Lord, and he was caught away by the Spirit of the Lord, and was carried down into the water, and was laid under the water, and was brought forth out of the water. And thus he was baptized, and the Spirit of God descended upon him, and thus he was born of the Spirit, and became quickened in the inner man."[d] Enoch preached the doctrine of repentance and baptism, and baptized the penitent believers; and as many as accepted these teachings and submitted to the requirements of the Gospel became sanctified in the sight of God.

The Special Purpose of Baptism is to afford admission to the Church of Christ with remission of sins. What need of more words to prove the worth of this divinely appointed ordinance? What gift could be offered the human race greater than a sure means of obtaining forgiveness for transgression? Justice forbids the granting of universal and unconditional pardon for sins committed except through obedience to ordained law; but means simple and effective are provided whereby the penitent sinner may enter into a covenant with God, sealing that covenant with the sign that commands recognition in heaven, that he will submit himself to the laws of God; thus he places himself within the reach of Mercy, under whose protecting influence he may win eternal life.

Biblical Proofs that baptism is designed as a means of securing to man a remission of his sins are abundant. John the Baptist was the special preacher of this doctrine, and the authorized administrator of the ordinance, in the days immediately preceding the Savior's ministry in the flesh; and the voice of this priest of the desert stirred Jerusalem and reverberated through all Judæa, proclaiming remission of sins as the fruits of acceptable baptism.[e]

[a] Alma 7:15.
[b] See Acts 2:37, 38.
[c] See Moroni 8:25.
[d] P.of G.P., Moses 6:52–65.
[e] See Mark 1:4; Luke 3:3.

Saul of Tarsus, a zealous persecutor of the followers of Christ, while journeying to Damascus intent on a further exercise of his ill-directed zeal, received a special manifestation of the power of God and was converted with signs and wonders. He heard and answered the voice of Christ, and thus became a special witness of his Lord. Yet even this unusual demonstration of divine favor was insufficient. Blinded through the glory that had been manifested unto him, humbled and earnest, awakening to the convicting fact that he had been persecuting his Redeemer, he exclaimed in anguish of soul: "What shall I do, Lord?"[f] He was directed to go to Damascus, there to learn more of the Lord's will concerning him. Gladly he received the Lord's messenger, devout Ananias, who ministered unto him so that he regained his sight, and then taught him baptism as a means of obtaining forgiveness.

Saul, known now as Paul, thereafter a preacher of righteousness and an apostle of the Lord Jesus Christ, taught to others the same great saving principle, that by baptism in water comes regeneration from sin.[g] In forceful language and attended with special evidences of divine power, Peter declared the same doctrine to the penitent multitude. Overcome with grief at the recital of what they had done to the Son of God, they cried out: "Men and brethren, what shall we do?" Promptly came the answer, with apostolic authority, "Repent, and be baptized every one of you in the name of Jesus Christ for the remission of sins."[h]

Book of Mormon Prophets gave the same testimony to the western fold of Christ. To this effect were the words of Nephi, son of Lehi, addressed to his brethren: "For the gate by which ye should enter is repentance and baptism by water; and then cometh a remission of your sins by fire and by the Holy Ghost."[i] So did Alma teach the people of Gideon, as already quoted.[j] Nephi, grandson of Helaman, immediately preceding Christ's advent upon earth went forth amongst his people, baptizing unto repentance; and from his ministry followed "a great remission of sins."[k] Nephi ordained assistants in the ministry, "that all such as should come unto them should be baptized with water, and this as a witness and a testimony before God, and unto the people, that they had repented and received a remission of their sins."[l] Mormon adds his own testimony, as commissioned of Christ, exhorting the people to forsake their sins and be baptized for remission thereof.[m]

Latter-day Revelation, concerning baptism and its object, shows that the same importance is ascribed by the Lord to the ordinance today as in earlier times. That there may be no question as to the application of this doctrine to the Church in the present dispensation, the principle has been restated, the law has been reenacted for our guidance. The elders of the Church are commissioned to preach the remission of sins as obtainable through the means of authorized baptism.[n]

Fit Candidates for Baptism—The prime object of baptism being admission to the Church with remission of sins, and this coming only through faith in God and true repentance before Him, it naturally follows that baptism can in justice be required of those only who are capable of exercising faith and of working repentance.[o] In a revelation on Church government given through

[f] See Acts 22:1–16.

[g] See Titus 3:5.

[h] Acts 2:36–38; see also 1 Pet. 3:21.

[i] 2 Nephi 31:17; read to end of chapter.

[j] See Alma 7:14, 15.

[k] 3 Nephi 1:23.

[l] 3 Nephi 7:24–26.

[m] See 3 Nephi 30:2.

[n] See D&C 19:31; 55:2; 68:27; 76:51, 52; 84:27, 74.

[o] See Appendix 6:1.

Joseph the Prophet, April, 1830, the Lord specifically states the conditions under which persons may be received into the Church through baptism: "All those who humble themselves before God, and desire to be baptized, and come forth with broken hearts and contrite spirits, and witness before the church that they have truly repented of all their sins, and are willing to take upon them the name of Jesus Christ, having a determination to serve him to the end, and truly manifest by their works that they have received of the Spirit of Christ unto the remission of their sins, shall be received by baptism into his church."[p]

These conditions exclude all who have not arrived at the age of discretion and accountability; and by direct commandment the Lord has forbidden the Church to receive any who have not attained to such age.[q] By revelation the Lord had designated eight years as the age at which children may be properly baptized into the Church; and parents are required to prepare their children for the ordinances of the Church by teaching them the doctrines of faith, repentance, baptism, and the laying on of hands for the gift of the Holy Ghost. Failure in this requirement is accounted by the Lord as a sin resting upon the heads of the parents.[r]

Infant Baptism—The Latter-day Saints are opposed to the practise of infant baptism, which indeed they believe to be a sacrilege. No one having faith in the word of God can look upon the child as culpably wicked; such an innocent being needs no initiation into the fold, for he has never strayed therefrom; he needs no remission of sins for he has committed no sin; and should he die before he has become contaminated by the sins of earth he will be received without baptism into the paradise of God. Yet there are many professedly Christian teachers who aver that as all children are born into a wicked world they are themselves wicked, and must be cleansed in the waters of baptism to be made acceptable to God. Such doctrine is heinous. The child to whom the Savior pointed as an example of emulation for those even who had received the holy apostleship,[s] the Lord's selected type of the kingdom of heaven, the favored spirits whose angels stand forever in the presence of the Father, faithfully reporting all that may be done unto their charges[t]—are such souls to be rejected and cast into torment because their earthly guardians failed to have them baptized? To teach such false doctrine is sin.

The History of Infant Baptism is instructive as throwing light upon the origin of this erratic practise. It is certain that the baptism of infants, or pedobaptism (Greek *paidos,* child, and *baptismos,* baptism) as it is styled in theological lore, was not taught by the Savior, nor by His apostles. Some point to the incident of Christ blessing children, and rebuking those who would forbid the little ones coming unto Him,[u] as an evidence in favor of infant baptism; but as has been wisely and tersely remarked: "From the action of Christ's blessing infants, to infer they are to be baptized, proves nothing so much as that there is a want of better argument; for the conclusion would with more probability be derived thus: Christ blessed infants, and so dismissed them, but baptized them not; therefore infants are not to be baptized."[v]

There is no authentic record of infant baptism having been practised during the first two centuries after Christ, and the custom probably did not become general before the fifth century; from

[p] D&C 20:37.
[q] See D&C 20:71.
[r] See D&C 68:25–27.
[s] See Matt. 18:1–6.
[t] See same, verse 10.
[u] See Matt. 19:13; Mark 10:13; Luke 18:15.
[v] This remark has been credited to Jeremy Taylor, an English bishop who died in 1667, but whether rightly or otherwise the present author is unable to say. The argument is sound, whoever worded it as above.

the time last named until the Reformation, however, it was accepted by the dominant church organization—the Roman Catholic. But even during that dark age many theological disputants raised their voices against this unholy rite.[w] In the early part of the sixteenth century, a sect rose into prominence in Germany, under the name of Anabaptists (Greek *ana,* again, and *baptizo,* baptize) distinguished for its opposition to the practise of infant baptism, and deriving its name from the requirement made of all its members who had been baptized in infancy that they be baptized again. The Baptists in general maintain a unity of belief in opposing the baptism of irresponsible children, but are not to be regarded as otherwise identical with the Anabaptist denomination.

Some pedobaptists have attempted to prove an analogy between baptism and circumcision, but without scriptural warrant. Circumcision was made the mark of a covenant between God and Abraham,[x] a symbol regarded by the posterity of Abraham as indicative of their freedom from the idolatry of the times, and of God's acceptance of them; and nowhere is circumcision made a means for remission of sins. That rite was applicable to males only; baptism is administered to both sexes. Circumcision was to be performed on the eighth day after birth, even though such should fall on the Sabbath.[y] In the third century a council of bishops was held under the presidency of Cyprian, Bishop of Carthage, at which it was gravely determined that to postpone baptism until the eighth day after birth was hazardous and consequently not to be allowed.

Infant Baptism is Forbidden in the Book of Mormon, from which fact we infer that disputation upon this subject had arisen among the Nephites. Mormon, having received special revelation from the Lord concerning the matter, wrote an epistle thereon to his son Moroni, in which he denounces the practise of infant baptism, and declares that any one who supposes that little children need baptism is in the gall of bitterness and in the bonds of iniquity, denying the mercies of Christ, and setting at naught His atonement and the power of His redemption.[z]

Baptism Essential to Salvation—Demonstrations concerning the object of baptism apply with equal force to the proposition that baptism is necessary for salvation; for, inasmuch as remission of sins constitutes a special purpose of baptism, and as no soul can be saved in the kingdom of God with unforgiven sins, it is plain that baptism is essential to salvation. Salvation is promised to man on condition of his obedience to the laws and ordinances of the Gospel; and, as the scriptures conclusively prove, baptism is one of the most important of such requirements. Baptism, being commanded of God, must be essential to the purpose for which it is instituted, for God deals not with unnecessary forms. Baptism is required of all who have attained to years of accountability; none are exempt.

Even Christ, standing as a man without sin in the midst of a sinful world, was baptized, "to fulfil all righteousness,"[aa] such being the purpose as declared by the Savior to the hesitating priest, who, zealous as he was for his great mission, yet demurred when asked to baptize one whom he considered sinless. Centuries before the great event, Nephi, prophesying among the people on the western continent, foretold the baptism of the Savior and explained how righteousness would be thereby fulfilled:[bb] "And now, if the Lamb of God, he being holy, should have need to be baptized by water, to fulfill all righteousness, O, then, how much more need have we, being unholy, to be baptized?"

[w] See Appendix 6:2.
[x] See Gen. 17:1–14.
[y] See John 7:22, 23.
[z] See Moroni, chap. 8; read the entire epistle.
[aa] See Matt. 3:15.
[bb] See 2 Nephi 31:5–8.

The words of the Savior, spoken while He ministered in the flesh, declare baptism to be essential to salvation. A certain ruler of the Jews, Nicodemus, came to Christ by night and made a profession of confidence in the ministry of Jesus, whom he designated as "a teacher come from God." Seeing his faith, Jesus taught unto him one of the chief laws of heaven, saying: "Except a man be born again, he cannot see the kingdom of God." A question by Nicodemus called forth the additional declaration: "Verily, verily, I say unto thee, Except a man be born of water and of the Spirit, he cannot enter into the kingdom of God."cc It is practically indisputable that the watery birth here referred to as essential to entrance into the kingdom is baptism. We learn further concerning Christ's attitude toward baptism that He required the ordinance of those who professed to become His disciples.dd When appearing to the eleven apostles in His resurrected state, giving them His farewell blessing and final commission, He commanded them: "Go ye, therefore, and teach all nations, baptizing them in the name of the Father, and of the Son, and of the Holy Ghost"ee and, concerning the results of baptism, He declared unto them, that "He that believeth and is baptized shall be saved; but he that believeth not shall be damned."ff

Plain as seems the spirit of these instructions and promises there are nevertheless many who, while professing to teach the doctrine of the Redeemer, evade the meaning of His precepts, and assume that because He said "he that believeth not shall be damned," instead of—he that is not baptized shall be damned—baptism is after all not an essential but a mere convenience or simple propriety in the plan of salvation. It is a mockery of faith to profess belief in Christ while refusing to abide by His commandments. To believe the word of God and do it not is to increase our culpability; such a course but adds hypocrisy to other sin. Surely the full penalty provided for wilful unbelief will fall to the lot of the professed believer who refuses to yield obedience to the very principles in which he boasts of having faith. Moreover, what can be said of the sincerity of one who refuses to obey the divine commands except penalties be specified for disobedience? Can such a one's repentance be sincere, when he is submissive only through fear of punishment? However, in stating this principle for the government of the saints in the present dispensation, the Lord's words are more specific: "And he that believeth and is baptized shall be saved, and he that believeth not, and is not baptized, shall be damned."gg

The same doctrine concerning the necessity of baptism was preached by the disciples of Christ, particularly those who were immediately associated with Him in the ministry. John the Baptist testified that he had been appointed to baptize with water;hh and concerning those who accepted John's teachings the Savior affirmed that they, even though they were publicans, justified God, while the Pharisees and lawyers who refused to be baptized "rejected the counsel of God against themselves"ii thereby, as we must conclude, forfeiting their claim to salvation. As already pointed out, Peter, the chief of the apostles, had but one answer to give to the eager multitude seeking to know the essentials of salvation, "Repent, and be baptized every one of you."jj

Christ's humble compliance with the will of His Father, by submitting to baptism even though He stood sinless, declares to the world in language more forceful than words that none

cc John 3:1–5.
dd See John 4:1, 2.
ee Matt. 28:19.
ff Mark 16:16.
gg D&C 112:29.
hh See John 1:33.
ii Luke 7:30.
jj Acts 2:38; see also 1 Pet. 3:21.

are exempt from this requirement, and that baptism indeed is a requisite for salvation. So, no evidence of divine favor, no bestowal of heavenly gifts, excuses man from obedience to this and other laws and ordinances of the Gospel. Saul of Tarsus, though permitted to hear the voice of the Redeemer, could only enter the Church of Christ through the portals of baptism by water and by the Holy Ghost.[kk] Afterward he preached baptism, declaring that by that ordinance may "we put on Christ," becoming the children of God. Cornelius, the centurion, was acknowledged of God through prayers and alms, and an angel came instructing him to send for Peter who would tell him what to do. The apostle, having been specially prepared by the Lord for this mission, entered the house of the penitent Gentile, though to do such was to violate the customs of the Jews, and taught him and his family concerning Christ Jesus. Even while Peter was speaking, the Holy Spirit fell upon his hearers, so that they testified by the gift of tongues and greatly glorified God.[ll] Yet the bestowal of such great gifts in no degree exempted them from compliance with the law of baptism; and Peter commanded them to be baptized in the name of the Lord.

Christ's ministers on the western continent were not less pronounced in promulgating the doctrine of baptism. Lehi[mm] and his son Nephi,[nn] each testified of the baptism of the Savior which was to follow, and of the absolute necessity of baptism by water and by the Holy Ghost on the part of all seekers after salvation. Nephi forcefully compared repentance and baptism by water and the Spirit to the gate leading into the fold of Christ.[oo] Alma preached baptism as indispensable to salvation, calling upon the people to witness unto the Lord, by their observance of this principle, that they covenanted to keep His commandments. The second Alma, son of the former, proclaimed baptism as a means of salvation and consecrated ministers to baptize.[pp]

During the last century preceding the birth of Christ, the work of God among the Lamanites was begun by the preaching of faith, repentance, and baptism. We find Ammon declaring this doctrine to King Lamoni and his people.[qq] Helaman preached baptism;[rr] and in the time of his ministry, less than half a century before Christ was born, we read that tens of thousands united themselves with the Church by baptism. So also preached Helaman's sons,[ss] and his grandson Nephi.[tt] These baptisms were administered in the name of the Messiah who was to come; but when He came to His western flock He directed that they should be baptized in the name of the Father, and of the Son, and of the Holy Ghost; and He conferred upon twelve men authority to officiate in the ordinance,[uu] promising salvation unto all who would comply with His law, and unto such only.

Evidence is abundant that the Savior regarded the baptized state as an essential condition of membership in His Church; thus, when instituting the sacrament of bread and wine among the Nephites He instructed His disciples to administer it unto those only who had been properly baptized.[vv] Further, we are informed that those who were baptized as Jesus had directed, were

kk See Acts 9:1–18; 22:1–16.
ll See Acts 10:30–48.
mm See 1 Nephi 10:7–10.
nn See 2 Nephi 31:4–14.
oo See 2 Nephi 31:17.
pp See Mosiah 18:8–17; Alma 5:61, 62; 9:27.
qq See Alma 19:35.
rr See Alma 62:45.
ss See Helaman 5:14–19.
tt See 3 Nephi 1:23.
uu See 3 Nephi 11:22–25; 12:1, 2.
vv See 3 Nephi 18:5, 11, 28–30.

called the Church of Christ.[ww] True to the Savior's promise, the Holy Ghost came to those who were baptized by His ordained authority, thus adding to water-baptism the higher baptism of the Holy Ghost;[xx] and many of them received specific manifestations of divine approval, seeing and hearing unspeakable things, not lawful to be written. The faith of the people showed itself in good works,[yy] by prayers and fasting,[zz] in acknowledgment of which Christ reappeared, this time manifesting Himself to the disciples whom He had called to the ministry. Unto them he reiterated the former promises regarding all who were baptized of Him; and to this He added, that, provided they endured to the end they should be held guiltless in the day of judgment.[aaa] On that occasion He repeated the commandment through obedience to which salvation is promised: "Repent, all ye ends of the earth, and come unto me and be baptized in my name, that ye may be sanctified by the reception of the Holy Ghost, that ye may stand spotless before me at the last day."[bbb]

Nearly four centuries later was heard the same proclamation from Mormon.[ccc] Then Moroni, his son, the solitary survivor of a once mighty people, while mourning the destruction of his kindred leaves what at the time he supposed would be his farewell testimony to the truth of this doctrine;[ddd] but being spared, contrary to his expectations, he reverts again to the sacred theme, realizing the incalculable worth of the doctrine unto any and all who would read his pages; and in what might be regarded as his last words, he testifies to baptism by water and of the Spirit as the means of salvation.[eee]

This fundamental principle, proclaimed of old, remains unaltered today; it is truth and changes not. The elders of the latter-day Church have been commissioned in almost the same words as were used in the authorization of the apostles of old: "Go ye into all the world, preach the gospel to every creature, acting in the authority which I have given you, baptizing in the name of the Father, and of the Son, and of the Holy Ghost. And he that believeth and is baptized shall be saved, and he that believeth not shall be damned."[fff] And again, hear the word of the Lord through Joseph the Prophet unto the elders of the Church: "Therefore, as I said unto mine apostles I say unto you again, that every soul who believeth on your words, and is baptized by water for the remission of sins, shall receive the Holy Ghost." But, "Verily, verily, I say unto you, they who believe not on your words, and are not baptized in water in my name, for the remission of their sins, that they may receive the Holy Ghost, shall be damned, and shall not come into my Father's kingdom where my Father and I am."[ggg] In obedience to these commands, the elders of this Church have continued to proclaim the Gospel among the nations, preaching faith, repentance, and baptism by water and of the Holy Ghost as essential to salvation.

We have examined the doctrines concerning baptism current among the Jews, the Nephites, and the Church of Jesus Christ in this age, and have found the principles taught to be ever the

---

ww See 3 Nephi 26:21.
xx See 3 Nephi 26:17, 18; 28:18; 4 Nephi 1.
yy See 3 Nephi 26:19, 20.
zz See 3 Nephi 27:1, 2.
aaa See 3 Nephi 27:16.
bbb See 3 Nephi 27:20.
ccc See Mormon 7:8–10.
ddd See Mormon 9:22, 23.
eee See Moroni 6:1–4.
fff D&C 68:8, 9.
ggg D&C 84:64, 74; see also 112:28, 29.

same. Indeed, we have gone farther back, even to the earliest history of the human race, and have learned that baptism was announced as a saving principle by which Adam was promised forgiveness and salvation. No one has reason to hope for salvation except by complying with the law of God, of which baptism is an essential part.

REFERENCES

Baptism for Remission of Sins

John the Baptist baptized and preached baptism of repentance for remission of sins—Mark 1:4; see also Luke 3:3 and compare 1:76, 77.

Repent, and be baptized in the name of Jesus Christ for remission of sins—Acts 2:38; see also 22:16; D&C 33:11.

The gate by which to enter is repentance and baptism, and then cometh remission of sins— 2 Nephi 31:17.

Be baptized unto repentance, that ye may be washed from your sins—Alma 7:14.

Baptizing unto repentance, in the which there was a great remission of sins—3 Nephi 1:23.

Christ taught the Nephites that through baptism they should receive remission—3 Nephi 12:2; see also 30:2.

Priesthood of Aaron holds authority to baptize by immersion for remission of sins—D&C 13:1.

Declare repentance and remission of sins by baptism—D&C 19:31; also 55:2.

Be baptized for a remission of your sins—D&C 33:11.

Gospel of repentance and of baptism, and remission of sins—D&C 84:27.

Baptism Essential to Salvation

Except a man be born of water and of the Spirit, he cannot enter into the kingdom of God—John 3:5.

He that believeth and is baptized shall be saved—Mark 16:16; 3 Nephi 11:33; D&C 112:29.

Pharisees and lawyers rejected the counsel of God, not being baptized of John—Luke 7:30.

By one Spirit are we baptized into one body—1 Cor. 12:13.

As many as have been baptized unto Christ have put on Christ—Gal. 3:27.

The like figure whereunto baptism doth save us—1 Peter 3:21.

One Lord, one faith, one baptism—Eph. 4:5.

All men must be baptized or they cannot be saved in the kingdom of God—2 Nephi 9:23.

Be baptized in my name; for he that believeth and is baptized shall be saved—Ether 4:18; also Moroni 7:34; 3 Nephi 21:6.

See that ye are not baptized unworthily—Mormon 9:29.

As many as repent, are baptized, and endure shall be saved—D&C 18:22.

Adam was taught that baptism is essential—Moses 6:52. Baptism of Adam—verses 64–68.

Jesus Christ was Baptized

To fulfil all righteousness—Matt. 3:15. Thus it is shown that baptism is required of all men; see also Mark 1:9; Luke 3:21.

If the Lamb of God, he being holy, should have need to be baptized, how much more need have we—2 Nephi 31:5.

Preparedness for Baptism—From foregoing citations it is shown that faith in the Lord Jesus Christ, and effective repentance are prerequisites to baptism. Knowledge is therefore necessary, and instruction is required.

Christ commanded the apostles *to teach* all nations, then to baptize them, and then to teach them further—Matt. 28:19, 20.

Those who gladly received Peter's instructions were baptized—Acts 2:41.

Those who believed Philip's teachings concerning the kingdom of God were baptized—Acts 8:12.

Peter instructed Cornelius and his household, before they were baptized—Acts 10:25–48.

Paul instructed the keeper of the prison and his household prior to their baptism—Acts 16:29–33.

John the Baptist required evidence of repentance before baptism—Luke 3:7–14.

Summary of requisite conditions—Moroni 6:1–4.

Little children, incapable of understanding or of repenting, are not to be baptized—Moroni, chap. 8.

Parents to teach their children, and thus prepare them for baptism when eight years old—D&C 68:25.

No one to be received into the Church who is unaccountable and incapable of repentance—D&C 20:71; see also verse 37.

7

BAPTISM—CONTINUED

ARTICLE 4

E BELIEVE that the first principles and ordinances of the Gospel are: * * * third, Baptism by immersion for the remission of sins; * * *

MODE OF BAPTISM

Method of Administering Baptism Important—In considering the object and necessity of baptism, we have seen the importance that the Lord attaches to this initiatory rite. It is not surprising that the mode of administering the ordinance should be specifically prescribed. Many Christian sects have some established rite of initiation, in which water figures as a necessary element; though with some the ceremony consists in nothing more than the placing of the priest's moistened finger on the forehead of the candidate, or in the pouring or sprinkling of water upon the face; while others consider immersion of the whole body as requisite. The Latter-day Saints hold that the scriptures are devoid of ambiguity regarding the acceptable mode of baptism; and they boldly declare their belief that bodily immersion by a duly commissioned servant or representative of the Savior is the only true form. Their reasons for this belief may be summed up as follows: The derivation and former usage of the word baptism, and its cognates, betoken immersion. The symbolism of the rite is preserved in no other form. Scriptural authority, the revealed word of God through the mouths of ancient and latter-day prophets, prescribes immersion as the true form of baptism.

The Verb "Baptize," from the Greek *bapto, baptizo,* meant literally to dip or to immerse. As is true in the case of every living language, words may undergo great changes of meaning; and some writers declare that the term in question may be as applicable to pouring or sprinkling with water as to actual immersion. It becomes interesting, therefore, to inquire as to the current meaning of the term at or near the time of Christ; for, as the Savior evidently deemed it unnecessary, in the course of His instructions concerning baptism, to enlarge upon the meaning of the term, it evidently conveyed a very definite meaning to those who received His teachings. From the use made of the original term by the Greek and Latin authors,[a] it is plain that they understood an actual immersion in water as the true signification. The modern Greeks understand baptism to mean a burial in water, and therefore, as they adopt the profession of Christianity, they practise immersion as the proper form in baptism.[b] Concerning this kind of argument, it should be remembered that philological evidence is not of the most decisive order. Let us pass then to the consideration of other and stronger reasons.

The Symbolism of the Baptismal Rite is preserved in no form other than immersion. The Savior compared baptism to a birth, and declared such to be essential to the life that leads to the kingdom of God.[c] None can say that a birth is typified by a sprinkling of water upon the face. Not the least of the distinctions that have contributed to Christ's preeminence as a teacher of teachers consists in His precise and forceful use of language; His comparisons and metaphors are always expressive, His parables convincing; and so inappropriate a similitude as is implied in such a misrepresentation of birth would be entirely foreign to the Lord's methods.

Baptism has also been very impressively compared to a burial, followed by a resurrection; and in this symbol of the bodily death and resurrection of His Son has God promised to grant remission of sins. In writing to the Romans, Paul says: "Know ye not, that so many of us as were baptized into Jesus Christ were baptized into his death? Therefore we are buried with him by baptism into death: that like as Christ was raised up from the dead by the glory of the Father, even so we also should walk in newness of life. For if we have been planted together in the likeness of his death, we shall be also in the likeness of his resurrection."[d] And again, the same apostle writes: "Buried with him in baptism, wherein also ye are risen with him through the faith of the operation of God, who hath raised him from the dead."[e] Among all the varied forms of baptism practised by man, immersion alone typifies a birth marking the beginning of a new career, or the sleep of the grave with subsequent victory over death.

Scriptural Authority warrants none other form than immersion. Jesus Christ was baptized by immersion. We read that following the ordinance, He "went up straightway out of the water."[f] That the baptism of the Savior was acceptable before His Father is abundantly proved by the manifestations immediately following—in the descent of the Holy Ghost, and the Father's declaration: "This is my beloved Son, in whom I am well pleased." John, surnamed because of his divine commission the Baptist, baptized in the river Jordan;[g] and shortly afterward we hear of him baptizing in Ænon, near to Salim, "because there was much water there;"[h] yet, had he been baptizing by sprinkling, a small quantity of water would have sufficed for a multitude.

[a] See Appendix 7:1.
[b] See Appendix 7:2.
[c] See John 3:3–5.
[d] Rom. 6:3–5.
[e] Col. 2:12.
[f] Matt. 3:16, 17; Mark 1:10, 11.
[g] See Mark 1:4, 5.
[h] John 3:23.

We read of baptism following the somewhat speedy conversion of an Ethiopian eunuch, treasurer to the queen Candace. To him Philip preached the doctrine of Christ as they rode together in the Ethiopian's chariot; the latter, believing the words of his inspired instructor, desired baptism, and Philip consenting, "he commanded the chariot to stand still: and they *went down both into the water*, both Philip and the eunuch; and he baptized him. And when they were come up out of the water, the Spirit of the Lord caught away Philip, that the eunuch saw him no more; and he went on his way rejoicing."[i]

History, other than Scriptural, proves that for more than two centuries after Christ immersion was the mode of baptism generally practised by professed Christians; and that not until near the close of the thirteenth century did other forms become general.[j] Distortions of ordinances instituted by authority may be expected if the outward form of such ordinances be attempted when the authority to minister in them is absent; yet such distortions are of gradual growth; deformities resulting from constitutional ailments do not develop in a day. We may look, therefore, for the closest approach to the true form of baptism, as likewise in the case of any other ordinance instituted by Christ, in the period immediately following His personal ministry and that of His apostles. Then, as the darkness of unbelief deepened, the authority given of Christ having been taken from the earth with His martyred servants, many innovations appeared; and dignitaries of the various churches became a law unto themselves and to their adherents. Early in the third century the Bishop of Carthage decided that persons of weak health might be acceptably baptized by sprinkling; and with the license thus given the true form of baptism gradually fell into disfavor, and unauthorized practises devised by man took its place.

Baptism among the Nephites was administered by immersion only. The wide extent to which baptism was preached and practised among the people from Lehi to Moroni has been already shown. When the Savior appeared to His people on the western continent, He gave them very explicit instructions as to the method of procedure in administering the ordinance. These are his words: "Verily I say unto you, that whoso repenteth of his sins through your words, and desireth to be baptized in my name, on this wise shall ye baptize them—Behold, ye shall go down and stand in the water, and in my name shall ye baptize them. And now behold, these are the words which ye shall say, calling them by name, saying: *Having authority given me of Jesus Christ, I baptize you in the name of the Father, and of the Son, and of the Holy Ghost. Amen.* And then shall ye immerse them in the water, and come forth again out of the water."[k]

Latter-day Baptism, as prescribed by revelation, is after the same pattern. The first baptisms in the present dispensation were those of Joseph Smith and Oliver Cowdery, who baptized each other according to the directions of the angel from whom they had received authority to administer this holy ordinance, and who was none other than John the Baptist of a former dispensation, the forerunner of the Messiah. Joseph Smith thus describes the event: "Accordingly we went and were baptized. I baptized him [Oliver Cowdery] first, and afterwards he baptized me— * * * Immediately on our coming up out of the water after we had been baptized, we experienced great and glorious blessings."[l]

[i] Acts 8:26–39.
[j] See Appendix 7:3.
[k] 3 Nephi 11:23–27.
[l] P.of G.P., pp. 57, 58.

In a revelation concerning Church government, dated April, 1830, the Lord prescribed the exact mode of baptism as He desires the ordinance administered in the present dispensation. He said: "Baptism is to be administered in the following manner unto all those who repent—The person who is called of God and has authority from Jesus Christ to baptize, shall go down into the water with the person who has presented himself or herself for baptism, and shall say, calling him or her by name: *Having been commissioned of Jesus Christ, I baptize you in the name of the Father, and of the Son, and of the Holy Ghost. Amen.* Then shall he immerse him or her in the water, and come forth again out of the water."[m]

The Lord would not have prescribed the words of this ordinance had He not intended that this form only should be used; therefore elders and priests of The Church of Jesus Christ of Latter-day Saints have no personal authority to change the form given of God, by additions, omissions, or alterations of any kind.

BAPTISM AND "REBAPTISM"

A Repetition of the Baptismal Ordinance to the same individual is allowable under certain specific conditions. Thus, if one, having entered the Church by baptism, withdraws from it or is excommunicated therefrom, and afterwards repents and desires to regain his standing in the Church, he can do so only through baptism. However, such is a repetition of the initiatory ordinance as previously administered. There is no ordinance of rebaptism in the Church distinct in nature, form, or purpose, from other baptism; and, therefore, in administering baptism to a subject who has been formerly baptized, the form of the ordinance is exactly the same as in first baptisms. The expression "I rebaptize you" in place of "I baptize you" and the additions "for the renewal of your covenants" or "for the remission of your sins" are not authorized. Dictates of reason unite with the voice of the presiding authorities of the Church in discountenancing any departures from the course prescribed by the Lord; changes in ordinances given by authority can be effected only by authority.

Rebaptisms Recorded in Scripture are few; and in every instance the existence of special circumstances justifying the action are apparent. Thus, we read of Paul baptizing certain disciples at Ephesus though they had already been baptized after the manner of John's baptism.[n] But in this case, the apostle had reason to doubt that the baptism of which these spoke had been administered by authorized hands, or after proper preliminary education of the candidates; for when he tested the efficacy of their baptism by asking "Have ye received the Holy Ghost since ye believed?" they answered him, "We have not so much as heard whether there be any Holy Ghost." Then asked he in surprise: "Unto what then were ye baptized?" and they replied: "Unto John's baptism." But Paul knew, as we know, that while John preached the baptism of repentance by water he declared that such was but preliminary to the greater baptism of the Holy Ghost, which Christ should bring. Therefore, in view of such unsatisfactory evidence concerning the validity of their baptism, Paul had baptism administered unto these twelve devout Ephesians in the name of the Lord Jesus, after which he laid his hands upon them, and they received the Holy Ghost.

The baptism instituted by Christ among the Nephites[o] was very largely a rebaptism; for, as we have already seen, the doctrine of baptism had been taught and practised among the people from the time of Lehi; and surely, Nephi, the first to whom the Savior gave authority to baptize after

[m] D&C 22:72–74.
[n] See Acts 19:1–6.
[o] See 3 Nephi 11:21–28.

His departure, had been previously baptized, for he and his colaborers in the ministry had been most zealous in preaching the necessity of baptism.[p] Yet in this case also there had probably arisen some impropriety in the manner and perhaps in the spirit of administering the ordinance; for the Savior in giving minute directions concerning the form of baptism reproved them for the spirit of contention and disputation that had previously existed among them regarding the ordinance.[q] Therefore, the baptism of these people was made valid by an authoritative administration after the manner prescribed by the Lord.

Repeated Baptisms of the Same Person are not sanctioned in the Church. It is an error to assume that baptism offers a means of gaining forgiveness of sins however oft repeated. Such a belief tends rather to excuse than to prevent sin, inasmuch as the hurtful effects may seem to be easily averted. Neither the written law nor the instructions of the living Priesthood designate baptism as a means of securing forgiveness by those who are already within the fold of Christ. Unto such, forgiveness of sin has been promised on confession and repentance with full purpose of heart; of them a repetition of the baptismal rite is not required; and, were subjects of this class repeatedly baptized, unto them remission of sins would in no wise come except they repent most sincerely. The frailties of mortality and our proneness to sin lead us continually into error; but if we covenant with the Lord at the waters of baptism, and thereafter seek to observe His law, He is merciful to pardon our little transgressions through repentance sincere and true; and without such repentance, baptism would avail us nothing.

BAPTISM FOR THE DEAD

Baptism Required of All—The universality of the law of baptism has been already dwelt upon. Compliance with the ordinance has been shown to be essential to salvation, and this condition applies to all mankind. Nowhere in scripture is a distinction made in this regard between the living and the dead. The dead are those who have lived in mortality upon earth; the living are mortals who yet shall pass through the ordained change that we call death. All are children of the same Father, all to be judged and rewarded or punished by the same unerring justice, with the same interpositions of benignant mercy. Christ's atoning sacrifice was offered, not alone for the few who lived upon the earth while He was in the flesh, nor for those who were to be born in mortality after His death, but for all inhabitants of earth then past, present, and future. He was ordained of the Father to be a judge of both quick and dead;[r] He is Lord alike of living and dead,[s] as men speak of dead and living, though all are to be placed in one class, for all live unto Him.[t]

The Gospel yet Unknown to Many—Of the multitudes of human beings who have already lived and died, but few have heard and fewer have obeyed the laws of the Gospel. In the course of the world's history there have been long periods of spiritual darkness, when the Gospel was not preached among men; when there was no authorized representative of the Lord officiating in the saving ordinances of the kingdom. Such a condition has never existed except as the result of unbelief and wickedness. When mankind have persistently trodden the pearls of truth into the mire and have sought to slay and rend the bearers of the jewels, in justice not more than in mercy these treasures of heaven have been taken and withheld until a more appreciative posterity would be

[p] See 3 Nephi 7:23–26, etc.
[q] See 3 Nephi 11:27–30.
[r] See Acts 10:42; 2 Tim. 4:1; 1 Peter 4:5.
[s] See Rom. 14:9.
[t] See Luke 20:36, 38.

raised up. It may very properly be asked, What provision is made in the economy of God for the eventual salvation of those who have thus neglected the requirements of the Gospel, and for those who have never heard it?

According to certain dogmas that have prevailed among many sects during the obscurity of the spiritual night, and which are yet zealously promulgated, neverending punishment or interminable bliss, unchanging in kind or degree, shall be the lot of every soul; the award being made according to the condition of the spirit at the time of bodily death; a life of sin being thus entirely nullified by a death-bed repentance; and an honorable career, if unmarked by ceremonies of the established sects, being followed by the tortures of hell without the hope of relief. Such a conception must rank with the dread heresy proclaiming the condemnation of innocent babes who have not been sprinkled by man's assumed authority.

It is blasphemous to thus attribute caprice and vindictiveness to the divine nature. In the justice of God no soul shall be condemned under any law that has not been made known unto him. True, eternal punishment has been decreed as the lot of the wicked; but the meaning of this expression has been given by the Lord Himself:[u] eternal punishment is God's punishment; endless punishment is God's punishment, for "Endless" and "Eternal" are among His names, and the words are descriptive of His attributes. No soul shall be kept in prison or continued in torment beyond the time requisite to work the needed reformation and to vindicate justice, for which ends alone punishment is imposed.[v] And no one will be permitted to enter any kingdom of glory to which he is not entitled through obedience to law.

The Gospel preached to the Dead—It is plain, then, that the Gospel must be proclaimed in the spirit world; and, that such work is provided for the scriptures abundantly prove. Peter, describing the mission of the Redeemer, thus declares this truth: "For this cause was the gospel preached also to them that are dead, that they might be judged according to men in the flesh, but live according to God in the spirit."[w] The inauguration of this work among the dead was effected by Christ in the interval between His death and resurrection. While His body lay in the tomb, His spirit ministered to the spirits of the departed: "By which also he went and preached unto the spirits in prison; Which sometime were disobedient, when once the longsuffering of God waited in the days of Noah, while the ark was a preparing, wherein few, that is, eight souls were saved by water."[x]

Other scriptures sustain the position, that while in a disembodied state, Christ went elsewhere than to the place usually termed heaven—the abode of His Father—and that He labored among the dead, who greatly needed His ministry. One of the malefactors, who suffered crucifixion by His side, through humility won from the dying Savior the promise: "Today shalt thou be with me in paradise."[y] And three days later, the Lord, then a resurrected being, declared to the sorrowing Magdalene: "I am not yet ascended to my Father."[z]

If it was deemed proper and just that the Gospel be carried to the spirits who were disobedient in the days of Noah, it is reasonable to conclude that like opportunities shall be placed within the reach of others who have rejected the word at different times. For the same spirit of neglect, disobedience, and opposition to divine law that characterized the time of Noah has existed

[u] D&C 19:10–12.

[v] See *Vitality of Mormonism,* article "How Long Shall Hell Last?" p. 263.

[w] 1 Peter 4:6.

[x] 1 Peter 3:18-20.

[y] Luke 23:39-43.

[z] John 20:17; see also *Jesus the Christ,* chap. 36.

since.[aa] Further, if, in the plan of God, provision be made for the redemption of the wilfully disobedient, those who actually spurn the truth, can we believe that the still greater multitudes of spirits who have never heard the Gospel are to be left in punishment eternally? No; God has decreed that even the heathen nations, and those that knew no law, shall be redeemed.[bb] The gifts of God are not confined to this sphere of action, but will be bestowed in justice throughout eternity. Upon all who reject the word of God in this life will fall the penalties provided; but after the debt has been paid the prison doors shall be opened, and the spirits once confined in suffering, then chastened and clean, shall come forth to partake of the glory provided for their class.

Christ's Work Among the Dead Foretold—Centuries before Christ came in the flesh, prophets rejoiced in the knowledge that through Him would salvation be carried to the dead as well as to the living. Speaking of the retribution to come upon the proud and haughty of the earth, Isaiah declares: "And they shall be gathered together, as prisoners are gathered in the pit, and shall be shut up in the prison, and after many days shall they be visited."[cc] The same prophet thus testifies concerning the work of the coming Redeemer—he is "to open the blind eyes, to bring out the prisoners from the prison, and them that sit in darkness out of the prison house."[dd] David, singing to the music of inspiration concerning the redemption from the grave, exclaims: "Therefore my heart is glad, and my glory rejoiceth: my flesh also shall rest in hope. For thou wilt not leave my soul in hell; neither wilt thou suffer thine Holy One to see corruption. Thou wilt shew me the path of life: in thy presence is fulness of joy; at thy right hand there are pleasures for evermore."[ee]

Work of the Living for the Dead—The redemption of the dead will be effected in accordance with the law of God, which is written in justice and framed in mercy. It is alike impossible for any spirit, in the flesh or disembodied, to obtain promise of eternal glory except on condition of obedience to the laws and ordinances of the Gospel. And, as baptism is essential to the salvation of the living, it is likewise indispensable to the dead. This was known by the saints of old, and hence the doctrine of baptism for the dead was taught among them. In an epistle addressed to the church at Corinth, Paul expounded the principles of the resurrection, whereby the bodies of the dead are to be brought forth from the graves—Christ the firstfruits, and afterward they that are Christ's—and as proof that this doctrine of the resurrection was included in the Gospel as they had received it, the apostle asks: "Else what shall they do which are baptized for the dead, if the dead rise not at all? Why are they then baptized for the dead?"[ff] These words are unambiguous, and the fact that they are presented without explanation or comment argues that the principle of baptism for the dead was understood among the people to whom the letter was addressed.

Herein is shown the necessity of vicarious work—the living ministering in behalf of the dead; the children doing for their progenitors what is beyond the power of the latter to do for themselves. Many and varied are the interpretations rendered by fallible human wisdom on this plain question by Paul; yet the simple and earnest student finds little difficulty in comprehending the meaning. In the closing sentences of the Old Testament, the prophet Malachi predicted the great work to be carried on in behalf of the dead during the latter days: "Behold, I will send you Elijah

aa See Luke 17:26.
bb See D&C 45:54.
cc Isa. 24:22.
dd Isa. 42:6, 7.
ee Ps. 16:9–11.
ff 1 Cor. 15:29; see *The House of the Lord,* chap. 4.

the prophet before the coming of the great and dreadful day of the Lord: And he shall turn the heart of the fathers to the children, and the heart of the children to their fathers, lest I come and smite the earth with a curse."[gg] It is a current belief among many Bible students that this prophecy had reference to the birth and ministry of John the Baptist,[hh] upon whom indeed rested and remained the spirit and power of Elias as the angel had foretold;[ii] but we have no record of Elijah ministering unto John; and moreover the results of the latter's ministry warrant no conclusion that in him did the prophecy find its full realization.

We must therefore look to a later date in the world's history for a fulfilment of Malachi's prediction. On September 21, 1823, Joseph Smith[jj] received the visitation of a resurrected being who announced himself as Moroni, sent from the presence of God. In the course of his instructions to the youth, he quoted the prophecy of Malachi, already referred to, but in language slightly different from and certainly more expressive than that appearing in the Bible; the angel's version is as follows: "For behold, the day cometh that shall burn as an oven, and all the proud, yea, and all that do wickedly shall burn as stubble; for they that come shall burn them, saith the Lord of Hosts, that it shall leave them neither root nor branch. * * * Behold I will reveal unto you the Priesthood by the hand of Elijah the prophet, before the coming of the great and dreadful day of the Lord. * * * And he shall plant in the hearts of the children the promises made to the fathers, and the hearts of the children shall turn to their fathers. If it were not so the whole earth would be utterly wasted at his coming."[kk]

In a glorious manifestation to Joseph Smith and Oliver Cowdery, given in the Kirtland Temple, April 3, 1836, there appeared unto them Elijah the prophet, who had been taken from earth without tasting death; he declared unto them: "Behold, the time has fully come, which was spoken of by the mouth of Malachi—testifying that he [Elijah] should be sent, before the great and dreadful day of the Lord come—To turn the hearts of the fathers to the children, and the children to the fathers, lest the whole earth be smitten with a curse—Therefore, the keys of this dispensation are committed into your hands; and by this ye may know that the great and dreadful day of the Lord is near, even at the doors."[ll]

Fathers and Children Mutually Dependent—One of the great principles underlying the doctrine of salvation for the dead is that of the mutual dependence of the fathers and the children, of ancestors and posterity. As the Prophet Joseph Smith taught the saints,[mm] but for the establishment of a connecting link between the departed fathers and the living children the earth would be smitten with a curse. The divine plan provides that neither the children nor the fathers can alone be made perfect; and the necessary union is effected through baptism and associated ordinances administered by the living in behalf of the dead. The manner in which the hearts of the children and those of the fathers are turned toward one another is made plain through these scriptures. As the children learn that without their progenitors they cannot attain perfection, their hearts will be opened, their faith will be strengthened, and good works will be attempted for the redemption of their dead; and the departed, learning from the ministers of the Gospel laboring

---

[gg] Mal. 4:5, 6; P.of G.P., p. 53.

[hh] See Matt. 11:14; 17:11; Mark 9:11; Luke 1:17.

[ii] See Luke 1:17; D&C 27:7; also *Jesus the Christ*, p. 375.

[jj] See pages 11, 12 herein.

[kk] Compare verses 1, 5, and 6, Mal., chap. 4; P.of G.P., pp. 52, 53.

[ll] D&C 110:13–16.

[mm] See D&C 128:18; see also this entire section and sec. 127.

among them that they depend upon their children as vicarious saviors, will seek to sustain their mortal representatives with faith and prayer for the perfecting of those labors of love.

Love, which is a power in itself, is thus intensified. Aside from the emotions stirred within the soul by the presence of the divine, there are few yearnings stronger and purer than the love for kindred. Heaven could not be all we wish were family love there unknown.[nn] Affection there will differ from its earthly type in being deeper, stronger, purer. Thus in the mercy of God, His erring, mortal children, who have taken upon themselves the name of Christ on earth, may become, in a limited sphere, each a savior in the house of his fathers, by vicarious labor and sacrifice, rendered in humility, and, as represented in the baptismal ordinance, typical of the death, burial, and resurrection of the Redeemer.

The Labor for the Dead is Twofold—That performed on earth would be incomplete but for its supplement and counterpart beyond the veil. Missionary labor is in progress there, whereby the tidings of the Gospel are carried to the departed spirits, who thus learn of the work done in their behalf on earth. So far as the divine law has been revealed, it requires that the outward ordinances, such as baptism in water, the laying on of hands for the bestowal of the Holy Ghost, and the higher endowments that follow, be attended to on earth, a proper representative in the flesh acting as proxy for the dead. The results of such labors are to be left with the Lord. It is not to be supposed that by these ordinances the departed are in any way compelled to accept the obligation, nor that they are in the least hindered in the exercise of their free agency. They will accept or reject according to their condition of humility or hostility in respect to the Gospel; but the work so done for them on earth will be of avail when wholesome teaching and real penitence have shown them their true position.[oo]

TEMPLES

Temples or Other Sacred Places are required for the administration of the ordinances pertaining to the salvation of the dead, and in certain ordinances for the living. It is but proper that such structures should be the best the people can build. In every age of the world the covenant people have been a temple-building people. Shortly after Israel's deliverance from the bondage of Egypt the Lord called upon the people to construct a sanctuary to His name, the plan of which He minutely specified. Though this was but a tent it was elaborately furnished and appointed, the choicest possessions of the people being used in its construction.[pp] The Lord accepted this offering by manifesting His glory therein, and there revealing Himself.[qq] When the people had settled in the promised land the Tabernacle of the Congregation was given a more permanent resting place;[rr] yet it still was honored for its sacred purpose until superseded by the Temple of Solomon as the sanctuary of the Lord.[ss]

This Temple, one of the most imposing structures ever erected by man for sacred service, was dedicated with solemn ceremonies. However, its splendor was of short duration; for, within less than forty years from the time of its completion, its glory declined, and finally it fell a prey to the flames. A partial restoration of the Temple was made after the Jews returned from their captivity;

[nn] See Appendix 7:4.
[oo] See *The House of the Lord*, chap. 3.
[pp] See Ex., chap. 25; 35:22; see *The House of the Lord*, chap. 2; Appendix 7:5.
[qq] See Ex. 40:34–38.
[rr] See Josh. 18:1.
[ss] See 1 Kings, chaps. 6–8

and through the friendly influence of Cyrus and Darius, the Temple of Zerubbabel was dedicated. That the Lord accepted this effort of His people to maintain a sanctuary to His name is fully shown by the spirit that actuated its officers, among whom were Zechariah, Haggai, and Malachi. This Temple remained standing for nearly five centuries; and but a few years before the birth of the Savior the reconstruction of the edifice was begun by Herod the Great, and the Temple of Herod began to figure in history.[tt] The veil of this Temple was rent at the time of the crucifixion,[uu] and in 70 A.D., as predicted, the destruction of the building was accomplished by Titus.

Latter-day Temples—From that time until the present dispensation, no other Temples have been reared on the eastern continent. It is true, imposing edifices have been erected for purposes of worship; but a colossal structure does not necessarily constitute a Temple. A Temple is more than church-building, meeting-house, tabernacle, or synagogue; it is a place specially prepared by dedication unto the Lord, and marked by His acceptance, for the solemnization of ordinances pertaining to the Holy Priesthood. The Latter-day Saints, true to the characteristics of the covenant people,[vv] have been from the first a temple-building organization. But a few months after the establishment of the Church in the present dispensation, the Lord made reference to a Temple that was to be built.[ww] In July, 1831, the Lord designated a spot in Independence, Mo., as the site of a future Temple;[xx] but the work of construction thereon has not yet been consummated, as is likewise the case with the temple-site at Far West, on which the cornerstones were laid July 4, 1838, and relaid April 26, 1839.

The Church of Jesus Christ of Latter-day Saints has constructed Temples, each an imposing and costly structure, at Kirtland, Ohio; Nauvoo, Illinois; St. George, Logan, Manti, and Salt Lake City, Utah; Cardston, Canada; Laie, Hawaiian Islands, and Mesa, Arizona. The Temples at Kirtland and Nauvoo were abandoned as the members of the Church who had built them, through sacrifices yet untold, were driven westward by the force of persecution. The building at Kirtland is now used as an ordinary meeting-house by a small sect that evinces no activity in the sacred labors for which Temples are required. The Temple at Nauvoo was destroyed through malicious incendiarism. The magnitude and grandeur of the sacred labors accomplished in the Temples of the present dispensation, for the salvation of both the living and the dead, give assurance of the Lord's gracious acceptance.[yy]

REFERENCES

Baptism by Immersion

Jesus, when he was baptized, went up *straightway out of the water*—Matt. 3:16.

People from all parts of Judea and from Jerusalem went to John, and were baptized of him *in the river of Jordan*. Jesus who was baptized of John *in Jordan*. And straightway *coming up out of the water*—Mark 1:5, 9, 10.

And John was baptizing in Ænon near to Salim, *because there was much water there*—John 3:23.

[tt] See Ezra, chaps. 1, 3, 6.
[uu] See Matt. 27:50, 51.
[vv] See D&C 124:39; see The House of the Lord, chap. 1.
[ww] See D&C 36:8.
[xx] See D&C 57:3.
[yy] For a comprehensive treatment see the author's work, *The House of the Lord — A Study of Holy Sanctuaries, Ancient and Modern;* 336 pp. with illustrations.

Philip and the eunuch *went down both into the water;* and came up out of the water—Acts 8:38.

Arise, and be baptized, *and wash away* thy sins—Acts 22:16; also D&C 39:10. But ye are washed—1 Cor. 6:11.

Adam was carried down *into the water,* laid *under the water,* and brought forth *out of the water* at his baptism—Moses 6:64, 65.

Account of baptisms at the waters of Mormon; Alma and Helam and the rest *were buried in the water*—Mosiah 18:8–16.

Many were baptized in the waters of Sidon—Alma 4:4.

The risen Lord's instructions to the Nephites: Ye shall go down and *stand in the water* * * * And then shall ye *immerse them in the water*—3 Nephi 11:22–26. Similar instructions have been given in the current dispensation—D&C 20:72–74.

Nephi went *down into the water* and was baptized, and *came up out of the water*—3 Nephi 19:11–13.

Symbolism of birth and burial, unto which baptism is likened is best typified by immersion. Jesus declared: Except a man *be born again,* he cannot see the kingdom of God—John 3:3; also verse 5. *Buried* with him by baptism into death—Rom. 6:4; see also Col. 2:12. Such as receive the celestial glory must have been *buried in the water* in Christ's name—D&C 76:51. And they shall *be born* of me, even of water and of the Spirit—D&C 5:16.

Baptism for the Dead

Else what shall they do which are baptized for the dead, if the dead rise not at all? Why are they then baptized for the dead?—1 Cor. 15:29.

Elijah to be sent in the latter days to minister in turning the heart of the fathers to the children, and the heart of the children to their fathers—Mal. 4:5; also 3 Nephi 25:5, 6; P. of G.P. p. 53; D&C, sec. 2. The mission of Elijah involved vicarious service by the living for their dead—D&C, 27:9.

Elijah has come and delivered this commission—D&C 110:13–16.

Baptism for the dead is an ordinance of the House of the Lord; hence the necessity of Temples—D&C 124:28–31, 36, 39. This ordinance was instituted before the foundation of the world—verse 33.

Records to be kept of baptisms for the dead—D&C 127:6; 128:1–7.

Scriptures relating to baptism for the dead—D&C 128:15–18.

Christ preached to the dead between his death and resurrection: He went and preached to the spirits in prison—1 Peter 3:18–20; also 4:6; as had been foreappointed—see Isa. 24:22. As baptism is essential to the salvation of men, and is an ordinance pertaining to life in mortality, it must be administered vicariously for the dead.

8

THE HOLY GHOST

ARTICLE 4

E BELIEVE that the first principles and ordinances of the Gospel are: * * * fourth, Laying on of hands for the gift of the Holy Ghost.

The Holy Ghost Promised—John the Baptist, proclaiming in the wilderness repentance and baptism by water, foretold a second and higher baptism, which he characterized as being of fire and the Holy Ghost; this was to follow his administration,[a] and was to be given by that Mightier One the latchet of whose shoes the Baptist considered himself unworthy to unloose. That the holder of this superior authority was none other than the Christ is proved by John's solemn record: "Behold the Lamb of God * * * This is he of whom I said, After me cometh a man which is preferred before me * * * And I knew him not: but he that sent me to baptize with water, the same said unto me, Upon whom thou shalt see the Spirit descending, and remaining on him, the same is he which baptizeth with the Holy Ghost."[b]

In declaring to Nicodemus[c] the necessity of baptism, the Savior did not stop with a reference to the watery birth alone, that being incomplete without the quickening influence of the Spirit. "Born of water and of the Spirit" is the necessary condition of him who is to gain admittance to the kingdom of God. Many of the scriptural pas-

[a] See Matt. 3:2, 3, 11; Mark 1:8; Luke 3:16.
[b] John 1:29–33.
[c] See John 3:3–5.

sages quoted in demonstration of the purpose and necessity of baptism show baptism of the Holy Ghost to be closely associated with the prescribed ordinance of immersion in water.

Christ's instructions to the apostles comprise repeated promises concerning the coming of the Comforter, and the Spirit of Truth,[d] by which expressive terms the Holy Ghost is designated. In His last interview with the apostles, at the close of which He ascended into heaven, the Lord repeated these assurances of a spiritual baptism, which was then soon to take place.[e] The fulfilment of this great prediction was realized at the succeeding Pentecost, when the apostles, having assembled together, were endowed with great power from heaven,[f] they being filled with the Holy Ghost so that they spoke in tongues other than their own as the Spirit gave them utterance. Among other manifestations of this spiritual endowment may be mentioned the appearance of flames of fire like unto tongues, which rested upon each of them. The promise so miraculously fulfilled upon themselves was repeated by the apostles to those who sought their instruction. Peter, addressing the Jews on that same day, declared, on the condition of their acceptable repentance and baptism, "Ye shall receive the gift of the Holy Ghost."[g]

Book of Mormon evidence is not less conclusive regarding the Holy Spirit's visitation unto those who obey the requirements of water baptism. Nephi, Lehi's son, bore solemn record of this truth[h] as made known to him by the voice of God. And the words of the resurrected Savior to the Nephites come in plainness indisputable, and with authority not to be questioned, proclaiming the baptism of fire and the Holy Ghost unto all those who obey the preliminary requirements.[i]

Unto the saints in the dispensation of the fulness of times, the same great promise has been made. "I say unto you again," spake the Lord in addressing certain elders of the Church, "that every soul who believeth on your words, and is baptized by water for the remission of sins, shall receive the Holy Ghost."[j]

Personality and Powers of the Holy Ghost—The Holy Ghost is associated with the Father and the Son in the Godhead. In the light of revelation, we are instructed as to the distinct personality of the Holy Ghost. He is a being endowed with the attributes and powers of Deity, and not a mere force, or essence. The term Holy Ghost and its common synonyms, Spirit of God,[k] Spirit of the Lord, or simply, Spirit,[l] Comforter,[m] and Spirit of Truth,[n] occur in the scriptures with plainly different meanings, referring in some cases to the person of God the Holy Ghost, and in other instances to the power or authority of this great Personage, or to the agencies through which He ministers. The context of such passages show which of these significations applies.

The Holy Ghost undoubtedly possesses personal powers and affections; these attributes exist in Him in perfection. Thus, He teaches and guides,[o] testifies of the Father and the Son,[p] reproves for

---

[d] See John 14:16, 17, 26; 15:26; 16:7, 13.

[e] See Acts 1:5.

[f] See Acts 2:1–4.

[g] See Acts 2:38.

[h] See 2 Nephi 31:8, 12–14, 17.

[i] See 3 Nephi 11:35; 12:2.

[j] D&C 84:64.

[k] See Matt. 3:16; 12:28; 1 Nephi 13:12.

[l] See 1 Nephi 4:6; 11:8; Mosiah 13:5; Acts 2:4; 8:29; 10:19; Rom. 8:10, 26; 1 Thess. 5:19.

[m] See John 14:16, 26; 15:26.

[n] See John 15:26; 16:13.

[o] See John 14:26; 16:13; Appendix 8:1.

[p] See John 15:26.

sin,[q] speaks, commands, and commissions,[r] makes intercession for sinners,[s] is grieved,[t] searches and investigates,[u] entices,[v] and knows all things.[w] These are not figurative expressions, but plain statements of the attributes and characteristics of the Holy Ghost. That the Spirit of the Lord is capable of manifesting Himself in the form and figure of man, is indicated by the wonderful interview between the Spirit and Nephi, in which He revealed Himself to the prophet, questioned him concerning his desires and belief, instructed him in the things of God, speaking face to face with the man. "I spake unto him," says Nephi, "as a man speaketh; for I beheld that he was in the form of a man; yet nevertheless, I knew that it was the Spirit of the Lord; and he spake unto me as a man speaketh with another."[x] However, the Holy Ghost does not possess a body of flesh and bones, as do both the Father and the Son, but is a personage of spirit.[y]

Much of the confusion existing in human conceptions concerning the nature of the Holy Ghost arises from the common failure to segregate His person and powers. Plainly, such expressions as being filled with the Holy Ghost,[z] and His falling upon persons, having reference to the powers and influences that emanate from God, and which are characteristic of Him; for the Holy Ghost may in this way operate simultaneously upon many persons even though they be widely separated, whereas the actual person of the Holy Ghost cannot be in more than one place at a time. Yet we read that through the power of the Spirit, the Father and the Son operate in their creative acts and in their general dealings with the human family.[aa] The Holy Ghost may be regarded as the minister of the Godhead, carrying into effect the decision of the Supreme Council.

In the execution of these great purposes, the Holy Ghost directs and controls the varied forces of nature, of which indeed a few, and these perhaps of minor order wonderful as even the least of them appears to man, have thus far been investigated by mortals. Gravitation, sound, heat, light, and the still more mysterious and seemingly supernatural power of electricity, are but the common servants of the Holy Ghost in His operations. No earnest thinker, no sincere investigator supposes that he has yet learned of all the forces existing in and operating upon matter; indeed, the observed phenomena of nature, yet wholly inexplicable to him, far outnumber those for which he has devised even a partial explanation. There are powers and forces at the command of God, compared with which electricity is as the pack-horse to the locomotive, the foot messenger to the telegraph, the raft of logs to the ocean steamer. With all his scientific knowledge man knows but little respecting the enginery of creation; and yet the few forces known to him have brought about miracles and wonders, which but for their actual realization would be beyond belief. These mighty agencies, and the mightier ones still to man unknown, and many, perhaps, to the present condition of the human mind unknowable, do not constitute the Holy Ghost, but are the agencies ordained to serve His purposes.

---

[q] See John 16:8.
[r] See Acts 10:19; 13:2; Rev. 2:7; 1 Nephi 4:6; 11:2–12.
[s] See Rom. 8:26.
[t] See Eph. 4:30.
[u] See 1 Cor. 2:4–10.
[v] See Mosiah 3:19.
[w] See Alma 7:13.
[x] 1 Nephi 11:11.
[y] D&C 130:22.
[z] See Luke 1:15, 67; 4:1; Acts 6:3; 13:9; Alma 36:24; D&C 107:56.
[aa] See Gen. 1:2; Neh. 9:20; Job 26:13; Ps. 104:30; Isa. 42:1; Acts 10:19; 1 Nephi 10:19; Alma 12:3; D&C 97:1; 105:36; Appendix 8:3.

Subtler, mightier, and more mysterious than any or all of the physical forces of nature are the powers that operate upon conscious organisms, the means by which the mind, the heart, the soul of man may be energized by spiritual forces. In our ignorance of the true nature of electricity we may speak of it as a fluid; and so by analogy the forces through which the mind is governed have been called spiritual fluids. The true nature of these manifestations of energy is unknown to us, for the elements of comparison and analogy, so necessary to our human reasoning, are wanting; nevertheless the effects are experienced by all. As the conducting medium in an electric circuit is capable of conveying but a limited current, the maximum capacity depending upon the resistance offered by the conductor, and, as separate circuits of different degrees of conductivity may carry currents of widely varying intensity, so human souls are of varied capacity with respect to the higher powers. But as the medium is purified, as obstructions are removed, so resistance to the energy decreases, and the forces manifest themselves with greater intensity. By analogous processes of purification our spirits may be made more susceptible to the forces of life, which are emanations from the Holy Spirit. Therefore are we taught to pray by word and action for a constantly increasing portion of the Spirit, that is, the power of the Spirit, which is a measure of this gift of God unto us.

The Office of the Holy Ghost in His ministrations among men is described in scripture. He is a teacher sent from the Father;[bb] and unto those who are entitled to His tuition He will reveal all things necessary for the soul's advancement. Through the influences of the Holy Spirit the powers of the human mind may be quickened and increased, so that things past may be brought to remembrance. He will serve as a guide in things divine unto all who will obey Him,[cc] enlightening every man,[dd] in the measure of his humility and obedience;[ee] unfolding the mysteries of God,[ff] as the knowledge thus revealed may effect greater spiritual growth; conveying knowledge from God to man;[gg] sanctifying those who have been cleansed through obedience to the requirements of the Gospel;[hh] manifesting all things;[ii] and bearing witness unto men concerning the existence and infallibility of the Father and the Son.[jj]

Not alone does the Holy Ghost bring to mind the past and explain the things of the present, but His power is manifested in prophecy concerning the future. "He will shew you things to come," declared the Savior to the apostles in promising the advent of the Comforter. Adam, the first prophet of earth, under the influence of the Holy Ghost "predicted whatsoever should befall his posterity unto the latest generation."[kk] The power of the Holy Ghost then, is the spirit of prophecy and revelation; His office is that of enlightenment of the mind, quickening of the intellect, and sanctification of the soul.

To Whom is the Holy Spirit Given? Not to all indiscriminately. Jesus Christ declared to the apostles of old: "I will pray the Father, and he shall give you another Comforter, that he may abide with you forever; Even the Spirit of truth; whom the world cannot receive, because it seeth him

bb John 14:26.
cc D&C 45:57.
dd D&C 84:45–47.
ee See D&C 136:33.
ff See 1 Nephi 10:19.
gg See D&C 121:43.
hh See Alma 13:12.
ii See D&C 18:18.
jj See John 15:26; Acts 5:32; 20:23; 1 Cor. 2:11; 12:3; 3 Nephi 11:32.
kk See D&C 107:56.

not, neither knoweth him."[ll] Clearly, then, a certain condition of the candidate is requisite before the Holy Spirit can be bestowed, that is to say, before the person can receive title to the companionship and ministrations of the Holy Ghost. God grants the gift of the Holy Ghost unto the obedient, and the bestowal of this gift follows faith, repentance, and baptism by water.

The apostles of old promised the ministration of the Holy Ghost unto those only who had received baptism by water for the remission of sins;[mm] John the Baptist gave assurances of the visitation of the Holy Ghost to those only who were baptized unto repentance.[nn] The instance of Paul's rebaptizing the twelve converts at Ephesus before he conferred upon them the Holy Ghost, on account of a probable lack of propriety or authority in their first baptism,[oo] has already been dwelt upon. We read of a remarkable manifestation of power among the people of Samaria,[pp] to whom Philip went and preached the Lord Jesus; the people with one accord accepted his testimony and sought baptism. Then came unto them Peter and John, through whose ministrations the Holy Ghost came upon the new converts, whereas upon none of them had the Spirit previously fallen, though all had been baptized.

The Holy Spirit dwells not in tabernacles unfit and unworthy. Paul makes the sublime declaration that man may become the temple of God, with the Spirit of God dwelling within him; and the apostle specifies the penalty prescribed for defiling a structure sanctified by so holy a presence.[qq] Faith in God leads to repentance of sin; this is followed by baptism in water for the remission of sins, and this in turn by the bestowal of the Holy Spirit, or the right and title to the personal association and inspiring ministration of the Holy Ghost, through whose power come sanctification and the specific gifts of God.

An Exception to this Sequence is shown in the case of the devout Gentile, Cornelius, unto whom, together with his family, came the Holy Ghost, with such power that they spake with new tongues to the glorification of God, and this before their baptism.[rr] But sufficient reason for this departure from the usual order is seen in the prejudice that existed among the Jews toward other nations, which, but for the Lord's direct instructions to Peter, would have hindered the apostle from ministering unto the Gentiles. As it was, his act was condemned by his own people; but he answered their criticisms with a recital of the lesson given him of God, and the undeniable evidence of the divine will as shown in the reception of the Holy Ghost by Cornelius and his family before baptism.

In another sense the Holy Ghost has frequently operated for good through persons that were unbaptized; indeed, some measure of His power is given to all mankind; for, as seen already, the Holy Spirit is the medium of intelligence, of wise direction, of development, of life. Manifestation of the power of God, as made plain through the operations of the Spirit, are seen in the triumphs of ennobling art, the discoveries of science, and the events of history; with all of which the carnal mind may believe that God takes no direct concern. Not a truth has ever been made the property of humankind except through the power of that great Spirit who exists to do the bidding of the Father and the Son. And yet the actual companionship of the Holy Ghost, the divinely-bestowed right to His ministrations, the sanctifying baptism with fire, are given as a permanent

[ll] John 14:16, 17.
[mm] See Acts 2:38.
[nn] See Matt.3:11; Mark 1:8.
[oo] See Acts 19:1-7; see pages 129, 130.
[pp] See Acts 8:5–8, 12, 14–17.
[qq] See 1 Cor. 3:16; see also 6:19; 2 Cor. 6:16; D&C 93:35.
[rr] See Acts, chap. 10.

and personal possession only to the faithful, repentant, baptized candidate for salvation; and with all such this gift shall abide unless it be forfeited through transgression.

The Bestowal of the Holy Ghost, which is to be regarded as a conferred right to His ministrations, is effected through the ordinance of an oral blessing pronounced upon the candidate by the specified authority of the Holy Priesthood, accompanied by the imposition of the hands of him or those officiating. That this was the mode followed by the apostles of old is evident from the Jewish scriptures; that it was practised by the early Christian Fathers is shown by history; that it was the acknowledged method among the Nephites is plainly attested by Book of Mormon record; and for the same practise in the present dispensation authority has come direct from heaven.

Among the instances recorded in the New Testament we may mention the following. Peter and John conferred the Holy Ghost upon Philip's converts at Samaria, and the ordinance was performed by prayer and the laying on of hands.[ss] Paul ministered in the same manner to the Ephesians whom he had caused to be baptized; and when he "had laid his hands upon them, the Holy Ghost came on them; and they spake with tongues, and prophesied."[tt] Paul also refers to this ordinance in his admonition to Timothy not to neglect the gift of God so bestowed.[uu] Furthermore we learn from the epistle to the Hebrews that the cardinal principles and ordinances of the Church of Christ include the laying on of hands as following baptism.[vv]

Alma so invoked the power of the Holy Ghost in behalf of his colaborers:[ww] "He clapped his hands upon all them who were with him. And behold, as he clapped his hands upon them, they were filled with the Holy Spirit." The Savior gave authority to the twelve Nephite disciples,[xx] by touching them one by one; they were thus commissioned to bestow the Holy Ghost.

In the current dispensation it has been made a duty of the Priesthood "to confirm those who are baptized into the church, by the laying on of hands for the baptism of fire and the Holy Ghost."[yy] The Lord has promised that the Holy Ghost shall follow these authoritative acts of His servants.[zz] The ordinance of laying on of hands for the bestowal of the Holy Ghost is associated with that of confirmation into the Church. The officiating elder, acting in the name and by the authority of Jesus Christ, says: *"Receive the Holy Ghost;"* and *"I confirm you a member of the Church of Jesus Christ of Latter-day Saints."* Even these words are not prescribed, but their meaning should be expressed; and to such may be added other words of blessing and invocation as the Spirit of the Lord may dictate to the officiating elder.

The authority to so bestow the Holy Ghost belongs to the higher or Melchizedek Priesthood,[aaa] whereas water baptism may be administered by a priest officiating in the ordinances of the lesser or Aaronic Priesthood.[bbb] This order of authority, as made known through revelation, explains that while Philip had authority to administer the ordinance of baptism to the converted Samaritans, others who held the higher Priesthood had to be sent to confer upon them the Holy Ghost.[ccc]

[ss] See Acts 8:14–17; read the account of Simon, the sorcerer, in the same chapter.
[tt] See Acts 19:2–6.
[uu] See 2 Tim. 1:6.
[vv] See Heb. 6:1, 2; see Appendix 8:2.
[ww] See Alma 31:36.
[xx] See 3 Nephi 18:36, 37.
[yy] D&C 20:41, 43; see Appendix 8:4.
[zz] See D&C 35:6; 39:6, 23; 49:11–14.
[aaa] See D&C 20:38–43.
[bbb] See D&C 20:46, 50.
[ccc] See Acts 8:5–17.

Gifts of the Spirit—As already pointed out, the special office of the Holy Ghost is to enlighten and ennoble the mind, to purify and sanctify the soul, to incite to good works, and to reveal the things of God. But, beside these general blessings, there are certain specific endowments promised in connection with the gifts of the Holy Ghost. The Savior said: "These signs shall follow them that believe; In my name shall they cast out devils; they shall speak with new tongues; They shall take up serpents; and if they drink any deadly thing, it shall not hurt them; they shall lay hands on the sick, and they shall recover."[ddd]

These gifts of the Spirit are distributed in the wisdom of God for the salvation of His children. Paul thus discourses upon them: "Now concerning spiritual gifts, brethren, I would not have you ignorant. * * * Now there are diversities of gifts, but the same Spirit. * * * But the manifestation of the Spirit is given to every man to profit withal. For to one is given by the Spirit the word of wisdom; to another the word of knowledge by the same Spirit; To another faith by the same Spirit; to another the gifts of healing by the same Spirit; To another the working of miracles; to another prophecy; to another discerning of spirits; to another divers kind of tongues; to another the interpretation of tongues: But all these worketh that one and the selfsame Spirit, dividing to every man severally as he will."[eee]

REFERENCES

The Holy Ghost One of the Personages in the Godhead
Baptism in the name of the Father and of the Son and of the Holy Ghost—Matt. 28:19; 3 Nephi 11:25; D&C 20:73; 68:8.
Three that bear record in heaven, the Father, the Word, and the Holy Ghost—1 John 5:7.
Blasphemy against the Holy Ghost not to be forgiven—Matt. 12:31, 32; also D&C 132:27.
Voice of the Son declaring that the Father will give the Holy Ghost—2 Nephi 31:12; see also verse 13.
Father, Son, and Holy Ghost, one God—D&C 20:28.
The Holy Ghost a personage of Spirit—D&C 130:22.

Holy Ghost Promised and Given to the Apostles
It is not ye that speak, but the Holy Ghost—Mark 13:11; see also Matt. 10:19, 20; Luke 21:14, 15.
For the Holy Ghost shall teach you in the same hour what ye ought to say—Luke 12:11, 12.
The resurrected Lord to the eleven apostles: Receive ye the Holy Ghost—John 20:22.
Concerning the Lord's promise of the Comforter then to come—John 14:16, 17, 26; 15:26; 16:7–14; Acts 1:5, 8.
Peter and others filled with the Holy Ghost spake the word of God with boldness—Acts 4:31.
Apostles endowed by the Holy Ghost at the Pentecost—Acts 2:1–4.
Preached with boldness being filled with the Holy Ghost—Acts 4:31; see also 5:12, 32; 7:51.

Ministry of the Holy Ghost Following Water Baptism
Descended in bodily shape upon Jesus Christ after baptism—Luke 3:22; see also Matt. 3:16; Mark 1:9–11; compare John 1:32, 33; 1 Nephi 11:27.
I indeed have baptized you with water, but he shall baptize you with the Holy Ghost—Mark 1:8; see also Acts 1:5; 11:16; 19:5, 6.

[ddd] Mark 16:17, 18; D&C 84:65–73.
[eee] 1 Cor. 12:1–11; see also Moroni 10:8–19.

After repentance and baptism: Ye shall receive the gift of the Holy Ghost—Acts 2:38.

About twelve were baptized at Ephesus, and when Paul laid his hands upon them the Holy Ghost came on them—Acts 19:1–7.

The Father to give the Holy Ghost to those who are baptized—2 Nephi 31:12; see also 31:13; 3 Nephi 11:33–36.

Whoso repents and is baptized according to the holy commandment shall receive the gift of the Holy Ghost—D&C 49:12–14; see also 33:15.

Remission of sins by baptism and by fire, yea, even the Holy Ghost—D&C 19:31.

Noah promised the Holy Ghost after faith, repentance and baptism—Moses 8:24.

Holy Ghost Invoked by Authorized Laying on of Hands

Peter and John laid their hands upon Samaritan converts and they received the Holy Ghost—Acts 8:14–17. Note that while Philip had authority to preach and baptize, men holding the higher authority were sent to confer the Holy Ghost upon the converts in Samaria. Here appears the distinction between the authority of the lesser or Aaronic and the higher or Melchizedek Priesthood.

Of the doctrine of baptisms, and of laying on of hands—Heb. 6:2.

The resurrected Christ by physical touch commissioned the Nephite disciples to confer the Holy Ghost—3 Nephi 18:36, 37. To him upon whom ye shall lay your hands ye shall give the Holy Ghost—Moroni, chap. 2.

He shall lay his hands upon thee, and thou shalt receive the Holy Ghost—D&C 25:8.

Gift of the Holy Ghost given to the baptized, by the laying on of the hands of the elders—D&C 49:14.

Promise of gift of the Holy Ghost to follow confirmation by laying on of hands—D&C 33:15.

Some of the Attributes and Operations of the Holy Ghost

The Holy Ghost shall teach you—Luke 12:12.

The Comforter, which is the Holy Ghost, shall teach you—John 14:26; see also John 16:7–15.

Christ through the Holy Ghost gave commandments unto the apostles—Acts 1:2.

Ye shall receive power, after that the Holy Ghost has come upon you—Acts 1:8.

The Holy Ghost a witness of the Christ—Acts 5:32; Heb. 10:15; 1 Nephi 12:18; 3 Nephi 28:11.

Directs the work of the ministry—Acts 13:2–4; 16:6.

Disciples were filled with joy and with the Holy Ghost—Acts 13:52.

Thus saith the Holy Ghost—Acts 21:11.

The Holy Ghost spake through Esaias the prophet—Acts 28:25.

Being sanctified by the Holy Ghost—Rom. 15:16.

Things which the Holy Ghost teacheth—1 Cor. 2:13.

No man can say that Jesus is the Lord but by the Holy Ghost—1 Cor. 12:3.

Knowledge, longsuffering, kindness, by the Holy Ghost—2 Cor. 6:6.

God bearing witness with gifts of the Holy Ghost—Heb. 2:4.

Holy men of old spake as they were moved by the Holy Ghost—2 Peter 1:21. Elders today to speak as moved upon by the Holy Ghost—D&C 68:3.

To minister unto the Gentiles—3 Nephi 20:27.

Is the spirit of revelation—D&C 8:2, 3.

Teacheth the peaceable things of the kingdom—D&C 39:6.

Prophets spake as they were inspired by the Holy Ghost—D&C 20:26.

Beareth record of the Father and the Son—D&C 20:27; Moses 1:24; 5:9.

Officers to be ordained by power of the Holy Ghost—D&C 20:60.

Inspires ordained men to speak scripture—D&C 68:4.

Knowledge given by the unspeakable gift of the Holy Ghost—D&C 121:26; see also 124:5.

Bore witness to Adam—Moses 5:9.

The Lord called upon men by the Holy Ghost in days of Adam—Moses 5:14.

Holy Ghost manifested His power upon Joseph Smith and Oliver Cowdery following their baptism—
    P.of G.P. p. 58.

Simon Dewey

9

THE SACRAMENT OF THE LORD'S SUPPER

I N CONNECTION WITH ARTICLE 4

The Sacrament—In the course of our study of the principles and ordinances of the Gospel, as specified in the fourth of the Articles of Faith, the subject of the Sacrament of the Lord's Supper[a] very properly claims attention, the observance of this ordinance being required of all who have become members of the Church of Christ through compliance with the requirements of faith, repentance, and baptism by water and of the Holy Ghost.

Institution of the Sacrament Among the Jews—The Sacrament of the Lord's Supper dates from the night of the Passover feast[b] immediately preceding the crucifixion of the Savior. On that solemn occasion Christ and the apostles were assembled in Jerusalem, keeping the feast in an upper room, which had been made ready by His express command.[c] As a Jew Christ appears to have been loyal to the established usages of His people; and it must have been with extraordinary feelings that He entered upon this commemorative feast, the last of its kind bearing the significance of the type of a future sacrifice as well as a reminder of the Lord's blessings to Israel in the past. Knowing well the terrible experiences immediately awaiting Him, Jesus communed with the Twelve in anguish of soul at the paschal board, prophesying concerning His betrayal, which was soon to be accomplished by the agency of one who there ate with Him. Then He took bread,

[a] See Appendix 9:1, 2.
[b] See Appendix 9:3.
[c] See Luke 22:8–13.

blessed it and gave it to the others, saying: "Take, eat; this is my body";[d] "This do in remembrance of me."[e] Afterward, taking the cup, He blessed its contents and administered it to them with the words: "Drink ye all of it; For this is my blood of the new testament, which is shed for many for the remission of sins."[f] It is enlightening to note that the account of the sacrament and its purport as given by Paul[g] resembles so closely as to be almost identical with the descriptions recorded by the evangelists. The designation of the sacrament as the Lord's Supper is used by no Biblical writer other than Paul.

Institution of the Sacrament Among the Nephites—On the occasion of His visit to the Nephites, which occurred shortly after the ascension from Mount Olives, Christ established the sacrament amongst this division of His flock. He directed the disciples whom He had chosen to bring bread and wine; then taking the bread, He brake it, blessed it, and gave it to them with the command that they should eat and afterward distribute to the multitude. Authority to administer this ordinance He promised to bestow. "And this shall ye always observe to do," He said, "even as I have done. * * * And this shall ye do in remembrance of my body, which I have shown unto you. And it shall be a testimony unto the Father that ye do always remember me. And if ye do always remember me ye shall have my Spirit to be with you."[h] The wine was administered in the same order, first to the disciples then by them to the people. This also was to be part of the standing ordinance among the people: "And ye shall do it in remembrance of my blood, which I have shed for you, that ye may witness unto the Father that ye do always remember me." Then followed a reiteration of the significant promise: "And if ye do always remember me, ye shall have my Spirit to be with you."[i]

Fit Partakers of the Sacrament—The divine instructions concerning the sacredness of this ordinance are explicit; and the consequent need of scrupulous care being exercised lest it be engaged in unworthily is apparent. In addressing the Corinthian saints Paul gave solemn warnings against hasty or unworthy action in partaking of the sacrament, and declares that the penalties of sickness and even death are visited upon those who violate the sacred requirements: "For as often as ye eat this bread, and drink this cup, ye do shew the Lord's death till he come. Wherefore whosoever shall eat this bread, and drink this cup of the Lord, unworthily, shall be guilty of the body and blood of the Lord. But let a man examine himself, and so let him eat of that bread, and drink of that cup. For he that eateth and drinketh unworthily, eateth and drinketh damnation to himself, not discerning the Lord's body. For this cause many are weak and sickly among you, and many sleep."[j]

When instructing the Nephites, Jesus laid great stress upon the fitness of those who partook of the sacrament; and moreover He placed responsibility upon the officers of the Church whose duty it was to administer it, that they should permit none whom they knew to be unworthy to participate in the ordinance: "And now behold, this is the commandment which I give unto you, that ye shall not suffer any one knowingly to partake of my flesh and blood unworthily, when ye shall minister it; For whoso eateth and drinketh my flesh and blood unworthily eateth and drinketh damnation to his soul; therefore if ye know that a man is unworthy to eat and drink of my flesh and blood ye shall forbid him."[k]

[d] Matt. 26:26.
[e] Luke 22:19; see also Mark 14:22–25.
[f] Matt. 26:27, 28; see *The Great Apostasy,* pp. 119, 120.
[g] See 1 Cor. 11:20–25.
[h] 3 Nephi 18:6, 7.
[i] 3 Nephi 18:11; see *Jesus the Christ,* chap. 39.
[j] 1 Cor. 11:26–30.
[k] 3 Nephi 18:28, 29.

The direct word of the Lord unto the saints in this dispensation instructs them to permit no one in transgression to partake of the sacrament until reconciliation has been made; nevertheless the saints are commanded to exercise abundant charity toward their erring fellows, not casting them out from the assemblies yet withholding the sacrament from them.[l] In our system of Church organization the local ecclesiastical officers are charged with the responsibility of administering the sacrament, and the people are required to keep themselves worthy to partake of the sacred emblems.

There is an absence of scriptural sanction for giving the sacrament to any who are not members in full fellowship in the Church of Jesus Christ. Christ administered the ordinance on the eastern continent to the apostles; and we have record of their giving it to those only who had assumed the name of Christ. Amongst His western fold, Christ established the law that only the actual members of His Church should partake. In promising to ordain one among them with power to officiate in the sacrament, the Savior specified that the one so chosen should give it unto the people of His Church, unto all those who believed and were baptized in His name.[m] Only those who had been so baptized were called the Church of Christ.[n] Continuing His instructions to the disciples concerning the sacrament, the Savior said: "This shall ye always do to those who repent and are baptized in my name."[o]

The same law is in force today. The members of the Church[p] are admonished to meet together often for the observance of the sacrament; and the Church comprises none of mature years who have not been baptized by the authority of the Holy Priesthood.[q]

Purpose of the Sacrament—From the scriptural citations already made, it is plain that the sacrament is administered to commemorate the atonement of the Lord Jesus, as consummated in His agony and death; it is a testimony before God that we are mindful of His Son's sacrifice made in our behalf; and that we still profess the name of Christ and are determined to strive to keep His commandments, in the hope that we may ever have His Spirit to be with us. Partaking of the sacrament worthily may be regarded therefore as a means of renewing our avowals before the Lord, of acknowledgment of mutual fellowship among the members, and of solemnly witnessing our claim and profession of membership in the Church of Jesus Christ. The sacrament has not been established as a specific means of securing remission of sins; nor for any other special blessing aside from that of a continuing endowment of the Holy Spirit, which, however, comprises all needful blessings. Were the sacrament ordained specifically for the remission of sins, it would not be forbidden to those who are in greatest need of forgiveness; yet participation in the ordinance is restricted to those whose consciences are void of serious offense, those, therefore, who are acceptable before the Lord, those indeed who are in as little need of special forgiveness as mortals can be.

The Sacramental Emblems—In instituting the sacrament among both the Jews and the Nephites, Christ used bread and wine as the emblems of His body and blood;[r] and in this, the dispensation of the fulness of times, He has revealed His will that the saints meet together often to partake of bread and wine in this commemorative ordinance.[s] But He has also shown that other forms of food and drink may be used in place of bread and wine. Soon after the Church had been organized in the present

[l] See D&C 46:4; see also 3 Nephi 18:30.
[m] See 3 Nephi 18:5.
[n] See 3 Nephi 26:21.
[o] 3 Nephi 18:11.
[p] See D&C 20:75.
[q] See D&C 20:37.
[r] See Matt. 26:27–29; 3 Nephi 18:1, 8.
[s] See D&C 20:75.

dispensation, the Prophet Joseph Smith was about to purchase wine for sacramental purposes, when a messenger from God met him and delivered the following instructions: "For, behold, I say unto you, that it mattereth not what ye shall eat or what ye shall drink when ye partake of the sacrament, if it so be that ye do it with an eye single to my glory—remembering unto the Father my body which was laid down for you, and my blood which was shed for the remission of your sins. Wherefore, a commandment I give unto you, that you shall not purchase wine neither strong drink of your enemies; Wherefore, you shall partake of none except it is made new among you; yea, in this my Father's kingdom which shall be built up on the earth."[t] Upon this authority, the Latter-day Saints administer water in their sacramental service, in preference to wine.

Manner of Administering the Sacrament—It is customary with the Latter-day Saints, in all wards or regularly organized branches of the Church, to hold sacramental meetings every Sabbath. The authority of the priest of the Aaronic order is requisite in consecrating the emblems; and, as a matter of course, any one who has been ordained to the higher order of Priesthood has authority to so officiate. The bread is first to be broken into small pieces, and placed in suitable receptacles on the sacramental table; and then, according to the Lord's direction, the elder or priest shall consecrate it, after this manner: "He shall kneel with the Church and call upon the Father in solemn prayer, saying:

"O God, the Eternal Father, we ask thee in the name of thy Son, Jesus Christ, to bless and sanctify this bread to the souls of all those who partake of it, that they may eat in remembrance of the body of thy Son, and witness unto thee, O God, the Eternal Father, that they are willing to take upon them the name of thy Son, and always remember him and keep his commandments which he has given them; that they may always have his Spirit to be with them. Amen."[u]

After the bread has been distributed to the congregation, in which service the teachers and deacons may take part under the direction of the officiating priest, the wine or water is consecrated in this manner:

"O God, the Eternal Father, we ask thee in the name of thy Son, Jesus Christ, to bless and sanctify this wine [or water] to the souls of all those who drink of it, that they may do it in remembrance of the blood of thy Son, which was shed for them; that they may witness unto thee, O God, the Eternal Father, that they do always remember him, that they may have his Spirit to be with them. Amen."[v]

The plainness of the Lord's instructions to the saints regarding this ordinance leaves no excuse for disputation concerning the proper procedure, for assuredly no one who officiates in these holy rites can feel that he is justified in changing the forms even by the alteration of a word. The records of the Nephites show that the manner of administering the sacrament in their day,[w] was the same as that revealed for the guidance of the saints in the dispensation of the fulness of times.

[t] D&C 27:2–4.
[u] D&C 20:76, 77; compare Moroni, chap. 4.
[v] D&C 20:78, 79; compare Moroni, chap. 5.
[w] See Moroni, chaps. 4, 5. For brief account of errors concerning the sacrament, see Appendix 9:4; for fuller treatment see *The Great Apostasy*, p. 119.

REFERENCES

Sacrament of the Lord's Supper

Instituted among the Jews by the Lord on the night of his betrayal—Matt. 26:26–28; Mark 14:22–25; Luke 22:19, 20.

Instituted among the Nephites by the resurrected Lord—3 Nephi 18:1–11. Administered among the Nephites a second time by the Savior—3 Nephi 20:3–5; and often thereafter—26:13.

Prefigurement of the sacrament—John 6:52–56.

Designated by Paul as the Lord's Supper—1 Cor. 11:20.

Jewish converts continued in the apostles' doctrine, and in the breaking of bread—Acts 2:42; see verse 46.

Upon the first day of the week, when the disciples came together to break bread, Paul preached to them—Acts 20:7.

Christ's institution of the sacrament revealed to Paul—1 Cor. 11:23–25.

Sin of partaking unworthily and its penalty—1 Cor. 11:26-34.

See that ye partake not of the sacrament of Christ unworthily—Mormon 9:29.

The communion of the blood and body of Christ—1 Cor. 10:16; the cup of the Lord and the Lord's table—verse 21.

He that thus eateth and drinketh doth eat and drink my body and blood to his soul—3 Nephi 20:8.

One to be ordained to administer the sacrament—3 Nephi 18:5.

Only members of the church to partake—3 Nephi 18:11.

Ye shall not suffer anyone knowingly to partake of my flesh and blood unworthily—3 Nephi 18:28, 29.

The church met together often to partake—Moroni 6:6.

Prescribed ritual for administering the emblems among the Nephites—Moroni, chaps. 4 and 5; among the saints in the current dispensation—D&C 20:75–79.

Emblems of the body and blood of Christ—D&C 20:40.

Priests may administer the sacrament—D&C 20:46; teachers and deacons have not authority to administer—verse 58.

Newly baptized members, duly instructed, are to partake—D&C 20:68.

Wine may be used—D&C 89:5, 6; but is not essential—27:1–5.

10

AUTHORITY IN THE MINISTRY

ARTICLE 5

W E BELIEVE that a man must be called of God, by prophecy, and by the laying on of hands, by those who are in authority, to preach the Gospel and administer in the ordinances thereof.

MEN CALLED OF GOD

Scriptural Examples—It is not less agreeable to the dictates of human reason than conformable to the plan of perfect organization that characterizes the Church of Jesus Christ, that all who minister in the ordinances of the Gospel should be called and commissioned for their sacred duties by divine authority. The scriptures sustain this view most thoroughly; they present to us an array of men whose divine callings are attested, and whose mighty works declare a power greater than that of unaided human capacity. On the other hand, not an instance is set down in Holy Writ of anyone taking to himself the authority to officiate in sacred ordinances and being acknowledged of the Lord in such administration.

Consider the case of Noah who "found grace in the eyes of the Lord"[a] in the midst of a wicked world. Unto him the Lord spake, announcing His displeasure with the wicked inhabitants of earth and the divine intention concerning the deluge, and instructed him in the manner of building and stocking the ark. That Noah declared the word of God unto his perverse contemporaries is

[a] Gen. 6:8.

shown in Peter's declaration of Christ's mission in the spirit world—that the Savior preached to those who had been disobedient during the period of God's longsuffering in the days of Noah, and who in consequence had endured the privations of the prison house in the interval.[b] None can question the divine source of Noah's authority, nor the justice of the retributive punishment following the wilful rejection of his teachings, for his words were the words of God.

So also with Abraham, whom the Lord called[c] and made covenant with for all generations of his posterity. Isaac[d] was similarly distinguished; likewise Jacob,[e] to whom, as he rested upon his pillow of stones in the desert, the Lord was manifest. Unto Moses[f] came the voice of God amidst the fierceness of fire, calling and commissioning the man to go into Egypt and deliver therefrom the people whose cries had come up with such effect before the Lord. In this work Aaron[g] was called to assist his brother; and later, Aaron and his sons[h] were chosen by divine direction from the midst of the children of Israel to minister in the priest's office. When Moses[i] saw that his days were numbered he solicited the Lord to appoint a successor in his holy station; and by command, Joshua, the son of Nun, was named for specific service.

Samuel, who became a great prophet in Israel, commissioned to consecrate, command, and rebuke kings, to direct armies and to serve as the oracle of God unto the people, was chosen while yet a boy and called by the voice of the Lord.[j] Such was the power that followed this call that all Israel from Dan to Beersheba knew that Samuel was established as the prophet of the Lord.[k] The scriptures tell of many other men of might, who received their power from God, and whose histories portray the honor with which the Lord regards His authorized ministers. Think of the heavenly vision by which Isaiah was called and directed in the duties of his prophetic office;[l] of Jeremiah, to whom the word of the Lord came in the days of Josiah;[m] of the priest Ezekiel, who first received the divine message in the land of the Chaldeans[n] and subsequently on other occasions; of Hosea,[o] and all the rest of the prophets to Zechariah[p] and Malachi.[q]

The apostles of the Lord were called by His own voice in the days of His ministry; and the Savior's authority is beyond question, vindicated as it is by the mighty works of the atonement, wrought through pain and the anguish of death, and by the declarations of the Father. Peter, and Andrew his brother, while casting their nets into the sea were called with the instruction: "Follow me, and I will make you fishers of men";[r] and soon afterward, James and John, sons of Zebedee, were similarly called. So with all of the Twelve who ministered with the Master; and unto the eleven apostles who had remained faithful He appeared after His resurrection, giving

[b] See 1 Peter 3:19, 20.
[c] See Gen., chaps. 12–25; P.of G.P., Abraham 2:6–11.
[d] See Gen. 26:2–5.
[e] See Gen. 28:10–15.
[f] See Ex. 3:2–10.
[g] See Ex. 4:14–16, 27.
[h] See Ex. 28:1.
[i] See Num. 27:15–23.
[j] See 1 Sam. 3:4–14.
[k] See 1 Sam. 3:20.
[l] See Isa. 1:1; 2:1; 6:8, 9.
[m] See Jer. 1:2–10.
[n] See Ezek. 1:3.
[o] See Hos. 1:1.
[p] See Zech. 1:1.
[q] See Mal. 1:1.
[r] Matt. 4:18–20.

them special commissions for the work of the kingdom.[s] Christ specifically affirms that He had chosen His apostles, and that He had ordained them in their exalted stations.[t]

In the period immediately following that of Christ's earthly mission, the ministers of the Gospel were all designated and set apart by unquestionable authority. Matthias was chosen, by lot but under invocation of the Lord's direction, to fill the vacancy in the body of the Twelve occasioned by the death of Judas Iscariot. Saul of Tarsus, afterward Paul the apostle, who had been converted with marvelous signs and wondrous manifestations,[u] had to be formally commissioned for the labor that the Lord desired him to perform; and we are told that the Holy Ghost spake to the prophets and teachers of the Church at Antioch, while they fasted before the Lord, saying: "Separate me Barnabas and Saul for the work whereunto I have called them."[v]

Ordination of Men to the Ministry, as sanctioned by scriptural precedent and established by direct revelation of God's will, is to be effected through the gift of prophecy and by the imposition of hands by those who are in authority. By prophecy is meant the right to receive and the power to interpret manifestations of the divine will. That the laying on of hands is usual as a part of the ordinance is seen in several of the instances already cited; nevertheless the scriptures record numerous ordinations to the offices of the Priesthood without specific statement concerning the imposition of hands or any other details. Such instances do not warrant the conclusion that the laying on of hands was omitted; and in the light of modern revelation it is clear that the imposition of hands was a usual accompaniment of ordination as also of confirming blessings[w] and of bestowing the Holy Ghost.

Thus, the Holy Priesthood descended from Adam to Noah under the hands of the fathers.[x] Enos was ordained by the hand of Adam; and the same was true of Mahalaleel, Jared, Enoch, and Methuselah. Lamech was ordained under the hand of Seth; Noah received his authority under the hand of Methuselah. And so may the Holy Priesthood by traced, bestowed as the spirit of prophecy directed, by the hand of one upon another, till the time of Moses. Melchizedek, who conferred this authority upon Abraham, received his own through the direct lineage of his fathers from Noah. Esaias, a contemporary of Abraham, received his ordination under the hand of God. Through the hand of Esaias, the authority passed to Gad, thence by the same means to Jeremy, Elihu, Caleb, and Jethro the priest of Midian under whose hand Moses was ordained.[y] Joshua the son of Nun was set apart as directed of God, through the imposition of hands by Moses.[z]

In the days of the apostles circumstances rendered it expedient to appoint special officers in the Church, to care for the poor and attend to the distribution of supplies; these were selected with care and were set apart through prayer and laying on of hands.[aa] Timothy was similarly ordained, as witness the admonitions given him by Paul: "Neglect not the gift that is in thee, which was given thee by prophecy, with the laying on of the hands of the presbytery,"[bb] and again, "Stir up the gift

---

[s] See Matt. 18:19, 20; Mark 16:15.

[t] See John 6:70; 15:16.

[u] Acts, ch. 9.

[v] See Acts 13:1, 2.

[w] See Gen. 48:14–19; compare 2 Kings 5:11; Matt. 8:15; Mark 6:5; 16:15–18.

[x] See D&C 107:40–52.

[y] See D&C 84:6–14.

[z] See Num. 27:18; Deut. 34:9.

[aa] See Acts 6:1–6.

[bb] 1 Timothy 4:14.

of God, which is in thee by the putting on of my hands."cc The Lord has bound Himself by covenant to acknowledge the acts of His authorized servants. Unto whomsoever the elders of the Church give promise after acceptable baptism, the Holy Ghost will come.dd Whatever the Priesthood shall bind or loose on earth, in accordance with the Lord's commands, is to be bound or loosed in heaven;ee the sick upon whom the elders lay their hands are to recover;ff and many other signs are to follow them that believe. So jealous is the Lord of the power to officiate in His name, that at the judgment all who have aided or persecuted His servants are to be rewarded or punished as if they had done those things unto Himself.gg

Unauthorized Ministrations in priestly functions are not alone invalid, but also grievously sinful. In His dealings with mankind God recognizes and honors the Priesthood established by His direction, and countenances no unauthorized assumption of authority. A lesson is taught by the case of Korah and his associates, in their rebellion against the authority of the Priesthood in that they falsely professed the right to minister in the priest's office. The Lord promptly visited them for their sins, causing the ground to cleave asunder and to swallow them up with all their belongings.hh

Consider also the affliction that fell upon Miriam, the sister of Moses, a prophetess among the people.ii She, with Aaron, railed against Moses, and they said: "Hath the Lord indeed spoken only by Moses? Hath he not spoken also by us? And the Lord heard it."jj Jehovah came down in a cloud and stood in the door of the tabernacle, denouncing their presumption and vindicating the authority of His oracle, Moses. When the cloud passed from the tabernacle Miriam was seen to be leprous, white as snow; and according to the law she was shut out from the camp of Israel. However, through the earnest entreaties of Moses, the Lord healed the woman and she was subsequently permitted to return to the company.

Consider the fate of Uzza, the Israelite who met sudden death through the anger of God because he put forth his hand to steady the ark of the covenant.kk This he did in spite of the law that none but the priests might touch the sacred accompaniments of the ark; we read that not even the appointed bearers of the vessel were allowed to touch its more sacred parts, on pain of death.ll

Think also of Saul who had been called from the field to be made king of the nation. When the Philistines were marshalled against Israel in Michmash, Saul waited for Samuel,mm under whose hand he had received his kingly anointingnn and to whom he had looked in the days of his humility for guidance; he asked that the prophet come and offer sacrifices to the Lord in behalf of the people. But, growing impatient at Samuel's delay, Saul prepared the burnt offering himself, forgetting that though he occupied the throne, wore the crown, and bore the scepter, these insignia of kingly power gave him no right to officiate even as a deacon in the Priesthood of God; and for this and other instances of his unrighteous presumption he was rejected of God and another was made king in his place.

cc 2 Tim. 1:6.
dd See Acts 2:38; 3 Nephi 11:35; 12:2; D&C 84:64.
ee See Matt. 16:19; D&C 1:8; 128:8–11.
ff See Mark 16:15–18.
gg See Matt. 18:4–6; 25:31-46; D&C 75:19–22; 84:88, 90.
hh See Num., chap. 16.
ii See Ex. 15:20.
jj Num., chap. 12.
kk See 1 Chr. 13:10.
ll See Num. 4:15.
mm See 1 Sam. 13:5–14.
nn See 1 Sam., chap. 10.

A striking instance of divine jealousy, which is righteous zeal, concerning priestly functions, is shown in the experience of Uzziah, king of Judah. He was placed upon the throne when but sixteen years old; and, as long as he sought the Lord he was greatly prospered, so that his name became a terror unto his enemies. But he allowed pride to grow in his heart, and indulged the delusion that in his kingship he was supreme. He entered the Temple and essayed to burn incense on the altar. Shocked at his blasphemous action, Azariah, the chief priest of the Temple, and fourscore priests with him, forbade the king, saying: "It appertaineth not unto thee, Uzziah, to burn incense unto the Lord, but to the priests the sons of Aaron, that are consecrated to burn incense: go out of the sanctuary; for thou hast trespassed." At this rebuke and condemnation from his subjects, though they were priests of the Lord, the king became angry; but immediately the scourge of leprosy fell upon him; the signs of the dread disease appeared in his forehead; and being now physically an unclean creature his presence tended the more to defile the holy place. So Azariah and his associate priests thrust the king out from the Temple; and he, a smitten thing, fled from the house of God never again to enter its sacred precincts. Concerning the rest of his punishment we read: "And Uzziah the king was a leper unto the day of his death, and dwelt in a several house, being a leper; for he was cut off from the house of the Lord."[oo]

A forceful illustration of the futility of false ceremonies, or of the mere form of sacred ordinances when the authority is absent, is shown in the New Testament record of the seven sons of Sceva. These in common with others had marveled at the miraculous power possessed by Paul, whom the Lord so blessed in his apostleship that through contact with handkerchiefs or aprons sent by him the sick were healed, and evil spirits were cast out. Sceva's sons, who are counted by the sacred chronicler among the exorcists and the vagabond Jews, sought also to expel an evil spirit: "We adjure you by Jesus whom Paul preacheth" said they; but the evil spirit derided them for their lack of authority, exclaiming: "Jesus I know, and Paul I know; but who are ye?" Then the afflicted person, in whom the evil spirit dwelt, leaped upon them and overcame them, so that when they escaped from the house they were naked and wounded.[pp]

Teachers True and False—None but those who are duly authorized to teach can be regarded as true expounders of the word of God. The remarks of Paul concerning high priests are applicable to every office of the Priesthood: "No man taketh this honor unto himself, but he that is called of God, as was Aaron."[qq] And Aaron, as we have already seen, was called through Moses unto whom the Lord revealed His will in the matter. This authority to act in the name of the Lord is given to those only who are chosen of God; it is not to be had for the mere asking; it is not to be bought with gold. We read of Simon, the sorcerer, who coveted the power possessed by the apostles; he offered them money, saying: "Give me also this power, that on whomsoever I lay hands he may receive the Holy Ghost." But Peter answered him with righteous indignation: "Thy money perish with thee, because thou hast thought that the gift of God may be purchased with money. Thou hast neither part nor lot in this matter: for thy heart is not right in the sight of God."[rr]

It was known to the apostles of old that men would seek to arrogate unto themselves the right to officiate in things divine, thus becoming servants of Satan. In addressing a conference of elders from Ephesus, Paul prophesied of these ill events and warned the shepherds of the flock to

[oo] 2 Chr., chap. 26.
[pp] See Acts 19:13–17.
[qq] Heb. 5:4.
[rr] Acts 8:18–24.

look well to their charge,[ss] and in an epistle to Timothy the apostle reiterated this prophecy. Encouraging to diligence in preaching the word, he declared: "For the time will come when they will not endure sound doctrine; but after their own lusts shall they heap to themselves teachers, having itching ears; And they shall turn away their ears from the truth, and shall be turned unto fables."[tt] Peter's declarations on the same subject are no less plain. Addressing himself to the saints of his time, he refers to the false prophets of old, and adds: "There shall be false teachers among you, who privily shall bring in damnable heresies; even denying the Lord that bought them * * * And many shall follow their pernicious ways; by reason of whom the way of truth shall be evil spoken of."[uu]

Divine Authority in the Present Dispensation—We claim that the authority to administer in the name of God is operative in The Church of Jesus Christ of Latter-day Saints today; and that this power or commission was conferred upon the first officers of the Church by ordination under the hands of those who had held the same power in earlier dispensations. That the authority of the Holy Priesthood was to be taken from the earth as the apostles of old were slain, and that of necessity it would have to be restored from heaven before the Church could be reestablished, may be shown by scripture. On May 15, 1829, while Joseph Smith and Oliver Cowdery were engaged in earnest prayer for instruction concerning baptism for the remission of sins, mention of which Joseph Smith had found in the plates from which he was then engaged in translating the Book of Mormon, a messenger from heaven descended in a cloud of light. He announced himself as John, called of old the Baptist, and said he had come under the direction of Peter, James, and John, who held the keys of the higher Priesthood. The angel laid his hands upon the two young men and ordained them to authority, saying: "Upon you my fellow servants, in the name of Messiah I confer the Priesthood of Aaron, which holds the keys of the ministering of angels, and of the gospel of repentance, and of baptism by immersion for the remission of sins; and this shall never be taken again from the earth, until the sons of Levi do offer again an offering unto the Lord in righteousness."[vv]

A short time after this event, Peter, James, and John appeared to Joseph Smith and Oliver Cowdery, and ordained the two to the higher or Melchizedek Priesthood, bestowing upon them the keys of the apostleship, which these heavenly messengers had held and exercised in the former Gospel dispensation. This order of Priesthood holds authority over all the offices in the Church, and includes power to administer in spiritual things;[ww] consequently all the authorities and powers necessary to the establishment and development of the Church were by this visitation restored to earth.

No one may officiate in any ordinances of The Church of Jesus Christ of Latter-day Saints unless he has been ordained to the particular order or office of Priesthood, by those possessing the requisite authority. Thus, no man receives the Priesthood except under the hands of one who holds that Priesthood himself; that one must have obtained it from others previously commissioned; and so every bearer of the Priesthood today can trace his authority to the hands of Joseph Smith the Prophet,[xx] who received his ordination under the hands of the apostles Peter, James, and John; and they had been ordained by the Lord Jesus Christ. That men who are called of God, to

[ss] See Acts 20:28–30.
[tt] 2 Tim. 4:2–4.
[uu] 2 Pet. 2:1–3.
[vv] P. of G. P., p. 57; D&C, sec. 13.
[ww] See D&C sec. 107.
[xx] See Appendix 10:1.

the authority of the ministry on earth, may have been selected for such appointment even before they took mortal bodies, is evident from the scriptures. This matter may properly claim attention in the present connection; and its consideration leads us to the subjects following.

FOREORDINATION AND PREEXISTENCE

Foreordination—In an interview with Abraham, the Lord revealed many things ordinarily withheld from mortals. Concerning this the patriarch wrote: "Now the Lord had shown unto me, Abraham, the intelligences that were organized before the world was; and among all these there were many of the noble and great ones; And God saw these souls that they were good, and he stood in the midst of them, and he said: These I will make my rulers; for he stood among those that were spirits, and he saw that they were good; and he said unto me: Abraham, thou art one of them; thou wast chosen before thou wast born."[yy] This is one of the many scriptural proofs that the spirits of mankind existed prior to their earthly probation—a condition in which these intelligences lived and exercised their free agency before they assumed bodily tabernacles. Thus the natures, dispositions, and tendencies of men are known to the Father of their spirits, even before they are born into mortality. The word of the Lord came unto Jeremiah, telling him that before he was conceived in the flesh he had been ordained to be a prophet unto the nations.[zz]

Evidence is abundant that Jesus Christ was chosen and ordained to be the Redeemer of the world, even in the beginning. We read of His foremost position amongst the sons of God in offering Himself as a sacrifice to carry into effect the will of the Father. He it was, "Who verily was foreordained before the foundation of the world."[aaa]

Paul taught the doctrine of divine selection and preappointment thus: "For whom he did foreknow, he also did predestinate to be conformed to the image of his Son. * * * Moreover whom he did predestinate, them he also called."[bbb] And again: "God hath not cast away his people which he foreknew."[ccc]

Alma, the Nephite prophet, spoke of the priests who had been ordained after the order of the Son, and added: "And this is the manner after which they were ordained—being called and prepared from the foundation of the world according to the foreknowledge of God, on account of their exceeding faith and good works; in the first place being left to choose good or evil; therefore they having chosen good, and exercising exceeding great faith, are called with a holy calling, yea, with that holy calling which was prepared with, and according to, a preparatory redemption for such."[ddd]

Foreordination Does Not Imply Compulsion—The doctrine of absolute predestination, resulting in a nullification of man's free agency, has been advocated with various modifications by different sects. Nevertheless, such teachings are wholly unjustified by both the letter and the spirit of sacred writ. God's foreknowledge concerning the natures and capacities of His children enables Him to see the end of their earthly career even from the first: "Known unto God are all his works from the beginning of the world."[eee] Many people have been led to regard this foreknowledge of God as a predestination whereby souls are designated for glory or condemnation even before their birth in the flesh, and irrespective of individual merit or demerit. This heretical

[yy] P.of G.P., Abraham 3:22, 23; see also Jer. 1:4, 5.
[zz] See Jer. 1:4.
[aaa] 1 Peter 1:20; see *Jesus the Christ*, chap. 2.
[bbb] Rom. 8:29, 30.
[ccc] Rom. 11:2.
[ddd] Alma 13:3; also 10, 11.
[eee] Acts 15:18.

doctrine seeks to rob Deity of mercy, justice, and love; it would make God appear capricious and selfish, directing and creating all things solely for His own glory, caring not for the suffering of His victims. How dreadful, how inconsistent is such an idea of God! It leads to the absurd conclusion that the mere knowledge of coming events must act as a determining influence in bringing about those occurrences. God's knowledge of spiritual and of human nature enables Him to conclude with certainty as to the actions of any of His children under given conditions; yet that knowledge is not of compelling force upon the creature.[fff]

Doubtless He knows of some spirits that they await only the opportunity of choice between good and evil to choose the latter and to accomplish their own destruction; these are they as spoken of by Jude, "who were before of old ordained to this condemnation."[ggg] To avert the fate of such their free agency would have to be taken away; they can be saved by force alone; and compulsion is forbidden by the laws of heaven alike for salvation and condemnation. There are others whose integrity and faithfulness have been demonstrated in their pristine state; the Father knows how unreservedly they may be trusted, and many of them are called even in their mortal youth to special and exalted labors as commissioned servants of the Most High.

Preexistence of Spirits—The facts already presented concerning foreordination furnish proof that the spirits of mankind passed through a stage of existence prior to their earthly probation. This antemortal period is oftentimes spoken of as the stage of primeval childhood or first estate. That these spirits existed as organized intelligences and exercised their free agency during that primeval stage is clear from the declaration of the Lord to Abraham: "And they who keep their first estate shall be added upon; and they who keep not their first estate shall not have glory in the same kingdom with those who keep their first estate; and they who keep their second estate shall have glory added upon their heads forever and ever."[hhh]

No one who accepts Jesus Christ as the Son of God can consistently deny His antemortal existence, or question His position as one of the Godhead before He came to earth as Mary's Son. The common interpretation given to the opening words of John's Gospel sustains the view of Christ's primeval Godship: "In the beginning was the Word, and the Word was with God, and the Word was God." We read further, "And the Word was made flesh, and dwelt among us."[iii] The affirmations of the Redeemer support this truth. When His disciples dissented concerning His doctrine of Himself, He said: "What and if ye shall see the Son of Man ascend up where he was before?"[jjj] On another occasion He spoke in this wise: "I came forth from the Father, and am come into the world: again, I leave the world, and go to the Father."[kkk] And His disciples, pleased with this plain declaration confirming the belief which, perchance, they already entertained at heart, rejoined, "Lo, now speakest thou plainly, and speakest no proverb * * * by this we believe that thou camest forth from God."[lll] To certain wicked Jews who boasted of their descent from Abraham, and sought to hide their sins under the protecting mantle of the great patriarch's name, the Savior declared: "Verily, verily, I say unto you, Before Abraham was, I am."[mmm] In solemn prayer the Son implored, "And now, O Father, glorify thou

[fff] See *Jesus the Christ,* pp. 18, 28; and *The Great Apostasy,* p. 19; also Appendix 10:2.
[ggg] Jude 4.
[hhh] P. of G.P., Abraham 3:26.
[iii] John 1:1, 14.
[jjj] John 6:62.
[kkk] John 16:28.
[lll] John 16:29, 30.
[mmm] John 8:58; see *Jesus the Christ,* pp. 37, 411.

me with thine own self with the glory which I had with thee before the world was."[nnn] Yet Christ was born a child among mortals; and it is consistent to infer that if His earthly birth was the union of a preexistent or antemortal spirit with a mortal body such also is the birth of every member of the human family.

But we are not left to mere inference on a basis of analogy; the scriptures plainly teach that the spirits of mankind are known and numbered unto God before their earthly advent. In his farewell administration to Israel Moses sang: "Remember the days of old * * * When the Most High divided to the nations their inheritance, when he separated the sons of Adam, he set the bounds of the people according to the number of the children of Israel."[ooo] From this we learn that the earth was allotted to the nations, according to the number of the children of Israel; it is evident therefore that the number was known prior to the existence of the Israelitish nation in the flesh; this is most easily explained on the basis of previous existence in which the spirits of the future nation were known.

No chance is possible, therefore, in the number or extent of the temporal creations of God.[ppp] The population of the earth is fixed according to the number of spirits appointed to take tabernacles of flesh upon this planet; when these have all come forth in the order and time appointed, then, and not till then, shall the end come.

REFERENCES

Authority in the Ministry

Prior to the Mosaic dispensation: Adam commissioned to teach—Moses 6:57, 58; he was after the order of God—verse 67. The Lord commanded Noah—Gen. 6:13, 14, 22; 7:1. And the Lord ordained Noah after his own order—Moses 8:19. The Lord commanded Abraham—Gen. 12:1; 15:9; 17:1–9. Abraham became a high priest—Abraham 1:2, 3. See book of Abraham in P.of G.P.. The Lord covenanted with Abraham as to the Priesthood—Abraham 2:9–11. Melchizedek, priest of the most high God—Gen. 14:18–20; see also Alma 13:18. Thou art a priest for ever after the order of Melchizedek—Ps. 110:4; Heb. 5:6–10; 6:20; 7:1–3. The Lord covenanted with Isaac— Gen. 26:2–5; and with Jacob—Gen. 28:10–15.

Authority to Moses and others: Moses commissioned to deliver the children of Israel— Ex. 3:4–17. I have made thee a god to Pharaoh—Ex. 7:1. Jethro, priest of Midian—Ex. chap. 18; conferred the Holy Priesthood upon Moses—D&C 84:6. Joshua ordained under hand of Moses—Num. 27:18–23; Deut. 34:9.

Note instances of retribution upon some who presumed to officiate without authority—Num. chap. 16; 1 Chr. 13:10; 1 Sam. 13:5-14; 2 Chr. chap. 26.

Priests which were anointed and consecrated to minister—Num. 3:3; Levites appointed—verse 9.

Seventy men of the elders of Israel—Num. 11:16, 25.

Them the Lord hath chosen to minister—Deut. 21:5.

Ye shall be named the Priests of the Lord—Isa. 61:6.

Jeremiah was ordained a prophet; the Lord's words in his mouth—Jer. 1:4–9.

Word of the Lord came expressly unto Ezekiel the priest—Ezek. 1:3.

[nnn] John 17:5; see also 2 Nephi 9:5; 25:12; Mos. 3:5; 13:33, 34; 15:1.
[ooo] Deut. 32:7, 8.
[ppp] See Appendix 10:3.

Then spake Haggai the Lord's messenger—Haggai 1:13.
Word of the Lord unto Zechariah—Zech. 1:1.
The priest is the messenger of the Lord of hosts—Mal. 2:7.

Authority Conferred by Jesus Christ While in Mortality
He gave power to twelve disciples—Matt. 10:1.
He ordained twelve—Mark 3:14; these twelve he named apostles—Luke 6:13.
I have chosen you, and ordained you—John 15:16; see also 17:18.
Christ appointed and sent out other seventy also—Luke 10:1, 17.
I will give unto thee (Peter) the keys of the kingdom of heaven—Matt. 16:19.
Commission to the apostles to baptize and teach—Matt. 28:19, 20.
Sins to be remitted or retained under authority given the apostles—John 20:21–23.

Ordination in Days of the Apostles
Matthias was numbered with the apostles—Acts 1:21–26.
Seven men chosen and ordained by the laying on of hands—Acts 6:2–6.
Philip ministered by authority, with signs following—Acts 8:5–12; compare 6:5. Note that Peter and John, apostles, administered the higher ordinances to the Samaritans converted through Philip's ministry—Acts 8:14–17.
Barnabas and Saul received the laying on of hands—Acts 13:1–3.
Elders ordained in every church—Acts 14:23; see also Titus 1:5.
Paul, called to be an apostle—Rom. 1:1; 1 Cor. 1:1; see also Rom. 1:5.
How shall they preach unless they are sent?—Rom. 10:14, 15.
Whereunto I am ordained a preacher, and an apostle—1 Tim. 2:7; also 2 Tim. 1:11.
Gift bestowed by prophecy with the laying on of the hands of the presbytery—1 Tim. 4:14; also 2 Tim. 1:6.
A chosen generation, a royal priesthood—1 Peter 2:9.
But he gave some, apostles, and some, prophets—Eph. 4:11.
Jesus Christ a high priest after the order of Melchizedek—Heb. 5:1–8.
If any man speak, let him speak as the oracle of God—1 Peter 4:11.
Nephi called to be a ruler and a teacher—1 Nephi 2:22; 3:29; 2 Nephi 5:19.
Nephi consecrated Jacob and Joseph to be priests—2 Nephi 5:26.
Jacob called of God and ordained after his holy order—2 Nephi 6:2.
Alma was consecrated the high priest over the church—Alma 4:4; 8:23; 16:5.
High priesthood after order of the Son of God—Alma 13:1–19.
Alma ordained priests and elders by the laying on of hands—Alma 6:1.
By all those who had been ordained by the holy order of God—Alma 49:30.
They of old were called after the holy order of God—Ether 12:10.
The Lord touched the twelve disciples with his hand and gave them power to give the Holy Ghost—3 Nephi 18:36, 37; Moroni chap. 2.
Other disciples ordained—4 Nephi 14.
The disciples ordained priests and teachers—Moroni, chap. 3.
Priesthood of Aaron conferred upon Joseph Smith and Oliver Cowdery by John the Baptist—D&C sec. 13.

Behold, this is mine authority, and the authority of my servants—D&C 1:6.

I will reveal unto you the priesthood, by the hand of Elijah the prophet—D&C 2:1.

Joseph Smith and Oliver Cowdery ordain each other as commanded—P. of G.P. pp. 57, 58, verse 71.

Ordinations required; each ordination must be under the hands of one having authority—D&C 42:11.

Bishops must be high priests, except they be literal descendants of Aaron; rights of the literal descendants of Aaron—D&C 68:14–21.

Through this priesthood, a savior unto my people Israel—D&C 86:11.

Revelation on Priesthood, giving lineage of the ancient patriarchs, and the duties of the several offices in the Priesthood—D&C sec. 84.

He that is ordained of me and sent forth to preach the word of truth—D&C 50:17.

Preach the Gospel, acting in the authority which I have given you—D&C 68:8.

The Lord took Moses out of the midst of Israel, and the Holy Priesthood also; and the lesser Priesthood continued—D&C 84:25, 26.

Whoso is faithful unto the obtaining these two priesthoods, become the sons of Moses and Aaron and the seed of Abraham—D&C 84:33, 34.

Wo unto all those who come not unto this priesthood—D&C 84:42.

The Twelve called to go into all the world to preach the gospel—D&C 18:27–29. Instructions relating to the Twelve—verses 31–36.

The Twelve a Traveling Presiding High Council to build up the church—D&C 107:33; the Seventy to act under the direction of the Twelve—verse 34.

The Twelve Apostles are special witnesses of the name of Christ in all the world—D&C 107:23.

Revelation dealing with the quorums of priesthood and their duties—D&C, sec. 107.

One man on the earth at a time holding the keys of the sealing power—D&C 132:7.

Same priesthood, which was in the beginning, shall be in the end of the world also—Moses 6:7.

The Lord said to Abraham: I will take thee, to put upon thee my name, even the priesthood of thy father—Abraham 1:18.

The records of the fathers, even the patriarchs, concerning the right of priesthood—Abraham 1:31.

Preexistence and Foreordination

God is the Father of the spirits of all flesh—Heb. 12:9; see also Num. 16:22; 27:16; Job 12:10.

After death the spirit is to return to God who gave it—Eccl. 12:7.

Jeremiah, before he was born, was known to God and was ordained—Jer. 1:5.

What and if ye shall see the Son of Man ascend up where he was before?—John 6:62.

I came forth from the Father; again, I leave the world, and go to the Father—John 16:28.

Christ prayed that he be glorified with the glory which he had with the Father before the world was—John 17:5.

Who did sin, this man, or his parents, that he was born blind?—John 9:2.

Consider the many instances of Jehovah, or Jesus Christ, manifesting himself to the ancient prophets of both hemispheres before his birth into the flesh.

Predictions that the Lord Omnipotent, who then reigned, would come down and dwell in a tabernacle of clay, and be born of Mary—Mosiah 3:5–8.

The Lord showed to Abraham the intelligences that were organized before the world was, for whom the earth was created—Abraham 3:22–26.

The resurrected Lord declared to the Nephites that he created the heavens and the earth and was with the Father from the beginning—3 Nephi 9:15.

The Lord declared to Nephi, son of Nephi, on the night before his birth: On the morrow come I into the world—3 Nephi 1:13.

Being called and prepared from the foundation of the world, according to the foreknowledge of God—Alma 13:3; prepared from eternity to all eternity, according to his foreknowledge—verse 7.

Christ, who was prepared from the foundation of the world—Mosiah 18:13. I am he who was prepared from the foundation of the world—Ether 3:14.

Elect according to the foreknowledge of God—1 Peter 1:2.

He hath chosen us in him before the foundation of the world—Eph. 1:4.

Being predestined according to the Lord's purpose—Eph. 1:11.

God foreordained that men should walk in good works—Eph. 2:10.

Ye are lawful heirs, and have been hid from the world with Christ in God—D&C 86:9, 10.

Things of God which were from the beginning, before the world was—D&C 76:13.

Ordained in the Council of the Eternal God before this world was—D&C 121:32.

The Lord chose from among the unembodied spirits those whom he would make his rulers in the flesh—Abraham 3:23.

11

THE CHURCH AND ITS PLAN
OF ORGANIZATION

ARTICLE 6

E BELIEVE in the same organization that existed in the Primitive Church, viz., apostles, prophets, pastors, teachers, evangelists, etc.

THE CHURCH IN FORMER
AND LATTER DAYS

The Primitive Church—In the dispensation of the meridian of time[a] Jesus Christ established His Church upon the earth, appointing therein the officers necessary for the carrying out of the Father's purposes. Every person so appointed was divinely commissioned with authority to officiate in the ordinances of his calling; and, after Christ's ascension, the same organization was continued, those who had received authority ordaining others to the various offices in the Priesthood. In this way were given unto the Church, apostles, prophets, evangelists, pastors,[b] high priests,[c] seventies,[d] elders,[e] bishops,[f] priests,[g] teachers,[h] and deacons.[i]

Besides these specific offices in the Priesthood, there were other callings of a more temporal nature, to which men were also set apart by authority; such for instance was the case of the seven

[a] See P. of G.P., Moses 5:57; D&C 20:26; 39:3.
[b] See Eph. 4:11.
[c] See Heb. 5:1–5.
[d] See Luke 10:1–11.
[e] See Acts 14:23; 15:6; 1 Peter 5:1.
[f] See 1 Tim. 3:1; Titus 1:7.
[g] See Rev. 1:6.
[h] See Acts 13:1.
[i] See 1 Tim. 3:8–12.

men of honest report who, in the days of the apostles, were appointed to minister to the poor, thus leaving the Twelve freer to attend to the particular duties of their office.[j] This special appointment illustrates the nature of the helps and governments[k] set in the Church, to assist in the work under the direction of the regular officers of the Priesthood.

The ministers so appointed and the members among whom they labor constitute the Church of Christ, which has been impressively compared to a perfect body, the individuals typifying the separate members, each with its own functions, all cooperating for the welfare of the whole.[l] Every office so established, every officer so commissioned, is necessary to the development of the Church and to the accomplishment of its work. An organization established of God comprises no superfluities; the eye, the ear, the hand, the foot, every organ of the body, is essential to the symmetry and perfection of the physical structure; in the Church no officer can rightly say to another: "I have no need of thee."[m]

The existence of these officers, and particularly their operation with accompaniments of divine assistance and power, may be taken as a distinguishing characteristic of the Church in any age of the world—a crucial test, whereby the validity or falsity of any claim to divine authority may be determined. The Gospel of Jesus Christ is the everlasting Gospel; its principles, laws and ordinances, and the Church organization founded thereon, must be ever the same. In searching for the true Church, therefore, one must look for an organization comprising the offices established of old, the callings of apostles, prophets, evangelists, high priests, seventies, pastors, bishops, elders, priests, teachers, deacons—not men bearing these names merely, but ministers able to vindicate their claim to position as officers in the Lord's service, through the evidences of power and authority accompanying their ministry.

Apostasy from the Primitive Church—Question may arise in the mind of the earnest investigator, as to whether these authorities, together with the attesting gifts of the Holy Spirit, have remained with men from the apostolic age to the present; in short, as to the existence of the Church of Jesus Christ upon the earth during this long interval. In answer, let the facts following be considered. Since the period immediately succeeding that of the ministrations of the apostles of old, and until the nineteenth century, no organization had maintained a claim to direct revelation from God; in fact, the teachings of professed ministers of the Gospel for centuries have been to the effect that such gifts of God have ceased, that the days of miracles have gone, and that the present depends for its guiding code wholly upon the past. A self-suggesting interpretation of history indicates that there has been a great departure from the way of salvation as laid down by the Savior, a universal apostasy from the Church of Christ.[n] Scarcely had the Church been organized by the Savior, whose name it bears, before the powers of darkness arrayed themselves for conflict with the organized body. Even in the days of our Lord's personal ministry in the flesh persecution was waged against Him and the disciples. Commencing with the Jews, and directed first against the Master and His few immediate associates, this tide of opposition soon enveloped every known follower of the Savior, so that the very name Christian was used as an epithet of derision.

---

j See Acts 6:1–6.

k See 1 Cor. 12:28.

l See 1 Cor. 12:12–27; Rom. 12:4, 5; Eph. 4:16.

m 1 Cor. 12:21.

n See Appendix 11:1, 2; also *The Great Apostasy,* chap. 9; and the instructive little work—*The Reign of Antichrist, or The Great "Falling Away,"* by Elder J. M. Sjodahl, Salt Lake City, 1913.

In the first quarter of the fourth century, however, a change in the attitude of paganism toward Christianity was marked by the so-called conversion of Constantine the Great, under whose patronage the Christian profession grew in favor and became in fact the religion of State. But what a profession, what a religion it was by this time! Its simplicity had departed; earnest devotion and self-sacrificing sincerity were no longer characteristic of the ministers of the Church. Those professed followers of the humble Prophet of Nazareth, those self-styled representatives of the Lord whose kingdom was not of earth earthy, those loudly proclaimed lovers of the Man of Sorrows acquainted with grief, lived amidst conditions strangely inconsistent with the life of their divine Exemplar. Church offices were sought after for the distinction of honor and wealth accompanying them; ministers of the Gospel affected the state of secular dignitaries; bishops exhibited the pomp of princes, archbishops lived as kings and popes like emperors. With these innovations came many changes in the ordinances of the so-called church—the rites of baptism were perverted; the sacrament was altered; public worship became an exhibition of art; men were canonized, martyrs were made subjects of adoration; blasphemy grew apace, in that men without authority essayed to exercise the prerogatives of God. Ages of darkness came upon the earth; the power of Satan seemed almost supreme.

For a special consideration of the evidence of a general apostasy from the Church of Christ the student must consult authorities on ecclesiastical history. While the fact of the apostasy is admitted by but few such writers, the historical events they chronicle reveal the awful truth. We may trace, from the days of the apostles down to near the close of the tenth century, a constantly changing form of Church organization, which at the later time named bore but little semblance to the Church established by the Savior. This falling away is admitted by some historians, and as we shall presently see, was definitely foretold by authoritative prophecy.

John Wesley, founder of an influential sect, declared that the distinctive gifts of the Holy Ghost were no longer with the Church, having been taken away on account of the unworthiness of professing Christians, whom he characterized indeed as heathen, with only a dead form of worship.[o] In the Church of England *Homily Against Peril of Idolatry* we read: "So that laity and clergy, learned and unlearned, all ages, sects, and degrees of men, women, and children of whole Christendom—an horrible and most dreadful thing to think—have been at once drowned in abominable idolatry; of all other vices most detested by God, and most damnable to man; and that by the space of eight hundred years and more." The *Book of Homilies* dates from about the middle of the sixteenth century; and in it is thus officially affirmed that the so-called Church and the whole religious world had been utterly apostate for eight centuries or more prior to the establishment of the Church of England.[p]

This Great Apostasy was Foretold—The foreknowledge of God made plain to Him even from the beginning this falling away from the truth; and, through inspiration the prophets of old uttered solemn warnings of the approaching dangers. Isaiah was contemplating the era of spiritual darkness when he declared: "The earth also is defiled under the inhabitants thereof; because they have transgressed the laws, changed the ordinance, broken the everlasting covenant."[q] Deeply impressive are the words of the Lord through Jeremiah: "For my people have committed two evils: they have forsaken me the fountain of living waters, and hewed them out cisterns, broken cisterns, that can hold no water."[r]

[o] See *John Wesley's Works*, 7, pp. 26, 27.
[p] See the author's *Philosophical Basis of "Mormonism,"* sec. 7, and *The Great Apostasy,* chap. 10.
[q] Isa. 24:5.
[r] Jer. 2:13.

The prophecies of the apostles relative to the false teachers then soon to trouble the flock show that the apostasy was at that early time approaching rapidly. Paul warned the saints of Thessalonica that they be not deceived by those who cried that the second coming of Christ was then at hand— "For," said the apostle, "that day shall not come except there come a falling away first, and that man of sin be revealed, the son of perdition; Who opposeth and exalteth himself above all that is called God, or that is worshiped; so that he as God sitteth in the temple of God, shewing himself that he is God."[s] This falling away had begun even in the days of the apostles: "Even now," says John, "are there many anti-Christs."[t] And Paul, in addressing the Galatians, declared, "There be some that trouble you, and would pervert the gospel of Christ."[u]

Not less conclusive are the prophecies contained in the Book of Mormon relating to this great falling away. Nephi, son of Lehi, predicted the oppression of the North American Indians at the hands of the Gentiles, and declared that at that time the people will be lifted up in self-pride, having departed from the ordinances of God's house; they will build to themselves many churches, but in these they will preach their own wisdom, with envyings, and strife, and malice, denying, however, the power and miracles of God.[v]

Restoration of the Church—From the facts already stated it is evident that the Church was literally driven from the earth; in the first ten centuries immediately following the ministry of Christ the authority of the Holy Priesthood was lost from among men, and no human power could restore it. But the Lord in His mercy provided for the reestablishment of His Church in the last days, and for the last time; and prophets of olden time foresaw this era of renewed enlightenment, and sang in joyous tones of its coming.[w] This restoration was effected by the Lord through the Prophet Joseph Smith, who, together with Oliver Cowdery, in 1829, received the Aaronic Priesthood under the hands of John the Baptist; and later the Melchizedek Priesthood under the hands of the former-day apostles, Peter, James, and John. By the authority thus bestowed the Church has been again organized with all its former completeness, and mankind once more rejoices in the priceless privileges of the counsels of God. The Latter-day Saints declare their high claim to the true Church organization, similar in all essentials to the organization effected by Christ among the Jews. This people of the last days profess to have the Priesthood of the Almighty, the power to act in the name of God, which power commands respect both on earth and in heaven.

PLAN OF GOVERNMENT IN THE RESTORED CHURCH

Orders and Offices in the priesthood[x]—The Church of Jesus Christ of Latter-day Saints recognizes two orders of Priesthood, the lesser called the Aaronic, the greater known as the Melchizedek order.

The Aaronic Priesthood is named after Aaron, who was given to Moses as his mouthpiece, to act under his direction in the carrying out of God's purposes respecting Israel.[y] For this reason it is sometimes called the Lesser Priesthood; but though lesser, it is neither small nor insignificant. While Israel journeyed in the wilderness, Aaron and his sons were called by prophecy and set apart for the duties of the priest's office.[z]

[s] 2 Thess. 2:3, 4.
[t] 1 John 2:18; see also 2 Peter 2:1–3; Jude 17, 18.
[u] Gal. 1:7; also Acts 20:29, 30; 1 Tim. 4:1–3; 2 Tim. 4:1–4; see *The Great Apostasy*, chap. 2.
[v] See 2 Nephi 26:19–22; see also 27:1; 28:3, 6; 29:3; 1 Nephi 13:5; 22:22, 23.
[w] See Dan. 2:44, 45; 7:27; Matt. 24:14; Rev. 14:6–8.
[x] See D&C, sec. 107.
[y] See Ex. 4:14–16.
[z] See Ex. 28:1.

At a later period the Lord chose the tribe of Levi to assist Aaron in the priestly functions, the special duties of the Levites being to keep the instruments and attend to the service of the tabernacle. The Levites were to take the place of the firstborn throughout the tribes, whom the Lord had claimed for His service from the time of the last dread plague in Egypt whereby the firstborn in every Egyptian house was slain while the eldest in every Israelitish house was hallowed and spared.[aa] The commission thus given to the Levites is sometimes called the *Levitical Priesthood;*[bb] it is to be regarded as an appendage to the Priesthood of Aaron, not comprising the highest priestly powers. The Aaronic Priesthood, as restored to the earth in this dispensation, includes the Levitical order.[cc] The Aaronic Priesthood holds the keys of the ministering of angels, and the authority to attend to the outward ordinances, the letter of the Gospel;[dd] it comprises the offices of deacon, teacher, and priest, with the bishopric holding the keys of presidency.

The Melchizedek Priesthood is named after the king of Salem, a great High Priest[ee] before whose day it was known as "the Holy Priesthood, after the Order of the Son of God. But out of respect or reverence to the name of the Supreme Being, to avoid the too frequent repetition of his name, they, the Church, in ancient days, called that priesthood after Melchizedek."[ff] This Priesthood holds the right of presidency in all the offices of the Church; its special functions lie in the administration of spiritual things, comprising the keys of all spiritual blessings of the Church, the right "to have the heavens opened unto them [the bearers of this Priesthood], to commune with the general assembly and Church of the Firstborn, and to enjoy the communion and presence of God the Father, and Jesus the mediator of the new covenant."[gg] The special offices of the Melchizedek Priesthood are those of apostle, patriarch or evangelist, high priest, seventy, and elder. Revelation from God has defined the duties associated with each of these callings; and the same high authority has directed the establishment of presiding officers appointed from among those who are ordained to the several offices in these two Priesthoods.[hh]

Special Duties in the Priesthood—The office of **Deacon** is the first or lowest in the Aaronic Priesthood. The duties of this calling are primarily of a temporal nature, pertaining to the care of houses of worship, the comfort of the worshipers, and ministration to the members of the Church as the bishop may direct. In all things, however, the deacon may be called to assist the teacher in his labors.[ii] Twelve deacons form a quorum;[jj] such a body is to be presided over by a president and counselors selected from among their number.

Teachers are local officers, whose function it is to mingle with the saints, exhorting them to their duties, and strengthening the Church by their constant ministry; they are to see that there is no iniquity in the Church; that the members do not cherish ill feelings toward one another, but

---

aa See Num. 3:12, 13, 39, 44, 45, 50, 51.

bb See Heb. 7:11.

cc See D&C 107:1.

dd See D&C 107:20.

ee See Gen. 14:18, Heb. 7:1–17.

ff D&C 107:2–4.

gg D&C 107:8, 18, 19.

hh See D&C 107:21.

ii See D&C 20:57; 107:85.

jj **Quorum**—This term has acquired a special meaning among the Latter-day Saints. It signifies, not alone a majority or such a number of persons of any organized body as is requisite for authoritative action, but the organized body itself. The Church regards a quorum as "a council or an organized body of the priesthood," e.g., *an elders' quorum: the quorum of the Twelve Apostles,* etc. (See *Standard Dictionary.*)

observe the law of God respecting Church duties. They may take the lead of meetings when no priest or higher officer is present. Both teachers and deacons may preach the word of God when properly directed so to do; but they have not the power to independently officiate in any spiritual ordinances, such as baptizing, administering the sacrament, or laying on of hands.[kk] Twenty-four teachers constitute a quorum, including a president and two counselors.

Priests are appointed to preach, teach, expound the scripture, to baptize, to administer the sacrament, to visit the homes of the members, exhorting them to diligence. When properly directed, the priest may ordain deacons, teachers, and other priests; and he may be called upon to assist the elder in his work. A quorum of priests comprises forty-eight members, and is under the personal presidency of a bishop.

Elders are empowered to officiate in any or all duties connected with lower callings in the Priesthood; and in addition, they may ordain other elders, confirm as members of the Church candidates who have been properly baptized, and confer upon them the Holy Ghost. Elders have authority to bless children in the Church, and to take charge of meetings, conducting the same as they are led by the Holy Ghost.[ll] The elder may officiate in the stead of the high priest when the latter is not present. Ninety-six elders form a quorum; three of these constitute the presidency of the body.[mm]

Seventies are primarily traveling elders, especially ordained to promulgate the Gospel among the nations of the earth, "unto the Gentiles first, and also unto the Jews." They are to act under the direction of the apostles in this specific labor.[nn] A full quorum comprises seventy members, including seven presidents.

High Priests are ordained with power to officiate, when set apart or otherwise authoritatively directed, in all the ordinances and blessings of the Church. They may travel as do the seventies, carrying the Gospel to the nations; but they are not especially charged with this duty; their particular calling being that of standing presidency and service. The high priests of any stake of the Church may be organized into a quorum, and this without limit as to number; over such a quorum, three of the members preside as president and counselors.[oo]

Patriarchs or Evangelists are charged with the duty of blessing the members of the Church; of course they have authority to officiate also in other ordinances. There is one "Patriarch to the Church," known officially as the Presiding Patriarch, with general jurisdiction throughout the whole organization; he holds the keys of the patriarchal office, and unto him the promise is given "that whoever he blesses shall be blessed, and whoever he curses shall be cursed, that whatsoever he shall bind on earth shall be bound in heaven, and whatsoever he shall loose on earth shall be loosed in heaven."[pp]

Concerning the patriarchal authority the Lord has said: "The order of this priesthood was confirmed to be handed down from father to son, and rightly belongs to the literal descendants of the chosen seed to whom the promises were made. This order was instituted in the days of Adam, and came down by lineage."[qq] But, besides this office of general patriarchal power, there are a number of local patriarchs appointed in the branches of the Church, all subject to counsel and instruction from the Presiding Patriarch as he is directed by the First Presidency or the Council of the Twelve,

[kk] See D&C 20:53–59; 107:86.
[ll] See D&C 20:38–45, 70; 107:11, 12.
[mm] See D&C 107:89.
[nn] See D&C 107:34, 35, 97, 98.
[oo] See D&C 107:10; 124:134, 135.
[pp] D&C 124:92, 93.
[qq] See D&C 107:40–57.

yet possessing the same privileges and authority within their districts as belong to the Presiding Patriarch throughout the Church. "It is the duty of the Twelve, in all large branches of the church, to ordain evangelical ministers, as they shall be designated unto them by revelation."[rr]

Apostles are called to be special witnesses of the name of Christ in all the world;[ss] they are empowered to build up and organize the branches of the Church; and may officiate in any and all of the sacred ordinances. They are to travel among the saints, regulating the affairs of the Church wherever they go, but particularly where there is no complete local organization. They are authorized to ordain patriarchs and other officers in the Priesthood, as they may be directed by the Spirit of God.[tt] In all their ministry they act under the direction of the First Presidency of the Church. Twelve Apostles, duly set apart, constitute the Quorum, or Council, of the Twelve.

Presidency and Quorum Organizations—The revealed word of God has provided for the establishment of presiding officers "growing out of, or appointed of or from among those who are ordained to the several offices in these two priesthoods."[uu] In accordance with the prevailing principles of order characteristic of all His work, the Lord has directed that the bearers of the Priesthood shall be organized into quorums, the better to aid them in learning and discharging the duties of their respective callings. Some of these quorums are general in extent and authority, others are local in jurisdiction. The General Authorities of the Church, and all officers whether of general or local jurisdiction, are to be sustained in their several positions by the vote of the people over whom they are appointed to preside. Stake and ward officers are so voted upon by the local organizations, the general authorities and general officers by the Church in conference assembled. Conferences of the Church are held at semiannual intervals, while both stake and ward conferences are convened quarterly; and at these conferences the vote of the people on nominations to office is an important feature. The principle of common consent is thus observed in all the organizations of the Church.[vv]

The First Presidency constitutes the presiding quorum of the Church. By divine direction, a president is appointed from among the members of the High Priesthood to preside over the entire Church. He is known as President of the High Priesthood of the Church, or Presiding High Priest over the High Priesthood of the Church.[ww] He is called "to be a seer, a revelator, a translator, and a prophet, having all the gifts of God which he bestows upon the head of the Church."[xx] His station is compared by the Lord to that of Moses of old, who stood as the mouthpiece of God unto Israel. In his exalted labors amongst the Church, the Presiding High Priest is assisted by two others holding the same Priesthood, and these three High Priests, when properly appointed and ordained and upheld by the confidence, faith, and prayers of the Church, "form a quorum of the Presidency of the Church."[yy]

The Quorum of the Twelve Apostles—Twelve men holding the apostleship, properly organized, constitute the Quorum of the Twelve Apostles, also designated The Council of the Twelve. These the Lord has named as the twelve traveling councilors;[zz] they form the Traveling Presiding High Council, to officiate under the direction of the First Presidency in all parts of the world. They

---

[rr] See D&C 107:39.
[ss] See D&C 107:23.
[tt] See D&C 107:39, 58; 20:38–44.
[uu] See D&C 107:21.
[vv] See Appendix 11:3.
[ww] See D&C 107:64–68.
[xx] D&C 107:91, 92.
[yy] D&C 107:22.
[zz] See D&C 107:23, 33.

constitute a quorum whose unanimous decisions are equally binding in power and authority with those of the First Presidency of the Church.[aaa] When the First Presidency is disorganized through the death or disability of the President, the directing authority in government reverts at once to the Quorum of the Twelve Apostles, by whom the nomination to the Presidency is made.

The Presiding Quorum of Seventy—The First Quorum of Seventies form a body whose unanimous decisions would be equally binding with those of the Twelve Apostles on matters properly brought before the Seventy for their official action. Many quorums of seventies may be required in the work of the Church. Each quorum is presided over by seven presidents. The seven presidents of the First Quorum of Seventies, however, preside over all the other quorums and their presidents.[bbb]

The Presiding Bishopric, as at present constituted, comprises the Presiding Bishop of the Church and two counselors. This body holds jurisdiction over the duties of other bishops in the Church, and of all activities and organizations pertaining to the Aaronic Priesthood. The oldest living representative among the sons of Aaron is entitled to this office of presidency, provided he be in all respects worthy and qualified; however, he must be designated and ordained by the First Presidency of the Church.[ccc] If such a literal descendant of Aaron be found and ordained, he may act without counselors except when he sits in judgment in a trial of one of the Presidents of the High Priesthood, in which case he is to be assisted by twelve High Priests.[ddd] But in the absence of any direct descendant of Aaron properly qualified, a High Priest of the Melchizedek Priesthood may be called and set apart by the First Presidency of the Church to the office of Presiding Bishop; he is to be assisted by two other High Priests properly ordained and set apart as his counselors.[eee]

Local Organizations of the Priesthood—Where the saints are permanently located, Stakes of Zion are organized, each stake comprising a number of wards or branches. Over each stake is placed a *Stake Presidency,* consisting of a president and two counselors, who are high priests set apart to this office. The Stake Presidency is assisted in judicial functions by a *Standing High Council,* composed of twelve high priests chosen and ordained to the office. This council is presided over by the Stake Presidency, and forms the highest judicial tribunal of the stake.

The presidents of stakes and bishops of wards are pastors to the fold; their duties are analogous to those of the pastors of former dispensations. The high priests and the elders in each stake are organized into quorums as already described, the former without limitation as to number, the latter forming one or more quorums, each of ninety-six members. *Patriarchs* are also set apart to officiate in their office among the people of the stake.

A Ward Bishopric is established in every fully organized ward of the Church. This body consists of three high priests, one of whom is ordained as a bishop and set apart to preside over the ward, the other two being set apart as counselors to the bishop. The bishop has jurisdiction over the quorums of the Lesser Priesthood in his ward, and also over holders of the Higher Priesthood as members of his ward; but he has no direct presidency over quorums of the Melchizedek order, as such, which may be embraced within his domain. As a presiding high priest, he properly presides over his entire ward. The ward comprises quorums of priests, teachers, and deacons, one or more of each as the numerical extent of the ward may determine, and also auxiliary organizations as noted hereinafter.

---

aaa See D&C 107:24.
bbb See D&C 107:25, 26, 34, 93–97.
ccc See D&C 68:18–20.
ddd See D&C 107:82, 83.
eee See D&C 68:19.

Church Auxiliaries—Beside these constituted authorities and offices in the Priesthood, there are secondary organizations established for moral, educational, and benevolent purposes. These include the following:

Primary Associations providing for the moral instruction and training of young children.

Mutual Improvement Associations comprising separate organizations for the sexes, and designed for the education and training of the youth in subjects of practical interest. Instruction is provided in literature and history, dramatics and music, science and art, the laws of health, and numerous other branches of useful knowledge; and facilities are provided for recreational activities of wide and varied range.

Sunday Schools include graded classes for the study of the scriptures and for training in theology, in moral and religious duties, and in the discipline of the Church. Sunday schools, while primarily designed for the young, are open to all and include kindergarten and parents' classes with all intermediate gradations.

Church Schools provide for both secular and religious instruction, and range from the grade of the kindergarten to that of the college.

Religion Classes—In these is provided a course of graded instruction in theology and religion, which is offered as supplement and complement to the secular teachings of the nondenominational schools. Theological seminaries are maintained for students of high school and college grades.

Relief Societies—These are composed of women whose duties relate to the care of the poor and the relief of suffering amongst the afflicted.

Most of these auxiliary organizations function in each ward of the Church, as also in the missions throughout the world. Officers are appointed to preside in the several auxiliaries of the ward, and while they are under the general supervision of the ward bishopric they look to the Stake and General Boards of the respective organizations for detailed instruction as to the plans and methods of their particular work. In line with the principle of common consent, which characterizes the Church administration in general, officers of the auxiliary institutions, while nominated by or with the approval of the administrative officers of the Priesthood, are sustained in their places by the vote of the members in the local or general units within which they are appointed to serve.

REFERENCES

The Church Before the Birth of Christ—It is a significant fact that the word "church" does not appear in our English version of the Old Testament. From the time of Moses to the coming of Christ the people lived under the jurisdiction of the *Law,* between which and the *Gospel,* as embodied in the Church established by Jesus Christ, there is important distinction. Among the Nephites, however, who were sequestered on the western continent, the Church did exist as an organized body prior to the advent of the Lord Jesus Christ.

As many as were baptized did belong to the church of God—Mosiah 25:18; see also 26:28.

Persecution against those who did belong to the church of God—Alma 1:19.

By way of commandment unto you that belong to the church—Alma 5:62.

Alma had consecrated teachers and priests and elders over the church—Alma 4:7; Alma retained the office of high priest—verse 18; Alma was the high priest over the church of God—Alma 8:23.

The people of the church did have great joy—Helaman 6:3; the church did spread throughout the face of all the land—Helaman 11:21.

The Primitive Church on the Eastern Continent

Upon this rock I will build my church—Matt. 16:18.

And if he shall neglect to hear them, tell it unto the church—Matt. 18:17.

And the Lord added to the church daily—Acts 2:47.

There was great persecution against the church which was at Jerusalem—Acts 8:1.

Herod the king stretched forth his hands to vex certain of the church—Acts 12:1.

Elders had been ordained in every church—Acts 14:23.

Then pleased it the apostles and elders, with the whole church—Acts 15:22.

Paul sent to Ephesus, and called the elders of the church—Acts 20:17; he instructed them to feed the church of God—verse 28.

And so ordain I in all churches—1 Cor. 7:17.

God hath set some in the church, first apostles, etc.—1 Cor. 12:28.

Christ is the head of the church—Eph. 5:23; as the church is subject under Christ—verse 24; even as Christ also loved the church—verse 25.

Let the sick call for the elders of the church—James 5:14.

John to the seven churches which are in Asia—Rev. 1:4.

I Jesus have sent mine angel to testify unto you these things in the churches—Rev. 22:16.

The Church Regulated and Continued by Christ on the Western Continent

The sacrament to be administered to the church of Christ—3 Nephi 18:5.

Even so shall ye pray in my church—3 Nephi 18:16.

If the Gentiles will repent the church of Christ is to be established amongst them—3 Nephi 21:22.

The church to be known and called by the name of Jesus Christ—3 Nephi 27:1–8.

And the church did meet together oft to partake of bread and wine—Moroni 6:5; see also verses 2, 4, 7, 9.

The Church of Jesus Christ Established in the Current Dispensation

Hearken, O ye people of my church—D&C 1:1.

Authority given to lay the foundation of the church, and to bring it out of obscurity—D&C 1:30; it being the only true and living church upon the face of the whole earth—same verse.

In this, the beginning of the rising up and the coming forth of my church out of the wilderness—D&C 5:14.

If this generation harden not their hearts, I will establish my church among them—D&C 10:53. Whosoever belongeth to my church need not fear—verse 55. Whosoever repenteth and cometh unto me, the same is my church—verse 67; see also verses 68–70.

Concerning the foundation of my church, my gospel, and my rock—D&C 18:4, 5.

The church of Christ organized and established April 6, 1830—D&C 20:1.

Elders of the church, the first and the second—D&C 20:2, 3.

Concerning duties of the several officers in the church—D&C, secs. 20 and 84.

Revelation given at the organization of the church—D&C, sec. 21.

None who belong to the church are exempt from law—D&C 70:10.

Duty of the church to preach the gospel—D&C 84:76; how the ancient apostles built up the church—verse 108.

Name of the church revealed: The Church of Jesus Christ of Latter-day Saints—D&C 115:4.

The First Presidency to receive the oracles for the whole church—D&C 124:126.

12

SPIRITUAL GIFTS

ARTICLE 7

W E BELIEVE in the gift of tongues, prophecy, revelation, visions, healing, interpretation of tongues, etc.

Spiritual Gifts Characteristic of the Church—It has been already affirmed, that all men who would officiate with propriety in the ordinances of the Gospel must be commissioned for their exalted duties by the authority of heaven. When so invested, these servants of the Lord will not be lacking in proofs of their divine commission; for it is characteristic of the ways of God that He manifests His power by the bestowal of a variety of ennobling graces, which are properly called gifts of the Spirit. These are oftentimes exhibited in a manner so different from the usual order of things as to be called miraculous and supernatural. In this way did the Lord make Himself known in the early times of scriptural history; and from the days of Adam until the present, prophets of God have generally been endowed with such power. Whenever the power of Priesthood has operated through an organized Church on the earth, the members have been strengthened in their faith and otherwise blessed in numerous related ways, by the possession of these gifts. We may safely regard the existence of these spiritual powers as one of the essential characteristics of the Church; where they are not, the Priesthood of God does not operate.

Mormon[a] solemnly declared that the days of miracles will not pass from the Church, as long as there shall be a man upon the earth to be saved. "For," says he, "it is by faith that miracles are wrought; and it is by faith that angels appear and minister unto men; wherefore, if these things have ceased wo be unto the children of men, for it is because of unbelief, and all is vain." And Moroni, standing in expectation of early departure from the earth, bore an independent testimony, that the gifts and graces of the Spirit will never be done away as long as the world shall stand, except it be through the unbelief of mankind.[b]

Hear the words of this prophet addressed to those "who deny the revelations of God, and say that they are done away, that there are no revelations, nor prophecies, nor gifts, nor healing, nor speaking with tongues, and the interpretation of tongues; Behold I say unto you, he that denieth these things knoweth not the gospel of Christ; yea, he has not read the scriptures; if so, he does not understand them. For do we not read that God is the same yesterday, today, and forever, and in him there is no variableness neither shadow of changing? And now, if ye have imagined up unto yourselves a god who doth vary, and in whom there is shadow of changing, then have ye imagined up unto yourselves a god who is not a God of miracles. But behold, I will show unto you a God of miracles, even the God of Abraham, and the God of Isaac, and the God of Jacob; and it is that same God who created the heavens and the earth, and all things that in them are."[c]

Nature of Spiritual Gifts—The gifts here spoken of are essentially endowments of power and authority, through which the purposes of God are accomplished, sometimes with accompanying conditions that may appear to be supernatural. By such the sick are healed, malignant influences overcome, spirits of darkness subdued; the saints, humble and weak, proclaim their testimonies and otherwise utter praises unto God in new and strange tongues while others interpret their words; human intellect is invigorated by the heavenly touch of spiritual vision and dreams to see and comprehend things ordinarily withheld from mortal senses; direct communication with the fountain of all wisdom is established, and the revelations of the divine are obtained.

These gifts have been promised of the Lord unto those who believe in His name,[d] and are to follow obedience to the requirements of the Gospel. Among believers they are to serve for encouragement, and as incentives to higher communion with the Spirit.[e] They are not given as signs to gratify carnal curiosity; nor to satisfy a morbid craving for the spectacular. Men have been led to the light through manifestations of the miraculous; but events in the lives of these show that they are either such as would have found a knowledge of the truth in some other way, or they are but superficially affected, and as soon as the novelty of the new sensation has exhausted itself they wander again into the darkness from which they had for the time emerged. Miracles are not primarily intended, surely they are not needed, to prove the power of God; the simpler occurrences, the more ordinary works of creation do that. But unto the heart already softened and purified by the testimony of the truth, to the mind enlightened through the Spirit's power and conscious of obedient service in the requirements of the Gospel, the voice of miracles comes with cheering tidings, with fresh and more abundant evidences of the magnanimity of an all-merciful God.[f]

Yet even to the unbeliever the testimony of miracles should appeal, at least to the extent of argument for an investigation of the power through which they are wrought; and in such cases

[a] Moroni 7:35–37.
[b] Moroni 10:19, 23–27.
[c] Mormon 9:7–11.
[d] Mark 16:17, 18; D&C 84:64–73.
[e] Matt. 12:38, 39; 16:1–4; Mark 8:11, 12; Luke 11:16–30.
[f] See Appendix 12:6; also *Jesus the Christ*, p. 147.

miracles are as "a loud voice addressed to those who are hard of hearing." The purpose of spiritual gifts in the Church is explicitly set forth in a revelation from the Lord through Joseph Smith: "Wherefore, beware lest ye are deceived; and that ye may not be deceived seek ye earnestly the best gifts, always remembering for what they are given; For verily I say unto you, they are given for the benefit of those who love me and keep all my commandments, and him that seeketh so to do; that all may be benefited that seek or that ask of me, that ask and not for a sign that they may consume it upon their lusts."[g]

Miracles are commonly regarded as occurrences in opposition to the laws of nature. Such a conception is plainly erroneous, for the laws of nature are inviolable. However, as human understanding of these laws is at best but imperfect, events strictly in accordance with natural law may appear contrary thereto. The entire constitution of nature is founded on system and order; the laws of nature, however, are graded as are the laws of man. The operation of a higher law in any particular case does not destroy the actuality of an inferior one. For example, society has enacted a law forbidding any man appropriating the property of another; yet oftentimes officers of the law forcibly seize the possessions of their fellowmen against whom judgments may have been rendered; and such acts are done to satisfy, not to violate justice. Jehovah commanded, "Thou shalt not kill," and mankind has reenacted the law, prescribing penalties for violation thereof. Yet sacred history testifies, that, in certain cases, the Lawgiver Himself has directly commanded that justice be vindicated by the taking of human life. The judge who passes the extreme sentence upon a convicted murderer, and the executioner who carries the mandate into effect act not in opposition to "Thou shalt not kill" but actually in support of this decree.

With some of the principles upon which the powers of nature operate we are in a degree acquainted; and in contemplating them we are no longer surprised, though deeper reflection may show that even the commonest phenomena are but little understood. But any event beyond the ordinary is regarded by the less thoughtful as miraculous, supernatural, if not indeed unnatural.[h] When the prophet Elisha caused the ax to float in the river,[i] he brought to his service a power superior to that of gravity. Without doubt the iron was heavier than the water; yet by the operation of this higher force it was supported, suspended, or otherwise sustained at the surface, as if it were held there by a human hand or rendered sufficiently buoyant by attached floaters.

Wine ordinarily consists of about four-fifths water, the rest being a variety of chemical compounds the elements of which are abundantly present in the air and soil. The ordinary method—what we term the natural method—of bringing these elements into proper combination is by planting the grape, then cultivating the vine till the fruit is ready to yield its juices in the press. But by a power not within purely human reach, Jesus Christ at the marriage in Cana[j] brought those elements together, and effected a chemical transmutation within the waterpots resulting in the production of wine. So, too, when the multitudes were fed, under His priestly touch and authoritative blessing the bread and fish substance increased as if months had been covered by their growth according to what we consider the natural order. In the healing of the leprous, the palsied, and the infirm, the disordered bodily parts were brought again into their normal and healthful state, the impurities operating as poisons in the tissues were removed by means more rapid and effectual than those which depend upon the action of medicine.

[g] D&C 46:8, 9.
[h] See Appendix 12:1.
[i] 2 Kings 6:5–7.
[j] John 2:1–11; see "Miracles" in *Jesus the Christ,* pp. 147, 151.

No earnest observer, no reasoning mind, can doubt the existence of intelligences and organisms that the unaided senses of man do not reveal. This world is the temporal embodiment of things spiritual. The Creator has told us that He formed all things spiritual before they were made temporal.[k] The flowers that flourish and die on earth are perhaps represented beyond by imperishable blossoms of beauty and fragrance. Man is shaped after the image of Deity; his mind, though darkened by custom and weakened by injurious habit, is still a fallen type of immortal thought; and though the space separating the human and the divine in thought, desire, and action, be as wide as that between sea and sky, for as the stars are above the earth so are the ways of God above those of man, yet we may affirm an analogy between the spiritual and the temporal. When the eyes of Elisha's servant were opened, the man saw the hosts of heavenly warriors covering the mountains about Dothan—footmen, horsemen, and chariots, armed for fight against the Syrians.[l] May we not believe that when Israel encompassed Jericho,[m] the captain of the Lord's host[n] and his heavenly train were there, and that before their supermortal agency, sustained by the faith and obedience of the human army, the walls were leveled?

Some of the latest and highest achievements of man in the utilization of natural forces approach the conditions of spiritual operations. To count the ticking of a watch thousands of miles away; to speak in but an ordinary tone and be heard across the continent; to signal from one hemisphere and be understood on the other though oceans roll and roar between; to bring the lightning into our homes and make it serve as fire and torch; to navigate the air and to travel beneath the ocean surface; to make chemical and atomic energies obey our will—are not these miracles? The possibility of such would not have been received with credence before their actual accomplishment. Nevertheless, these and all other miracles are accomplished through the operation of the laws of nature, which are the laws of God.

An Enumeration of the Gifts of the Spirit cannot be made complete by man; yet the more common of these spiritual manifestations have been specified by inspired writers, and by the word of revelation. Paul writing to the Corinthian saints,[o] Moroni inditing his last appeal to the Lamanites,[p] and the voice of the Lord directed to the people of His Church in this dispensation,[q] each names many of the specific gifts of the Spirit. From these scriptures we learn that every man has received some gift from God; and in the great diversity of gifts all do not receive the same. "To some it is given by the Holy Ghost to know the differences of administration * * * And again, it is given by the Holy Ghost to some to know the diversities of operations, whether they be of God, that the manifestations of the Spirit may be given to every man to profit withal. And again, verily I say unto you, to some is given, by the Spirit of God, the word of wisdom. To another is given the word of knowledge, that all may be taught to be wise and to have knowledge. And again, to some it is given to have faith to be healed; And to others it is given to have faith to heal. And again, to some is given the working of miracles; And to others it is given to prophesy; And to others the discerning of spirits. And again, it is given to some to speak with tongues; And to another is given the interpretation of tongues. And all these gifts come from God, for the benefit of the children of God."[r]

[k] See Appendix 10:3.
[l] 2 Kings 6:13–18.
[m] Josh., chap. 6.
[n] Josh. 5:13, 14.
[o] 1 Cor. 12:4–11.
[p] Moroni 10:7–19.
[q] D&C 46:8–29.
[r] D&C 46:11–26; see also 1 Cor. 12:4–11.

The Gift of Tongues and Interpretation—The gift of tongues constituted one of the first miraculous manifestations of the Holy Ghost unto the apostles of old. It was included by the Savior among the special signs appointed to follow the believer: "In my name," said He, "they shall speak with new tongues."[s] The early fulfilment of this promise in the case of the apostles themselves was realized at the succeeding Pentecost, when they were filled with the Holy Ghost and began to speak in strange tongues.[t] When the door of the Gospel was first opened to the Gentiles, the converts rejoiced in the Holy Ghost which had fallen upon them and which gave them utterance in tongues.[u] This gift with others manifested itself among certain disciples at Ephesus[v] on the occasion of their receiving the Holy Ghost. In the present dispensation, this gift, again promised to the saints, is not infrequently manifest. Its chief employment is in the function of praise rather than that of instruction and preaching; and this is agreeable to Paul's teaching: "For he that speaketh in an unknown tongue speaketh not unto men but unto God."[w] An unusual manifestation of the gift was witnessed on the occasion of the Pentecostal conversion of the Jews, already referred to, when the apostles addressing the multitude were understood by all the diversified company, each listener hearing in his own tongue.[x] This special gift was here associated with higher endowments of power; the occasion was one of instruction, admonition, and prophecy. The gift of interpretation may be possessed by the one speaking in tongues, though more commonly the separate powers are manifested by different persons.

The Gift of Healing was exercised extensively in the times of the Savior and the apostles; indeed, healing constituted by far the greater part of the recorded miracles wrought in that period. By authoritative ministrations the eyes of the blind were opened, the dumb were made to speak, the deaf to hear, the lame to leap for joy; afflicted mortals, bowed with infirmity, were lifted erect and enjoyed the vigor of youth; the palsied were made well; lepers were cleansed, impotence was banished, and fevers were assuaged. In the present day, the dispensation of the fulness of times, this power is possessed in the Church and its manifestation is of frequent occurrence among the Latter-day Saints. Thousands of recipients can testify to the fulfilment of the Lord's promise, that if His servants lay hands on the sick they shall recover.[y]

The usual method of administering to the afflicted is by the imposition of hands of those who possess the requisite authority of the Priesthood, this being agreeable to the Savior's instructions in former days[z] and according to divine revelation in the present day.[aa] This part of the ordinance is usually preceded by an anointing with oil previously consecrated. The Latter-day Saints profess to abide by the counsel of James of old:[bb] "Is any sick among you? Let him call for the elders of the church; and let them pray over him, anointing him with oil in the name of the Lord: And the prayer of faith shall save the sick, and the Lord shall raise him up; and if he have committed sins, they shall be forgiven him."

[s] Mark 16:17.
[t] Acts 2:4.
[u] Acts 10:46.
[v] Acts 19:6.
[w] 1 Cor. 14:2.
[x] Acts 2:6–12.
[y] Mark 16:18; see also D&C 84:68.
[z] The same; see also James 5:14, 15.
[aa] D&C 42:43–44.
[bb] James 5:14, 15.

Though the authority to administer to the sick belongs to the elders of the Church in general, some possess this power in an unusual degree, having received it as an especial endowment of the Spirit. Another gift, allied to this, is that of having faith to be healed,[cc] which is manifested in varying degrees. Not always are the administrations of the elders followed by immediate healings; the afflicted may be permitted to suffer in body, perhaps for the accomplishment of good purposes,[dd] and in the time appointed all must experience bodily death. But let the counsels of God be observed in administering to the afflicted; then if they recover, they live unto the Lord; and the assuring promise is added that those who die under such conditions die unto the Lord.[ee]

Visions and Dreams have constituted a means of communication between God and men in every dispensation of the Priesthood. In general, visions are manifested to the waking senses whilst dreams are given during sleep. In the vision, however, the senses may be so affected as to render the person practically unconscious, at least oblivious to ordinary occurrences, while he is able to discern the heavenly manifestation. In the earlier dispensations, the Lord frequently communicated through dreams and visions, oftentimes revealing to prophets the events of the future even to the latest generations. Consider the case of Enoch,[ff] unto whom the Lord spoke face to face, showing him the course of the human family unto and beyond the second coming of the Savior. The brother of Jared[gg] because of his righteousness was so blessed of God as to be shown all the inhabitants of the earth, both those who had previously existed and those who were to follow. Unto Moses the will of God was made known with the visual manifestation of fire.[hh] Lehi received through dreams his instructions to leave Jerusalem;[ii] and on many subsequent occasions the Lord communicated with this patriarch of the western world by dreams and visions. The Old Testament prophets were generally so favored; e.g., Jacob the father of all Israel,[jj] Job the patient sufferer,[kk] Jeremiah,[ll] Ezekiel,[mm] Daniel,[nn] Habakkuk,[oo] Zechariah.[pp]

The dispensation of Christ and the apostles was marked by similar manifestations. The birth of John the Baptist was foretold to his father while officiating in priestly functions.[qq] Joseph, betrothed to the Virgin, received through an angel's visit[rr] tidings of the Christ yet to be born; and on subsequent occasions he received warnings and instructions in dreams concerning the welfare of the Holy Child.[ss] The wise men from the East, returning from their pilgrimage of worship, were warned in dreams of Herod's treacherous designs.[tt] Saul of Tarsus was shown in a vision the messenger whom

---

[cc] D&C 46:19; 42:48-51; see also Acts 14:9; Matt. 8:10; 9:28, 29.

[dd] See instances of Job.

[ee] D&C 42:44–46.

[ff] P. of G.P., Moses 6:27–39.

[gg] Ether, chap. 3.

[hh] Ex. 3:2.

[ii] 1 Nephi 2:2–4.

[jj] Gen. 46:2.

[kk] Job 4:12–21.

[ll] Jer. 1:11–16.

[mm] Ezek. 1:1; 2:9, 10; 3:22, 23; 37:1–10, etc.

[nn] Dan., chaps. 7, 8.

[oo] Hab. 2:2, 3.

[pp] Zech. 1:8–11, 18–21; 2:1, 2; chaps.4, 5; 6:1–8.

[qq] Luke 1:5–22.

[rr] Matt. 1:20.

[ss] Matt. 2:13, 19, 22.

[tt] Matt. 2:12.

God was about to send to him to minister in the ordinances of the Priesthood;[uu] and other visions followed.[vv] Peter was prepared for the ministry to the Gentiles through a vision;[ww] and John was so favored of God in this respect that the book of Revelation is occupied by the record.

Most of the visions and dreams recorded in scripture have been given through the ministering Priesthood; but there are exceptional instances of such manifestations unto some, who, at the time, had not entered the fold. Such, for example, was the case with Saul and Cornelius; but in these instances the divine manifestations were immediately preliminary to conversion. Dreams with special import were given to Pharaoh,[xx] Nebuchadnezzar,[yy] and others; but it required a higher power than their own to interpret them, and Joseph and Daniel were called to officiate. The dream given to the Midianite soldier, and its interpretation by his fellow,[zz] betokening the victory of Gideon, were true manifestations, as also the dream of Pilate's wife[aaa] in which she learned of the innocence of the accused Christ.

The Gift of Prophecy distinguishes its possessor as a prophet—literally, one who speaks for another, specifically, one who speaks for God.[bbb] It is distinguished by Paul as one of the most desirable of spiritual endowments, and its preeminence over the gift of tongues he discusses at length.[ccc] To prophesy is to receive and declare the word of God, and the statement of His will to the people. The function of prediction, often regarded as the sole essential of prophecy, is but one among many characteristics of this divinely given power. The prophet may have as much concern with the past as with the present or the future; he may use his gift in teaching through the experience of preceding events as in foretelling occurrences. The prophets of God are entrusted with His confidences, being privileged to learn of His will and designs. The statement appears that the Lord will do nothing except He reveal His secret purposes unto His servants, the prophets.[ddd] These oracles stand as mediators between God and mortals, pleading for or against the people.[eee]

No special ordination in the Priesthood is essential to man's receiving the gift of prophecy; bearers of the Melchizedek Priesthood, Adam, Noah, Moses, and a multitude of others were prophets, but not more truly so than others who were specifically called to the Aaronic order, as exemplified in the instance of John the Baptist.[fff] The ministrations of Miriam[ggg] and Deborah[hhh] show that this gift may be possessed by women also. In the time of Samuel the prophets were organized into a special order, to aid their purposes of study and improvement.[iii]

In the current dispensation this gift is enjoyed in a fulness equal to that of any preceding time. The Lord's will concerning present duties is made known through the mouths of prophets, and events of great import have been foretold.[jjj] The fact of the present existence and vitality of the

---

[uu] Acts 9:12.
[vv] Acts 16:9; 18:9, 10; 22:17–21.
[ww] Acts 10:10–16; 11:5–10.
[xx] Gen., chap. 41; see other instances in Gen., chap. 40.
[yy] Dan., chap. 2.
[zz] Judges 7:13, 14.
[aaa] Matt. 27:19.
[bbb] See Appendix 12:2.
[ccc] 1 Cor. 14:1–9.
[ddd] Amos 3:7.
[eee] 1 Kings 18:36, 37; Rom. 11:2, 3; James 5:16-18; Rev. 11:6.
[fff] Matt. 11:8–10.
[ggg] Ex. 15:20.
[hhh] Judges 4:4.
[iii] See Appendix 12:3.
[jjj] See D&C 1:4; sec. 87.

Church is an undeniable testimony of the actuality of latter-day prophecy. The Church today constitutes a body of witnesses, numbering hundreds of thousands, to the effect of this, one of the great gifts of God.

Revelation is the communication or disclosure of the will of God directly to man. Under circumstances best suiting the divine purposes, through the dreams of sleep or in waking visions of the mind, by voices without visional appearance or by actual manifestations of the Holy Presence before the eye, God makes known His designs, and instructs His revelators. Under the influence of inspiration, or its more potent manifestation, revelation, man's mind is enlightened and his energies are quickened to the accomplishment of wonders in the work of human progress; touched with a spark from the heavenly altar, the revelator preserves the sacred fire within his soul and imparts it to others as he may be instructed to do; he is the channel through which the will of God is conveyed. The words of him who speaks by revelation in its highest degree are not his own; they are the words of God Himself; the mortal mouthpiece is but the trusted conveyer of these heavenly messages. With the authoritative "Thus saith the Lord," the revelator delivers the burden committed to his care.

The Lord observes the principle of order and fitness in giving revelation to His servants. Though it is the privilege of any person to live so as to merit this gift in the affairs of his special calling, only those appointed and ordained to the offices of presidency are to be revelators to the people at large. Concerning the President of the Church, who at the time of the revelation here referred to was the Prophet Joseph Smith, the Lord has said to the elders of the Church: "And this ye shall know assuredly, that there is none other appointed unto you to receive commandments and revelations until he be taken, if he abide in me. * * * And this shall be a law unto you, that ye receive not the teachings of any that shall come before you as revelations or commandments; And this I give unto you that you may not be deceived, that you may know they are not of me."[kkk]

The Testimony of Miracles—The Savior's promise in a former day[lll] as in the present dispensation[mmm] is definite, to the effect that specified gifts of the Spirit are to follow the believer as signs of divine acknowledgment. The possession of such gifts may be taken therefore as essential features of the Church of Jesus Christ.[nnn] Nevertheless, we are not justified in regarding the evidence of miracles as proof of authority from heaven; on the other hand, the scriptures aver that spiritual powers of the baser sort have wrought miracles, and will continue so to do, to the deceiving of many who lack discernment. If miracles be accepted as infallible evidence of godly power, the magicians of Egypt, through the wonders which they accomplished in opposition to the ordained plan for Israel's deliverance, have as good a claim to our respect as has Moses.[ooo] John the Revelator saw in vision a wicked power working miracles, and thereby deceiving many, doing great wonders, even bringing fire from heaven.[ppp] Again, he saw unclean spirits, whom he knew to be "the spirits of devils, working miracles."[qqq]

Consider in connection with this the prediction made by the Lord: "There shall arise false Christs, and false prophets, and shall shew great signs and wonders; insomuch that, if it were

---

kkk D&C 43:3, 5, 6.
lll Mark 16:17, 18.
mmm D&C 84:65–73.
nnn See Appendix 12:4, 5.
ooo Ex. chaps. 7–11.
ppp Rev. 13:11–18.
qqq Rev. 16:13, 14.

possible, they shall deceive the very elect."[rrr] The invalidity of miracles as proof of divinely appointed ministry is declared in an utterance of Jesus Christ regarding the events of the great judgment: "Many will say to me in that day, Lord, Lord, have we not prophesied in thy name? and in thy name have cast out devils? and in thy name done many wonderful works? And then will I profess unto them, I never knew you: depart from me, ye that work iniquity."[sss] The Jews to whom these teachings were addressed knew that wonders could be wrought by evil powers, for they charged Christ with working miracles by the authority of Beelzebub the prince of devils.[ttt]

If the working of miracles were exclusively a characteristic of the Holy Priesthood, we would look for the testimony of wondrous manifestations in connection with the work of every prophet and authorized minister of the Lord; yet we fail to find record of miracles in the case of Zechariah, Malachi, and certain other prophets; while of John the Baptist, whom Christ declared to be more than a prophet,[uuu] it was plainly said that he did no miracle;[vvv] nevertheless, in rejecting John's doctrine the unbelievers were ignoring the counsel of God against their own souls.[www] To be valid as a testimony of truth, miracles must be wrought in the name of Jesus Christ, and to His honor in furtherance of the plan of salvation. As stated, they are not given to satisfy the curious and the lustful, nor as a means of gaining notoriety for him through whom they are accomplished. These gifts of the true Spirit are manifested in support of the message from heaven, in corroboration of the words spoken by authority, and to the blessing of individuals.

Imitations of Spiritual Gifts—The instances already cited of miraculous achievements by powers other than of God, and the scriptural predictions concerning such deceptive manifestations in the last days, ought to be an effective warning against spurious imitations of the Holy Spirit. Satan has shown himself to be an accomplished strategist and a skilful imitator; the most deplorable of his victories are due to his simulation of good, whereby the undiscerning have been led captive. Let no one be deluded with the thought that any act, the immediate result of which appears to be benign, is necessarily productive of permanent good. It may serve the dark purposes of Satan to play upon the human sense of goodness, even to the extent of healing the body and apparently of thwarting death.

The restoration of the Priesthood to earth in this age of the world was followed by a phenomenal growth of the vagaries of spiritualism, whereby many were led to put their trust in Satan's counterfeit of God's eternal power. The development of the healing gift in the Church today is imitated in a degree comparable to that with which the magicians simulated the miracles of Moses, by the varied faith cures and their numerous modifications. For those to whom miraculous signs are all-sufficient, the imitation will answer as well as would the real; but the soul who regards the miracle in its true nature as but one element of the system of Christ, possessing value as a positive criterion only as it is associated with the numerous other characteristics of the Church, will not be deceived.

Spiritual Gifts in the Church Today—The Latter-day Saints claim to possess within the Church all the sign-gifts promised as the heritage of the believer. They point to the unimpeached testimonies of thousands who have been blessed with direct and personal manifestations of

[rrr] Matt. 24:24.
[sss] Matt. 7:22, 23.
[ttt] Matt. 12:22–30; Mark 3:22; Luke 11:15; see *Jesus the Christ,* p. 265.
[uuu] Matt. 11:9.
[vvv] John 10:41.
[www] Luke 7:30.

heavenly power; to the once blind, deaf, dumb, halt, and weak in body, who have been freed from their infirmities through their faith and by the ministrations of the Holy Priesthood; to a multitude who have voiced their testimony in tongues with which they were naturally unfamiliar, or who have demonstrated their possession of the gift by a phenomenal mastery of foreign languages when such was necessary to the discharge of their duties as preachers of the word of God; to many who have enjoyed personal communion with heavenly beings; to others who have prophesied in words that have found speedy vindication in literal fulfilment; and to the Church itself, whose growth has been guided by the voice of God, made known through the gift of revelation.[xxx]

REFERENCES

Spiritual Gifts Characteristic of the Church of Christ

And these signs shall follow them that believe; In my name shall they cast out devils, etc.—Mark 16:16–18.

The Lord's promise: He that believeth on me, the works that I do shall he do also; and greater works than these shall he do—John 14:12.

Now concerning spiritual gifts—1 Cor. 12:1–11, 27–31; see also 14:1, 12.

The apostles spoke with other tongues as the Spirit gave them utterance—Acts 2:4–8; see also verses 9–18.

For they heard them speak with tongues, and magnify God—Acts 10:46.

And when Paul had laid his hands upon them, the Holy Ghost came on them; and they spake with tongues, and prophesied—Acts 19:6.

To another the working of miracles; to another prophecy; to another discerning of spirits; to another divers kinds of tongues; to another the interpretation of tongues—1 Cor. 12:10; see also verses 28, 30 and 13:1; 14:2–28.

Citation of prophecy by Joel respecting the gifts of prophecy, visions and dreams—Acts 2:16, 17; see also Joel 2:28, 29.

Excellence of the gift of prophecy—1 Cor. 14:1-5, 24–39.

The gift of vision and revelation, manifested to Saul, afterward known as Paul the apostle—Acts, chap. 9.

Then spake the Lord to Paul in the night by a vision—Acts 18:9. And the night following the Lord stood by him, and said: Be of good cheer, Paul—Acts 23:11; see also Acts 27:23, 24.

Communication of the Lord's will to Peter while in vision—Acts 10:10, 17; see also 11:5.

The Revelation of Jesus Christ unto his servant John—Rev. 1:1.

They shall lay hands on the sick, and they shall recover—Mark 16:18.

In the name of Jesus Christ of Nazareth rise up and walk—Acts 3:6.

Saul recovered his sight through the administration of Ananias—Acts 9:17, 18.

Healings through the instrumentality of Paul—Acts 14:9–11; 28:8.

Is there any sick among you? Let him call for the elders of the church; and let them pray over him, anointing him with oil in the name of the Lord—James 5:14, 15.

Christ gave unto his twelve disciples power against unclean spirits, to cast them out, and to heal all manner of sickness and all manner of disease—Matt. 10:1.

Healing of the repentant Zeezrom through Alma—Alma 15:6-12.

[xxx] See Appendix 12:7.

The sick healed and evil spirits cast out among the repentant Nephites—3 Nephi 7:22.

Nephite sick and afflicted were brought to the resurrected Christ and were healed—3 Nephi 17:9, 10.

The resurrected Christ ascended after having wrought many miracles of healing and having raised a man from the dead—3 Nephi 26:15.

Timothy raised from the dead by his brother Nephi—3 Nephi 19:4.

The ordinance of healing at the request of the afflicted—D&C 24:13, 14.

Manner of administering the healing ordinance—D&C 42:44.

Faith requisite to the manifestation of the healing power—D&C 42:48.

The gift to have faith to be healed, and that of having faith to heal—D&C 46:19, 20: an enumeration of other spiritual gifts appears in verses 8–18 and 21–31.

That ye may not be deceived seek ye earnestly the best gifts—D&C 46:8.

The Lord has promised unto his servants in the current dispensation that in his name they shall do many wonderful works—D&C 84:64–73.

There are many gifts, and to every man is given a gift by the Spirit of God—D&C 46:11.

That unto some it may be given to have all those gifts, that there may be a head—D&C 46:29.

Abundance multiplied through the manifestations of the Spirit—D&C 70:13.

The Spirit giveth light to every man that cometh into the world—D&C 84:46.

Through the Spirit your whole bodies shall be filled with light—D&C 88:66, 67.

If not equal in temporal things the abundance of the manifestations of the Spirit shall be withheld—D&C 70:14.

All spiritual administrations to be done in the name of Christ—D&C 46:31.

Man cannot see God except as quickened by the Spirit of God—D&C 67:11.

Unto as many as received me gave I power to do many miracles—D&C 45:8.

Working of miracles a gift of God—D&C 46:21.

God has not ceased to be a God of miracles—Mormon 9:15.

Prediction of a day when it should be said that miracles are done away—Mormon 8:26.

The Lord affirms that he will show miracles, signs, and wonders—D&C 35:8.

13

THE HOLY BIBLE

ARTICLE 8

E BELIEVE the Bible to be the word of God as far as it is translated correctly. * * *

Our Acceptance of the Bible—The Church of Jesus Christ of Latter-day Saints accepts the Holy Bible as the foremost of her standard works, first among the books which have been proclaimed as her written guides in faith and doctrine. In the respect and sanctity with which the Latter-day Saints regard the Bible they are of like profession with Christian denominations in general, but differ from them in the additional acknowledgment of certain other scriptures as authentic and holy, which others are in harmony with the Bible, and serve to support and emphasize its facts and doctrines.

The historical and other data upon which is based the current Christian faith as to the genuineness of the Biblical record are accepted as unreservedly by the Latter-day Saints as by the members of any sect; and in literalness of interpretation this Church probably excels.

Nevertheless, the Church announces a reservation in the case of erroneous translation, which may occur as a result of human incapacity; and even in this measure of caution we are not alone, for Biblical scholars generally admit the presence of errors of the kind—both of translation and of transcription of the text. The

Latter-day Saints believe the original records to be the word of God unto man, and, as far as these records have been translated correctly, the translations are regarded as equally authentic. The English Bible professes to be a translation made through the wisdom of man; in its preparation the most scholarly men have been enlisted, yet not a version has been published in which errors are not admitted. However, an impartial investigator has cause to wonder more at the paucity of errors than that mistakes are to be found at all.

There will be, there can be, no absolutely reliable translation of these or other scriptures unless it be effected through the gift of translation, as one of the endowments of the Holy Ghost. The translator must have the spirit of the prophet if he would render in another tongue the prophet's words; and human wisdom alone leads not to that possession. Let the Bible then be read reverently and with prayerful care, the reader ever seeking the light of the Spirit that he may discern between truth and the errors of men.

The Name "Bible"—In present usage, the term *Holy Bible* designates the collection of sacred writings otherwise known as the Hebrew Scriptures, containing an account of the dealings of God with the human family; which account is confined wholly, except in the record of antediluvian events, to the eastern hemisphere. The word *Bible,* though singular in form, is the English representative of a Greek plural, *Biblia,* signifying literally *books.* The use of the word probably dates from the fourth century, at which time we find Chrysostom[a] employing the term to designate the scriptural books then accepted as canonical by the Greek Christians. It is to be noted that the idea of a collection of books predominates in all early usages of the word *Bible*; the scriptures were, as they are, composed of the special writings of many authors, widely separated in time; and, from the harmony and unity prevailing throughout these diverse productions, strong evidence of their authenticity may be adduced.

The word *Biblia* was thus endowed with a special meaning in the Greek, signifying the holy books as distinguishing sacred scriptures from other writings; and the term soon became current in the Latin, in which tongue it was used from the first in its special sense. Through Latin usage, perhaps during the thirteenth century, the word came to be regarded as a singular noun signifying *the book,* this departure from the plural meaning, invariably associated with the term in the Greek original, tends to obscure the facts. It may appear that the derivation of a word is of small importance; yet in this case the original form and first use of the title now current as that of the sacred volume must be of instructive interest, as throwing some light upon the compilation of the book in its present form.

It is evident that the name *Bible,* with its current signification, cannot be of itself a Biblical term; its use as a designation of the Hebrew scriptures is wholly external to those scriptures themselves. In its earliest application, which dates from post-apostolic times, it was made to embrace most if not all the books of the Old and the New Testament. Prior to the time of Christ, the books of the Old Testament were known by no single collective name, but were designated in groups as (1) the Pentateuch, or five books of the Law; (2) the Prophets; and (3) the Hagiographa, comprising all sacred records not included in the other divisions. But we may the better consider the parts of the Bible by taking the main divisions separately. A very natural division of the Biblical record is effected by the earthly ministry of Jesus Christ; the written productions of pre-Christian times came to be known as the Old Covenant; those of the days of the Savior and the years immediately following, as the New Covenant.[b] The term *Testament* gradually grew in favor until the designations *Old* and *New Testaments* became common.

a See Appendix 13:1.
b See 1 Cor. 11:25; compare Jer. 31:31–33.

THE OLD TESTAMENT

Its Origin and Growth—At the time of our Lord's ministry in the flesh, the Jews were in possession of certain scriptures regarded by them as canonical or authoritative. There can be little doubt as to the authenticity of those works, for they were frequently quoted by both Christ and the apostles, by whom they were designated as "the scriptures."[c] The Savior specifically refers to them under their accepted terms of classification as the law of Moses, the prophets, and the psalms.[d] The books thus accepted by the people in the time of Christ are sometimes spoken of as the Jewish Canon of Scripture. The term *canon,* now generally current, suggests not books that are merely credible, authentic or even inspired, but such books as are recognized as authoritative guides in profession and practise. The term is instructive in its derivation. Its Greek original, *kanon,* signified a straight measuring rod, and hence it came to mean a standard of comparison, a rule, a test, as applied to moral subjects as well as to material objects.

As to the formation of the Jewish Canon, or the Old Testament, we read that Moses wrote the first part of it, viz., the Law; and that he committed it to the care of the priests, or Levites, with a command that they preserve it in the ark of the covenant,[e] to be a witness against Israel in their transgressions. Foreseeing that a king would some day govern Israel, Moses commanded that the monarch should make a copy of the Law for his guidance.[f] Joshua, who succeeded Moses in some of the functions pertaining to leadership in Israel, wrote further of the dealings of God with the people and of the divine precepts; and this writing he evidently appended to the Law as recorded by Moses.[g] Three centuries and a half after the time of Moses, when the theocracy had been replaced by a monarchy, Samuel, the approved prophet of the Lord, wrote of the change "in a book, and laid it up before the Lord."[h] Thus the law of Moses was augmented by later authoritative records. From the writings of Isaiah we learn that the people had access to the Book of the Lord; for the prophet admonished them to seek it out, and read it.[i] It is evident, then, that in the time of Isaiah the people had a written authority in doctrine and practise.

Nearly four centuries later, 640–630 B.C., while the righteous King Josiah occupied the throne of Judah as a part of divided Israel, Hilkiah, the high priest and father of the prophet Jeremiah, found in the Temple "a book of the law of the Lord,"[j] which was read before the kings.[k] Then, during the fifth century B.C., in the days of Ezra, the edict of Cyrus permitted the captive people of Judah, a remnant of once united Israel, to return to Jerusalem,[l] there to rebuild the Temple of the Lord, according to the law[m] of God then in the hand of Ezra. From this we may infer that the written law was then known; and to Ezra is usually attributed the credit of compiling the books of the Old Testament as far as completed in his day, to which he added his own writings.[n] In this work of compilation he was probably assisted by Nehemiah and the members of the Great Synagogue—a Jewish college of a hundred and twenty scholars.[o] The book of

[c] John 5:39; Acts 17:11.
[d] See Luke 24:44.
[e] See Deut. 31:9, 24–26.
[f] See Deut. 17:18.
[g] See Joshua 24:26.
[h] 1 Sam. 10:25.
[i] See Isa. 34:16.
[j] 2 Chr. 34:14, 15; see also Deut. 31:26.
[k] See 2 Kings 22:8–10.
[l] See Ezra 1:1–3.
[m] See Ezra 7:12–14.
[n] See The Book of Ezra.
[o] This historical information is given in certain of the apocryphal books; see 2 Esdras.

Nehemiah, which gives a continuation of the historical annals recorded by Ezra, is supposed to have been written by the prophet whose name it bears, in part at least during the life of Ezra. Then, a century later, Malachi,[p] the last of the prophets of note who flourished before the opening of the dispensation of Christ, added his record, completing and virtually closing the pre-Christian canon, with a prophetic promise of the Messiah and of the messenger whose commission would be to prepare the way of the Lord, particularly as to the last days, now current.

Thus, it is evident that the Old Testament grew with the successive writings of authorized and inspired scribes from Moses to Malachi, and that its compilation was a natural and gradual process, each addition being deposited, or, as the sacred record gives it, "laid up before the Lord" in connection with the previous writings. Undoubtedly there were known to the Jews many other books not included in our present Old Testament; references to such are abundant in the scriptures themselves, which references prove that many of those extra-canonical records were regarded as of considerable authority. But concerning this we will inquire further in connection with the Apocrypha. The recognized canonicity of the Old Testament books is attested by the numerous references in the later to the earlier books, and by the many quotations from the Old Testament occurring in the New. About two hundred and thirty quotations or direct references have been listed, and in addition to these, hundreds of less direct allusions occur.

Language of the Old Testament—Nearly all the books of the Old Testament were originally written in Hebrew. Scholars profess to have found evidence that small portions of the books of Ezra and Daniel were written in the Chaldee language; but the prevalence of Hebrew as the language of the original scriptures has given to the Old Testament the common appellation, Hebrew or Jewish Canon. Of the Pentateuch, two versions have been recognized—the Hebrew proper and the Samaritan,[q] the latter of which was preserved in the most ancient of Hebrew characters by the Samaritans, between whom and the Jews there was enmity.

The Septuagint and the Peshito—We recognize first the important translation of the Hebrew canon known as the *Septuagint.*[r] This was a Greek version of the Old Testament, translated from the Hebrew at the instance of an Egyptian monarch, probably Ptolemy Philadelphus, about 286 B.C. The name *Septuagint* connotes the number seventy, and is said to have been given because the translation was made by a body of seventy-two elders, in round numbers seventy; or, as other traditions indicate, because the work was accomplished in seventy, or seventy-two days; or, according to yet other stories, because the version received the sanction of the Jewish ecclesiastical council, the Sanhedrin, which comprised seventy-two members. Certain it is that the Septuagint, sometimes indicated by the Roman numerals LXX, was the current version among the Jews in the days of Christ's earthly ministry, and was quoted by the Savior and the apostles in their references to the old canon. It is regarded as the most authentic of the ancient versions, and is accepted at the present time by the Greek Catholics and other eastern churches. It is evident, then, that from a time nearly three hundred years before Christ, the Old Testament has been current in both Hebrew and Greek; and this duplication has been an effective means of protection against alterations.

Another compilation, the *Peshito,* was made, according to tradition, at an early but undetermined date and is referred to as "the oldest Syriac version of the Bible." It contains the canonical books of the Old Testament and many New Testament books, omitting, however, 2 Peter, 2 and 3 John, Jude and Revelation. The Peshito is regarded by scholars as of great critical value.

p Mal., chaps. 3, 4.
q See Appendix 13:2.
r See Appendix 13:3.

The Present Compilation recognizes thirty-nine books in the Old Testament; these were originally combined as twenty-two books, corresponding to the letters in the Hebrew alphabet. The thirty-nine books as at present constituted may be conveniently classified as follows:

The Pentateuch or Books of the Law   5
The Historical Books   12
The Poetical Books   5
The Books Of the Prophets   17

The Books of the Law—The first five books in the Bible are collectively designated as the *Pentateuch* (*pente*—five, *teuchos*—volume) and were known among the early Jews as the *Torah,* or the law. Their authorship is traditionally ascribed to Moses,[s] and in consequence the "Five Books of Moses" is another commonly used designation. They give the history, brief though it be, of the human race from the creation to the flood, and from Noah to Israel; then a more particular account of the Israelites through their period of Egyptian bondage; thence during the journey of four decades in the wilderness to the encampment on the farther side of Jordan.

The Historical Books, twelve in number, comprise: Joshua, Judges, Ruth, the two books of Samuel, the two of Kings, the two of Chronicles, Ezra, Nehemiah, Esther. They tell the story of the Israelites entering the land of promise, and their subsequent career through three distinct periods of their existence as a people—(1) as a theocratic nation, with a tribal organization, all parts cemented by ties of religion and kinship; (2) as a monarchy, at first a united kingdom, later a nation divided against itself; (3) as a partly conquered people, their independence curtailed by their victors.

The Poetical Books number five: Job, Psalms, Proverbs, Ecclesiastes, and the Song of Solomon. They are frequently spoken of as the doctrinal or didactic works, and the Greek designation Hagiographa (*hagios*—holy, and *graphe*—a writing) is still applied.[t] These are of widely different ages, and their association in the Bible is probably due to their common use as guides in devotion amongst the Jewish churches.

The Books of the Prophets comprise the larger works—Isaiah, Jeremiah, including his Lamentations, Ezekiel, and Daniel, commonly known as the works of the four *Major Prophets;* and the twelve shorter books—Hosea, Joel, Amos, Obadiah, Jonah, Micah, Nahum, Habakkuk, Zephaniah, Haggai, Zechariah, and Malachi, known as the books of the *Minor Prophets.* These give the burden of the Lord's word to His people, encouragement, warning and reproof, as suited their condition, before, during, and after their captivity.[u]

The Apocrypha embrace a number of books of doubtful authenticity, though such have been at times highly esteemed. Thus, they were added to the Septuagint, and for a time were accorded recognition among the Alexandrine Jews. However, they have never been generally admitted, being of uncertain origin. They are not quoted in the New Testament. The designation *apocryphal,* meaning hidden, or secret, was first applied to the books by Jerome. The Roman church professes to acknowledge them as scripture, action to this end having been taken by the Council of Trent (1546); though doubt as to the authenticity of the works seems still to exist even among Roman Catholic authorities. The sixth article in the Liturgy of the Church of England defines the

---

[s] See Ezra 6:18; 7:6; Neh. 8:1; John 7:19.

[t] As stated, the Hagiographa, or "sacred writings," are generally understood to include the five poetical works of the Old Testament. By some authorities, the list is extended to include all the books mentioned in the Talmud as hagiographa; viz., Ruth, Chronicles, Ezra and Nehemiah, Esther, Job, Psalms, Proverbs, Ecclesiastes, Song of Solomon, Lamentations, and Daniel.

[u] See Appendix 13:4. For writings referred to in the Bible but not included therein see Appendix 13:8.

orthodox view of the church as to the meaning and intent of Holy Scripture; and, after specifying the books of the Old Testament which are regarded as canonical, proceeds in this wise: "And the other books (as Hierome [Jerome] saith) the church doth read for example of life and instruction of manners; but yet doth it not apply them to establish any doctrine; such are these following:—The Third Book of Esdras; The Fourth Book of Esdras; The Book of Tobias; The Book of Judith; The rest of the Book of Esther; The Book of Wisdom; Jesus, the Son of Sirach; Baruch the Prophet; The Song of the Three Children; The Story of Susanna; Of Bel and the Dragon; The Prayer of Manasses; The First Book of Maccabees; The Second Book of Maccabees."

THE NEW TESTAMENT

Its Origin and Authenticity—Since the latter part of the fourth century of our current era, there has arisen scarcely a question of importance regarding the authenticity of the books of the New Testament as at present constituted. During these centuries the New Testament has been accepted as a canon of scripture by professed Christians.[v] In the fourth century there were generally current several lists of the books of the New Testament as we now have them; of these may be mentioned the catalogues of Athanasius, Epiphanius, Jerome, Rufinus, and Augustine of Hippo, and the list announced by the third Council of Carthage. To these may be added four others, which differ from the foregoing in omitting the Revelation of John in three cases, and the Epistle to the Hebrews in one.

This abundance of evidence relating to the constitution of the New Testament in the fourth century is a result of the anti-Christian persecution of that period. At the beginning of the century in question, the oppressive measures of Diocletian, emperor of Rome, were directed not alone against the Christians as individuals and as a body, but against their sacred writings, which the fanatical monarch sought to destroy.[w] Some degree of leniency was extended to those persons who yielded up the holy books that had been committed to their care; and not a few embraced this opportunity of saving their lives. When the rigors of persecution were lessened the churches sought to judge their members who had weakened in their allegiance to the faith, as shown by their surrender of the scriptures, and all such were anathematized as traitors. Inasmuch as many books that had been thus given up under the pressure of threatening death were not at that time generally accepted as holy, it became a question of first importance to decide just which books were of such admitted sanctity that their betrayal would make a man a traitor.[x] Hence we find Eusebius designating the books of the Messianic and apostolic days as of two classes: (1) Those of acknowledged canonicity: the Gospels, the epistles of Paul, Acts, 1 John, 1 Peter, and probably the Apocalypse. (2) Those of disputed authenticity: the epistles of James, 2 Peter, 2 and 3 John, and Jude. To these classes he added a third class, including books that were admittedly spurious.[y]

The list published by Athanasius, which dates from near the middle of the fourth century, gives the constitution of the New Testament as we now have it; and at that time all doubts as to the correctness of the enumeration seem to have been put to rest; and we find the Testament of common acceptance by Christians in Rome, Egypt, Africa, Syria, Asia Minor, and Gaul. The testimony of Origen, who flourished in the third century, and that of Tertullian, who lived during

[v] See Appendix 13:5, 6.
[w] See *The Great Apostasy,* p. 73.
[x] See Tregelles' *Historic Evidence of the Origin * * * of the Books of the New Testament,* p. 12.
[y] See Eusebius, *Ecclesiastical History* 3:25.

the second, were tested and pronounced conclusive by the later writers in favor of the canonicity of the Gospels and the apostolic writings. Each book was tested on its own merits, and all were declared by common consent to be authoritative and binding on the churches.

If there be need to go farther back, we may note the testimony of Irenæus, distinguished in ecclesiastical history as Bishop of Lyons; he lived in the latter half of the second century, and is known as a disciple of Polycarp, who was personally associated with the Revelator, John. His voluminous writings affirm the authenticity of most of the books of the New Testament and define their authorship as at present admitted. To these testimonies may be added those of the saints in Gaul, who wrote to their fellow sufferers in Asia, quoting freely from Gospels, epistles, and the Apocalypse;[z] the declarations of Melito, Bishop of Sardis, who journeyed to the East to determine which were the canonical books, particularly of the Old Testament;[aa] and the solemn attest of Justin Martyr, who embraced Christianity as a result of his earnest and learned investigations, and who suffered death for his convictions. In addition to individual testimony we have that of ecclesiastical councils and official bodies, by whom the question of authenticity was tried and decided. In this connection may be mentioned the Council of Nice, 325 A.D.; the Council of Laodicea, 363 A.D.; the Council of Hippo, 393 A.D.; the third and the sixth Councils of Carthage, 397 and 419 A.D.

Since the date last named, no dispute as to the authenticity of the New Testament has claimed much attention. The present is too late a time and the separating distance too vast to encourage the reopening of the question. The New Testament must be accepted for what it claims to be; and though, perhaps, many precious parts have been suppressed or lost, while some corruptions of the texts may have crept in, and errors have been inadvertently introduced through the incapacity of translators, the volume as a whole must be admitted as authentic and credible, and as an essential part of the Holy Scriptures.[bb]

Classification of the New Testament—The New Testament comprises twenty-seven books, conveniently classified as:

Historical 5

Didactic 21

Prophetic 1

The Historical Books include the four Gospels and the Acts of the Apostles. The authors of these works are spoken of as the evangelists, Matthew, Mark, Luke, and John; to Luke is ascribed the authorship of the Acts.

The Didactic Books comprise the epistles; and these we may arrange thus: *(1) The Epistles of Paul,* comprising *(a)* his doctrinal letters addressed to Romans, Corinthians, Galatians, Ephesians, Philippians, Colossians, Thessalonians, Hebrews; *(b)* his pastoral communications to Timothy, Titus, and Philemon. *(2) The General Epistles* of James, Peter, John, and Jude.

The Prophetic Works, consisting of the Revelation of John, also known as the Apocalypse.

[z] See Eusebius, book 4.

[aa] Eusebius 4:26.

[bb] Compare John 5:39.

Early Versions of the Bible—Many versions of the Old Testament and of the combined Testaments have appeared at different times. The Hebrew text with the Samaritan duplication of the Pentateuch, and the Greek translation, or the Septuagint, have been already noted with mention of the Peshito. Revisions and modified translations competed for favor with the Septuagint during the early ages of the Christian era; Theodotian, Aquila, and Symmachus each issued a new version. One of the first translations into Latin was the *Italic Version,* probably prepared in the second century; this was later improved and amended, and became known as the *Vulgate;* and this is still held by the Roman Catholic church to be the authentic version. This includes both Old and New Testaments.

Many Modern Versions in English, some fragmentary, others complete, have appeared since the beginning of the thirteenth century. About A.D. 1380, Wycliffe presented an English translation of the New Testament, made from the Vulgate; the Old Testament was afterward added. About A.D. 1525, Tyndale's translation of the New Testament appeared; this was included in Coverdale's Bible, printed in 1535, which constituted the first version of the complete Bible in English. Matthew's Bible dates from 1537; Taverner's Bible from 1539, and Cranmer's Great Bible from the same year. In 1560 the Geneva Bible appeared; in 1568 the Bishops' Bible, the first English version having chapter and verse divisions; and in 1611 the Authorized English Version, or King James' translation, this being a new translation of Old and New Testaments from the Hebrew and Greek, made by forty-seven scholars at the command of King James I. This has superseded all earlier versions, and is the form now in current use among Protestants. But even this was found to contain many and serious blemishes; and in 1885 a Revised Version was issued, which, however, has not yet been accorded general acceptance.

Genuineness and Authenticity of the Bible—However interesting and instructive these historical and literary data of the Hebrew scriptures may be, the consideration of such is subordinate to that of the authenticity of the books; for as we, in common with the rest of the Christian world, have accepted them as the word of God, it is eminently proper that we should inquire into the genuineness of the records upon which our faith is so largely founded. All evidences furnished by the Bible itself, such as its language, historical details, and the consistency of its contents, unite in supporting its claim to genuineness as the actual works of the authors to whom the separate parts are ascribed. In a multitude of instances comparisons are easy between the Biblical record and history not scriptural, particularly in regard to biography and genealogy; and, in such cases, general agreement has been found.[cc] Further evidence appears in the individuality maintained by each writer, resulting in a marked diversity of style; while the unity pervading the whole declares the operation of some guiding influence throughout the ages of the record's growth; and this can be nothing less than the power of inspiration, which operated upon all who were accepted as instruments in the divine hand to prepare this book of books. Tradition, history, literary analysis, and above and beyond all these, the test of prayerful research and truth-seeking investigation, unite to prove the authenticity of this volume of scripture, and to point the way, defined within its covers, leading men back to the Eternal Presence.

Book of Mormon Testimony Regarding the Bible—The Latter-day Saints accept the Book of Mormon as a volume of sacred scripture, which, like the Bible, embodies the word of God. In the next chapter the Book of Mormon will receive especial attention; but it may be profitable to

[cc] See Appendix 13:7.

refer here to the collateral evidence furnished by that work regarding the authenticity of the Jewish scriptures, and of the general integrity of these latter in their present form. According to the Book of Mormon record, the Prophet Lehi, with his family and some others, left Jerusalem by the command of God 600 B.C., during the first year of King Zedekiah's reign. Before departing from the land of their nativity, the travelers secured certain records, which were engraved on plates of brass. Among these writings were a history of the Jews and some of the scriptures then accepted as authentic.

Lehi examined the records: "And he beheld that they did contain the five books of Moses, which gave an account of the creation of the world, and also of Adam and Eve, who were our first parents; And also a record of the Jews from the beginning, even down to the commencement of the reign of Zedekiah, king of Judah; And also the prophecies of the holy prophets, from the beginning, even down to the commencement of the reign of Zedekiah; and also many prophecies which have been spoken by the mouth of Jeremiah."[dd] This direct reference to the Pentateuch and to certain of the Jewish prophets is valuable external evidence concerning the authenticity of those parts of the Biblical record.

Nephi, son of Lehi, learned in vision of the future of God's plan regarding the human family; and saw that a book of great worth, containing the word of God and the covenants of the Lord with Israel, would go forth from the Jews to the Gentiles.[ee] It is further stated that Lehi's company, who, as we shall see, were led across the waters to the western continent, whereon they established themselves and afterward grew to be a numerous and powerful people, were accustomed to study the scriptures engraved on the plates of brass; and, moreover, their scribes embodied long quotations therefrom in their own growing record.[ff] So much for Book of Mormon recognition of the Old Testament, or at least of such parts of the Jewish canon as had been completed when Lehi's migrating colony left Jerusalem, during the ministry of the Prophet Jeremiah.

But further, concerning the New Testament scriptures this voice from the West is not silent. In prophetic vision many of the Nephite prophets saw and then foretold the ministry of Christ in the meridian of time, and recorded predictions concerning the principal events of the Savior's life and death, all with striking fidelity and detail. This testimony is recorded of Nephi,[gg] Benjamin,[hh] who was both prophet and king, Abinadi,[ii] Samuel the converted Lamanite,[jj] and others. In addition to these and many more prophecies regarding the mission of Jesus Christ, all of which agree with the New Testament record of their fulfilment, we find in the Book of Mormon an account of the risen Lord's ministrations among the Nephite people, during which He established with them His Church, after the pattern recorded in the New Testament; and, moreover, He gave them instructions in words almost identical with those of His teachings among the Jews in the East.[kk]

dd 1 Nephi 5:10–13.
ee See 1 Nephi 13:21–23.
ff See 1 Nephi, chaps. 20–21; 2 Nephi, chaps. 7, 8; chaps. 12–24.
gg See 1 Nephi 10:4, 5; see also chaps. 11–14; 2 Nephi 25:26; 26:24.
hh See Mosiah, chap. 3; 4:3.
ii See Mosiah, chaps. 13–16.
jj See Helaman 14:12.
kk See 3 Nephi, chaps. 9–26; compare for New Testament references with Matt., chaps. 5–7, etc; and for Old Testament mention with Isa., chap. 54; Mal., chaps. 3, 4.

REFERENCES

Holy Scriptures

Ye do err, not knowing the scriptures, nor the power of God—Matt. 22:29.

Search the scriptures; for in them ye think ye have eternal life—John 5:39; see also verse 46.

Abraham said unto him: They have Moses and the prophets—Luke 16:29.

Instances of Christ citing scripture—Matt. 4:4; Mark 12:10; Luke 24:27.

Holy scripture given through the Holy Ghost—Acts 1:16.

All scripture is given by inspiration of God, and is profitable—2 Tim. 3:16.

Prophecy came not by the will of man: but holy men of God spake as they were moved by the Holy Ghost—2 Peter 1:21.

The scriptures testify of Christ—John 5:39; Acts 10:43; 18:28; 1 Cor. 15:3.

That we through patience and comfort of the scriptures might have hope—Rom. 15:4.

Now is made manifest, and by the scriptures of the prophets—Rom. 16:26.

For as yet they knew not the scripture, that he must rise again—John 20:9.

But these are written, that ye might believe that Jesus is the Christ—John 20:31.

Scriptures appealed to and cited by the apostles—Acts, chaps. 2 and 3; 8:32; 17:2; see also 18:24, 28:23.

No prophecy of the scripture is of any private interpretation—2 Peter 1:20.

Holy scriptures which are able to make thee wise unto salvation through faith—2 Tim. 3:15.

What does the scripture mean, which saith that God placed cherubim?—Alma 12:21.

For thus saith the scripture: Choose ye this day—Alma 30:8.

Nephi read to the people from the book of Moses, and from Isaiah, and did liken all scriptures unto their conditions—1 Nephi 19:23.

For my soul delighteth in the scriptures, and my heart pondereth them—2 Nephi 4:15.

This people understand not the scriptures, for they seek to excuse themselves—Jacob 2:23.

And I said unto him: Believest thou the scriptures?—Jacob 7:10. Alma confounded Zeezrom by unfolding the scriptures unto him—Alma, chap. 12.

The scriptures are before you; if ye will wrest them it shall be to your own destruction—Alma 13:20.

Ye do greatly err, and ye ought to search the scriptures—Alma 33:2.

Now in this thing they did err, having not understood the scriptures—3 Nephi 1:24.

After Jesus had expounded all these scriptures unto the Nephites—3 Nephi 23:6; see also verse 14.

Have they not read the scriptures, which say ye must take upon you the name of Christ?—3 Nephi 27:5.

Scriptures engraven upon the plates of brass brought from Jerusalem—2 Nephi 4:15.

The Bible referred to in divine revelation to Nephi: They shall have a Bible; and it shall proceed forth from the Jews—2 Nephi 29:3–6. Other scriptures to come forth—verses 7–14.

Because that ye have a Bible ye need not suppose that it contains all my words—2 Nephi 29:10.

Part of the Biblical record found upon the brass plates brought from Jerusalem—1 Nephi 5:10–13.

Ancient records containing scripture spoken by the manifestation of the Spirit—D&C 8:1.

And whatsoever they shall speak when moved upon by the Holy Ghost shall be scripture—D&C 68:4.

Through Satan's influence people wrest the scriptures and do not understand them—D&C 10:63.

Latter-day admonitions to study the scriptures—D&C 11:22.

Proving to the world that the holy scriptures are true—D&C 20:11.

Principles of the gospel contained in the Bible and the Book of Mormon—D&C 42:12.

The holy scriptures are given for instruction; and the power of the Spirit quickeneth all things—D&C 33:16.

Holy scriptures quoted by the Angel Moroni to Joseph Smith—P. of G.P. pp. 52, 53.

A book of remembrance was kept, recorded in the language of Adam—Moses 6:5; written according to the pattern given by the finger of God—verse 46.

THE BOOK OF MORMON

ARTICLE 8

E ALSO BELIEVE the Book of Mormon to be the word of God.

DESCRIPTION AND ORIGIN

What is the Book of Mormon?—The Book of Mormon is a divinely inspired record, made by the prophets of the ancient peoples who inhabited the American continent for centuries before and after the time of Christ, which record has been translated in the present generation through the gift of God and by His special appointment. The authorized and inspired translator of these sacred scriptures, through whose instrumentality they have been given to the world in modern language, is Joseph Smith, whose first acquaintance with the plates received mention in our first chapter. As stated, during the night of September 21–22, 1823, Joseph Smith received, in answer to fervent prayer, a visitation from a resurrected personage[a] who gave his name as Moroni. Subsequent revelations showed him to be the last of a long line of prophets whose translated writings constitute the Book of Mormon; by him the ancient records had been closed; by him the engraved plates had been deposited in the earth; and through his ministration they were brought into the possession of the latter-day prophet and seer whose work of translation is before us.

On the occasion of his first visit to Joseph Smith, Moroni told of

[a] See statement of Joseph Smith, *HC,* vol. 3, p. 28.

the existence of the record, which, he said, was engraved on plates of gold, at that time lying buried in the side of a hill near Joseph's home. The hill, which was known by one division of the ancient peoples as Cumorah, by another as Ramah, is situated near Palmyra in the State of New York. The precise spot where the plates lay was shown to Joseph in vision; and he had no difficulty in finding it on the day following the visitation referred to Joseph Smith's statement of Moroni's declaration concerning the plates is as follows: "He said there was a book deposited, written upon gold plates, giving an account of the former inhabitants of this continent, and the source from which they sprang. He also said that the fulness of the everlasting Gospel was contained in it, as delivered by the Savior to the ancient inhabitants; Also, that there were two stones in silver bows—and these stones, fastened to a breastplate, constituted what is called the Urim and Thummim—deposited with the plates; and the possession and use of these stones were what constituted 'seers' in ancient or former times; and that God had prepared them for the purpose of translating the book."[b]

Joseph found a large stone at the indicated spot on the hill Cumorah; beneath the stone was a box, also of stone; the lid of this he raised by means of a lever; then he saw within the box the plates and the breastplate with the Urim and Thummim, as described by the angel. As he was about to remove the contents of the box, Moroni again appeared before him and forbade him taking the sacred things at that time, saying that four years must pass before they would be committed to his personal care; and that, in the meantime, Joseph would be required to visit the place at yearly intervals. This the youthful revelator did, receiving on each occasion additional instruction concerning the record and God's purposes with regard to it. On September 22, 1827, Joseph received from the angel Moroni the plates and the Urim and Thummim with the breastplate. He was instructed to guard them with strict care, and was promised that if he used his best efforts to protect them they would be preserved inviolate in his hands, and that on the completion of the labor of translation Moroni would visit him again and receive the plates.

The reason prompting the caution regarding Joseph's care of the plates and other objects soon appeared, for in the course of his short journey homeward with the sacred relics he was attacked; but by divine aid he was enabled to withstand his assailants and finally reached his home with the plates and other articles unharmed. These assaults were but the beginning of a siege of persecution, which was relentlessly waged against him as long as the plates remained in his custody. News that he had the plates in his possession soon spread; and numerous attempts, many of them violent, were made to wrest them from his hands. But they were preserved; and, slowly, with many hindrances incident to persecution by the wicked, and to the conditions of his own poverty, which made it necessary for him to toil and left little leisure for the appointed labor, Joseph proceeded with the translation; and in 1830 the Book of Mormon was first published to the world.

The Title Page of the Book of Mormon—Our best answer to the question—What is the Book of Mormon?—is found on the title page to the volume. Thereon we read:

THE
BOOK OF MORMON
An Account Written by
THE HAND OF MORMON
UPON PLATES

---

[b] P. of G.P., pp. 52–59; see also HC, vol. 1, chap. 2. See further chaps. 8–11 of *Essentials of Church History*, by Joseph Fielding Smith, Church Historian, Salt Lake City, 1922.

Wherefore, it is an abridgment of the record of the people of Nephi, and also of the Lamanites—Written to the Lamanites, who are a remnant of the house of Israel; and also to Jew and Gentile—Written by way of commandment, and also by the spirit of prophecy and of revelation—Written and sealed up, and hid up unto the Lord, that they might not be destroyed—To come forth by the gift and power of God unto the interpretation thereof—Sealed by the hand of Moroni, and hid up unto the Lord, to come forth in due time by way of the Gentile—The interpretation thereof by the gift of God.

An abridgment taken from the Book of Ether also, which is a record of the people of Jared, who were scattered at the time the Lord confounded the language of the people, when they were building a tower to get to heaven—Which is to show unto the remnant of the House of Israel what great things the Lord hath done for their fathers; and that they may know the covenants of the Lord, that they are not cast off forever—And also to the convincing of the Jew and Gentile that JESUS is the CHRIST, the ETERNAL GOD, manifesting himself unto all nations—And now, if there are faults they are the mistakes of men; wherefore, condemn not the things of God, that ye may be found spotless at the judgment-seat of Christ.

This combined title and preface is a translation from the last page of the plates, and was presumably written by Moroni, who, as before stated, sealed and hid up the record in former days.[c]

Main Divisions of the Book—From the title page, we learn that in the Book of Mormon we have to deal with the histories of two nations, who flourished in America as the descendants of small colonies brought hither from the eastern continent by divine direction. Of these we may conveniently speak as the Nephites and the Jaredites.

The Nephite Nation was the later, and in point of the fulness of the records, the more important. The progenitors of this people were led from Jerusalem in the year 600 B.C., by Lehi, a Jewish prophet of the tribe of Manasseh. His immediate family, at the time of their departure from Jerusalem, comprised his wife Sariah, and their sons Laman, Lemuel, Sam, and Nephi; at a later stage of the history daughters are mentioned, but whether any of these were born before the family exodus we are not told. Beside his own household, the colony of Lehi included Zoram and Ishmael, the latter an Israelite of the tribe of Ephraim.[d] Ishmael, with his family, joined Lehi's company in the wilderness, and his descendants were numbered with the nation of whom we are speaking. It appears that the company journeyed somewhat east of south, keeping near the borders of the Red Sea; then, changing their course to the eastward, crossed the peninsula of Arabia; and there, on the shores of the Arabian Sea, built and provisioned a vessel in which they committed themselves to divine care upon the waters. It is believed that their voyage must have carried them eastward across the Indian Ocean, then over the Pacific to the western coast of America, whereon they landed about 590 B.C. The landing place is not described in the book itself with such detail as to warrant definite conclusions.

The people established themselves on what to them was the land of promise; many children were born, and in the course of a few generations a numerous posterity held possession of the land. After the death of Lehi a division occurred, some of the people accepting as their leader, Nephi, who had been duly appointed to the prophetic office; while the rest proclaimed Laman, the eldest of Lehi's sons, as their chief. Thenceforth the divided people were known as Nephites and

[c] See Appendix 14:1.
[d] See Appendix 15:1.

Lamanites respectively. At times they observed toward each other a semblance of friendly relations; but generally they were opposed, the Lamanites manifesting implacable hatred and hostility toward their Nephite kindred. The Nephites advanced in the arts of civilization, built large cities, and established prosperous commonwealths; yet they often fell into transgression, and the Lord chastened them by permitting their hereditary enemies to be victorious. It is traditionally believed that they spread northward, occupying a considerable area in Central America, and then expanded eastward and northward over part of what is now the United States of America. The Lamanites, while increasing in numbers, fell under the curse of divine displeasure; they became dark in skin and benighted in spirit, forgot the God of their fathers, lived a wild nomadic life, and degenerated into the fallen state in which the American Indians—their lineal descendants—were found by those who rediscovered the western continent in later times.

The final struggles between Nephites and Lamanites were waged in the vicinity of the Hill Cumorah, in what is now the State of New York, resulting in the destruction of the Nephites as a nation, about 400 A.D. The last Nephite representative was Moroni, who, wandering for safety from place to place, daily expecting death from the victorious Lamanites, wrote the concluding parts of the Book of Mormon, and hid the record in Cumorah. It was this same Moroni who, as a resurrected being, gave the records into the hands of Joseph Smith in the present dispensation.

The Jaredite Nation—Of the two nations whose histories constitute the Book of Mormon, the first in order of time consisted of the people of Jared, who followed their leader from the Tower of Babel at the time of the confusion of tongues. Their history was written on twenty-four plates of gold by Ether, the last of their prophets, who, foreseeing the destruction of his people because of their wickedness, hid away the historic plates. They were afterward found, about B.C. 122, by an expedition sent out by King Limhi, a Nephite ruler. The record engraved on these plates was subsequently abridged by Moroni, and the condensed account was attached by him to the Book of Mormon record; it appears in the modern translation under the name of the Book of Ether.

The first and chief prophet of the Jaredites is not specified by name in the record as we have it; he is known only as the brother of Jared. Of his people we learn that, amidst the confusion of Babel, Jared and his brother importuned the Lord that they and their associates be spared from the impending disruption. Their prayer was heard, and the Lord led them with a considerable company, who, like themselves, were free from the taint of idolatry, away from their homes, promising to conduct them to a land choice above all other lands. Their course of travel is not given with exactness; we learn only that they reached the ocean and there constructed eight vessels, called barges, in which they set out upon the waters. These vessels were small and dark within; but the Lord made certain stones luminous, and these gave light to the imprisoned voyagers. After a passage of three hundred and forty-four days, the colony landed on the American shores.

Here they became a flourishing nation; but, giving way in time to internal dissensions, they divided into factions, which warred with one another until the people were totally destroyed. This destruction, which occurred near the Hill Ramah, afterward known among the Nephites as Cumorah, probably took place at about the time of Lehi's landing, near 590 B.C. The last representative of the ill-fated race was Coriantumr, the king, concerning whom Ether had prophesied that he should survive all his subjects and live to see another people in possession of the land. This prediction was fulfilled in that the king, whose people had been exterminated, came, in the course of his solitary wanderings, to a region occupied by the people of Mulek, who are to be mentioned here as the third ancient colony of emigrants from the eastern continent.

Mulek was the son of Zedekiah, king of Judah, an infant at the time of his brothers' violent deaths and his father's cruel torture at the hands of the king of Babylon.[e] Eleven years after Lehi's departure from Jerusalem, another colony was led from the city, amongst whom was Mulek. The colony took his name, probably on account of his recognized rights of leadership by virtue of lineage. The Book of Mormon record concerning Mulek and his people is scant; we learn, however, that the colony was brought across the waters to a landing, probably on the northern part of the American continent. The descendants of this colony were discovered by the Nephites under Mosiah; they had grown numerous, but, having had no scriptures for their guidance had fallen into a condition of spiritual darkness. They joined the Nephites and their history is merged into that of the greater nation.[f] The Nephites gave to a part of North America the name Land of Mulek.

THE ANCIENT PLATES AND THE TRANSLATION

The Plates of the Book of Mormon as delivered by the angel Moroni to Joseph Smith, according to the description given by the latter-day prophet, were, as far as he knew, of gold, of uniform size, each about seven inches wide by eight inches long, and in thickness a little less than that of ordinary sheet tin. They were fastened together by three rings running through the plates near one edge; together they formed a book nearly six inches in thickness, but not all has been translated, a part having been sealed. Both sides of the plates were engraved with small characters, described by those who examined them as of curious workmanship, with the appearance of ancient origin.

Three classes of plates are mentioned on the title page of the Book of Mormon:

1. *The Plates of Nephi,* which, as will be shown, were of two kinds: (a) the larger plates; (b) the smaller plates.
2. *The Plates of Mormon,* containing an abridgment from the plates of Nephi, with additions made by Mormon and his son Moroni.
3. *The Plates of Ether,* containing the history of the Jaredites.
    To these may be added another set of plates, as being mentioned in the Book of Mormon, and in point of time the oldest of all:
4. *The Brass Plates of Laban,* brought by Lehi's people from Jerusalem, and containing Jewish scriptures and genealogies, many extracts from which appear in the Nephite records. We have now to consider more particularly the plates of Nephi and Mormon's abridgment thereof.

The Plates of Nephi are so named from the fact that they were prepared and their record was begun by Nephi, son of Lehi. These plates were of two kinds,[g] which may be distinguished as the larger plates and the smaller plates. Nephi began his labors as a recorder by engraving on his plates a historical account of his people from the time his father left Jerusalem. This account recited the story of their wanderings, their prosperity and distress, the reigns of their kings and the wars and contentions of the people; the record was in the nature of a secular history. These plates were handed from one recorder to another throughout the generations of the Nephite people, so that,

[e] See 2 Kings 25:7.
[f] See Omni 12–19.
[g] See 1 Nephi, chap. 9; 19:15; 2 Nephi 5:30; Jacob 1:14; Words of Mormon 3–7.

at the time of their abridgment by Mormon, the record covered a period of about a thousand years, dating from 600 B.C., the time of Lehi's exodus from Jerusalem. Although these plates bore the name of the first of the writers thereon, the separate work of each recorder is known in general by his specific name, so that the record is made up of several distinct books.

By command of the Lord, Nephi made other plates, upon which he recorded particularly what may be called in a broad sense the ecclesiastical history of his people, citing only such instances of other events as seemed necessary to the proper sequence of the narrative. "I have received a commandment of the Lord," says Nephi, "that I should make these plates, for the special purpose that there should be an account engraven of the ministry of my people."[h] The object of this double line of history was unknown to Nephi; it was enough for him that the Lord required the labor; that it was for a wise purpose will be shown.

Mormon's Abridgment—In the course of time the records that had accumulated passed into the hands of Mormon,[i] who undertook to make an abridgment of these extensive works, upon plates made with his own hands.[j] By such a course a record was prepared more concise and more nearly uniform in style, language, and treatment than could possibly have been the case with the varied writings of so many authors as had contributed to the great history during the many centuries of its growth. Mormon recognizes and testifies to the inspiration of God by which he was moved to undertake the great labor.[k] In preparing this shorter history, Mormon preserved the division of the record into books according to the arrangement of the originals; and thus, though the language may be that of Mormon, except in cases of quotations from the plates of Nephi, which are indeed numerous, we find the Books of Nephi, the Book of Alma, the Book of Helaman, etc., the form of speech known as the first person being generally preserved.

When Mormon, in the course of his work of abridging the voluminous records, had reached the time of King Benjamin's reign, he was deeply impressed with the account engraved on the smaller plates of Nephi—the history of God's dealings with the people during the period of about four centuries, extending from the time of Lehi's exodus from Jerusalem down to the time of King Benjamin. This record, comprising so much of prophecy concerning the mission of the Savior, was regarded by Mormon with great reverence. Of these plates he attempted no transcript, but included the originals with his own abridgment of the larger plates, making of the two one book. The record as compiled by Mormon contained, therefore, a double account of the descendants of Lehi for the first four hundred years of their history—the brief secular history condensed from the larger plates, and the full text on the smaller plates. In solemn language, and with an emphasis that subsequent events have shown to be significant, Mormon declares the hidden wisdom of the Lord's purpose in this duplication: "And I do this for a wise purpose; for thus it whispereth me, according to the workings of the Spirit of the Lord which is in me. And now, I do not know all things; but the Lord knoweth all things which are to come; wherefore, he worketh in me to do according to his will."[l]

The Lord's Purpose in the matter of preparing and preserving the smaller plates as testified of by Mormon and also by Nephi,[m] is rendered plain from certain circumstances in this latter-day dispensation attending the translation of the records by Joseph Smith. After the prophet had prepared

[h] 1 Nephi 9:3.
[i] See Words of Mormon 11; Mormon 1:1–4; 4:23.
[j] See 3 Nephi 5:8–11.
[k] See 3 Nephi 5:14–19.
[l] Words of Mormon 7.
[m] See 1 Nephi 9:5.

a translation of the first part of the writings of Mormon, the manuscript was won from his custody through the unrighteous solicitations of Martin Harris, to whom he considered himself indebted for material assistance while he was devoting his time to the work. This manuscript, in all one hundred and sixteen pages, was never returned to Joseph; but, through the dark schemes of evil powers, it fell into the hands of enemies, who straightway laid a wicked plan to ridicule the translator and thwart the purposes of God. This design was that the conspirators wait until Joseph had retranslated the missing matter, when the stolen manuscript, which in the meantime had been altered so that the words were made to express the contrary of the true record, would be set forth as a proof that the prophet was unable to translate the same passages twice alike. But the Lord's wisdom interposed to bring to naught these dark designs.

Having chastened the prophet by depriving him for a season of his gift to translate, as also of the custody of the sacred records, and this for his dereliction in permitting the writings to pass into unappointed hands, the Lord graciously restored His penitent servant to favor, and revealed to him the designs of his enemies,[n] at the same time showing how these evil machinations should be made to fail. Joseph was instructed not to attempt a retranslation of that part of Mormon's abridgment, the first translation of which had been stolen; but instead, to translate from the plates of Nephi the record of the same period—the set of smaller plates which Mormon had incorporated with his own writings. The translation so made was therefore published as the record of Nephi, and not as the writing of Mormon; and thus no second translation was made of the parts from which the stolen manuscript had been prepared.

The Translation of the Book of Mormon was effected through the power of God manifested in the bestowal of the gift of revelation. The book professes not to be dependent upon the wisdom or learning of man; its translator was not versed in linguistics; his qualifications were of a different and of a more efficient order. With the plates, Joseph Smith received from the angel other sacred treasures, including a breastplate, to which were attached the Urim and Thummim,[o] called by the Nephites *Interpreters;* and by the use of these he was enabled to translate the ancient records into our modern tongue. The details of the work of translation have not been recorded, beyond the statement that the translator examined the engraved characters by means of the sacred instruments, and then dictated to the scribe the English sentences.

Joseph began his work with the plates by patiently copying a number of characters, adding his translation to some of the pages thus prepared. The prophet's first assistant in the labor, Martin Harris, obtained permission to take away some of these transcripts, with the purpose of submitting them to the examination of men learned in ancient languages. He placed some of the sheets before Professor Charles Anthon, of Columbia College, who, after examination, certified that the characters were in general of the ancient Egyptian order, and that the accompanying translations appeared to be correct. Hearing how this ancient record came into Joseph's hands, Professor Anthon requested Mr. Harris to bring the original book for examination, stating that he would undertake the translation of the work; then, learning that a part of the book was sealed, he remarked, "I cannot read a sealed book"; and thus unwittingly did this man fulfil the prophecy of Isaiah concerning the coming forth of the volume: "And the vision of all is become unto you as the words of a book that is sealed, which men deliver to one that is learned, saying, Read this, I pray thee: and he saith, I cannot; for it is sealed."[p] Another linguist, a Doctor Mitchell, of New

[n] See D&C, sec. 10; also *HC,* vol. 1, chap. 3.
[o] See D&C 10:1; 17:1; 130:8, 9; Mos. 8:13–19; Ether 3:23–28.
[p] Isa. 29:11.

York, having examined the characters, gave concerning them a testimony in all important respects corresponding to that of Professor Anthon.

Arrangement of the Book of Mormon—The Book of Mormon comprises fifteen separate parts, which with a single exception are called books, and are distinguished by the names of their principal authors. Of these, the first six books, viz., First and Second Nephi, Jacob, Enos, Jarom, and Omni, are literal translations from corresponding portions of the smaller plates of Nephi. The body of the volume, from the book of Mosiah to Mormon, chapter 7, inclusive, is the translation of Mormon's abridgment of the larger plates of Nephi. Between the books of Omni and Mosiah, the "Words of Mormon" occur, connecting the record of Nephi, as engraved on the smaller plates, with Mormon's abridgment of the larger plates for the periods following. The Words of Mormon may be regarded as a brief explanation of the preceding portions of the work and a preface of the parts then to follow. The last part of the Book of Mormon, from the beginning of Mormon, chapter 8, to the end of the volume, is in the language of Moroni, son of Mormon, who first proceeds to finish the record of his father, and then adds an abridgment of a set of plates which contained an account of the Jaredites; this appears as the book of Ether.

At the time of Moroni's writing he stood alone—the sole surviving representative of his people, excepting the many who had identified themselves with the Lamanites. The last of the fratricidal wars between Nephites and Lamanites had resulted in the annihilation of the former as a people; and Moroni supposed that his abridgment of the book of Ether would be his last literary work; but, finding himself miraculously preserved at the conclusion of that undertaking, he added the part known to us as the book of Moroni, containing accounts of procedure in ordination, baptism, and administration of the sacrament, and a record of certain utterances and writings of his father Mormon.

The Genuineness of the Book of Mormon will appear as the result of impartial investigation into the circumstances attending its coming forth. The fanciful theories of its origin, advanced by prejudiced opponents, are in general too inconsistent, and in most instances too thoroughly puerile, to merit serious consideration. Assumptions that the Book of Mormon is the production of a single author or of men working in collusion, a work of fiction, or in any manner a modern composition, are their own refutation.[q] The sacred character of the plates forbade their display as a means of gratifying personal curiosity; nevertheless a number of reputable witnesses examined them, and these men have given to the world their solemn testimony of the facts. In June, 1829, the prophecies respecting the witnesses by whose testimony the word of God as set forth in the Book of Mormon was to be established,[r] saw its fulfilment in a manifestation of divine power, demonstrating the genuineness of the record to three men, whose affirmations accompany all editions of the book.

THE TESTIMONY OF THREE WITNESSES

BE IT KNOWN unto all nations, kindreds, tongues, and people, unto whom this work shall come: That we, through the grace of God the Father, and our Lord Jesus Christ, have seen the plates which contain this record, which is a record of the people of Nephi, and also of the Lamanites, their brethren, and also of the people of Jared, who came from the tower of which hath been spoken. And we also know that they have been translated by the gift and power of God, for his voice hath declared it unto us; wherefore we know of a surety that the work is true. And we also testify that we have seen the engravings which are upon the plates; and they have been shown unto us by the power of God,

[q] See Appendix 14:2.
[r] See 2 Nephi 11:3, 27:12, 13; Ether 5:3, 4; see also D&C 5:11–15; sec. 17.

and not of man. And we declare with words of soberness, that an angel of God came down from heaven, and he brought and laid before our eyes, that we beheld and saw the plates, and the engravings thereon; and we know that it is by the grace of God the Father, and our Lord Jesus Christ, that we beheld and bear record that these things are true. And it is marvelous in our eyes. Nevertheless, the voice of the Lord commanded us that we should bear record of it; wherefore, to be obedient unto the commandments of God, we bear testimony of these things. And we know that if we are faithful in Christ, we shall rid our garments of the blood of all men, and be found spotless before the judgment-seat of Christ, and shall dwell with him eternally in the heavens. And the honor be to the Father, and to the Son, and to the Holy Ghost, which is one God. Amen.

OLIVER COWDERY
DAVID WHITMER
MARTIN HARRIS

The testimony so declared was never revoked, nor even modified by any one of the witnesses whose names are subscribed to the foregoing,[s] though all of them withdrew from the Church, and developed feelings amounting almost to hatred toward Joseph Smith. To the last of their lives they maintained the same solemn declaration of the angelic visit, and of the testimony that had been implanted in their hearts. Shortly after the witnessing of the plates by the three, other eight persons were permitted to see and handle the ancient records; and in this also was prophecy fulfilled, in that it was of old declared, that beside the three, "God sendeth more witnesses,"[t] whose testimony would be added to that of the three. Joseph Smith showed the plates to the eight whose names are attached to the following certificate, presumably in July, 1829.

THE TESTIMONY OF EIGHT WITNESSES

BE IT KNOWN unto all nations, kindreds, tongues, and people, unto whom this work shall come: That Joseph Smith, Jun., the translator of the work, has shown unto us the plates of which hath been spoken, which have the appearance of gold; and as many of the leaves as the said Smith has translated we did handle with our hands; and we also saw the engravings thereon, all of which has the appearance of ancient work, and of curious workmanship. And this we bear record with words of soberness, and that the said Smith has shown unto us, for we have seen and hefted, and know of a surety that the said Smith has got the plates of which we have spoken. And we give our names unto the world, to witness unto the world that which we have seen. And we lie not, God bearing witness of it.

CHRISTIAN WHITMER
JACOB WHITMER
PETER WHITMER, JUN.
JOHN WHITMER
HIRAM PAGE
JOSEPH SMITH, SEN.
HYRUM SMITH
SAMUEL H. SMITH

[s] See Appendix 14:3.
[t] 2 Nephi 11:3; also Appendix 14:4.

Three of the eight witnesses died out of the Church, yet not one of the whole number ever was known to deny his testimony concerning the Book of Mormon.[u]

Here, then, are proofs of varied kinds regarding the reliability of this volume. The translator gives simple and circumstantial account of the bringing forth of the ancient plates, and avers that the translation was effected by the power of God; learned linguists pronounce the engraved characters genuine; eleven men of honest report, beside the translator, make solemn affirmation as to the appearance of the plates; and the nature of the book[v] itself sustains the claim that it is nothing other than a translation of ancient records.[w]

[u] See Appendix 14:4.
[v] See Appendix 14:5.
[w] See *Vitality of "Mormonism,"* articles "A Messenger from the Presence of God" and "Scriptures of the American Continent," pp. 128–137.

15

THE BOOK OF MORMON—CONTINUED

ARTICLE 8
E ALSO BELIEVE the Book of Mormon to be the word of God.

ITS AUTHENTICITY
The Authenticity of the Book of Mormon constitutes our most important consideration of the work. This subject is one of vital interest to every earnest investigator of the word of God, to every sincere searcher after truth. Claiming to be, as far as the present dispensation is concerned, a new scripture, presenting prophecies and revelations not heretofore recognized in modern theology, announcing to the world the message of a departed people, written by way of commandment, and by the spirit of prophecy and revelation—this book is entitled to the most thorough and impartial examination. Not only does the Book of Mormon merit such consideration, it claims, even demands the same; for no one professing belief in the power and authority of God can receive with unconcern the announcement of a new revelation, professedly bearing the seal of divine authority. The question of the authenticity of the Book of Mormon is therefore one in which the world is concerned.

The Latter-day Saints base their belief in the authenticity of the book on the following proofs:
1. The general agreement of the Book of Mormon with the Bible in all related matters.

2. The fulfilment of ancient prophecies accomplished by the bringing forth of the Book of Mormon.
3. The strict agreement and consistency of the Book of Mormon with itself.
4. The evident truth of its contained prophecies.
   To these may be added certain external, or extra-scriptural evidences, amongst which are:
5. Corroborative testimony furnished by archeology and ethnology.

1. THE BOOK OF MORMON AND THE BIBLE

The Nephite and the Jewish Scriptures are found to agree in matters of tradition, history, doctrine, and prophecy which the separate records treat. These two volumes of scripture were prepared on opposite hemispheres, under widely diverse conditions; yet between them there exists surprising harmony, confirmatory of divine inspiration in both. The Book of Mormon contains a number of quotations from the ancient Jewish scriptures, a copy of which, as far as they had been compiled at the time of Lehi's exodus from Jerusalem, was brought to the western continent as part of the record engraved on the plates of Laban. In the case of such passages there is no essential difference between Biblical and Book of Mormon versions, except in instances of probable error in translation—usually apparent through inconsistency or lack of clearness in the Biblical reading. There are, however, numerous minor variations in corresponding parts of the two volumes; and between such, examination usually demonstrates the superior clearness of the Nephite scripture.

In a careful comparison of the prophecies of the Bible with corresponding predictions contained in the Book of Mormon, e.g., those relating to the birth, earthly ministry, sacrificial death, and second coming of Christ Jesus; with others referring to the scattering and subsequent gathering of Israel; and with such as relate to the establishment of Zion and the rebuilding of Jerusalem in the last days, each of the records is corroborative of the other. True, there are many predictions in one that are not found in both, but in no instance has contradiction or inconsistency been pointed out. Between the doctrinal parts of the two volumes of scripture the same perfect harmony is found to prevail.ᵃ

2. PROPHECIES REGARDING THE BOOK OF MORMON

Ancient Prophecy has been literally fulfilled in the coming forth of the Book of Mormon. One of the earliest utterances directly bearing upon this subject is that of Enoch, an antediluvian prophet unto whom the Lord revealed His purposes for all time. Witnessing in vision the corruption of mankind, after the ascension of the Son of Man, Enoch cried unto his God: "Wilt thou not come again upon the earth? * * * And the Lord said unto Enoch: As I live, even so will I come in the last days. * * * And the day shall come that the earth shall rest, but before that day the heavens shall be darkened, and a veil of darkness shall cover the earth; and the heavens shall shake, and also the earth; and great tribulations shall be among the children of men, but my people will I preserve; And righteousness will I send down out of heaven; and truth will I send forth out of the earth, to bear testimony of mine Only Begotten. * * * And righteousness and truth will I cause to sweep the earth as with a flood, to gather out mine elect from the four quarters of the earth, unto a place which I shall prepare."ᵇ The Latter-day Saints regard the coming forth of the Book of Mormon, together with the restoration of the Priesthood by the direct ministration of heavenly messengers, as a fulfilment of this prophecy, and of similar predictions contained in the Bible.

a See Appendix 14:5.
b P.of G.P., Moses 7:59–62.

David, who sang his psalms over a thousand years before the "meridian of time," predicted: "Truth shall spring out of the earth; and righteousness shall look down from heaven."[c] And so also declared Isaiah.[d] Ezekiel saw in vision[e] the coming together of the stick of Judah, and the stick of Joseph, signifying the Bible and the Book of Mormon. The passage last referred to reads, in the words of Ezekiel: "The word of the Lord came again unto me, saying, Moreover, thou son of man, take thee one stick, and write upon it, For Judah, and for the children of Israel his companions: then take another stick, and write upon it, For Joseph, the stick of Ephraim, and for all the house of Israel his companions: And join them one to another into one stick; and they shall become one in thine hand."

When we call to mind the ancient custom in the making of books—that of writing on long strips of parchment and rolling the same on rods or sticks, the use of the word "stick" as equivalent to "book" in the passage becomes apparent.[f] At the time of this utterance, the Israelites had divided into two nations known as the kingdom of Judah and that of Israel, or Ephraim. Plainly the separate records of Judah and Joseph are here referred to.[g] Now, as we have seen, the Nephite nation comprised the descendants of Lehi who belonged to the tribe of Manasseh, of Ishmael who was an Ephraimite,[h] and of Zoram whose tribal relation is not definitely stated. The Nephites were then of the tribes of Joseph; and their record or "stick" is as truly represented by the Book of Mormon as is the "stick" of Judah by the Bible.

That the bringing forth of the record of Joseph or Ephraim was to be accomplished through the direct power of God is evident from the Lord's exposition of the vision of Ezekiel, wherein He says: "Behold, *I will take* the stick of Joseph * * * and will put them with him, even with the stick of Judah."[i] That this union of the two records was to be a characteristic of the latter days is evident from the prediction of an event which was to follow immediately, viz., the gathering of the tribes from the nations among which they had been dispersed.[j] Comparison with other prophecies relating to the gathering will conclusively prove that the great event was predicted to take place in the latter times, preparatory to the second coming of Christ.[k]

Reverting to the writings of Isaiah, we find that prophet voicing the Lord's threatenings against Ariel, or Jerusalem, "the city where David dwelt." Ariel was to be distressed, burdened with heaviness and sorrow; then the prophet refers to some people, other than Judah who occupied Jerusalem, for he makes the comparison with the latter, saying: "And it shall be unto me *as* Ariel." Concerning the fate decreed against this other people we read: "And thou shalt be brought down, and shalt speak out of the ground, and thy speech shall be low out of the dust, and thy voice shall be, as of one that hath a familiar spirit, out of the ground, and thy speech shall whisper out of the dust."[l]

Of the fulfilment of these and associated prophecies, a latter-day apostle has written: "These predictions of Isaiah could not refer to Ariel, or Jerusalem, because their speech has not been 'out of the ground,' or 'low out of the dust'; but it refers to the remnant of Joseph who were destroyed

---

[c] Ps. 85:11.

[d] See Isa. 45:8.

[e] See Ezek., Chap. 37, particularly verses 15–20.

[f] See a corresponding use of the word "roll" in Jeremiah 36:1, 2; and its synonym "book" in verses 8, 10, 11, and 13.

[g] Compare with Lehi's prediction made to his son Joseph, 2 Nephi 3:12.

[h] See Appendix 15:1.

[i] Ezek. 37:19.

[j] same, verse 21.

[k] See chap. 18 herein.

[l] Isa. 29:4—read verses 1–6.

in America upwards of fourteen hundred years ago. The Book of Mormon describes their down-fall, and truly it was great and terrible. At the crucifixion of Christ, 'the multitude of their terri-ble ones,' as Isaiah predicted, 'became as chaff that passeth away,' and it took place as he further predicts, 'at an instant suddenly.' * * * This remnant of Joseph in their distress and destruction became *as* Ariel. As the Roman army lay siege to Ariel, and brought upon her great distress and sorrow, so did the contending nations of ancient America bring upon each other the most direful scenes of blood and carnage. Therefore the Lord could, with the greatest propriety, when speak-ing in reference to this event, declare that, 'It shall be unto me as Ariel.'"[m]

Isaiah's striking prediction that the nation thus brought down should "speak out of the ground," with speech "low out of the dust" was literally fulfilled in the bringing forth of the Book of Mormon, the original of which was taken out of the ground, and the voice of the record is as that of one speak-ing from the dust. In continuation of the same prophecy we read: "And the vision of all is become unto you as the words of a book that is sealed, which men deliver to one that is learned, saying, Read this, I pray thee: and he saith, I cannot; for it is sealed: And the book is delivered to him that is not learned, saying, Read this, I pray thee: and he saith, I am not learned."[n] The fulfilment of this prediction is claimed in the presentation of the transcript from the plates—"the words of a book," not the book itself—to the learned Professor Charles Anthon, whose reply, almost in the words of the text, has been cited in the last chapter; and in the delivery of the book itself to the unlettered youth, Joseph Smith.

3. CONSISTENCY OF THE BOOK OF MORMON

The Internal Consistency of the Book of Mormon sustains belief in its divine origin. The parts bear evidence of having been written at different times and under widely varying conditions. The style of the component books is in harmony with the times and circumstances of their production. The por-tions that were transcribed from the plates bearing Mormon's abridgment contain numerous interpo-lations as comments and explanations of the transcriber; but in the first six books, which, as already explained, are the verbatim record of the smaller plates of Nephi, no such interpolations occur. The book maintains consistency throughout; no contradictions, no disagreements have been pointed out.

Diversity of Style characterizes the different books.[o] From what has been said regarding the several sets of plates that constitute the original accumulation of records from which the Book of Mormon was translated, it is evident that the volume contains the compiled writings of a long line of inspired scribes extending through a thousand years, this time-range being exclusive of the earlier years of Jaredite history. Unity of style is not to be expected under such conditions.

4. THE BOOK OF MORMON SUSTAINED BY THE FULFILMENT OF ITS CONTAINED PROPHECIES

Book of Mormon Predictions are numerous and important. Amongst the most conclusive proofs of the authenticity of the book is that furnished by the demonstrated truth of its contained prophecies. Prophecy is best proved in the light of its own fulfilment. The predictions contained within the Book of Mormon may be classed as (1) Prophecies relating to the time covered by the book itself, the fulfilment of which is recorded therein; and (2) Prophecies relating to times beyond the limits of the history chronicled in the book.

[m] Orson Pratt, *Divine Authenticity of the Book of Mormon,* pp. 293, 294 (Utah ed., 1891). For details of fulfilment of part of the prophecy, see 3 Nephi, chaps. 8, 9.
[n] Isa. 29:11, 12.
[o] See Appendix 15:2.

Prophecies of the First Class named, the fulfilment of which is attested by the Book of Mormon record, are of minor value as proof of the authenticity of the work; for, had the book been written by human design as fiction, both prediction and fulfilment would have been provided for with equal care and ingenuity. Nevertheless, to the studious and conscientious reader the genuineness of the book will be apparent; and the literal realization of the numerous and varied predictions relating to the fate, then future, of the people whose history is given in the record, as also of prophecies concerning details of the birth and death of the Savior, and of His appearing to that people in a resurrected state, must, by their accuracy and consistency, appeal with force as evidence of inspiration and authority in the record.

Prophecies of the Second Class, relating to a time which to the writers was far future, are numerous and explicit. Many of them have special reference to the last days—the dispensation of the fulness of times—and of these, some have been already literally accomplished, others are now in process of actual realization, while yet others are awaiting fulfilment under specified conditions that seem now to be rapidly approaching. Among the most remarkable of the Book of Mormon predictions incident to the last dispensation are those that relate to its own coming forth and the effect of its publication amongst mankind. Ezekiel's prophecy concerning the coming together of the "sticks," or records, of Judah and of Ephraim has received attention. Consider the promise made to Joseph who was sold into Egypt, repeated by Lehi to his son Joseph—a prediction that couples the prophecy concerning the book with that of the seer through whose instrumentality the miracle was to be accomplished: "But a seer will I raise up out of the fruit of thy loins; and unto him will I give power to bring forth my word unto the seed of thy loins—and not to the bringing forth my word only, saith the Lord, but to the convincing them of my word, which shall have already gone forth among them. Wherefore, the fruit of thy loins shall write; and the fruit of the loins of Judah shall write; and that which shall be written by the fruit of thy loins, and also that which shall be written by the fruit of the loins of Judah, shall grow together, unto the confounding of false doctrines and laying down of contentions, and establishing peace among the fruit of thy loins, and bringing them to the knowledge of their fathers in the latter days, and also to the knowledge of my covenants, saith the Lord. And out of weakness he shall be made strong, in that day when my work shall commence among all my people, unto the restoring thee, O house of Israel, saith the Lord."[p] The literal fulfilment of these utterances in the bringing forth of the Book of Mormon through Joseph Smith is apparent.

Unto Nephi the Lord showed what would be an effect of the new publication, declaring that in the day of Israel's gathering—plainly then the day of the fulness of times, as attested by the Jewish scriptures—the words of the Nephites should be given to the world, and should "hiss forth unto the ends of the earth, for a standard" unto the house of Israel; and that then the Gentiles, forgetting even their debt to the Jews from whom they had received the Bible in which they profess such faith, would revile and curse that branch of the covenant people, and would reject the new scripture, exclaiming: "A Bible! a Bible! we have got a Bible, and there cannot be any more Bible."[q] Is this not the burden of the frenzied objections raised by the Gentile world against the Book of Mormon—that it is of necessity void because new revelation is not to be expected?

Now, in olden times, two witnesses were required to establish the truth of an allegation; and, said the Lord concerning the dual records witnessing of Himself: "Wherefore murmur ye, because that ye shall receive more of my word? Know ye not that the testimony of two nations is a witness

p 2 Nephi 3:11–13.
q 2 Nephi 29:3; read the chapter.

unto you that I am God, that I remember one nation like unto another? Wherefore, I speak the same words unto one nation like unto another. And when the two nations shall run together the testimony of the two nations shall run together also."[r]

Associated with these predictions of the joint testimony of Jewish and Nephite scriptures is another prophecy, the consummation of which is now expectantly yet patiently awaited by the faithful. Additional scriptures are promised, specifically the records of the Lost Tribes. Note this word of promise: "Wherefore, because that ye have a Bible ye need not suppose that it contains all my words; neither need ye suppose that I have not caused more to be written. * * * For behold, I shall speak unto the Jews and they shall write it; and I shall also speak unto the Nephites and they shall write it; and I shall also speak unto the other tribes of the house of Israel, which I have led away, and they shall write it; and I shall also speak unto all nations of the earth, and they shall write it. And it shall come to pass that the Jews shall have the words of the Nephites, and the Nephites shall have the words of the Jews; and the Nephites and the jews shall have the words of the lost tribes of Israel; and the lost tribes of Israel shall have the words of the Nephites and the Jews."[s]

5. CORROBORATIVE EVIDENCE FURNISHED BY MODERN DISCOVERIES

The Archeology and Ethnology of the western continent contribute some corroborative evidence in support of the Book of Mormon. These sciences are confessedly unable to explain in any decisive manner the origin of the native American races; nevertheless, investigation in this field has yielded results that are fairly definite, and with the most important of these the Book of Mormon account is in general accord. No exhaustive treatment will be attempted here, as such would require space far beyond present limitations. For detailed consideration of the subject the student should consult works especially devoted thereto.[t] Among the most significant of the discoveries respecting the aboriginal inhabitants, are the following:

1. That America was peopled in very ancient times, probably soon after the building of the Tower of Babel.
2. That the continent has been successively occupied by different peoples, at least by two classes, or so-called races, at widely separated periods.
3. That the aboriginal inhabitants came from the East, probably from Asia, and that the later occupants, or those of the second period, were closely allied to, if not identical with, the Israelites.
4. That the existing native races of America form a common stock.

From the outline already given of the historical part of the Book of Mormon, it is seen that each of these discoveries is fully sustained by that record. Thus it is stated therein:

1. That America was settled by the Jaredites, who came direct from the scenes of Babel.
2. That the Jaredites occupied the land for about eighteen hundred and fifty years, and that at about the time of their extinction, near 590 B.C., Lehi and his company came to this continent, where

[r] 2 Nephi 29:8.
[s] 2 Nephi 29:10, 12.
[t] The student is especially referred to the comprehensive work by Elder B. H. Roberts, *New Witnesses for God,* vol. 2, chaps. 24 to 29 inclusive, and vol. 3, chaps. 30 to 34 inclusive.

they developed into the segregated nations Nephites and Lamanites, the former becoming extinct near 385 A.D.—about a thousand years after Lehi's arrival on these shores—the latter continuing in a degenerate condition until the present, and being represented by the Indian tribes.

3. That Lehi, Ishmael, and Zoram, the progenitors of both Nephites and Lamanites, were undoubtedly Israelites, Lehi being of the tribe of Manasseh while Ishmael was an Ephraimite, and that the colony came direct from Jerusalem, in Asia.

4. That the existing Indian tribes are descendants of the immigrants whose history is contained in the Book of Mormon, and that therefore they have sprung from progenitors who were of the house of Israel.

Now, let us examine some of the evidence bearing on these points presented by investigators, most of whom knew nothing of the Book of Mormon, and none of whom accept the book as authentic.[u]

1. **Concerning the Ancient Colonization of America**—A recognized authority on American antiquities gives the following evidence and inference: "One of the arts known to the builders of Babel was that of brick-making. This art was also known to the people who built the works in the west. The knowledge of copper was known to the people of the plains of Shinar; for Noah must have communicated it, as he lived a hundred and fifty [350] years among them after the flood. Also copper was known to the antediluvians. Copper was also known to the authors of the western monuments. Iron was known to the antediluvians. It was also known to the ancients of the west. However, it is evident that very little iron was among them, as very few instances of its discovery in their works have occurred; and for this very reason we draw a conclusion that they came to this country soon after the dispersion."[v]

Lowry, in his "Reply to official inquiries respecting the Aborigines of America," concludes concerning the peopling of the western continent, "that the first settlement was made shortly after the confusion of tongues at the building of the Tower of Babel."[w]

Professor Waterman of Boston says of the progenitors of the American Indians: "When and whence did they come? Albert Galatin, one of the profoundest philologists of the age, concluded that, so far as language afforded any clue, the time of their arrival could not have been long after the dispersion of the human family."[x]

Pritchard writes of America's ancient inhabitants, that "the era of their existence as a distinct and isolated race must probably be dated as far back as that time which separated into nations the inhabitants of the old world, and gave to each branch of the human family its primitive language and individuality."[y]

A native Mexican author, Ixtilxochitl, "fixes the date of the first people of America about the year 2000 B.C.; this closely accords with that given by the Book of Mormon, which positively

---

[u] Many of the citations which follow, used in connection with the extra-scriptural evidence supporting the Book of Mormon, have been brought together by writers among our people, particularly by Elder George Reynolds; see also series of articles entitled "American Antiquities," in *Millennial Star,* Liverpool, vol. 21; a series of articles on "The Divine Origin of the Book of Mormon," in *Contributor,* Salt Lake City, vol. 2, by Moses Thatcher; and a tract, *A Prophet of Latter Days,* Liverpool, 1898, Edwin F. Parry.

[v] Priest, *American Antiquities,* 1834, p. 219.

[w] Schoolcraft's *Ethnological Researches,* vol. 3 (1853).

[x] Extract from lecture by Prof. Waterman, delivered in Bristol, England, 1849; quoted in pamphlet by Edwin F. Parry, *A Prophet of Latter Days* (Liverpool, 1898).

[y] Pritchard, *National History of Man* (London, 1845).

declares that it occurred at the time of the dispersion, when God in His anger scattered the people upon the face of the whole earth."[z] "Referring to the quotations from Ixtilxochitl, seventeen hundred and sixteen years are said to have elapsed from the creation to the flood. Moses places it sixteen hundred and fifty-six, a difference of only sixty years.[aa] They agree exactly as to the number of cubits, fifteen, which the waters prevailed over the highest mountains. Such a coincidence can lead to but one conclusion, the identity of origin of the two accounts."[bb]

John T. Short, quoting from Clavigero, says: "The Chiapanese have been the first peoplers of the New World, if we give credit to their traditions. They say that Votan, the grandson of that respectable old man who built the great ark to save himself and family from the deluge, and one of those who undertook the building of that lofty edifice, which was to reach up to heaven, went by express command of the Lord to people that land. They say also that the first people came from the quarter of the north, and that when they arrived at Soconusco, they separated, some going to inhabit the country of Nicaragua, and others remaining at Chiapas."[cc]

2. **Concerning the Successive Occupation of America by Different Peoples in Ancient Times**—It has been stated by eminent students of American archeology that two distinct classes, by some designated as separate races of mankind, inhabited this continent in early times. Professor F. W. Putnam[dd] is even more definite in his assertion that one of these ancient races spread from the north, the other from the south. Henry C. Walsh, in an article entitled "Copan, a City of the Dead,"[ee] gives many interesting details of excavation and other work prosecuted by Gordon under the auspices of the Peabody expedition; and adds, "All this points to successive periods of occupation, of which there are other evidences."[ff]

3. **Concerning the Advent of at Least One Division of the Ancient Americans from the East, Probably from Asia; and Their Israelitish Origin**—Confirmatory evidence of the belief that the aboriginal Americans sprang from the peoples of the eastern hemisphere is found in the similarity of record and tradition on the two continents, regarding the creation, the deluge, and other great events of history. Boturini,[gg] who is quoted by writers on American archeology, says: "There is no Gentile nation that refers to primitive events with such certainty as the Indians do. They give us an account of the creation of the world, of the deluge,[hh] of the confusion of languages at the Tower of Babel, and of all other periods and ages of the world, and of the long peregrinations which their people had in Asia representing the specific years by their characters; and in the seven Conejos (rabbits) they tell us of the great eclipse that occurred at the death of Christ, our Lord."

---

[z] Moses Thatcher, *Contributor,* vol. 2, p. 227, Salt Lake City, 1881.

[aa] See Appendix 15:3.

[bb] Moses Thatcher, *Contributor,* Vol. 2, p. 228.

[cc] John T. Short, *North Americans of Antiquity,* p. 204; Harper Bros., New York; 2nd ed., 1888. See also *Contributor,* Salt Lake City, vol. 2, p. 259.

[dd] See Putnam, "Prehistoric Remains in the Ohio Valley," *Century Magazine,* March, 1890.

[ee] See *Harper's Weekly* (New York), September, 1897, p. 879; article by Henry C. Walsh.

[ff] See Appendix 15:4.

[gg] Chevalier Boturini; he spent several years investigating the antiquities of Mexico and Central America, and collected many valuable records, of most of which he was despoiled by the Spanish; he published a work on the subject of his studies in 1746. His mention of a "great eclipse" at the time of the crucifixion has reference to the "darkness over all the land" (Matt. 27:45), which could not have been due to a solar eclipse, as this phenomenon is possible only at new moon, and the Jewish Passover, in the time of which the crucifixion occurred, came at full moon.

[hh] See Appendix 15:5.

Similar evidence of the common source of eastern and western traditions of great events in primitive times is furnished in the writings of Short, already quoted, and by Baldwin,[ii] Clavigero,[jj] Kingsborough,[kk] Sahagun,[ll] Prescott,[mm] Schoolcraft,[nn] Squiers,[oo] and others.[pp]

John T. Short adds his testimony to the evidence of the aboriginal inhabitants of America being of "Old World origin," but admits his inability to determine when or whence they came to this continent.[qq] Waterman, before cited, says: "This people could not have been created in Africa, for its inhabitants were widely dissimilar from those of America; nor in Europe, which was without a native people agreeing at all with American races; then to Asia alone could they look for the origin of the Americans."[rr]

Lord Kingsborough, in his comprehensive and standard work, refers to a manuscript by Las Casas, the Spanish Bishop of Chiapa, which writing is preserved in the convent of St. Dominic, Mexico; in this the bishop states that a knowledge of the Godhead was found to exist among the natives of Yucatan. One of the bishop's emissaries wrote: "He had met with a principal lord who, on his questioning him respecting the faith and ancient religion which prevailed in that country, informed him that they knew and believed in God who resided in heaven; and that this God was the Father, Son, and Holy Ghost; and that the Father was named Ycona, who had created men and all things; and that the Son was called Bacab, who was born of a virgin named Chibirias, who was in heaven with God; and that the name of the mother of Chibirias was Ischel; and that the Holy Ghost was called Echuah. Bacab, the Son, they said, was put to death by Eopuco, who scourged him and put a crown of thorns upon his head, and placed him with his arms stretched out upon a beam of wood, to which they believed that he had not been nailed but tied: and that he died there, and remained during three days dead; and that on the third day he came to life and ascended into heaven, where he is with his Father: and immediately afterwards Echuah came, who is the Holy Ghost, and filled the earth with whatsoever it stood in need of."[ss]

Rosales affirms a tradition among the Chileans to the effect that their forefathers were visited by a wonderful personage, full of grace and power, who wrought many miracles among them, and taught them of the Creator who dwelt in heaven in the midst of glorified hosts.[tt] Prescott refers to the symbol of the cross, which was found by the followers of Cortez to be common among the natives of Mexico and Central America. In addition to this sign of a belief in Christ, a ceremony suggestive of analogy to the sacrament of the communion was witnessed with astonishment by the invaders. Aztec priests were seen to prepare a cake of flour, mixed with blood, which they consecrated and gave to the people, who, as they ate, "showed signs of humiliation and sorrow, declaring it was the flesh of Deity."[uu]

[ii] Baldwin, *Ancient America* (Harper Bros., New York, 1871).

[jj] Clavigero, quoted by Prof. Short in *North Americans of Antiquity,* p. 140.

[kk] Lord Kingsborough, *Mexican Antiquities* (1830-37), vol. 6.

[ll] Bernardo de Sahagun, Historia *Universal de Nueva Espana.*

[mm] W. H. Prescott, *Conquest of Mexico.*

[nn] Schoolcraft, *Ethnological Researches* (1851); see vol. 1.

[oo] Squiers, *Antiquities of the State of New York,* 1851.

[pp] See Bancroft's *Native Races,* etc., vols. 3 and 5; Donnelly's *Atlantis,* p. 391; 1882; see also Appendix 15:7.

[qq] John T. Short, *North Americans of Antiquity,* p. 517 (1879).

[rr] Extract from lecture by Prof. Waterman, delivered in Bristol, England, 1849; quoted in pamphlet by Edwin F. Parry, *A Prophet of Latter Days,* Liverpool, 1898.

[ss] Kingsborough's *Antiquities of Mexico,* vol. 6, pp. 160, 161.

[tt] Rosales, *History of Chile;* see Pres. Taylor's *Mediation and Atonement,* pp. 200–202.

[uu] Prescott, *Conquest of Mexico,* vol. 2; Appendix, part 1, p. 389.

The Mexicans recognize a Deity in Quetzalcoatl, the traditional account of whose life and death is closely akin to our history of the Christ, so that, says President John Taylor, "we can come to no other conclusion than that Quetzalcoatl and Christ are the same being."[vv] Lord Kingsborough speaks of a painting of Quetzalcoatl, "in the attitude of a person crucified, with the impression of nails in his hands and feet, but not actually upon the cross." The same authority further says: "The seventy-third plate of the Borgian MS. is the most remarkable of all, for Quetzalcoatl is not only represented there as crucified upon a cross of Greek form, but his burial and descent into hell are also depicted in a very curious manner." And again: "The Mexicans believe that Quetzalcoatl took human nature upon him, partaking of all the infirmities of man, and was not exempt from sorrow, pain, or death, which he suffered voluntarily to atone for the sins of man."[ww]

The source of this knowledge of Christ and the Godhead is apparent to the student of the Book of Mormon. We learn from that scripture that the progenitors of the native American races, for centuries prior to the time of Christ's birth, lived in the light of direct revelation, which, coming to them through their authorized prophets, showed the purposes of God respecting the redemption of mankind; and, moreover, that the risen Redeemer ministered unto them in person, and established His Church among them with all its essential ordinances. The people have fallen into a state of spiritual degeneracy; many of their traditions are sadly distorted and disfigured by admixture of superstition and human invention; yet the origin of their knowledge is plainly authentic.

4. **Concerning a Common Origin of Native American Races**—That the many tribes and nations among the Indians are of common parentage is generally admitted; the conclusion is based on the evident close relationship in their languages, traditions, and customs. "Mr. Lewis H. Morgan finds evidence that the American aborigines had a common origin in what he calls 'their system of consanguinity and affinity.' He says, 'The Indian nations from the Atlantic to the Rocky Mountains, and from the Arctic sea to the Gulf of Mexico, with the exception of the Esquimaux, have the same system. It is elaborate and complicated in its general form and details; and, while deviations from uniformity occur in the systems of different stocks, the radical features are in the main constant. This identity in the essential characteristics of a system so remarkable tends to show that it must have been transmitted with the blood to each stock from a common original source. It affords the strongest evidence yet obtained of unity in origin of the Indian nations within the regions defined.'"[xx]

Bradford's summary of conclusions regarding the origin and characteristics of the ancient Americans sets forth: "That they were all of the same origin, branches of the same race, and possessed of similar customs and institutions."[yy]

Written Language of the Ancient Americans—To these secular, or extra-scriptural, evidences of the authenticity of the Book of Mormon may be added the agreement of the record with discoveries regarding the written language of these ancient peoples. The prophet Nephi states that he made his record on the plates in "the language of the Egyptians,"[zz] and we are further told that the brazen plates of Laban were inscribed in the same.[aaa] Mormon, who abridged the voluminous writings of his predecessors, and prepared the plates from which the modern translation was made, also employed Egyptian characters. His son Moroni, who completed the record, declares

---

[vv] *Mediation and Atonement,* p. 201.
[ww] Lord Kingsborough, *Antiquities of Mexico,* see quotations by Pres. John Taylor, *Mediation and Atonement,* p. 202.
[xx] Baldwin's *Ancient America,* p. 66.
[yy] Bradford's *American Antiquities,* under title "Conclusions," p. 431, 1841.
[zz] 1 Nephi 1:2.
[aaa] See Mosiah 1:4.

this fact; but, recognizing a difference between the writing of his day and that on the earlier plates, he attributed the change to the natural mutation through time, and speaks of his own record and that of his father, Mormon, as being written in the "reformed Egyptian."[bbb]

But the Egyptian is not the only eastern language found to be represented in the relics of American antiquities; the Hebrew occurs in this connection with at least equal significance. That the Hebrew tongue should have been used by Lehi's descendants is most natural, inasmuch as they were of the House of Israel, transferred to the western continent directly from Jerusalem. That the ability to read and write in that language continued with the Nephites until the time of their extinction is evident from Moroni's statement regarding the language used on the plates of Mormon: "And now, behold, we have written this record according to our knowledge, in the characters which are called among us the reformed Egyptian, being handed down and altered by us, according to our manner of speech. And if our plates had been sufficiently large we should have written in Hebrew; but the Hebrew hath been altered by us also."[ccc]

The following instances are taken from an instructive array brought together by Elder George Reynolds.[ddd] Several of the early Spanish writers claim that the natives of some portions of the land were found speaking a corrupt Hebrew. "Las Casas so affirms with regard to the inhabitants of the island of Hayti. Lafitu wrote a history wherein he maintained that the Caribbee language was radically Hebrew. Isaac Nasci, a learned Jew of Surinam, says of the language of the people of Guiana, that all their substantives are Hebrew." Spanish historians record the early discovery of Hebrew characters on the western continent. "Malvenda says that the natives of St. Michael had tombstones, which the Spaniards digged up, with several ancient Hebrew inscriptions upon them."

In all such writings, the characters and the language are allied to the most ancient form of Hebrew, and show none of the vowel signs and terminal letters which were introduced into the Hebrew of the eastern continent after the return of the Jews from the Babylonian captivity. This is consistent with the fact that Lehi and his people left Jerusalem shortly before the captivity, and therefore prior to the introduction of the changes in the written language.[eee]

Another Test—Let not the reader of the Book of Mormon content himself with such evidences as have been cited concerning the authenticity of this reputed scripture. There is promised a surer and a more effectual means of ascertaining the truth or falsity of this volume. Like other scriptures, the Book of Mormon is to be comprehended through the spirit of scripture, and this is obtainable only as a gift from God. But this gift is promised unto all who shall seek for it. Then to all let us commend the counsel of the last writer in the volume, Moroni, the solitary scribe who sealed the book, afterward the angel of the record who brought it forth: "And when ye shall receive these things, I would exhort you that ye would ask God, the Eternal Father, in the name of Christ, if these things are not true; and if ye shall ask with a sincere heart, with real intent, having faith in Christ, he will manifest the truth of it unto you, by the power of the Holy Ghost. And by the power of the Holy Ghost ye may know the truth of all things."[fff]

[bbb] Mormon 9:32.

[ccc] Mormon 9:32, 33. See especially articles entitled "Egyptology and the Book of Mormon," by Robert C. Webb, in *Improvement Era*, vol. 26, Salt Lake City, February, March, April, 1923; also article "The Book of Mormon Plates," by J. M. Sjodahl in the April issue, same volume; and Appendix 15:6.

[ddd] Reynolds, "The Language of the Book of Mormon," in *The Contributor*, Salt Lake City, vol. 17, p. 236.

[eee] See an instructive series of articles in *Improvement Era*, Salt Lake City, vol. 17, by Thomas W. Brookbank, entitled "Hebrew Idioms and Analogies in the Book of Mormon."

[fff] Moroni 10:4, 5.

REFERENCES

Biblical Allusions to the Book of Mormon

For out of Jerusalem shall go forth a remnant, and they that escape out of Mount Zion: the zeal of the Lord of Hosts shall do this—2 Kings 19:31.

The vision of all is become as the words of a book that is sealed; this is delivered to the learned and the unlearned—Isa. 29:11, 12.

Note that at the foretold time of the coming forth of this book people would be led away from the doctrines of God by the precepts of men—Isa. 29:13; compare the words of the Lord Jesus Christ to Joseph Smith: They teach for doctrines the commandments of men—P. of G.P. p. 49.

The people spoken of in the book were to be brought down and their speech was to be low out of the dust—Isa. 29:4. Compare: Truth shall spring out of the earth; and righteousness shall look down from heaven—Ps. 85:11.

The stick or record of Judah and the children of Israel his companions; also the stick of Joseph, called also the stick of Ephraim, and for all the house of Israel his companions, these to be one in the Lord's hands—Ezek. 37:16–19.

And other sheep I have, which are not of this fold: they shall hear my voice—John 10:16. Compare the words of the resurrected Lord to the Nephites that they were the other sheep of another fold—3 Nephi 15:17–24.

Book of Mormon Testimony Relating to Itself

The words of the Lord to Nephi, son of Lehi, relating to the bringing forth of scriptures other than the Holy Bible: Unto the Gentiles in this day, much of the gospel, plain and precious, to be given; the Nephites to write many things, which, after the destruction of the people as a nation, were to be hidden up, later to come forth unto the Gentiles; these writings to contain the record of the gospel—1 Nephi 13:34–37.

Nephi, who had kept the records of his people, was commanded by the Lord to make other plates and to engrave upon them as directed—2 Nephi 5:29–33.

The word of the Lord through Nephi, son of Lehi, that those who are to be destroyed shall yet speak out of the ground, with speech low out of the dust; their book to be brought forth in a day when the Gentiles had built up many churches—2 Nephi 26:16–22. Compare Ps. 85:10–13 cited above.

The prayer of Enos that the Lord would preserve a record of his people and bring it forth in due time—Enos 13–18.

Mormon, who abridged and compiled the ancient records, predicts their coming forth—Mormon 5:12–15.

Moroni, son of Mormon, completes his father's record, and testifies to its coming forth—Mormon 8:13–17; 25–32.

Nephi, son of Lehi, predicts the bringing forth of a book which contains the words of them that have slumbered; the one appointed to bring it forth is to deliver the words of the book, but not the book, to another—2 Nephi 27:6–11.

The book itself to be hid from the world, but to be shown to three witnesses, and afterward to a few according to the will of God. The unsealed part to be translated, the sealed part to remain for a season—2 Nephi 27:12–25.

The book to come forth among the Gentiles shall establish the truth of the first, or the Holy Bible; and both shall be established in one—1 Nephi 13:39–42.

Concerning him who was appointed to bring forth the book in the last days—2 Nephi 3:6–16; 27:9–12, 15, 19; Mormon 8:14–16.

Many of the Gentiles reject the book, saying: A Bible! A Bible! We have got a Bible, and there cannot be any more Bible—2 Nephi, chap. 29. Note that the Gentile world has derisively called the Book of Mormon the "Mormon Bible."

The resurrected Christ commanded the Nephites to write the words he had given unto them—3 Nephi 16:4; read the entire chapter.

Latter-day Revelation Concerning the Book of Mormon

To Joseph Smith was given the power to translate the ancient records constituting the Book of Mormon—D&C 1:29; see also 20:8–12; 135:3.

Concerning the loss of certain manuscripts containing the translation of parts of the writings of Mormon—D&C, sec. 3. Compare 2 Nephi 5:30; 1 Nephi, chap. 9; Words of Mormon 7.

Concerning the testimony of the three witnesses to the Book of Mormon—D&C 5:1–18.

Joseph Smith called and chosen to bring forth the Book of Mormon—D&C 24:1.

And with Moroni, whom I have sent unto you to reveal the Book of Mormon—D&C 27:5.

Elders of the Church to teach the principles of the gospel contained in the Bible and the Book of Mormon—D&C 42:12.

Account of the revelation to Joseph Smith concerning the existence of the ancient records, and incidents relating to its translation—P.of G.P. pp. 51–57.

And he has translated the book, even that part which I have commanded him, and as your Lord and your God liveth it is true—D&C 17:6; read the entire section, which is directed to the three witnesses prior to their viewing the plates.

A knowledge of the Savior attested by both the Bible and the Book of Mormon—D&C 3:16–20.

16

REVELATION, PAST, PRESENT, AND FUTURE

ARTICLE 9

E BELIEVE all that God has revealed, all that He does now reveal, and we believe that He will yet reveal many great and important things pertaining to the Kingdom of God.

Revelation and Inspiration—In a theological sense the term *revelation* signifies the making known of divine truth by communication from the heavens. The Greek word, *apocalypsis,* which in meaning closely corresponds with our word *revelation,* expresses an uncovering or a disclosure of that which had been wholly or in part hidden—the drawing aside of a veil. An Anglicized form of the Greek term—*Apocalypse*—is sometimes used to designate the particular Revelation given to John upon the Isle of Patmos, the record of which forms the last book of the New Testament. Divine revelation, as illustrated by numerous examples in scripture, may consist of disclosures or declarations concerning the attributes of Deity, or of an expression of the will of God regarding the affairs of men.

The word *inspiration* is sometimes invested with a signification almost identical with that of *revelation,* though by origin and early usage it possessed a distinctive meaning. To inspire is literally to animate with the spirit; a man is inspired when under the influence of a power other than his own. Divine inspiration may be regarded as a lower or less directly intensive operation of spiritual influence upon man than is shown in revelation. The difference therefore is rather one of degree than of kind. By neither of these directing processes does the Lord deprive the human subject of agency or individuality,[a] as is proved by the marked peculiarities of style and method characterizing the several books of scripture. Yet, in the giving of revelation, a more direct influence operates upon the human recipient than under the lesser, though no less truly divine, effect of inspiration.[b]

The directness and plainness with which God may communicate with man is dependent upon the conditions of receptivity of the person. One may be susceptible to inspiration in its lower and simpler phases only; another may be so thoroughly responsive to this power as to be capable of receiving direct revelation; and this higher influence again may manifest itself in varying degrees, and with a greater or lesser shrouding of the divine personality. Consider the Lord's words to Aaron and Miriam, who had been guilty of disrespect toward Moses the revelator: "And the Lord came down in the pillar of the cloud, and stood in the door of the tabernacle, and called Aaron and Miriam: and they both came forth. And he said, Hear now my words: If there be a prophet among you, I the Lord will make myself known unto him in a vision, and will speak unto him in a dream. My servant Moses is not so, who is faithful in all mine house. With him will I speak mouth to mouth, even apparently, and not in dark speeches; and the similitude of the Lord shall he behold."[c]

We have seen that among the most conclusive proofs of the existence of a Supreme Being is that afforded by direct revelation from Him; and that some knowledge of the divine attributes and personality is essential to the rational exercise of faith in God. We can but imperfectly respect an authority whose very existence is a matter of uncertainty with us; therefore, if we are to implicitly trust and truly revere our Creator, we must know something of Him. Though the veil of mortality, with all its thick obscurity, may shut the light of the divine presence from the sinful heart, that separating curtain may be drawn aside and the heavenly light may shine into the righteous soul. By the listening ear, attuned to the celestial music, the voice of God has been heard declaring His personality and will; to the eye that is freed from the motes and beams of sin, single in its search after truth, the hand of God has been made visible; within the soul properly purified by devotion and humility the mind of God has been revealed.

Communication from God to Man—We have no record of a period of time during which an authorized minister of Christ has dwelt on earth, when the Lord did not make known to that servant the divine will concerning his appointed ministry. No man can take upon himself the honor and dignity of the ministry. To become an authorized minister of the Gospel, "a man must be called of God, by prophecy, and by the laying on of hands, by those who are in authority," and those in authority must have been similarly called. When thus commissioned, he speaks by a power greater than his own in preaching the Gospel and in administering the ordinances thereof; he may verily become a prophet unto the people. The Lord has consistently recognized and honored His servants so appointed. He has magnified their office in proportion to their worthiness, making them living oracles of the divine will. This has been true of every dispensation of the work of God.

It is a privilege of the Holy Priesthood to commune with the heavens, and to learn the immediate will of the Lord; this communion may be effected through the medium of dreams and visions, by Urim and Thummim, through the visitation of angels, or by the higher endowment

---

a See Appendix 16:1, 2.
b See Appendix 16:3.
c Num. 12:5–8.

of face to face communication with the Lord.[d] The inspired utterances of men who speak by the power of the Holy Ghost are scripture unto the people.[e] In specific terms the promise was made in olden times that the Lord would recognize the medium of prophecy through which to make His will and purposes known unto man: "Surely the Lord God will do nothing, but he revealeth his secret unto his servants the prophets."[f] Not all men may attain the position of special revelators: "The secret of the Lord is with them that fear him; and he will show them his covenant."[g] Such men are oracles of truth, privileged counselors, friends of God.[h]

Revelation in Ancient Times—Unto Adam, the patriarch of the race, to whom were committed the keys of the first dispensation, God revealed His will and gave commandments.[i] While living in a state of innocence prior to the fall, Adam had direct communication with the Lord; then, through transgression the man was driven from Eden, but he took with him some remembrance of his former happy state, including a personal knowledge of the existence and attributes of his Creator. While sweating under the penalty foretold and fulfilled upon him, tilling the earth in a struggle for food, he continued to call upon the Lord. As Adam and his wife, Eve, prayed and toiled, "they heard the voice of the Lord from the way toward the Garden of Eden, speaking unto them, and they saw him not; for they were shut out from his presence. And he gave unto them commandments."[j]

The patriarchs who succeeded Adam were blessed with the gift of revelation in varying degrees. Enoch, the seventh in the line of descent, was particularly endowed. We learn from Genesis that Enoch "walked with God," and that when he had reached the age of three hundred and sixty-five years "he was not; for God took him."[k] From the New Testament we learn something more regarding his ministry;[l] and the Writings of Moses furnish us a yet fuller account of the Lord's dealings with this richly endowed seer.[m] Unto him were made known the plan of redemption, and the prospective history of the race down to the meridian of time, thence to the Millennium and the final judgment. Unto Noah the Lord revealed His intentions regarding the impending deluge; by this prophetic voice the people were warned and urged to repent; disregarding it and rejecting the message, they were destroyed in their iniquity. With Abraham God's covenant was established; unto him was revealed the course of creative events;[n] and this covenant was confirmed unto Isaac and Jacob.

Through revelation God commissioned Moses to lead Israel from bondage. From the burning bush on Horeb the Lord declared to the man thus chosen: "I am the God of thy father, the God of Abraham, the God of Isaac, and the God of Jacob."[o] In all the troublous scenes between Moses and Pharaoh the Lord continued His communications unto His servant, who appeared amidst the glory of the divine endowment as a veritable god unto the heathen king.[p] And

d See chapter 12 herein.
e See D&C 68:4.
f Amos 3:7; see also 1 Nephi 22:2.
g Ps. 25:14.
h See John 15:14, 15.
i See Gen. 2:15–20; P.of G.P., Moses 3:16.
j P.of G.P., Moses 5:4, 5.
k Gen. 5:18–24.
l See Jude 14.
m See P.of G.P., Moses, chaps. 6, 8.
n See Gen., chaps. 17, 18; P.of G.P., Abraham, especially chaps. 3, 4, 5.
o Ex. 3:2–6.
p See Ex. 7:1; see also 4:16.

throughout the wearisome journey of four decades in the wilderness, the Lord ceased not to honor His prophet. So may we trace the line of revelators—men who have stood, each in his time, as the medium between God and the people, receiving instruction from the heavens and transmitting it to the masses—from Moses to Joshua, and on through the Judges to David and Solomon, thence to John, who was the immediate forerunner of the Messiah.

Christ Himself was a Revelator—Notwithstanding His personal authority, God though He had been and was, while Jesus Christ lived as a man among men He declared His work to be that of One greater than Himself, by whom He had been sent and from whom He received instructions. Note His words: "For I have not spoken of myself; but the Father which sent me, he gave me a commandment, what I should say, and what I should speak. And I know that his commandment is life everlasting: whatsoever I speak therefore, even as the Father said unto me, so I speak."[q] Further: "I can of mine own self do nothing: as I hear, I judge: and my judgment is just; because I seek not mine own will, but the will of the Father which hath sent me."[r] And again: "The words that I speak unto you I speak not of myself: but the Father that dwelleth in me, he doeth the works. * * * And as the Father gave me commandment, even so I do."[s]

The Apostles Likewise, left to bear the burden of the Church after the departure of the Master, looked to heaven for guidance, expected and received the word of revelation to direct them in their exalted ministry. Paul writing to the Corinthians said: "But God hath revealed them [divine truths] unto us by his Spirit: for the Spirit searcheth all things, yea, the deep things of God. For what man knoweth the things of a man, save the spirit of man which is in him? Even so the things of God knoweth no man, but the Spirit of God. Now we have received, not the spirit of the world, but the spirit which is of God; that we might know the things that are freely given to us of God."[t]

John affirms that the book known specifically as *The Revelation* was not written of his own wisdom, but that it is: "The Revelation of Jesus Christ, which God gave unto him, to shew unto his servants things which must shortly come to pass; and he sent and signified it by his angel unto his servant John."[u]

Current Revelation Necessary—The scriptures are conclusive as to the fact that, from Adam to John the Revelator, God directed the affairs of His people by personal communication through commissioned servants. As the written word—the record of revelation previously given—grew with time, it became a law unto the people, but in no period was that deemed sufficient. While the revelations of the past are indispensable as guides to the people, showing forth, as they do, the plan and purpose of God's dealings under particular conditions, they may not be universally and directly applicable to the circumstances of succeeding times. Many of the revealed laws are of general application to all men in all ages; e.g., the commandments—Thou shalt not steal; Thou shalt not kill; Thou shalt not bear false witness—and other injunctions regarding the duty of man toward his fellows, most of which are so plainly just as to be approved by the human conscience even without the direct word of divine command. Other laws may be equally general in application, yet they derive their validity as God-given ordinances from the fact that they have been authoritatively instituted as such. As examples of this class we may consider the requirements concerning the sanctity of the Sabbath, the necessity of baptism as a means of securing forgiveness of

---

[q] John 12:49, 50.
[r] John 5:30.
[s] John 14:10, 31.
[t] 1 Cor. 2:10–12.
[u] Rev. 1:1.

sins, the ordinances of confirmation, the sacrament, and others. Revelations of yet another kind are of record, such as have been given to meet the conditions of particular times, and these may be regarded as special, or circumstantial revelations, e.g., the instructions to Noah regarding the building of the ark and the warning of the people; the requirement made of Abraham that he leave the land of his nativity and sojourn in a strange country; the command to Moses, and through him to Israel, relative to the exodus from Egypt; the revelations given to Lehi directing the departure of his company from Jerusalem, their journeying in the wilderness, the building of a ship and the voyage on the great waters to another hemisphere.

It is at once unreasonable, and directly contrary to our conception of the unchangeable justice of God, to believe that He will bless the Church in one dispensation with a present living revelation of His will and in another leave the Church, to which He gives His name, to live as best it may according to the laws of a bygone age. True, through apostasy the authority of the Priesthood may have been taken from the earth for a season, leaving the people in a condition of darkness with the windows of heaven shut against them; but at such times God has recognized no earthly Church as His own, nor any prophet to declare with authority "Thus saith the Lord."

In support of the doctrine that revelation especially adapted to existing conditions is characteristic of God's dealings, we have the fact of laws having been ordained, and subsequently repealed when a more advanced stage of the divine plan had been reached. Thus, the law of Moses[v] was strictly binding upon Israel from the time of the exodus to that of Christ's ministry; but its repeal was declared by the Savior Himself,[w] and a higher law than that of carnal commandments, which had been given because of transgression, was instituted in its stead.

From the scriptures cited, and from numerous other assurances of holy writ, it is evident that revelation from God to man has been a vital characteristic of the living Church. It is equally plain that revelation is essential to the existence of the Church in an organized state on the earth. If to have authority to preach the Gospel and administer in the ordinances of the same a man must be called of God, "by prophecy"[x] it is evident that in the absence of direct revelation the Church would be left without authorized officers, and in consequence would become extinct. The prophets and patriarchs of old, the judges, the priests, and every authorized servant from Adam to Malachi, were called by direct revelation manifested through the special word of prophecy. This was true also of John the Baptist,[y] of the apostles,[z] and of lesser officers[aa] of the Church, as long as an organization recognized of God remained on the earth. Without the gift of continual revelation there can be no authorized ministry on the earth; and without officers duly commissioned there can be no Church of Christ.

Revelation is essential to the Church, not only for the proper calling and ordination of its ministers but also that the officers so chosen may be guided in their administrations—to teach with authority the doctrines of salvation, to admonish, to encourage, and if necessary to reprove the people, and to declare unto them by prophecy the purposes and will of God respecting the Church, present and future. The promise of salvation is not limited by time, place, or persons. So taught Peter on Pentecost day, assuring the multitude of their eligibility to blessing: "For the promise is

[v] See Ex., chap. 21; Lev., chap 1; Deut., chap. 12.
[w] See Matt. 5:17–48.
[x] See chapter 10 herein.
[y] See Luke 1:13–20.
[z] See John, chap. 15; Acts 1:12–26.
[aa] See Acts 20:28; 1 Tim. 4:14; Titus 1:5.

unto you," said he, "and to your children, and to all that are afar off, even as many as the Lord our God shall call."[bb] Salvation, with all the gifts of God, was of old for Jew and Greek alike;[cc] the same Lord over all, rich unto those who would call upon Him, without difference.[dd]

Alleged Objections in Scripture—The opponents of the doctrine of continual revelation quote, with gross perversion of meaning, certain scriptural passages to sustain their heresy; among such scriptures are the following. The words of John with which he approaches the conclusion of his book are these: "For I testify unto every man that heareth the words of the prophecy of this book, If any man shall add unto these things, God shall add unto him the plagues that are written in this book: And if any man shall take away from the words of the book of this prophecy, God shall take away his part out of the book of life, and out of the holy city, and from the things which are written in this book."[ee] To apply these sayings to the Bible as it was afterward compiled is wholly unjustified, for John did not write his book as the concluding section of any such compilation of the scriptures as we now possess in our Bible. John had reference to his own prophecies, which, having come to him by revelation, were sacred; and to alter such, by omission or addition, would be to modify the words of God. The sin of altering any other part of the revealed word would be equally great. Moreover, in this oft-quoted passage, no intimation is given that the Lord may not add to or take from the word therein revealed; the declaration is that no man may change the record and escape the penalty. A similar injunction against altering the message of divine command was uttered by Moses, over fifteen centuries before the date of John's writing,[ff] and with a similarly restricted application.

Another alleged objection to modern revelation is offered in Paul's words to Timothy, regarding the scriptures "which are able to make thee wise unto salvation,"[gg] and which are "profitable for doctrine, for reproof, for correction, for instruction in righteousness: That the man of God may be perfect, thoroughly furnished unto all good works."[hh] The remarks of the apostle to the elders of Ephesus are quoted with the same intent: "Ye know * * * how I kept back nothing that was profitable unto you, but have shewed you, and have taught you publicly, and from house to house * * * For I have not shunned to declare unto you all the counsel of God."[ii] It is argued that if the scriptures known to Timothy were all-sufficient to make him "wise unto salvation," and the man of God "perfect, thoroughly furnished unto all good works," the same scriptures are sufficient for all men to the end of time; and that if the doctrines preached to the Ephesian elders represented "all the counsel of God," no further counsel is to be expected. In reply, it is perhaps sufficient to say that the objectors to continued revelation who defend their unscriptural position by strained interpretation of such passages, if consistent, would be compelled to reject all revelation given through the apostles after the date of Paul's utterances, including even the Revelation of John.

Equally inconsistent is the assertion that Christ's dying exclamation "It is finished" meant that revelation was at an end; for we find the same Jesus afterward revealing Himself, as the resurrected Lord, promising the apostles further revelation,[jj] and assuring them that He would be with

---

[bb] Acts 2:39.
[cc] See Rom. 10:12; Gal. 3:28; Col. 3:11.
[dd] See Rom. 3:22.
[ee] Rev. 22:18, 19; see also D&C 20:35.
[ff] See Deut. 4:2; 12:32.
[gg] 2 Tim. 3:15.
[hh] 2 Tim. 3:16, 17.
[ii] Acts 20:18–27.
[jj] See Luke 24:49.

them even unto the end.[kk] Moreover, were the words of the Crucified One susceptible of any such intent, the apostles, who taught as they were directly and specifically led by revelation as long as they lived, must be classed as impostors.

To justify the anathema with which the opponents of modern revelation seek to persecute those who believe in the continual flow of God's word to His Church, the following prophecy of Zechariah is quoted: "And it shall come to pass in that day, saith the Lord of hosts, that I will cut off the names of the idols out of the land, and they shall no more be remembered; and also I will cause the prophets and the unclean spirit to pass out of the land. And it shall come to pass, that when any shall yet prophesy, then his father and his mother that begat him shall say unto him, Thou shalt not live; for thou speakest lies in the name of the Lord: and his father and his mother that begat him shall thrust him through when he prophesieth. And it shall come to pass in that day, that the prophets shall be ashamed every one of his vision, when he hath prophesied."[ll] The day here spoken of appears to be yet future, for the idols and the unclean spirits still have influence; and, moreover, the fact that the prophets here spoken of are false ones is shown by Zechariah's associating them with idols and unclean spirits.

Such attempts to refute the doctrine of continued revelation as have been made on the authority of the foregoing scriptures are pitiably futile; they carry their own refutation, and leave untouched the truth that belief in current revelation is wholly reasonable and strictly scriptural.[mm]

Latter-day Revelation—In the light of our knowledge concerning the continuity of revelation as an essential characteristic of the Church, it is as reasonable to look for new revelation today as to believe in the actuality of the gift during ancient times. "Where there is no vision, the people perish"[nn] was declared of old; and it is proper to include with vision, revelation also, since the latter gift is often manifested through dreams and visions. Nevertheless, in spite of abundant and most explicit testimony of scripture, so-called Christian sects of the day are practically a unit in declaring that direct revelation ceased with the apostles or even before their time; that further communication from the heavens is unnecessary; and that to expect such is unscriptural. In assuming this position the discordant sects of the day are but following the path that was trodden by unbelievers in earlier times. The recreant Jews rejected the Savior because He came to them with a new revelation. Had they not Moses and the prophets to guide them, and what more could they need? They openly boasted: "We are Moses' disciples" and added: "We know that God spake unto Moses: as for this fellow, we know not from whence he is."[oo]

The scriptures, far from asserting a cessation of revelation in latter times, expressly declare the restoration and latter-day operation of that gift. John foresaw the bringing anew of the Gospel in the last days, through angelic ministration; and having seen in vision what was then future, he voiced the prediction in the past tense as though already accomplished: "And I saw another angel fly in the midst of heaven, having the everlasting gospel to preach unto them that dwell on the earth, and to every nation, and kindred, and tongue, and people."[pp] He knew further that the voice of God would be heard in the last days, calling His people from Babylon to a place of safety: "And I heard another voice from heaven saying, Come out of her, my people, that ye be not partakers of her sins, and that ye receive not of her plagues."[qq]

[kk] See Matt. 28:20; see also Mark 16:20.
[ll] Zech. 13:2–4.
[mm] See Appendix 16:2.
[nn] Prov. 29:18.
[oo] John 9:28, 29.
[pp] Rev. 14:6.
[qq] Rev. 18:4.

The Book of Mormon is not less explicit in declaring that direct revelation shall abide as a blessing upon the Church in the latter days. Note the prophecy given through Ether the Jaredite; the context shows that the time spoken of is that of the last dispensation: "And in that day that they [the Gentiles] shall exercise faith in me, saith the Lord, even as the brother of Jared did, that they may become sanctified in me, then will I manifest unto them the things which the brother of Jared saw, even to the unfolding unto them all my revelations, saith Jesus Christ, the Son of God, the Father of the heavens and of the earth, and all things that in them are. * * * But he that believeth these things which I have spoken, him will I visit with the manifestations of my Spirit, and he shall know and bear record."[rr]

Lehi, instructing his sons, quoted a prophecy of Joseph the son of Jacob, which is not recorded in the Bible; it has special reference to the work of Joseph the modern prophet: "Yea, Joseph truly said: thus saith the Lord unto me: A choice seer will I raise up out of the fruit of thy loins; and he shall be esteemed highly among the fruit of thy loins. And unto him will I give commandment that he shall do a work for the fruit of thy loins, his brethren, which shall be of great worth unto them, even to the bringing of them to the knowledge of the covenants which I have made with thy fathers."[ss]

Nephi, son of Lehi, spoke by prophecy of the last days, in which the Gentiles should receive a testimony of Christ with many signs and wondrous manifestations: "He manifesteth himself unto all those who believe in him, by the power of the Holy Ghost; yea, unto every nation, kindred, tongue, and people, working mighty miracles, signs, and wonders, among the children of men according to their faith. But behold, I prophesy unto you concerning the last days; concerning the days when the Lord God shall bring these things forth unto the children of men."[tt]

The same prophet, apostrophizing with warning words the unbelievers of the last days, predicted the coming forth of additional scriptures: "And it shall come to pass that the Lord God shall bring forth unto you the words of a book, and they shall be the words of them which have slumbered. And behold the book shall be a revelation from God, from the beginning of the world to the ending thereof."[uu]

The Savior, addressing the Nephites, repeated the prediction of Malachi concerning the revelation to be given through Elijah, before the day of the Lord's second coming: "Behold, I will send you Elijah the prophet before the coming of the great and dreadful day of the Lord; And he shall turn the heart of the fathers to the children, and the heart of the children to their fathers, lest I come and smite the earth with a curse."[vv]

By revelation in the present day the Lord has confirmed and fulfilled His earlier promises, and has specifically rebuked those who would close His mouth and estrange His people from Him. His voice is heard today, "proving to the world that the holy scriptures are true, and that God does inspire men and call them to his holy work in this age and generation, as well as in generations of old; Thereby showing that he is the same God yesterday, today, and forever."[ww]

Revelation Yet Future—In view of the demonstrated facts that revelation between God and man has ever been and is a characteristic of the Church of Jesus Christ, it is reasonable to await

---

[rr] Ether 4:7, 11.

[ss] 2 Nephi 3:7.

[tt] 2 Nephi 26:13, 14.

[uu] 2 Nephi 27:6, 7.

[vv] 3 Nephi 25:5, 6; see also Mal. 4:5, 6; and for the fulfilment, D&C 110:13–16.

[ww] D&C 20:11, 12; see also 1:11; 11:25; 20:26-28; 35:8; 42:61; 50:35; 59:4; 70:3; and the entire volume, as evidence of the continuation of revelation in the Church today.

with confident expectation the coming of other messages from heaven, even until the end of man's probation on earth. The Church is, and shall continue to be, as truly founded on the rock of revelation as it was in the day of Christ's prophetic blessing upon Peter, who through this gift of God was able to testify of his Lord's divinity.[xx] Current revelation is equally plain with that of former days in predicting the yet future manifestations of God through this appointed channel.[yy] The canon of scripture is still open; many lines, many precepts, are yet to be added; revelation, surpassing in importance and glorious fulness any that has been recorded, is yet to be given to the Church and declared to the world.

What justification or pretense of consistency can man claim for denying the power and purposes of God to reveal Himself and His will in these days as He assuredly did in former times? In every department of human knowledge and activity, in everything for which man arrogates glory to himself, he prides himself in the possibilities of enlargement and growth; yet in the divine science of theology he holds that progress is impossible and advancement forbidden. Against such heresy and blasphemous denial of divine prerogatives and power, God has proclaimed His edict in words of piercing import: "Wo be unto him that shall say: We have received the word of God, and we need no more of the word of God, for we have enough!"[zz] "Deny not the spirit of revelation, nor the spirit of prophecy, for wo unto him that denieth these things."[aaa]

REFERENCES

Direct Communication from God to Man—Many scriptural passages relating to this subject have been cited; see references following Chapter 12.

The Lord revealed himself to Adam, both before and after the fall—Gen., chaps. 2, 3, and others; Moses, chaps. 4, 5, etc.

Surely the Lord God will do nothing, but he revealeth his secret unto his servants the prophets—Amos 3:7.

Christ declared to Peter that the church should be built upon revelation—Matt. 16:15–19.

The God of heaven to set up a kingdom which shall never be destroyed—Dan. 2:44.

The Lord foretold future revelation to his people—Jer. 31:33, 34.

The Lord predicted that he would plead with his people face to face—Ezek. 20:35, 36.

Revelation through Elijah the prophet promised—Mal. 4:5, 6; compare P.of G.P. pp. 52, 53; D&C 2:1; 27:9; 110:14, 15; 128:17; 110:13.

A promise that the Spirit of truth should show things to come—John 16:13.

That God may give the spirit of wisdom and revelation—Eph. 1:17.

Paul testifies to revelation personally received—Eph. 3:3-5.

The Lord gave thanks that the Father had given revelations—Matt. 11:25.

But God hath revealed them unto us by his Spirit—1 Cor. 2:10.

For I neither received it of man, neither was I taught it, but by the revelation of Jesus Christ—Gal. 1:12.

Divine revelation may be given to correct error—Philip. 3:15.

[xx] See Matt. 16:16-19; Mark 8:27–29; Luke 9:18–20; John 6:69.
[yy] See D&C 20:35; 35:8; and the D&C references last cited.
[zz] 2 Nephi 28:29; see also verse 30, and 29:6–12.
[aaa] D&C 11:25; see also Appendix 16:4.

The saints kept by the power of God through faith unto salvation ready to be revealed in the last time—1 Peter 1:5; see also 4:13.

The revelation of Jesus Christ unto his servant John—the Book of Revelation.

Abraham received all things by revelation and commandment—D&C 132:29.

Promise of revelation from God as in times of old—1 Nephi 10:19.

Consult References following chapter 15—"Book of Mormon Testimony Relating to Itself."

Gifts of the Spirit, including wisdom, knowledge, and prophecy, are not to cease except through the transgressions of the people—Moroni 10:24; consider the entire chapter.

God will give his word, line upon line, precept upon precept—2 Nephi 28:29, 30.

Manifestations of the Eternal Father and his Son Jesus Christ to Joseph Smith in the year 1820—P. of G. P. pp. 49, 50.

I will speak unto you and prophesy, as unto men in days of old—D&C 45:15.

The Lord to reveal things of the kingdom from days of old and for ages to come—D&C 76:7–10.

Commissioned by ordination to teach the revelations received and those yet to be received—D&C 43:7.

Revelations of God which shall come hereafter—D&C 20:35.

I deign to reveal unto my church things which have been kept hid from before the foundation of the world—D&C 124:40–42.

A time to come in the which nothing shall be withheld, but all shall be manifest—D&C 121:28–32.

A revelation through vision given to Joseph Smith and Sidney Rigdon, 1832—D&C, sec. 76.

Revelation and personal manifestations to Joseph Smith and Oliver Cowdery in the Temple at Kirtland, Ohio, 1836—D&C, sec. 110.

Men ordained to the priesthood are to speak as they are moved upon by the Holy Ghost—D&C 68:3–6.

Revelation dealing with the affairs of the saints in Zion, Jackson County, Missouri—D&C, sec. 97.

Deny not the spirit of revelation nor the spirit of prophecy, for wo unto him that denieth these things—D&C 11:25.

17

THE DISPERSION OF ISRAEL

ARTICLE 10

E BELIEVE in the literal gathering of Israel and in the restoration of the Ten Tribes; * * *

Israel—The combined name and title, *Israel,* in the original sense of the word, expressed the thought of one who had succeeded in his supplication before the Lord; "soldier of God," "one who contends with God," "a prince of God," are among the common English equivalents. The name first appears in sacred writ as a title conferred upon Jacob, when the latter prevailed in his determination to secure a blessing from his heavenly visitor in the wilderness, receiving the promise: "Thy name shall be called no more Jacob, but Israel: for as a prince hast thou power with God and with men, and hast prevailed."[a] We read further: "And God appeared unto Jacob again, when he came out of Padan-aram, and blessed him. And God said unto him, Thy name is Jacob: thy name shall not be called any more Jacob, but Israel shall be thy name: and he called his name Israel."[b]

But the name-title thus bestowed under conditions of solemn dignity acquired a wider application, and came to represent the posterity of Abraham, through Isaac and Jacob,[c] with each of whom the Lord had covenanted that through his descendants should all nations of the earth be blessed.[d] The name of the individual patriarch thus grew into the designation of a people,

[a] Gen. 32:28.
[b] Gen. 35:9, 10.
[c] See 1 Sam. 25:1; Isa. 48:1; Rom. 9:4; 11:1.
[d] See Gen. 12:1–3; 17:1-8; 26:3, 4; 28:13–15.

And yet other tribulations were to follow, against which the people were warned lest they alienate themselves entirely from the God of their fathers: "And what will ye do in the day of visitation, and in the desolation which shall come from far? To whom will ye flee for help?"[q] The prophet directs the attention of his erring people to the fact that their tribulations are from the Lord: "Who gave Jacob for a spoil, and Israel to the robbers? Did not the Lord, he against whom we have sinned? For they would not walk in his ways, neither were they obedient unto his law. Therefore he hath poured upon him the fury of his anger, and the strength of battle."[r]

After the captivity of Ephraim, or the kingdom of Israel specifically so called, the people of Judah needed yet further admonishments. Through Jeremiah the fate of their brethren was brought to their remembrance; then, as a result of their continued and increasing wickedness, the Lord said: "And I will cast you out of my sight, as I have cast out all your brethren, even the whole seed of Ephraim."[s] Their land was to be despoiled; all the cities of Judah were to be consigned to desolation,[t] and the people were to be scattered among the kingdoms of the earth.[u] Other prophets[v] revealed the Lord's words of anger and dire warning; and the divine decree is recorded: "I will sift the house of Israel among all nations, like as corn is sifted in a sieve;"[w] and again: "I will sow them among the people: and they shall remember me in far countries."[x]

Book of Mormon Predictions—The record made by the division of the house of Israel that took its departure from Jerusalem and made its way to the western hemisphere about 600 B.C., contains many references to the dispersions that had already taken place, and to the continuation of the scattering which was to the writers of the Book of Mormon yet future. In the course of the journey to the coast, and while encamped with his company in the valley of Lemuel on the borders of the Red Sea, the Prophet Lehi declared what he had learned by revelation of the future "dwindling of the Jews in unbelief," of their crucifying the Messiah, and of their scattering "upon all the face of the earth."[y] He compared Israel to an olive-tree,[z] the branches of which were to be broken off and distributed; and he recognized the exodus of his colony and their journeying afar as an incident in the general course of dispersion.[aa] Nephi, son of Lehi, also beheld in vision the scattering of the covenant people of God, and on this point added his testimony to that of his prophet-father.[bb] He saw also that the posterity of his brethren, subsequently known as the Lamanites, would be chastened for their unbelief, and that they were destined to become subject to the Gentiles, and to be scattered before them.[cc] Down the prophetic vista of years he saw also the bringing forth of sacred records, other than those then known, "unto the convincing of the Gentiles and the remnant of the seed of my brethren,[dd] and also the Jews who were scattered upon all the face of the earth."[ee]

[q] Isa. 10:3.

[r] Isa. 42:24, 25.

[s] Jer. 7:12, 15.

[t] See Jer. 9:11; 10:22.

[u] See Jer. 34:17.

[v] See Ezek. 20:23; 22:15; 34:6; 36:19; Amos 7:17; 9:9; Micah 3:12.

[w] Amos 9:9.

[x] Zech. 10:9.

[y] 1 Nephi 10:11, 12.

[z] See 1 Nephi 15:12, 13; see also Jacob, chaps. 5, 6.

[aa] See 1 Nephi 10:13.

[bb] See 1 Nephi 14:14.

[cc] See 1 Nephi 13:11–14.

[dd] A division of Lehi's posterity, known at a later date as Lamanites.

[ee] 1 Nephi 13:39.

After their arrival on the promised land, the colony led by Lehi received further information regarding the dispersion of Israel. The prophet Zenos,[ff] quoted by Nephi, had predicted the unbelief of the house of Israel, in consequence of which the people were to "wander in the flesh, and perish, and become a hiss and a byword, and be hated among all nations."[gg] The brothers of Nephi, skeptical in regard to these teachings, asked whether the things of which he spake were to come to pass in a spiritual sense or more literally, and were informed that "the house of Israel, sooner or later, will be scattered upon all the face of the earth, and also among all nations"; and further, in reference to dispersions then already accomplished, that "the more part of all the tribes have been led away; and they are scattered to and fro upon the isles of the sea";[hh] and then, by way of prediction concerning further division and separation, Nephi adds that the Gentiles shall be given power over the people of Israel, "and by them shall our seed be scattered."[ii] Though an ocean lay between the country of their nativity and the land to which they had been miraculously brought, the children of Lehi learned through revelation by the mouth of Jacob, Nephi's brother, of the captivity of the Jews whom they had left at Jerusalem.[jj] By Nephi they were further told of troubles then impending over the city of their birth, and of a further dispersion of their kindred, the Jews.[kk]

The Lamanites, a division of Lehi's posterity, were also to be disrupted and scattered, as witness the words of Samuel, a prophet of that benighted people.[ll] Nephi, the third prophet of that name, grandson of Helaman, emphasizes the dispersion of his people by declaring that their "dwellings shall become desolate."[mm] Jesus Himself, after His resurrection, while ministering to the division of His flock on the western hemisphere, refers solemnly to the remnant who were to be "scattered forth upon the face of the earth because of their unbelief."[nn]

From these citations it is plain that the followers of Lehi, including his own family, and Zoram,[oo] together with Ishmael and his family,[pp] from whom sprang the mighty peoples the Nephites, who suffered extermination as a nation because of their unfaithfulness, and the Lamanites, who, now known as the American Indians, have continued in troubled existence until the present day, were informed by revelation of the dispersion of their former compatriots in the land of Palestine, and of their own certain doom if they continued in disobedience to the laws of God. We have said that the transfer of Lehi and his followers from the eastern to the western hemisphere was itself a part of the general dispersion. It should be remembered that another colony of Jews came to the west, the start dating about eleven years after the time of Lehi's departure. This second company was led by Mulek, a son of Zedekiah, who was the last king of Judah; they left Jerusalem immediately after the capture of the city by Nebuchadnezzar, about 588 B.C.[qq]

The Fulfilment of These Prophecies—The sacred scriptures, as well as other writings for which the claim of direct inspiration is not asserted, record the literal fulfilment of prophecy in the desolation of the house of Israel. The dividing of the nation into the separate kingdoms of

[ff] See Appendix 17:3.
[gg] 1 Nephi 19:12–14.
[hh] 1 Nephi 22:1–4.
[ii] 1 Nephi 22:7.
[jj] See 2 Nephi 6:8.
[kk] See 2 Nephi 25:14, 15.
[ll] See Helaman 15:12.
[mm] 3 Nephi 10:7.
[nn] 3 Nephi 16:4.
[oo] See 1 Nephi 4:20–26, 30–37.
[pp] See 1 Nephi 7:2–6, 19, 22; 16:7.
[qq] See Omni 14–19; Mos. 25:2–4; Alma 22:30-32; Hel. 6:10; 8:21, p. 262.

Judah and Israel led to the downfall of both. As the people grew in their disregard for the laws of their fathers their enemies were permitted to triumph over them. After many minor losses in war the kingdom of Israel met an overwhelming defeat at the hands of the Assyrians, in or about the year 721 B.C. We read that Shalmanezer IV, king of Assyria, besieged Samaria, the third and last capital of the kingdom,[rr] and that after three years the city was taken by Sargon, Shalmanezer's successor. The people of Israel were carried captive into Assyria and distributed among the cities of the Medes.[ss] Thus was the dread prediction of Ahijah to the wife of Jeroboam fulfilled. Israel was scattered beyond the river,[tt] probably the Euphrates, and from the time of this event the Ten Tribes are lost to history.

The sad fate of the kingdom of Israel had some effect in partially awakening among the people of Judah a sense of their own impending doom. Hezekiah reigned as king for nine and twenty years, and proved himself a bright exception to a line of wicked rulers who had preceded him. Of him we are told that "he did that which was right in the sight of the Lord."[uu] During his reign, the Assyrians under Sennacherib invaded the land; but the Lord's favor was in part restored to the people and Hezekiah roused them to a reliance upon their God, bidding them take courage and fear not the Assyrian king nor his hosts, "for," said this righteous prince, "there be more with us than with him: With him is an arm of flesh; but with us is the Lord our God to help us, and to fight our battles."[vv] The Assyrian army was miraculously destroyed.[ww] But Hezekiah died, and Manasseh ruled in his stead; this king did evil in the sight of the Lord,[xx] and the wickedness of the people continued for half a century or more, broken only by the good works of one righteous king, Josiah.[yy]

While Zedekiah occupied the throne, Nebuchadnezzar, king of Babylon, laid siege to Jerusalem,[zz] took the city about 588 B.C., and soon thereafter led the people captive into Babylon, thus virtually putting an end to the kingdom of Judah. The people were scattered among the cities of Asia, and groaned under the vicissitudes of the Babylonian captivity for nearly seventy years, after which they were given permission by Cyrus the Persian, who had subdued the Babylonians, to return to Jerusalem. Multitudes of the exiled Jews availed themselves of this opportunity, though many remained in the land of their captivity; and while those who did return earnestly sought to reestablish themselves on a scale of their former power they were never again a truly independent people. They were assailed by Syria and Egypt, and later became tributary to Rome, in which condition they were during the personal ministry of Jesus Christ amongst them.

Jeremiah's prophecy still lacked a complete fulfilment, but time proved that not a word was to fail. "Judah shall be carried away captive, all of it; it shall be wholly carried away captive";[aaa] this was the prediction. A rebellious disturbance among the Jews gave a semblance of excuse for chastisement to be visited upon them by their Roman masters, which culminated in the destruction of Jerusalem, A.D. 71. The city fell after a six months' siege before the Roman arms led by Titus, son

[rr] Shechem was the first capital of the kingdom of Israel (1 Kings 12:25); later, Tirzah became the capital; it was famous for its beauty (1 Kings 14:17; 15:33; 16:8, 17, 23; Song of Sol. 6:4); and lastly Samaria (1 Kings 16:24).
[ss] See 2 Kings 17:5, 6; 18:9–11.
[tt] 1 Kings 14:15.
[uu] 2 Kings 18:1–3; 2 Chr. 29:1–11.
[vv] 2 Chr. 32:7, 8.
[ww] See 2 Chr. 32:21, 22.
[xx] See 2 Chr. 33:1–10; 2 Kings 21:1–9.
[yy] See 2 Kings 22:1; 2 Chr. 34:1.
[zz] See 2 Kings 25:1–3; 2 Chr. 36:17.
[aaa] Jer. 13:19.

of the Emperor Vespasian. Josephus, the famous historian to whom we owe most of our knowledge as to the details of the struggle, was himself a resident in Galilee and was carried to Rome among the captives. From his record we learn that more than a million Jews lost their lives through the famine incident to the siege; many more were sold into slavery, and uncounted numbers were forced into exile. The city was utterly destroyed, and the site upon which the Temple had stood was plowed up by the Romans in their search for treasure. Thus literally were the words of Christ fulfilled: "There shall not be left here one stone upon another, that shall not be thrown down."[bbb]

Since the destruction of Jerusalem and the final disruption of the Jewish autonomy, the Jews have been wanderers upon the face of the earth, a people without a country, a nation without a home. The prophecy uttered by Amos of old has had its literal fulfilment—truly have Israel been sifted among all nations "like as corn is sifted in a sieve."[ccc] Let it be remembered, however, that coupled with this dread prediction was the promise: "Yet shall not the least grain fall upon the earth."

The Lost Tribes—As already stated, in the division of the Israelites after the death of Solomon ten tribes established themselves as an independent kingdom. This, the kingdom of Israel, was terminated as far as history is concerned by the Assyrian captivity, 721 B.C. The people were led into Assyria and later disappeared so completely that they have been called the Lost Tribes. They seem to have departed from Assyria, and while we lack definite information as to their final destination and present location, there is abundant evidence that their journey was toward the north.[ddd] The Lord's word through Jeremiah promises that the people shall be brought back "from the land of the north,"[eee] and a similar declaration has been made through divine revelation in the present dispensation.[fff]

In the writings of Esdras or Ezra, which, however, are not included among the canonical books of the Bible but are known as apocryphal, we find references to the northbound migration of the Ten Tribes, which they undertook in accordance with a plan to escape the heathen by going to "a farther country where never man dwelt, that they might there keep their statues which they never kept in their own land."[ggg] The same writer informs us that they journeyed a year and a half into the north country, but he gives us evidence that many remained in the land of their captivity.

The resurrected Christ, while ministering among the Nephites on this hemisphere, specifically mentioned "the other tribes of the house of Israel, whom the Father hath led away out of the land;"[hhh] and again He referred to them as "other sheep which are not of this land, neither of the land of Jerusalem; neither in any parts of that land round about whither I have been to minister."[iii] Christ announced a commandment of the Father that He should reveal Himself to them. The present location of the Lost Tribes has not been revealed.

REFERENCES

Dispersion of Israel Foretold—Biblical Predictions
Prediction that the descendants of Joseph should be as branches that run over the wall—Gen. 49:22.

[bbb] Matt. 24:1, 2; see also Luke 19:44; see *Jesus the Christ,* pp. 563, 567, 586.
[ccc] Amos 9:9.
[ddd] See Jer. 3:12.
[eee] Jer. 16:15; 23:8; 31:8.
[fff] See D&C 133:26, 27.
[ggg] 2 Esdras 13; see Appendix 17:4.
[hhh] 3 Nephi 15:15.
[iii] 3 Nephi 16:1.

And I will scatter you among the heathen—this conditioned on the wickedness of the people—Lev. 26:33; see also Deut. 4:27.

Israel to flee before their enemies, and to be removed into all the kingdoms of the earth—Deut. 28:25. The people to become an astonishment, a proverb, and a byword, among all nations whither the Lord would lead them—verse 37. And the Lord shall scatter thee among all people, from the one end of the earth even unto the other—verse 64.

Because of their wickedness the Lord would smite Israel, and root them up out of the good land, and scatter them beyond the river—1 Kings 14:15.

The Lord removed Israel out of his sight, as he had said by all his servants the prophets. So was Israel carried away out of their own land to Assyria—2 Kings 17:23.

To the kingdom of Judah the Lord spake: And I will cast you out of my sight, as I have cast out all your brethren, even the whole seed of Ephraim—Jer. 7:15. Judah shall be carried away captive all of it, it shall be wholly carried away captive—13:19; see also 15:14. Judah to be delivered, to be removed to all the kingdoms of the earth, to be a curse, and an astonishment, and a hissing, and a reproach, among all the nations whither the Lord would drive them—29:16–19.

And I will scatter thee among the heathen, and disperse thee in the countries—Ezek. 22:15.

I will sift the house of Israel, among all nations, like as corn is sifted in a sieve, yet shall not the least grain fall upon the earth—Amos 9:9.

And I will sow them among the people: and they shall remember me in far countries—Zech. 10:9.

Woes to fall upon the people in the day of visitation, and in the desolation which would come from far—Jer. 5:15.

Israel shall surely go into captivity—Amos 7:17.

The people who remained until the time of Christ were to be further scattered: Shall be led away captive into all nations: and Jerusalem shall be trodden down of the Gentiles, until the times of the Gentiles be fulfilled—Luke 21:24.

Book of Mormon Prophecies of the Dispersion

Lehi predicted the Babylonian captivity, and that the people should be scattered on all the face of the earth, and recognized the bringing of himself and his colony to the western continent as part of the decreed scattering—1 Nephi 10:3, 12–14.

Scattering of the descendants of Lehi shown in vision to Nephi—1 Nephi 13:14, 15.

Scattering of the Jews following the crucifixion of Christ foretold by Jacob—2 Nephi 10:5, 6; compare verse 22.

The Voice from heaven proclaimed further scattering unless the people would repent—3 Nephi 10:7.

The Gentiles to contribute to the scattering of the house of Israel—3 Nephi 20:27; see also Mormon 5:9, 20.

The Dispersion Successively Accomplished

The kingdom of Israel removed, and none but those of Judah left; all the seed of Israel delivered into the hand of spoilers—2 Kings 17:20.

And the king of Assyria did carry away Israel unto Assyria—2 Kings 18:9–11.

The Lord gave Jacob for a spoil, and Israel to the robbers, because of the sins of the people—Isa. 42:24.

Zion a wilderness and Jerusalem a desolation—Isa. 64:10, 11.

I lifted up mine hand unto them also in the wilderness, that I would scatter them among the heathen, and disperse them through the countries—Ezek. 20:23, 24; see also 36:19; compare 34:5, 6.

And them that had escaped from the sword carried he away to Babylon—2 Chr. 36:17-20.

But I scattered them with a whirlwind among all the nations whom they knew not—Zech. 7:13, 14; compare Joel 3:2; James 1:1.

Nephi proclaimed part of the dispersion already accomplished and predicted further scattering—1 Nephi 22:3–5, 7, 8.

The Lord revealed to Jacob that the Jews had been carried away captive—2 Nephi 6:8.

Consider the allegory of the olive-tree, and the pruning of the vineyard—Jacob, chaps. 5, 6.

18

THE GATHERING OF ISRAEL

ARTICLE 10

E BELIEVE in the literal gathering of Israel and in the restoration of the Ten Tribes; * * *

The Gathering Predicted—Dire as was the chastisement decreed on Israel for their waywardness, amounting, as it did, to their dissolution as a nation, fearful as has been their denunciation by Him who delighted to call them His people, yet through all their sufferings and privations, while wandering as outcasts among alien nations who have never ceased to treat them with contumely and insult, when their very name has been made a hiss and a byword in the earth, they have been sustained by the sure word of promise, that a day of glorious deliverance and blessed restoration awaits them. Associated with the curses, under which they writhed and groaned, were assurances of blessings. From the heart of the people, as from the soul of their king in the day of his affliction, has poured forth a song of tearful rejoicing: "Thou wilt not leave my soul in hell."[a] The sufferings of Israel have been but necessary chastening by a grieved yet loving Father, who planned by these effective means to purify His sin-stained children. To them He has freely told His purpose in thus permitting them to be afflicted; and in His punishments they have seen His love: "For whom the Lord loveth he chasteneth"[b] and "Blessed is the man whom thou chastenest, O Lord."[c]

[a] Ps. 16:10; Acts 2:27.
[b] Heb. 13:6.
[c] Ps. 94:12; see also Prov. 3:12; James 1:12; Rev. 3:19.

Though smitten of men, a large part of them gone from a knowledge of the world, Israel are not lost unto their God. He knows whither they have been led or driven; toward them His heart still yearns with paternal love; and surely will He bring them forth, in due time and by appointed means, into a condition of blessing and influence befitting His covenant people. In spite of their sin and notwithstanding the tribulations that they were bringing upon themselves, the Lord said: "And yet for all that, when they be in the land of their enemies, I will not cast them away, neither will I abhor them, to destroy them utterly, and to break my covenant with them: for I am the Lord their God."[d] As complete as was the scattering, so shall be the gathering of Israel.

Biblical Prophecies Concerning the Gathering—We have examined a few of the Biblical predictions concerning the dispersion of Israel; in all cases the blessing of eventual restoration was associated with the curse. Among the early prophecies we hear the Lord declaring that it shall come to pass that when thou, Israel, "shalt return unto the Lord thy God, and shalt obey his voice according to all that I command thee this day, thou and thy children, with all thine heart, and with all thy soul; That then the Lord thy God will turn thy captivity, and have compassion upon thee, and will return and gather thee from all the nations, whither the Lord thy God hath scattered thee. If any of thine be driven out unto the outmost parts of heaven, from thence will the Lord thy God gather thee, and from thence will he fetch thee: And the Lord thy God will bring thee into the land which thy fathers possessed, and thou shalt possess it; and he will do thee good, and multiply thee above thy fathers."[e]

Nehemiah pleaded in fasting and prayer that the Lord would remember His promise of restoration if the people would turn unto righteousness.[f] Isaiah spoke with no uncertain words of the assured return and reunion of scattered Israel, saying: "And it shall come to pass in that day, that the Lord shall set his hand again the second time to recover the remnant of his people, which shall be left. * * * And he shall set up an ensign for the nations, and shall assemble the outcasts of Israel, and gather together the dispersed of Judah from the four corners of the earth."[g]

The restoration is to be comprehensive; there shall be a united people, no longer two kingdoms each at enmity with the other; for: "The envy also of Ephraim shall depart, and the adversaries of Judah shall be cut off: Ephraim shall not envy Judah, and Judah shall not vex Ephraim."[h] With the words of a fond father the Lord thus speaks of His treatment of Israel and brightens their desolation with promise: "For a small moment have I forsaken thee; but with great mercies will I gather thee. In a little wrath I hid my face from thee for a moment; but with everlasting kindness will I have mercy on thee, saith the Lord thy Redeemer."[i]

After having given a fearful recital of the sins of the people and of the penalties to follow, Jeremiah thus voiced the will and purpose of God concerning the subsequent deliverance: "Therefore, behold, the days come, saith the Lord, that it shall no more be said, The Lord liveth, that brought up the children of Israel out of the land of Egypt; But, The Lord liveth, that brought up the children of Israel from the land of the north, and from all the lands whither he had driven them: and I will bring them again into their land that I gave unto their fathers. Behold, I will send for many fishers, saith the Lord, and they shall fish them; and after will I send for many hunters, and they shall hunt them from every

[d] Lev. 26:44; see also Deut. 4:27–31.
[e] Deut. 30:2–5.
[f] See Neh. 1:9.
[g] Isa. 11:11, 12.
[h] Same, verse 13; see also Ezek. 37:21, 22.
[i] Isa. 54:7, 8.

mountain, and from every hill, and out of the holes of the rocks."[j] And again: "Behold, I will bring them from the north country, and gather them from the coasts of the earth. * * * Hear the word of the Lord, O ye nations, and declare it in the isles afar off, and say, He that scattered Israel will gather him, and keep him, as a shepherd doth his flock. For the Lord hath redeemed Jacob, and ransomed him from the hand of him that was stronger than he. Therefore they shall come and sing in the height of Zion, and shall flow together to the goodness of the Lord."[k]

"Backsliding Israel," "treacherous Judah" are the terms of reproof with which the Lord addressed His recreant people; then He commanded the prophet, saying: "Go and proclaim these words toward the north, and say, Return, thou backsliding Israel, saith the Lord; and I will not cause mine anger to fall upon you: for I am merciful, saith the Lord, and I will not keep anger for ever. Only acknowledge thine iniquity, that thou hast transgressed against the Lord thy God, and hast scattered thy ways to the strangers under every green tree, and ye have not obeyed my voice, saith the Lord. Turn, O backsliding children, saith the Lord; for I am married unto you: and I will take you one of a city, and two of a family, and I will bring you to Zion: And I will give you pastors according to mine heart, which shall feed you with knowledge and understanding. And it shall come to pass, when ye be multiplied and increased in the land, in those days, saith the Lord, they shall say no more, The ark of the covenant of the Lord: neither shall it come to mind: neither shall they remember it; neither shall they visit it; neither shall that be done any more. At that time they shall call Jerusalem the throne of the Lord; and all the nations shall be gathered unto it, to the name of the Lord, to Jerusalem: neither shall they walk any more after the imagination of their evil heart. In those days the house of Judah shall walk with the house of Israel, and they shall come together out of the land of the north to the land that I have given for an inheritance unto your fathers."[l]

To Ezekiel the Lord also declared the plan of Israel's restoration: "Thus saith the Lord God; Behold, I will take the children of Israel from among the heathen, whither they be gone, and will gather them on every side, and bring them into their own land: And I will make them one nation in the land upon the mountains of Israel; and one king shall be king to them all: and they shall be no more two nations, neither shall they be divided into two kingdoms any more at all."[m]

That the reestablishment is to be a permanent one is evident from the revelation given through Amos, wherein we read that the Lord said: "And I will bring again the captivity of my people of Israel, and they shall build the waste cities, and inhabit them; and they shall plant vineyards, and drink the wine thereof; they shall also make gardens, and eat the fruit of them. And I will plant them upon their land, and they shall no more be pulled up out of their land which I have given them, saith the Lord thy God."[n]

As a fitting close to our selection of Biblical prophecies, let the words of Jesus of Nazareth be pondered, spoken while He lived among men: "And he shall send his angels with a great sound of a trumpet, and they shall gather together his elect from the four winds, from one end of heaven to the other."[o]

Book of Mormon prophecies—The gathering of Israel claimed the attention of many prophets whose teachings are recorded in the Book of Mormon, and not a little direct revelation

[j] Jer. 16:12–16.
[k] Jer. 31:7, 8, 10–12.
[l] Jer. 3:12–18; see also 23:8; 25:34; 30:3; 32:37.
[m] Ezek. 37:21, 22; see also 11:17; 20:34–42; 28:25; 34:11–13.
[n] Amos 9:14, 15.
[o] Matt. 24:31.

concerning the subject is preserved within the pages of that volume. We have noted Lehi's discourse in the valley of Lemuel, in which that patriarch-prophet compared the house of Israel to an olive-tree, the branches of which were to be broken off and scattered; now we may add his prediction regarding the subsequent grafting-in of the branches. He taught that, "after the house of Israel should be scattered they should be gathered together again; or, in fine, after the Gentiles had received the fulness of the Gospel, the natural branches of the olive-tree, or the remnants of the house of Israel, should be grafted in, or come to a knowledge of the true Messiah, their Lord and their Redeemer."[p]

Nephi, quoting the words of the prophet Zenos,[q] emphasizes the declaration that, when purified through suffering, Israel shall come again into the favor of the Lord, and then shall they be gathered from the four quarters of the earth, and the isles of the sea shall be remembered.[r] Jacob, brother of Nephi, testified to the truth of the prophecies of Zenos, and indicated the time of the gathering as a characteristic sign of the last days. Consider his words: "And the day that he shall set his hand again the second time to recover his people, is the day, yea, even the last time, that the servants of the Lord shall go forth in his power, to nourish and prune his vineyard; and after that the end soon cometh."[s]

Among the most comprehensive predictions regarding the restoration of the Jews is this utterance of Nephi: "Wherefore, the Jews shall be scattered among all nations; yea, and also Babylon shall be destroyed; wherefore, the Jews shall be scattered by other nations. And after they have been scattered, and the Lord God hath scourged them by other nations for the space of many generations, yea, even down from generation to generation until they shall be persuaded to believe in Christ, the Son of God, and the atonement, which is infinite for all mankind—and when that day shall come that they shall believe in Christ, and worship the Father in his name, with pure hearts and clean hands, and look not forward any more for another Messiah, then, at that time, the day will come that it must needs be expedient that they should believe these things. And the Lord will set his hand again the second time to restore his people from their lost and fallen state. Wherefore, he will proceed to do a marvelous work and a wonder among the children of men."[t]

Nephi, commenting on the words of Isaiah regarding the sufferings and subsequent triumph of the people of Israel, states the condition upon which their gathering is predicated, and says of God: "That he has spoken unto the Jews, by the mouth of his holy prophets, even from the beginning down, from generation to generation, until the time comes that they shall be restored to the true church and fold of God; when they shall be gathered home to the lands of their inheritance, and shall be established in all their lands of promise."[u]

It is evident from these and many other scriptures that the time of the full recovery or redemption of the Jews is to be determined by their acceptance of Christ as their Lord. When that time comes, they are to be gathered to the land of their fathers; and in the work of gathering, the Gentiles are destined to take a great and honorable part, as witness the further words of Nephi: "But behold, thus saith the Lord God: When the day cometh that they shall believe in me, that

[p] 1 Nephi 10:14; see also Jacob, chap. 5.
[q] See Appendix 17:3.
[r] See 1 Nephi 19:16; see also 1 Nephi 22:11, 12, 25; 2 Nephi 6:8–11.
[s] Jacob 6:2.
[t] 2 Nephi 25:15–17.
[u] 2 Nephi 9:2; see also 1 Nephi 15:19, 20; 19:13–16; 2 Nephi 25:16, 17, 20; 3 Nephi 5:21–26; 21:26–29; chap. 29; Mormon 5:14.

I am Christ, then have I covenanted with their fathers that they shall be restored in the flesh, upon the earth, unto the lands of their inheritance. And it shall come to pass that they shall be gathered in from their long dispersion, from the isles of the sea, and from the four parts of the earth; and the nations of the Gentiles shall be great in the eyes of me, saith God, carrying them forth to the land of their inheritance. Yea, the kings of the Gentiles shall be nursing fathers unto them, and their queens shall become nursing mothers; wherefore, the promises of the Lord are great unto the Gentiles, for he hath spoken it, and who can dispute?"[v]

The assistance which the Gentiles are to give in the preparation of the Jews, and of the remnant of the house of Israel established on the western continent, is affirmed by several Book of Mormon prophets; and, moreover, the blessings which the Gentiles may thus bring upon themselves are described in detail.[w] A single quotation must suffice for our present purpose; and this the declaration of the risen Lord, during His brief ministration among the Nephites: "But if they [the Gentiles] will repent, and hearken unto my words, and harden not their hearts, I will establish my church among them, and they shall come in unto the covenant and be numbered among this the remnant of Jacob, unto whom I have given this land for their inheritance; And they shall assist my people, the remnant of Jacob, and also as many of the house of Israel as shall come, that they may build a city, which shall be called the New Jerusalem. And then shall they assist my people that they may be gathered in, who are scattered upon all the face of the land, in unto the New Jerusalem. And then shall the power of heaven come down among them; and I also will be in the midst. And then shall the work of the Father commence at that day, even when this gospel shall be preached among the remnant of this people. Verily I say unto you, at that day shall the work of the Father commence among all the dispersed of my people, yea, even the tribes which have been lost, which the Father hath led away out of Jerusalem. Yea, the work shall commence among all the dispersed of my people, with the Father, to prepare the way whereby they may come unto me, that they may call on the Father in my name. Yea, and then shall the work commence, with the Father, among all nations, in preparing the way whereby his people may be gathered home to the land of their inheritance."[x]

Latter-day Revelation Concerning the Gathering—We have found abundant proof of the severely literal fulfilment of prophecies relating to the dispersion of Israel. The predictions relative to the gathering have been but partly fulfilled; for, while the work of concentration has been well begun, and is now in active progress, the consummation is yet future. It is reasonable, then, to look for revelation and prophecy concerning the subject in modern scripture as well as in the inspired writings of former times. Speaking to the elders of the Church in this dispensation, the Lord declares the purpose of gathering His people "even as a hen gathereth her chickens under her wings"[y] and adds: "And ye are called to bring to pass the gathering of mine elect; for mine elect hear my voice and harden not their hearts; Wherefore the decree hath gone forth from the Father that they shall be gathered in unto one place upon the face of this land, to prepare their hearts and be prepared in all things against the day when tribulation and desolation are sent forth upon the wicked."[z]

Hear further the word of the Lord unto the Church in the present day, not only predicting the gathering of the saints to Zion, but announcing that the hour for the gathering has come: "Wherefore, prepare ye, prepare ye, O my people; sanctify yourselves; gather ye together, O ye

[v] 2 Nephi 10:7–9; see also Isa. 49:23; 2 Nephi 30:7; 3 Nephi 5:26; 20:29–33.
[w] See 3 Nephi 21:21–27; Ether 13:8–10.
[x] 3 Nephi 21:22–28.
[y] Revelation, given 1830, D&C 29:2; see also 10:65; 43:24.
[z] D&C 29:7, 8; see also 31:8; 33:6; 38:31; 45:25; 77:14; 84:2; 133:7.

people of my Church * * * Yea, verily I say unto you again, the time has come when the voice of the Lord is unto you: Go ye out of Babylon; gather ye out from among the nations, from the four winds, from one end of heaven to the other."[aa]

Extent and Purpose of the Gathering—Some of the prophecies already cited have special reference to the restoration of the Lost Tribes; others relate to the return of the people of Judah to the land of their inheritance; yet others refer to the rehabilitation of Israel in general, without mention of tribal or other divisions; while many passages in the revelations of the present dispensation deal with the gathering of the saints who have numbered themselves with the Church of Christ as reestablished. It is evident that the plan of gathering comprises:

1. Assembling in the land of Zion of the people of Israel from the nations of the earth.
2. Return of the Jews to Jerusalem.
3. Restoration of the Lost Tribes.

The sequence of these events as here presented is that of convenience and has no significance as to the order in which the several gatherings are to be accomplished. The division first named constitutes an important part of the current work of the Church, though the labor of assisting in the restoration of the Lost Tribes is included. We are informed by revelation, given in the Kirtland Temple, that the appointment to and the authority for the work were solemnly committed to the Church. And through none could such authority be more fittingly conferred than through him who had received it by divine commission in a former dispensation of united Israel. Moses, who was the representative of Israel's God when the Lord set His hand the first time to lead His people to the land of their appointed inheritance, has come in person and has committed to the latter-day Church the authority to minister in the work now that the Lord has "set his hand the second time" to recover His people.

Joseph Smith and Oliver Cowdery, each of whom had been duly ordained to the apostleship, testify of the manifestations made to them, in these words: "The heavens were again opened unto us; and Moses appeared before us, and committed unto us the keys of the gathering of Israel from the four parts of the earth, and the leading of the Ten Tribes from the land of the north."[bb] The importance of the work thus required of the Church was emphasized by a later revelation, in which the Lord gave this command: "Send forth the elders of my church unto the nations which are afar off; unto the islands of the sea; send forth unto foreign lands; call upon all nations, first upon the Gentiles, and then upon the Jews. And behold, and lo, this shall be their cry, and the voice of the Lord unto all people: Go ye forth unto the land of Zion * * * Let them, therefore, who are among the Gentiles flee unto Zion. And let them who be of Judah flee unto Jerusalem, unto the mountain of the Lord's house. Go ye out from among the nations, even from Babylon, from the midst of wickedness, which is spiritual Babylon."[cc]

The last sentence of the foregoing quotation expresses the purpose for which this work of gathering the saints from the nations of the earth has been ordained. The Lord would have His people separate themselves from the sins of the world and depart from spiritual Babylon, that they may learn the ways of God and serve Him the more fully. John the Revelator, while in exile on Patmos, saw in vision the fate of the sinful world. An angel came down from heaven, "and he cried

---

[aa] D&C 133:4, 7.
[bb] D&C 110:11.
[cc] D&C 133:8, 9, 12–14.

mightily with a strong voice, saying, Babylon the great is fallen, is fallen, and is become the habitation of devils, and the hold of every foul spirit, and a cage of every unclean and hateful bird. * * * And I heard another voice from heaven, saying, Come out of her, my people, that ye be not partakers of her sins, and that ye receive not of her plagues. For her sins have reached unto heaven, and God hath remembered her iniquities."[dd]

The faith of the Latter-day Saints teaches that in the day of the Lord's righteous fury safety will be found in Zion. The importance which they associate with the work of gathering, and the fidelity with which they seek to discharge the duty enjoined upon them by divine authority in the matter of warning the world of the impending dangers, as described in the Revelator's vision, are sufficiently demonstrated by the great extent of the missionary labor as at present prosecuted by this people.[ee]

Israel the Covenant People—The Lord has designated the people of Israel as especially His own.[ff] With Abraham He entered into a covenant and said: "I will make of thee a great nation, and I will bless thee, and make thy name great; and thou shalt be a blessing: And I will bless them that bless thee, and curse him that curseth thee: and in thee shall all families of the earth be blessed."[gg] This was to be an everlasting covenant.[hh] It was confirmed upon Isaac,[ii] and in turn upon Jacob who was called Israel.[jj] The promises regarding the multitudinous posterity, amongst whom were to be counted many of exalted rank, have been literally fulfilled. No less certain is the realization of the second part of the prediction, that in and through Abraham's descendants should all nations of the earth be blessed. For, by worldwide dispersion the children of Israel have been mingled with the nations; and the blood of the covenant people has been sprinkled among the peoples.[kk] And now, in this the day of gathering, when the Lord is again bringing His people together to honor and bless them above all that the world can give, every nation with the blood of Israel in the veins of its members will partake of the blessings.

But there is another and a more striking proof of blessings flowing to all nations through the house of Israel. The Redeemer was born in the flesh through the lineage of Abraham; and the blessings of that divine birth are extended, not only to the nations and families of the earth collectively, but to every individual in mortality.

Restoration of the Lost Tribes—From the scriptural passages already considered, it is plain that, while many of those belonging to the Ten Tribes were diffused among the nations, a sufficient number to justify the retention of the original name were led away as a body and are now in existence in some place where the Lord has hidden them. To them the resurrected Christ went to minister after His visit to the Nephites, as before stated. Their return constitutes a very important part of the gathering, characteristic of the dispensation of the fulness of times.

To the scriptures already quoted as relating to their return, the following should be added. As a feature of the work of God in the day of restoration we are told: "And they who are in the north countries shall come in remembrance before the Lord; and their prophets shall hear his voice, and shall no longer stay themselves; and they shall smite the rocks, and the ice shall flow down at their

---

[dd] Rev. 18:2, 4, 5.
[ee] See Appendix 18:1.
[ff] See Appendix 18:2.
[gg] Gen. 12:2, 3; see also Gal. 3:14, 16.
[hh] See Gen. 17:6–8.
[ii] See Gen. 26:3, 4.
[jj] See Gen. 35:11, 12.
[kk] See Appendix 18:3.

presence. And an highway shall be cast up in the midst of the great deep. Their enemies shall become a prey unto them, And in the barren deserts there shall come forth pools of living water; and the parched ground shall no longer be a thirsty land. And they shall bring forth their rich treasures unto the children of Ephraim, my servants. And the boundaries of the everlasting hills shall tremble at their presence. And there shall they fall down and be crowned with glory, even in Zion, by the hands of the servants of the Lord, even the children of Ephraim. And they shall be filled with songs of everlasting joy. Behold, this is the blessing of the everlasting God upon the tribes of Israel, and the richer blessing upon the head of Ephraim and his fellows."[ll]

From the express and repeated declaration, that in their exodus from the north the Ten Tribes are to be led to Zion, there to receive honor at the hands of those who are of Ephraim, who necessarily are to have previously gathered there, it is plain that Zion is to be first established. The establishment of Zion will receive attention in the next chapter.

REFERENCES

Biblical Prophecies Concerning the Gathering of Israel

The Lord promises not to forget Israel in their scattered condition—Lev. 26:44.

Then the Lord thy God will turn thy captivity, and have compassion upon thee, and will return and gather thee from all the nations whither the Lord thy God hath scattered thee—Deut. 30:1–5.

Supplication that the Lord will remember his words: Yet will I gather them from thence, and will bring them unto the place that I have chosen to set my name there—Neh. 1:8, 9.

When the Lord bringeth back the captivity of his people, Jacob shall rejoice, and Israel shall be glad—Ps. 14:7; see also 107:3.

The Lord will lift up an ensign to the nations from far, and will hiss unto them from the end of the earth: and, behold, they shall come with speed swiftly—Isa. 5:25, 26.

In that day, that the Lord shall set his hand again the second time to recover the remnant of his people—Isa. 11:11, 12.

And the ransomed of the Lord shall return, and come to Zion—Isa. 35:10.

The Lord promises to have mercy on Jacob and to choose Israel and set them in their own land—Isa. 14:1; see also 35:4; 43:5; 54:7; 61:4.

The Lord promised to restore both the house of Judah and the house of Israel—Jer. 3:12–18.

After that I have plucked them out I will return, and have compassion on them, and will bring them again, every man to his heritage, and every man to his land—Jer. 12:14, 15.

The Lord liveth, that brought up the children of Israel from the land of the north, and from all the lands whither he had driven them—Jer. 16:15, 16.

And I will gather the remnant of my flock out of all countries whither I have driven them, and will bring them again to their folds—Jer. 23:3.

I will bring again the captivity of my people Israel and Judah, saith the Lord; and I will cause them to return to the land that I gave to their fathers—Jer. 30:3; see also 31:7–12; 32:37, 38; 33:7-11; 50:4.

I will even gather you from the people, and assemble you out of the countries where ye have been scattered—Ezek. 11:17; see also 20:34.

[ll] D&C 133:26–34.

The Lord's promise of great blessings when he shall have gathered the house of Israel from the people among whom they are scattered—Ezek. 28:25, 26; 34:13; 37:21-27; Amos 9:14, 15.

At that time will I bring you again, even in the time that I gather you—Zeph. 3:20.

And they shall be as though I had not cast them off—Zech. 10:6.

Angels to gather together the Lord's elect from the four winds, from one end of heaven to the other—Matt. 24:31.

Come out of her, my people, that ye be not partakers of her sins, and that ye receive not of her plagues—Rev. 18:4.

Book of Mormon Prophecies Concerning the Gathering of Israel

And after the house of Israel should be scattered, they should be gathered together again—1 Nephi 10:14.

All the people who are of the house of Israel will I gather in, saith the Lord—1 Nephi 19:15, 16.

He will bring them again out of captivity, and they shall be gathered together to the lands of their inheritance—1 Nephi 22:11, 12; see verse 25.

When the Jews come to the knowledge of their Redeemer, they shall be gathered together again to the lands of their inheritance—2 Nephi 6:11; see also 9:2; 10:7.

He shall set his hand again the second time to recover his people—Jacob 6:2.

They shall be gathered in from their long dispersion, from the isles of the sea, and from the four parts of the earth—2 Nephi 10:8.

A remnant of the seed of Joseph to be gathered in from the four quarters of the earth—3 Nephi 5:23–26.

The gathering of Israel in the last days to be a sign of other great occurrences—3 Nephi 21:1–7.

The Father's purpose—to restore the Jews, or all the house of Israel, to the land of their inheritance—Mormon 5:14.

Latter-day Revelation Concerning the Gathering of Israel

The Church commissioned to bring about the gathering of the elect into one place upon the face of the land—D&C 29:7, 8.

The covenant people to be gathered in one—D&C 42:36.

The restoration of the scattered Israel to be shown—D&C 45:17; see also verses 25, 43, 69.

The land of Missouri appointed and consecrated for the gathering of the saints—D&C 57:1, 2.

And they that have been scattered shall be gathered—D&C 101:13.

Moses appeared in the Kirtland Temple and committed unto Joseph Smith and Oliver Cowdery the keys of the gathering of Israel from the four parts of the earth—D&C 110:11.

This is Elias which was to come to gather together the tribes of Israel and restore all things—D&C 77:9; see also verse 14.

Let them who are among the Gentiles flee unto Zion, and those of Judah flee unto Jerusalem—D&C 133:12, 13.

The Lost Tribes to Be Restored

They shall come together out of the land of the north—Jer. 3:18; see also 31:8.

Other sheep besides the Jews and the Nephites—3 Nephi 16:1–3.

The resurrected Christ announced that he was about to show himself unto the lost tribes of Israel—3 Nephi 17:4.

The work of the Father to be wrought among the tribes which have been lost—3 Nephi 21:26.

The records of the lost tribes of Israel shall be had among the Nephites and the Jews—2 Nephi 29:13.

Blessed conditions following the bringing back of the tribes from the north country—Ether 13:11.

Moses committed to Joseph Smith and Oliver Cowdery the keys of authority for the leading of the ten tribes from the land of the north—D&C 110:11.

And they who are in the north countries shall come in remembrance before the Lord—D&C 133:26–34; compare Isa. 35:3–10.

19

ZION

ARTICLE 10

ᴇ ʙᴇʟɪᴇᴠᴇ * * * that Zion will be built upon this [the American] continent; * * *

Two Gathering Places—Some of the passages quoted in connection with the dispersion and the subsequent gathering of Israel make reference to Jerusalem, which is to be reestablished, and Zion, which is to be built. True, the latter name is in many cases used as a synonym of the first, owing to the fact that a certain hill within the Jerusalem of old was known specifically as Zion, or Mount Zion; and the name of a part is often used figuratively to designate the whole; but in other passages the separate and distinctive meaning of the terms is clear. The prophet Micah, "full of power by the spirit of the Lord, and of judgment, and of might"[a] predicted the destruction of Jerusalem and its associated Zion, the former to "become heaps," and the latter to be "plowed as a field";[b] and then announced a new condition that is to exist in the last days, when another "mountain of the house of the Lord" is to be established, and this is to be called Zion.[c] The two places are mentioned separately in the prophecy: "For the law shall go forth of Zion, and the word of the Lord from Jerusalem."[d]

Joel adds this testimony regarding the two places from which the Lord shall rule over His people: "The Lord also shall roar out of Zion, and utter his voice from Jerusalem."[e] Zephaniah breaks forth

[a] Micah 3:8.
[b] Micah 3:12; see also page 293 of this book.
[c] See Micah 4:1.
[d] Micah 4:2; Isa. 2:2–3.
[e] Joel 3:16.

into song, with the triumph of Israel as his theme, and apostrophizes the daughters of both cities: "Sing, O daughter of Zion; shout, O Israel; be glad and rejoice with all the heart, O daughter of Jerusalem." Then, the prophet predicts separately of each place: "In that day it shall be said to Jerusalem, Fear thou not: and to Zion, Let not thine hands be slack."[f] Furthermore, Zechariah records the revealed will in this way: "And the Lord shall yet comfort Zion, and shall yet choose Jerusalem."[g]

When the people of the house of Jacob are prepared to receive the Redeemer as their rightful king, when the scattered sheep of Israel have been sufficiently humbled through suffering and sorrow to know and to follow their Shepherd, then, indeed, will He come to reign among them. Then a literal kingdom will be established, wide as the world, with the King of kings on the throne; and the two capitals of this mighty empire will be Jerusalem in the east and Zion in the west. Isaiah speaks of the glory of Christ's kingdom in the latter days, and ascribes separately to Zion and to Jerusalem the blessings of triumph:[h] "O Zion, that bringest good tidings, get thee up into the high mountain; O Jerusalem, that bringest good tidings, lift up thy voice with strength; lift it up, be not afraid; say unto the cities of Judah, Behold your God!"[i]

The Name "Zion" is used in several distinct senses. By derivation *Zion,* or, as written by the Greeks, *Sion,* probably meant bright, or sunny; but this commonplace signification is lost in the deeper and more affecting meaning that the word as a name and title came to acquire. As stated, a particular hill within the site of the city of Jerusalem was called Zion. When David gained his victory over the Jebusites he captured and occupied the "stronghold of Zion," and named it the city of David.[j] "Zion" then was the name of a place; and it has been applied as follows:

1. To the hill itself, or Mount Zion, and, by extension of meaning, to Jerusalem.
2. To the location of the "mountain of the house of the Lord," which Micah predicts shall be established in the last days, distinct from Jerusalem. To these we may add another application of the name as made known through modern revelation, viz.:
3. To the City of Holiness, founded by Enoch, the seventh patriarch in descent from Adam, and called by him Zion.[k]
4. Yet another use of the term is to be noted—a metaphorical one—by which the Church of God is called Zion, comprising, according to the Lord's own definition, the pure in heart.[l]

Jerusalem—As a fitting introduction to our study regarding the new Zion, yet to be built as we shall presently see on the western hemisphere, let us briefly consider the history and destiny of Jerusalem,[m] the Zion of the eastern continent. "Jerusalem" is generally believed to mean by derivation the foundation or city of peace. We meet it for the first time as Salem, the abode of Melchizedek, high priest and king, to whom Abram paid tithes.[n] We find a direct statement concerning the identity of Salem and Jerusalem by Josephus.[o] As noted, the city was wrested from the

f Zeph. 3:14–16.
g Zech. 1:17; see also 2:7–12.
h See Isa. 4:3, 4.
i Isa. 40:9.
j See 2 Sam. 5:6, 7; see also 1 Kings 2:10, and 8:1.
k See P. of G.P., Moses 7:18–21.
l See D&C 97:21.
m See Appendix 19:1.
n See Gen. 14:18–20.
o See Ant. of the Jews 1, chapter 10.

Jebusites by David;[p] this was about 1048 B.C. During the reigns of David and Solomon, the city as the capital of the kingdom of undivided Israel acquired great fame for its riches, beauty, and strength, its chief attraction being the imposing Temple of Solomon which adorned Mount Moriah.[q] After the division of the kingdom as a unit, Jerusalem remained the capital of the smaller kingdom of Judah.

Among its many and varied vicissitudes incident to the fortunes of war,[r] may be mentioned: the destruction of the city and the enslaving of the inhabitants by Nebuchadnezzar, 588–585 B.C.;[s] its reestablishment at the close of the Babylonian captivity,[t] about 515 B.C., and its final overthrow at the disruption of the Jewish nation by the Romans, 70–71 A.D. In importance and in the love of the Jews the city was the very heart of Jewry; and in the estimation of Christians it is invested with sanctity. It occupied an important place in the earthly works of the Redeemer, and was the scene of His death, resurrection, and ascension. The Savior's high regard for the chief city of His people is beyond question. He forbade that any should swear by it, "for it is the city of the great King;"[u] and because of its sins, He lamented over it as a father for a wayward child.[v] But, great as is Jerusalem's past, a yet greater future awaits her. Again will the city become a royal seat, her throne that of the King of kings, with permanency of glory assured.

The Latter-day Zion; New Jerusalem—Biblical statements concerning the Zion of the last days, as separate from both the ancient and the reestablished Jerusalem of the east, are silent regarding the geographical location of this second and latter-day capital of Christ's kingdom. We learn something, however, from the Bible as to the physical characteristics of the region wherein Zion is to be built. Thus, Micah, after predicting the desolation of the hill, Mount Zion, and of Jerusalem in general, describes in contrast the new Zion, at which the house of the Lord is to be built in the last days. These are his words: "But in the last days it shall come to pass, that the mountain of the house of the Lord shall be established in the top of the mountains, and it shall be exalted above the hills; and people shall flow unto it. And many nations shall come, and say, Come, and let us go up to the mountain of the Lord, and to the house of the God of Jacob; and he will teach us of his ways, and we will walk in his paths: for the law shall go forth of Zion, and the word of the Lord from Jerusalem."[w]

The prophecy of Isaiah is not less explicit regarding the mountainous character of the country of modern Zion;[x] and, furthermore, this writer assures us that the righteous man only shall be able to dwell amid the fiery splendor of this new abode; and of him the prophet says: "He shall dwell on high: his place of defense shall be the munitions of rocks;" and adds the statement that the land shall be very far off.[y] In another passage he mentions a gathering place "beyond the rivers of Ethiopia," and, "on the mountains" where the Lord is to set up an ensign to the world.[z]

p See 2 Sam. 5:6, 7.

q See 1 Kings, chaps. 5–8; 2 Chr., chaps. 2–7.

r See 1 Kings 14:25; 2 Kings 14:13, 14; chap. 25; 2 Chr. 12:25; 36:14-21; Jer. 39:5-8.

s See Jer. 52:12–15.

t See Ezra, chaps. 1–3; Neh., chap. 2.

u Matt. 5:35; see also Ps. 48:2; 87:3.

v See Matt. 23:37; Luke 13:34.

w Micah 4:1, 2.

x See Isa. 2:2, 3.

y See Isa. 33:15–17.

z See Isa. 18:1–3.

established on the chosen site; she "shall not be moved out of her place," and the pure in heart shall return "with songs of everlasting joy, to build up the waste places of Zion."[oo]

But gathered Israel cannot be confined to the "center place," nor to the region immediately adjacent; other places have been and will be appointed, and these are called Stakes of Zion.[pp] Many stakes have been established in the regions inhabited by the Latter-day Saints, to be permanent possessions; and thence will go those who are appointed from among the worthy to receive possessions of their inheritances. Zion is to be chastened, but only for a little season,[qq] then will come the time of her redemption.

That time will be appointed of God, yet it is to be determined according to the faithfulness of the people. Wickedness causes the Lord to tarry; for, saith He: "Therefore, in consequence of the transgressions of my people, it is expedient in me that mine elders should wait for a little season for the redemption of Zion."[rr] And again: "Zion shall be redeemed in mine own due time."[ss] But the Lord's time in giving blessings is dependent upon the prospective recipients. As long ago as 1834 came the word of the Lord unto the Church: "Behold, I say unto you, were it not for the transgressions of my people, speaking concerning the church and not individuals, they might have been redeemed even now."[tt]

REFERENCES

Two Gathering Places—Note that the two capitals of the kingdom of the world over which Christ shall reign are designated as Zion and Jerusalem; and further observe that the names of these two cities are sometimes used distinctively, and sometimes interchangeably in the figurative sense.

The mountain of the Lord's house to be established, and all nations to flow unto it—Isa. 2:2, 3.
He that is left in Zion, and he that remaineth in Jerusalem, shall be called holy—Isa. 4:3.
O Zion, and O Jerusalem, that bringest good tidings—Isa. 40:9.
Put on thy strength, O Zion; put on thy beautiful garments, O Jerusalem—Isa. 52:1.
In mount Zion and in Jerusalem shall be deliverance—Joel 2:32. The Lord shall roar out of Zion, and utter his voice from Jerusalem—3:16, 17.
The Lord shall yet comfort Zion, and shall yet choose Jerusalem—Zech. 1:17; see also 2:7–12.
The New Jerusalem is specifically mentioned: But ye are come unto mount Sion, and unto the city of the living God, the heavenly Jerusalem—Heb. 12:22.
The name of the city of God, the New Jerusalem, which cometh down out of heaven from God—Rev. 3:12.
The new heaven and the new earth, and the holy city, or New Jerusalem—Rev., chap. 21.
Ether saw the days of Christ; and he spake concerning a New Jerusalem upon the western continent—Ether 13:4–8.
The resurrected Lord confirmed earlier prophecies as to the establishment of a New Jerusalem on the western continent—3 Nephi 20:22.

[oo] D&C 101:17, 18; see also 101:43, 74, 75; 103:1, 11, 13, 15; 105:1, 2, 9, 13, 16, 34; 109:47; 136:18.
[pp] See D&C 101:21; see page 192 herein.
[qq] See D&C 100:13.
[rr] D&C 105:9; also 136:31.
[ss] D&C 136:18.
[tt] D&C 105:1, 2.

The Gentiles, if repentant, are to be permitted to assist the house of Israel in building the city to be called the New Jerusalem—3 Nephi 21:14–24.

The time for establishing the city of the New Jerusalem to be revealed—D&C 42:9; see also verses 62 and 67.

Lands to be purchased for the building of the New Jerusalem—D&C 42:35.

Characteristics of the New Jerusalem, to be called Zion—D&C 45:66–71.

The Lord will hasten the building of the city in its time—D&C 52:43.

The saints to stand upon Mount Zion, which shall be the city of the New Jerusalem—D&C 84:2–5.

The building of the New Jerusalem delayed—D&C 124:51, 52.

Prediction that in Zion alone shall there be safety—D&C 45:68, 69.

Blessed are they whose feet stand upon the land of Zion—D&C 59:3.

The rebellious shall not inherit the land of Zion—D&C 64:35.

The pure in heart to return to Zion with songs of everlasting joy—D&C 101:18.

Stakes of Zion organized—D&C 68:26; foundation to be laid for a stake of Zion—94:1.

Stakes, so-called, for the curtains or the strength of Zion—D&C 101:21; see also 109:59; Zion and her stakes—115:6; also verse 18; the people to gather that the stakes of Zion may be strengthened—133:9.

The Zion of Enoch: Why the Lord so called his people—Moses 7:18; taken into heaven—verse 23; taken to the bosom of the Lord—verse 31; see also verse 69.

20

CHRIST'S REIGN ON EARTH

ARTICLE 10

E BELIEVE * * * that Christ will reign personally upon the earth; * * *

First and Second Advents—The facts of our Lord's birth in the flesh, of His thirty and three years of life among mortals, of His ministry, sufferings, and death, are accepted as attested history. Not alone do the records regarded distinctively by the Christian world as sacred and inspired bear testimony concerning these facts, but the history written by man, and in contrast called profane, is in general harmony with the Biblical account. Even those who reject the doctrine of Christ's divinity and refuse to accept Him as their Redeemer admit the historical facts of His marvelous life, and acknowledge the incalculable effect of His precepts and example upon the human family.

In the "meridian of time" Christ was born to earth, amid humble surroundings—in obscurity, indeed, to all except the faithful few who had been watching for the promised event. His coming had been heralded through the previous centuries, even from the dawn of human existence; prophets of God had borne record of the great events that were to characterize His advent. Every important incident connected with His birth, life, death, triumphal resurrection, and ultimate glory as King, Lord, and God, had been predicted; and even circumstantial details were given with exactness.

Judah and Israel had been told to prepare for the coming of the Anointed One;[a] yet when He came to His own they received Him not. Persecuted and despised, He trod the thorny path of duty, "a man of sorrows and acquainted with grief"; and finally condemned by His people, who clamored to an alien power for authority to execute their own unjust sentence upon their Lord, He went to death by the torturing crucifixion prescribed for malefactors.

To human judgment it must have appeared that the mission of Jesus Christ had been nullified, that His work had failed, and that the powers of darkness had triumphed. Blind, deaf, and hard of heart were those who refused to see, hear, and comprehend the purport of the Savior's mission. Similarly benighted are they who reject the prophetic evidence of His second coming, and who fail to read the signs of the times, which declare the event, at once glorious and terrible, to be near at hand. Both before and after His death Christ prophesied of His appointed return to earth; and His faithful followers are today waiting and watching for the signs of the great fulfilment. The heavens are flaming with those signals, and the burden of inspired teaching is again heard—Repent, repent, for the kingdom of heaven is at hand.

Christ's Second Coming Predicted and Signs Described; Biblical Prophecies—The prophets of the Old Testament and those of Book of Mormon record who lived and wrote before the era of Christ, had little to say regarding the second coming of the Lord, little indeed in comparison with their numerous and explicit predictions concerning His first advent. As they looked into the sky of futurity their vision was dazzled with the brilliancy of the meridian sun, and saw little of the glorious luminary beyond, whose proportions and radiance were reduced by distance. A few of them saw and so testified, as the following passages show. The Psalmist sang: "Our God shall come, and shall not keep silence: a fire shall devour before him, and it shall be very tempestuous round about him."[b] These conditions did not attend the coming of the Babe of Bethlehem, and are yet future.

Isaiah cried: "Say to them that are of a fearful heart, Be strong, fear not: behold, your God will come with vengeance, even God with a recompense; he will come and save you."[c] Aside from the evident fact that these conditions were not characteristic of the first coming of Christ, the context of the prophet's words show that he applied them to the last days, the time of restitution, the day of the "ransomed of the Lord," and of triumph of Zion.[d] Again Isaiah spake: "Behold, the Lord God will come with strong hand, and his arm shall rule for him: behold, his reward is with him, and his work before him."[e]

The prophet Enoch, who lived twenty centuries before the first of those whose words are given above, spoke with vigor on the subject. His teachings do not appear under his own name in the Bible, though Jude, a New Testament writer, cites them.[f] From the Writings of Moses we learn concerning the revelation given to Enoch: "And the Lord said unto Enoch: As I live, even so will I come in the last days, in the days of wickedness and vengeance, to fulfil the oath which I have made unto you concerning the children of Noah."[g]

[a] See Appendix 20:1.
[b] Ps. 50:1, 3.
[c] Isa. 35:4.
[d] Same, verses 5–10.
[e] Isa. 40:10.
[f] See Jude 14, 15.
[g] P.of G.P., Moses 7:60.

Jesus taught the disciples that His mission in the flesh was to be of short duration, and that He would come again to earth, for we find them inquiring in this wise: "Tell us, when shall these things be? And what shall be the sign of thy coming, and of the end of the world?"[h] In reply, our Lord detailed many of the signs of the latter times, the last and greatest of which He thus stated: "And this gospel of the kingdom shall be preached in all the world for a witness unto all nations; and then shall the end come."[i] With great clearness, Jesus spoke of the worldliness in which the children of men had continued to indulge, even to the eve of deluge, and on the day of the fiery destruction which befell the Cities of the Plains, and added: "Even thus shall it be in the day when the Son of Man is revealed."[j]

Another of our Lord's predictions concerning His second coming is as follows: "And they [the disciples] asked him, saying, Master, but when shall these things be? And what sign will there be when these things shall come to pass? And he said, Take heed that ye be not deceived: for many shall come in my name, saying, I am Christ; and the time draweth near: Go ye not therefore after them. But when ye shall hear of wars and commotions, be not terrified: for these things must first come to pass; but the end is not by and by. Then said he unto them, Nation shall rise against nation, and kingdom against kingdom: And great earthquakes shall be in divers places, and famines, and pestilences; and fearful sights and great signs shall there be from heaven. But before all these, they shall lay their hands on you, and persecute you, delivering you up to the synagogues, and into prisons, being brought before kings and rulers for my name's sake. And it shall turn to you for a testimony. Settle it therefore in your hearts, not to meditate before what ye shall answer: For I will give you a mouth and wisdom, which all your adversaries shall not be able to gainsay nor resist. And ye shall be betrayed both by parents, and brethren, and kinsfolks, and friends; and some of you shall they cause to be put to death. And ye shall be hated of all men for my name's sake. * * * And there shall be signs in the sun, and in the moon, and in the stars; and upon the earth distress of nations, with perplexity; the sea and the waves roaring; Men's hearts failing them for fear, and for looking after those things which are coming on the earth: for the powers of heaven shall be shaken. And then shall they see the Son of Man coming in a cloud with power and great glory. And when these things begin to come to pass, then look up, and lift up your heads; for your redemption draweth nigh."[k]

Many of these dire predictions were realized at the destruction of Jerusalem; and the oft-quoted twenty-fourth chapter of Matthew undoubtedly has a double application—to the judgment brought upon Israel in the complete overthrow of the Jewish autonomy, and in the events now current immediately preceding the Lord's coming, when He shall take His rightful place as Ruler.

Again, by way of warning, the Lord said: "Whosoever therefore shall be ashamed of me and of my words in this adulterous and sinful generation; of him also shall the Son of Man be ashamed, when he cometh in the glory of his Father with the holy angels."[l]

At the time of the ascension, as the apostles stood gazing into the firmament where a cloud had hidden the resurrected Lord from sight, they became aware of the presence of two visitants in white apparel, who said: "Ye men of Galilee, why stand ye gazing up into heaven? This same

[h] Matt. 24:3; see *Jesus the Christ,* chap. 32.
[i] Matt. 24:14.
[j] Luke 17:26–30. For exposition of "The Son of Man" see *Jesus the Christ,* p. 142; see also chap. 32.
[k] Luke 21:7–28; see also Mark 13:14–26; Rev. 6:12–17; P.of G.P., pp. 43-46. For more detailed treatment see *Jesus the Christ,* chap. 32.
[l] Mark 8:38.

Jesus, which is taken up from you into heaven, shall so come in like manner as ye have seen him go into heaven."[m] Paul instructed the churches in the doctrines of Christ's second advent, and described the glory of His coming.[n] So also did others of the apostles.[o]

Among Book of Mormon Prophecies concerning our present subject, it is sufficient to consider here the personal assurances of Christ at the time of His ministrations to the Nephites in His resurrected state. To the multitude He explained many matters, "even from the beginning until the time that he should come in his glory."[p] In promising the three disciples the desire of their hearts, which was that they might be spared in the flesh to continue the work of the ministry, the Lord said to them: "Ye shall live to behold all the doings of the Father unto the children of men, even until all things shall be fulfilled according to the will of the Father, when I shall come in my glory with the powers of heaven."[q]

The Word of Modern Revelation is no less sure regarding the appointed advent of the Redeemer. To servants, specially commissioned, instructions were given to this effect: "Wherefore, be faithful, praying always, having your lamps trimmed and burning, and oil with you,[r] that you may be ready at the coming of the Bridegroom—For behold, verily, verily, I say unto you, that I come quickly."[s] And further: "Cry repentance unto a crooked and perverse generation, preparing the way of the Lord for his second coming. For behold, verily, verily, I say unto you, the time is soon at hand that I shall come in a cloud with power and great glory."[t]

In a revelation to the people of the Church, March 7, 1831, the Lord speaks of the signs of His coming, and counsels diligence: "Ye look and behold the fig-trees, and ye see them with your eyes, and ye say when they begin to shoot forth, and their leaves are yet tender, that summer is now nigh at hand; Even so it shall be in that day when they shall see all these things, then shall they know that the hour is nigh. And it shall come to pass that he that feareth me shall be looking forth for the great day of the Lord to come, even for the signs of the coming of the Son of Man. And they shall see signs and wonders, for they shall be shown forth in the heavens above, and in the earth beneath. And they shall behold blood, and fire, and vapors of smoke. And before the day of the Lord shall come, the sun shall be darkened, and the moon be turned into blood, and the stars fall from heaven. And the remnant shall be gathered unto this place; And then they shall look for me, and, behold, I will come; and they shall see me in the clouds of heaven, clothed with power and great glory, with all the holy angels; and he that watches not for me shall be cut off."[u]

A distinctive characteristic of the revelations given in the present dispensation, regarding the second coming of our Lord, is the emphatic and oft-repeated declaration that the event is near at hand.[v] The call is, "Prepare ye, prepare ye, for that which is to come; for the Lord is nigh." Instead of the cry of one man in the wilderness of Judea, the voice of thousands is heard authoritatively warning the nations and inviting them to repent and flee to Zion for safety. The fig-tree is rapidly putting forth its leaves; the signs in heaven and earth are increasing; the great and dreadful day of the Lord is near.

[m] Acts 1:11; see *Jesus the Christ,* p. 695.

[n] See 1 Thess. 4:16; 2 Thess. 1:7, 8; Heb. 9:28.

[o] See 1 Peter 4:13; 1 John 2:28; 3:2.

[p] 3 Nephi 26:3; see also 25:5.

[q] 3 Nephi 28:7; see also verse 8; see *Jesus the Christ,* chap. 39.

[r] An allusion to the parable of the Ten Virgins; see Matt. 25:1–13.

[s] D&C 33:17.

[t] D&C 34:6, 7.

[u] D&C 45:37–44; see also paragraphs 74, 75.

[v] See the numerous references in connection with D&C 1:12; see *Jesus the Christ,* chap. 42.

The Precise Time of Christ's Coming has not been made known to man. By learning to comprehend the signs of the times, by watching the development of the work of God among the nations, and by noting the rapid fulfilment of significant prophecies, we may perceive the progressive evidence of the approaching event: "But the hour and the day no man knoweth, neither the angels in heaven, nor shall they know until he comes."[w] His coming will be a surprise to those who have ignored His warnings, and who have failed to watch. "As a thief in the night"[x] will be the coming of the day of the Lord unto the wicked. "Watch therefore, for ye know neither the day nor the hour wherein the Son of Man cometh."[y]

Christ's Reign; The Kingdom—We have seen that, according to the words of holy prophets ancient and modern, Christ is to come in a literal sense and so manifest Himself in person in the last days. He is to dwell among His saints. "Yea, even I will be in the midst of you,"[z] He declared to the people on this continent, whom He promised to establish in the land of the New Jerusalem; and similar assurances were given through the prophets of the east.[aa] In this prospective ministration among His gathered saints, Jesus Christ is to be at once their God and their King. His government is to be that of a perfect theocracy; the laws of righteousness will be the code, and control will be administered under one authority, undisputed because indisputable.

The scriptures abound with declarations that the Lord will yet reign among his people. To this effect sang Moses before the host of Israel after their miraculous passage through the Red Sea: "The Lord shall reign forever and ever;"[bb] and the psalmist echoes the refrain, "The Lord is King forever and ever."[cc] Jeremiah calls Him "an everlasting king" before whose wrath the earth shall tremble, and the nations yield;[dd] and Nebuchadnezzar, humbled through tribulations, rejoiced in honoring the King of heaven, "whose dominion is an everlasting dominion, and his kingdom is from generation to generation."[ee]

Even the covenant people, Israel, were not always willing to accept the Lord as their king. Remember how they protested that Samuel, the anointed prophet and judge, was old—a poor excuse for their clamor, as the old man ministered with vigor among them for thirty-five years beyond that time—and how they cried for a king to rule them, that they might be like other nations.[ff] Note the pathos with which the Lord replied to Samuel's prayer regarding this demand of the people: "Hearken unto the voice of the people in all that they say unto thee; for they have not rejected thee, but they have rejected me, that I should not reign over them."[gg] But the Lord will not be ever rejected by His people; at the time appointed He will come with power and great glory, and will assume His rightful place of authority as King of earth.

Daniel interpreted the dream of Nebuchadnezzar, and spoke of the many kingdoms and divisions of kingdoms that were to be established; then he added: "And in the days of these kings shall the God of heaven set up a kingdom, which shall never be destroyed: and the kingdom shall not

[w] D&C 49:7.

[x] 2 Peter 3:10; 1 Thess. 5:2.

[y] Matt. 25:13; see also 24:42, 44; Mark 13:33, 35; Luke 12:40; see *Jesus the Christ,* chap. 42.

[z] 3 Nephi 20:22; see also 21:25.

[aa] See Ezek. 37:26, 27; Zech. 2:10, 11; 8:3; 2 Cor 6:16.

[bb] Ex. 15:18.

[cc] Ps. 10:16; see also 29:10; 145:13; 146:10.

[dd] See Jer. 10:10.

[ee] Dan. 4:34–37.

[ff] See 1 Sam. 8:5.

[gg] Same, verse 7; see also 10:19; Hosea 13:10, 11.

be left to other people, but it shall break in pieces and consume all these kingdoms, and it shall stand forever."[hh] Touching the extent of the great kingdom to be established the same prophet declared: "And the kingdom and dominion, and the greatness of the kingdom under the whole heaven, shall be given to the people of the saints of the Most High, whose kingdom is an everlasting kingdom, and all dominions shall serve and obey him."[ii]

Speaking of the restoration of Judah and Israel in the last days, Micah prophesied: "And the Lord shall reign over them in mount Zion from henceforth, even forever."[jj] In the annunciation to the Virgin, the angel said of the unborn Christ: "He shall reign over the house of Jacob forever; and of his kingdom there shall be no end."[kk] In the visions of Patmos, the Apostle John saw the glorious consummation, and a universal recognition of the eternal King: "And the seventh angel sounded; and there were great voices in heaven, saying, The kingdoms of this world are become the kingdoms of our Lord, and of his Christ: and he shall reign forever and ever."[ll] Modern revelation is rich in evidence of an approaching reign of righteousness, with Christ as King; witness the following: "And also the Lord shall have power over his saints, and shall reign in their midst."[mm] "For in mine own due time will I come upon the earth in judgment, and my people shall be redeemed and shall reign with me on earth."[nn]

Kingdom and Church—In the Gospel according to Matthew, the phrase "kingdom of heaven" is of frequent occurrence; while in the books of the other evangelists, and throughout the epistles, the equivalent expression is "kingdom of God," "kingdom of Christ," or simply "kingdom." It is evident that these words may be used interchangeably without violence to the true meaning. However, the term kingdom is used in more senses than one, and a careful study of the context in each instance may be necessary to a proper comprehension of the writer's intent. The most common usages are two: An expression synonymous with "the Church" having reference to the followers of Christ without distinction as to their temporal organizations; and the designation of the literal kingdom over which Jesus Christ is to reign upon the earth in the last days.

When we contemplate the kingdom in the latter and more general sense, the Church must be regarded as a part thereof; an essential indeed, for it is the germ from which the kingdom is to be developed, and the very heart of the organization. The Church has existed and now continues in an organized form, without the kingdom as an established power with temporal authority in the world; but the kingdom cannot be maintained without the Church.

In modern revelation, the expressions "kingdom of God" and "kingdom of heaven" are sometimes used with distinctive meanings—the former phrase signifying the Church, and the latter the literal kingdom which is to supersede and comprise all national or racial divisions. In this sense, the kingdom of God has been set up already in these the last days; its beginning in and for the present dispensation was the establishment of the Church on its latter-day and permanent foundation. This is consistent with our conception of the Church as the vital organ of the kingdom in general. The powers and authority committed to the Church are, then, the keys of the kingdom. Such meaning is made clear in the following revelation to the Church: "The keys of the

[hh] Dan. 2:44.
[ii] Dan. 7:27.
[jj] Micah 4:7; see also Isa. 24:23.
[kk] Luke 1:33.
[ll] Rev. 11:15.
[mm] D&C 1:36.
[nn] D&C 43:29; see also 84:119.

kingdom of God are committed unto man on the earth, and from thence shall the gospel roll forth unto the ends of the earth, as the stone which is cut out of the mountain without hands[oo] shall roll forth, until it has filled the whole earth. * * * Call upon the Lord, that his kingdom may go forth upon the earth, that the inhabitants thereof may receive it, and be prepared for the days to come, in the which the Son of Man shall come down in heaven, clothed in the brightness of his glory, to meet the kingdom of God which is set up on the earth. Wherefore, may the *kingdom of God* go forth, that *the kingdom of heaven* may come, that thou, O God, mayest be glorified in heaven so on earth, that thine enemies may be subdued; for thine is the honor, power and glory, forever and ever."[pp]

At the time of His glorious advent, Christ will be accompanied by the hosts of righteous ones who have already passed from earth; and saints who are still alive on earth are to be quickened and caught up to meet Him, then to descend with Him as partakers of His glory.[qq] With Him too will come Enoch and his band of the pure in heart; and a union will be effected with the kingdom of God, or that part of the kingdom of heaven previously established as the Church of Jesus Christ on earth; and the kingdom on earth will be one with that in heaven. Then will be realized a fulfilment of the Lord's own prayer, given as a pattern to all who pray: "Thy kingdom come. Thy will be done in earth, as it is in heaven."[rr]

The disputed question—Is the kingdom already set up on earth or are we to wait for its establishment until the time of the future advent of Christ, the King?—may properly receive answer either affirmative or negative, according to the sense in which the term "kingdom" is understood. The kingdom of God as identical with the Church of Christ has been established; its history is that of the Church in these the last days; its officers are divinely commissioned, their power is that of the Holy Priesthood. They claim an authority that is spiritual, but also temporal in dealing with the members of the organization—Church or kingdom as one may choose to call it—but they make no attempt, nor do they assert the right, to assail, modify, or in any way interfere with existing governments, far less to subdue nations or to set up rival systems of control. The kingdom of heaven, including the Church, and comprising all nations, will be set up with power and great glory when the triumphant King comes with His heavenly hosts to personally rule and reign on the earth, which He has redeemed at the sacrifice of His own life.

As seen, the kingdom of heaven will comprise more than the Church. The honorable and honest among men will be accorded protection and the privileges of citizenship under the perfect system of government which Christ will administer; and this will be their lot whether they are members of the Church or not. Law-breakers and men of impure heart will receive judgment according to their sin; but those who live according to the truth as they have been able to receive and comprehend it will enjoy the fullest liberty under the benign influences of a perfect administration. The special privileges and blessings associated with the Church, the right to hold and exercise the Priesthood with its boundless possibilities and eternal powers, will be, as now they are, for those only who enter into the covenant and become part of the Church of Jesus Christ.

The Millennium—In connection with scriptural mention of Christ's reign on earth, a duration of a thousand years is frequently specified. While we cannot regard this as indicating a time

[oo] Allusion to Daniel's interpretation of the dream of Nebuchadnezzar; see Dan. 2:34, 44.
[pp] D&C 65:2, 5, 6.
[qq] See D&C 88:91–98.
[rr] Matt. 6:10; Luke 11:2.

limit to the kingdom's existence, or a measure of the Savior's administration of power, we are justified in the belief that the thousand years immediately following the establishment of the kingdom are to be specially characterized, and so be different from both preceding and succeeding time. The gathering of Israel and the establishment of an earthly Zion are to be effected preparatory to His coming. His advent is to be marked by a destruction of the wicked, and by the inauguration of an era of peace. The Revelator saw the souls of the martyrs, and of other righteous men, in power, living and reigning with Christ a thousand years.[ss] At the beginning of this period Satan is to be bound, "that he should deceive the nations no more, till the thousand years should be fulfilled."[tt] Certain of the dead are not to live again until the thousand years are past;[uu] while the righteous "shall be priests of God and of Christ, and shall reign with him a thousand years."[vv] Among the most ancient of revelations regarding the Millennium is that given to Enoch: "And it came to pass that Enoch saw the day of the coming of the Son of Man, in the last days, to dwell on the earth in righteousness for the space of a thousand years."[ww]

It is evident, then, that in speaking of the Millennium we have to consider a definite period, with important events marking its beginning and its close, and conditions of unusual blessedness extending throughout. It will be a sabbatical era[xx]—a thousand years of peace. Enmity between man and beast shall cease; the fierceness and venom of the brute creation shall be done away,[yy] and love shall rule.[zz] A new condition of affairs will prevail later, as was declared in the word of the Lord to Isaiah: "For, behold, I create new heavens and a new earth: and the former shall not be remembered, nor come into mind."[aaa]

Concerning the state of peace, prosperity, and duration of human life, characteristic of that period, we read: "There shall be no more thence an infant of days, nor an old man that hath not filled his days: for the child shall die an hundred years old, but the sinner being an hundred years old shall be accursed. And they shall build houses, and inhabit them; and they shall plant vineyards, and eat the fruit of them. They shall not build, and another inhabit; they shall not plant, and another eat: for as the days of a tree are the days of my people, and mine elect shall long enjoy the work of their hands. They shall not labor in vain, nor bring forth for trouble; for they are the seed of the blessed of the Lord, and their offspring with them. And it shall come to pass, that before they call, I will answer; and while they are yet speaking, I will hear. The wolf and the lamb shall feed together, and the lion shall eat straw like the bullock: and dust shall be the serpent's meat. They shall not hurt nor destroy in all my holy mountain, saith the Lord."[bbb]

The Lord's voice is heard today declaring the same prophetic truths, as shown in the revelations touching the Millennium given in the present dispensation of the Church.[ccc] In 1831, He thus addressed the elders of His Church: "For the great Millennium, of which I have spoken by the mouth of my servants, shall come. For Satan shall be bound, and when he is loosed again he

[ss] See Rev. 20:4; see also verse 6.
[tt] Rev. 20:2, 3.
[uu] Same, verse 5.
[vv] Same, verse 6.
[ww] P. of G.P., Moses 7:65.
[xx] See D&C 77:12.
[yy] See Isa. 11:6–9; 65:25.
[zz] See Appendix 20:2, 3.
[aaa] Isa. 65:17.
[bbb] Isa. 65:20–25.
[ccc] See D&C 63:49–51.

shall only reign for a little season, and then cometh the end of the earth."[ddd] On another occasion these words were spoken: "For I will reveal myself from heaven with power and great glory, with all the hosts thereof, and dwell in righteousness with men on earth a thousand years, and the wicked shall not stand. * * * And again, verily, verily, I say unto you that when the thousand years are ended, and men again begin to deny their God, then will I spare the earth but for a little season; And the end shall come."[eee]

During the millennial period conditions will be propitious for righteousness; Satan's power will be restrained; and men, relieved to some degree from temptation, will be mostly zealous in the service of their reigning Lord. Nevertheless, sin will not be wholly abolished, nor will death be banished; though children will live to reach maturity in the flesh, and then may be changed to a condition of immortality in the "twinkling of an eye."[fff] Both mortal and immortal beings will tenant the earth, and communion with heavenly powers will be common. The Latter-day Saints believe that during the millennial era they will be privileged to continue the vicarious work for the dead, which constitutes so important and so characteristic a feature of their duty,[ggg] and that the facilities for direct communication with the heavens will enable them to carry on their labor of love without hindrance. When the thousand years are passed Satan will again be permitted to assert his power, and those who are not then numbered among the pure in heart will yield to his influence. But the liberty thus recovered by "the prince of the power of the air"[hhh] will be of short duration; his final doom will speedily follow, and with him will go to the punishment that is everlasting, all who are his. Then the earth will pass to its celestial condition and become a fit abode for the glorified sons and daughters of our God.[iii]

REFERENCES

Prophecies of and Conditions to Attend the Lord's Coming

The Lord said unto Enoch: As I live, even so will I come in the last days—Moses 7:60; Enoch saw the day of the coming of the Son of Man, in the last days, to dwell on earth for a thousand years—verse 65.

Enoch prophesied, saying: Behold, the Lord cometh with ten thousands of his saints—Jude 14, 15.

For I know that my Redeemer liveth, and that he shall stand at the latter day upon the earth—Job 19:25.

Our God shall come, and shall not keep silence—Ps. 50:3; note that verses 4 and 5 tell of conditions that shall attend the Lord's future coming.

He shall have dominion also from sea to sea, and from the river unto the ends of the earth—Ps. 72:8; see also verse 17; 82:8.

When the Lord shall build up Zion, he shall appear in his glory—Ps. 102:16.

The Lord of Hosts shall reign in mount Zion, and in Jerusalem—Isa. 24:23.

The Lord God will come with strong hand—Isa. 40:10.

The Lord shall reign in mount Zion even forever—Micah 4:7; see also Zech. 14:9, 20, 21.

---

ddd D&C 43:30, 31.
eee D&C 29:11, 22, 23.
fff D&C 63:50–51.
ggg See "Baptism for the Dead," chap. 7 herein.
hhh Eph. 2:2.
iii See *Jesus the Christ*, concluding part of chap. 42.

The Lord to come suddenly; but who may abide the day of his coming?—Mal. 3:1–4.

Elijah the prophet to be sent before the great and dreadful day of the Lord—Mal. 4:5, 6.

The Son of Man to come in the glory of his Father—Matt. 16:27.

The Son of Man to come in glory and to judge the nations—Matt. 25:31–46.

Then shall appear the sign of the Son of Man in heaven—Matt. 24:30.

Of the day and hour of the Lord's coming no man knoweth—Matt. 24:36.

Then shall they see the Son of Man coming in the clouds with great power and glory—Mark 13:26; see also verses 32, 33, 37. Of him also shall the Son of Man be ashamed, when he cometh in the glory of his Father with the holy angels—8:38.

After many tribulations the people shall see the Son of Man coming in a cloud with power and great glory—Luke 21:27; read verse 10 and the verses following; also 17:26–30.

Be ye therefore ready also: for the Son of Man cometh at an hour when ye think not—Luke 12:40.

But the day of the Lord will come as a thief in the night—2 Peter 3:10; see also 1 Thess. 5:2.

This same Jesus shall so come in like manner as ye have seen him go into heaven—Acts 1:11.

And he shall send Jesus Christ, which before was preached unto you—Acts 3:20.

Therefore judge nothing before the time, until the Lord come—1 Cor. 4:5; compare 11:26.

From whence also we look for the Savior, the Lord Jesus Christ—Philip. 3:20.

At the coming of our Lord Jesus Christ with all his saints—1 Thess. 3:13; see also 2:19.

For the Lord himself shall descend from heaven with a shout, with the voice of the archangel, and with the trump of God—1 Thess. 4:16.

When the Lord Jesus shall be revealed from heaven with his mighty angels—2 Thess. 1:7; see also 2:1; 1 Tim. 6:14; Titus 2:13; Heb. 9:28.

Stablish your hearts: for the coming of the Lord draweth nigh—James 5:8.

That we may have confidence, and not be ashamed before him at his coming—1 John 2:28; see also 3:2.

Behold, he cometh with clouds; and every eye shall see him, and they also which pierced him—Rev. 1:7; see also 6:12–17.

The Holy One of Israel must reign in dominion, and might and power, and great glory—1 Nephi 22:24; see also verse 26.

The bands of death to be broken and the Son to reign—Mosiah 15:20.

Elijah to come before the great and dreadful day of the Lord—3 Nephi 25:5.

Christ expounded to the Nephites things that should occur until he should come in his glory—3 Nephi 26:3.

The power of heaven to come down with Christ in the midst—3 Nephi 21:25; compare 20:22; see also 24:1–3.

The Three Nephites to remain in the flesh until the Lord shall come in his glory with the powers of heaven—3 Nephi 28:7.

Ye need not say that the Lord delays his coming—3 Nephi 29:2.

Christ to reveal himself from heaven with power and great glory, with all the hosts thereof—D&C 29:11; see also 45:44; 65:5.

The time is soon at hand when I shall come in a cloud with power and great glory—D&C 34:7, 8, 12.

When he shall come in the clouds of heaven to reign on the earth over his people—D&C 76:63.

The Lord to be in the midst of the saints in glory, and to be their king and lawgiver—D&C 45:59; see also 1:36.

The Son of Man now reigneth in the heavens, and will reign on the earth—D&C 49:6.

The Lord will come down from the presence of the Father to take judgment upon the wicked—D&C 63:34.

Preparing the way of the Lord for his second coming—D&C 34:6; see also 39:20; 77:12.

The Son of Man to come in an hour you think not—D&C 61:38.

The time of the Lord's coming nigh at hand—D&C 35:15; 43:17; 133:17.

Hour and day of the Lord's coming no man knoweth, neither the angels—D&C 49:7; 39:21; 133:11.

The good and the meek shall be looking for the time of the Lord's coming—D&C 35:15. He that feareth me shall be looking for the great day of the Lord to come—D&C 45:39; see also verses 40-56, and verses 74, 75.

Unto some it shall be given to know the signs of the coming of the Son of Man—D&C 68:11.

I come quickly—D&C 34:12; 35:27; 39:24; 41:4; 49:28; 51:20; 54:10; 68:35; 87:8; 99:5; 112:34.

The Millennium

Conditions to prevail during the Millennium—Isa. 11:6–9; see also 65:25.

Satan to be bound during the thousand years—Rev. 20:1–7.

And they lived and reigned with Christ a thousand years—Rev. 20:4. But the rest of the dead lived not again until the thousand years were finished—verse 5.

And hast made us unto our God kings and priests: and we shall reign on the earth—Rev. 5:10.

For the space of a thousand years the earth shall rest—Moses 7:64. Enoch saw the day of the coming of the Son of Man to dwell on the earth for a thousand years—verse 65.

The Lord to dwell on earth with men a thousand years—D&C 29:11.

For the great Millennium, of which I have spoken, shall come—D&C 43:30; read also verses 31–35.

Conditions when the thousand years are ended—D&C 29:22, 23.

Satan not to be loosed for the space of a thousand years, then to muster his armies—D&C 88:110–116.

21

REGENERATION AND RESURRECTION

ARTICLE 10

E BELIEVE * * * that the earth will be renewed and receive its paradisiacal glory.

RENEWAL OF THE EARTH

The Earth Under the Curse—The blessed conditions under which the earth shall exist and man shall live during the millennial era are almost beyond human powers of comprehension, so different are they from all to which history testifies and experience confirms. A reign of righteousness throughout the earth has never yet been known to the fallen race of man. So marked has been the universal curse, so great the power of the tempter, so bitter the selfish strife betwixt man and man and between nation and nation; so general has been the enmity of the animal creation, amongst its own members and toward the being who, though in a degraded state, yet holds the divine commission to the authority of dominion; so prolific has been the soil in bringing forth thorns, thistles, and noxious weeds—that the description of Eden is to us as the story of another world, an orb of a higher order of existence, wholly unlike this dreary sphere. Yet we learn that Eden was in reality a feature of our planet, and that the earth is destined to become a celestialized body fit for the abode of the most exalted intelligences. The Millennium, with all its splendor, is but a more advanced stage of preparation, by which the earth and its inhabitants will approach foreordained perfection.

its surface a heterogeneous mass of fragmental material; he reads, in the record inscribed on its stony pages, the story of past development through many successive stages of progress, each making the globe more fit for habitation by man; he witnesses the work of constructive and destructive agencies now in operation, land masses yielding to the lowering action of air and water and by their destruction furnishing material for other formations now in process of construction—the general effect of all such being to level the surface by degrading the hills and raising the valleys. On the other hand, he observes volcanic and other agencies operating to increase the inequality of level by violent eruption and crustal elevation or depression. He confesses inability, from his observations of the present and his deductions concerning the past of the earth, to predict even a probable future. The epoch-making declaration of an acknowledged leader in the science is in point: Geology furnishes "no traces of a beginning, no prospect of an end."[m]

The astronomer, studying the varied conditions of other worlds, may seek by analogy to learn of the probable fate of our own. Gazing into space with greatly augmented vision, he sees, within the system to which the earth belongs, spheres exhibiting a great range of development—some in their formative stage, unfit for the abode of beings constituted as are we; others in a state more nearly resembling that of the earth; and yet others that appear old and lifeless. Of the vast systems beyond the comparatively small company under control of our own sun he knows little beyond the fact of their existence. But nowhere has he discovered a celestialized world; and mortal eye could not discern such an orb even if it were within the limits of unaided or telescopic vision as determined by distance alone. We may readily believe in the existence of worlds other than those of structure so gross as to be visible to our dull eyes. In regard to the revealed word concerning the regeneration of earth, and the acquirement of a celestial glory by our planet, science has nothing to offer either by way of support or contradiction. Let us not, because of this, disparage science nor decry the labors of its votaries. No one realizes more fully than does the mind trained to scientific method how much we do not know.

RESURRECTION OF THE BODY

Resurrection from the Dead—Closely associated with, and analogous to, the ordained rejuvenation of earth, whereby our planet is to pass from its present dreary and broken state to a condition of glorified perfection, is the resurrection of the bodies of all beings who have had an existence upon it. The Church of Jesus Christ of Latter-day Saints teaches the doctrine of a literal resurrection; an actual reunion of the spirits of the dead and the tabernacles with which they were clothed during mortal probation; and transition from mortality to immortality in the case of some who will be in the flesh at the time of the Lord's advent, and who, because of individual righteousness, are to be spared the sleep of the grave. The Bible is replete with testimony regarding the quickening of the dead. Human knowledge of the resurrection rests wholly upon revelation. Pagan peoples have little or no conception of an actual coming forth of the dead unto life.[n]

In accepting the doctrine of a resurrection we are to be guided by faith, which, however, is supported by abundant revelation, given in a manner unequivocal and sure. Science, the result of human research, fails to afford us any indication of such an event in the history of living things, and men have sought in vain for an exact analogy in external nature. True, comparisons have been made, metaphors have been employed and similes pressed into service, to show in nature some counterpart or semblance

[m] James Hutton.
[n] See Appendix 21:2.

of the immortalizing change to which the Christian soul looks forward with unwavering confidence; but all such figures are defective in application, and untrue in their professed analogies.

The return of spring after the death-like sleep of winter; the passing of the crawling caterpillar into the corpse-like chrysalis, and the subsequent emergence of the winged butterfly; the coming forth of a living bird from the tomb-like recess of the egg—these and other natural processes of development have been used as illustrative of the resurrection. Each of them falls short, for in no instance of such awakening has there been actual death. If the tree die it will not resume its leafage with the return of the sun; if the pupa within the chrysalis, or the life-germ within the egg be killed, no butterfly or bird will emerge. When we indulge such illustrations without discrimination, we are apt to conceive the thought that the body predestined to resurrection is not truly dead; and that therefore the quickening that is to follow is not what the revealed word declares it to be. Observation proves that the separation of the spirit from the body leaves the latter veritably inanimate, no longer able to resist the processes of physical and chemical dissolution. The body, deserted by its immortal tenant, is literally dead; it resolves itself into its natural components, and its substance enters again upon the round of universal circulation of matter. Yet the resurrection from the dead is assured; the faith of those who trust in the word of revealed truth will be vindicated, and the divine decree will be carried into full effect.

Predictions Concerning the Resurrection—The prophets in the past dispensations of the world's history have foreseen and foretold the final conquest of death. Some of them testified specifically of Christ's victory over the tomb; others have dwelt upon the resurrection in a general way. Job, the man of patience under tribulation, sang joyously even in his agony: "For I know that my Redeemer liveth, and that he shall stand at the latter day upon the earth: And though after my skin worms destroy this body, yet in my flesh shall I see God,"[o] Enoch, to whom the Lord revealed His plan for the redemption of mankind, foresaw the resurrection of Christ, the coming forth of the righteous dead with Him, and the eventual resurrection of all men.[p]

Nephi testified to his brethren that the Redeemer's death was a foreordained necessity, provided in order that resurrection from the dead might be given to man. These are his words: "For as death hath passed upon all men, to fulfil the merciful plan of the great Creator, there must needs be a power of resurrection, and the resurrection must needs come unto man by reason of the fall; and the fall came by reason of transgression; and because man became fallen they were cut off from the presence of the Lord. * * * And this death of which I have spoken, which is the spiritual death, shall deliver up its dead; which spiritual death is hell; wherefore, death and hell must deliver up their dead, and hell must deliver up its captive spirits, and the grave must deliver up its captive bodies, and the bodies and the spirits of men will be restored one to the other; and it is by the power of the resurrection of the Holy One of Israel. O how great the plan of our God! For on the other hand, the paradise of God must deliver up the spirits of the righteous, and the grave deliver up the body of the righteous; and the spirit and the body is restored to itself again, and all men become incorruptible, and immortal, and they are living souls, having a perfect knowledge like unto us in the flesh, save it be that our knowledge shall be perfect."[q]

Samuel, the Lamanite prophet, predicted the Savior's birth, ministry, death, and resurrection, and explained the resulting resurrection of mankind: "For behold, he surely must die that salva-

[o] Job 19:25, 26; see also Isa. 26:19; Ezek. 37:11–14; Hos. 13:14.
[p] See P. of G. P., Moses 7:56, 57.
[q] 2 Nephi 9:6, 12, 13.

tion may come; yea, it behooveth him and becometh expedient that he dieth, to bring to pass the resurrection of the dead, that thereby men may be brought into the presence of the Lord. Yea, behold, this death bringeth to pass the resurrection, and redeemeth all mankind from the first death—that spiritual death; for all mankind, by the fall of Adam being cut off from the presence of the Lord, are considered as dead, both as to things temporal and of things spiritual. But, behold, the resurrection of Christ redeemeth mankind, yea, even all mankind, and bringeth them back into the presence of the Lord."[r]

The New Testament shows that the doctrine of the resurrection was understood during the time of Christ's earthly mission, and in the succeeding apostolic era.[s] The Master Himself proclaimed these teachings. In reply to the hypercritical Sadducees,[t] He said: "But as touching the resurrection of the dead, have ye not read that which was spoken unto you by God, saying, I am the God of Abraham, and the God of Isaac, and the God of Jacob? God is not the God of the dead, but of the living."[u] To the Jews who sought His life because of His deeds and doctrine He spoke in this way: "Verily, verily, I say unto you, He that heareth my word, and believeth on him that sent me, hath everlasting life, and shall not come into condemnation; but is passed from death unto life. Verily, verily, I say unto you, The hour is coming, and now is, when the dead shall hear the voice of the Son of God: and they that hear shall live."[v]

That Christ fully comprehended the purpose of His approaching martyrdom, and the resurrection that was to follow, is proved by His own utterances while yet in the flesh. To Nicodemus He said: "And as Moses lifted up the serpent in the wilderness, even so must the Son of Man be lifted up: That whosoever believeth in him should not perish, but have eternal life."[w] And to Martha, bewailing the death of her brother Lazarus, He declared: "I am the resurrection, and the life: he that believeth in me, though he were dead, yet shall he live."[x] Of His own resurrection He prophesied freely, specifying the time during which His body would be entombed.[y]

Two General Resurrections are mentioned in the scriptures, and these may be specified as first and final, or as the resurrection of the just and the resurrection of the unjust. The first was inaugurated by the resurrection of Jesus Christ; immediately following which many of the saints came forth from their graves. A continuation of this, the resurrection of the just, has been in operation since,[z] and will be greatly extended, or brought to pass in a general way, in connection with the coming of Christ in His glory. The final resurrection will be deferred until the end of the thousand years of peace, and will be in connection with the last judgment.

The First Resurrection—Christ's Resurrection, and That Immediately Following— The facts of Christ's resurrection from the dead are attested by such an array of scriptural proofs that no doubt of the reality finds place in the mind of any believer in the inspired records. To the women who came early to the sepulchre, the angel who had rolled the stone from the door of the tomb spoke, saying:

[r] Helaman 14:15–17; see also Mosiah 15:20–24, and Alma 40:26, 16–24.

[s] See Matt. 14:1,2; John 11:24.

[t] See Appendix 21:3.

[u] Matt. 22:31, 32; see also Luke 14:14.

[v] John 5:24, 25; see also verse 21, and 11:23–25.

[w] John 3:14, 15.

[x] John 11:25.

[y] See Matt. 12:40; 16:21; 17:23; 20:19.

[z] Note the fact that Moroni, the last of the Nephite prophets, who died in the first quarter of the fifth century A.D., appeared as a resurrected being to Joseph Smith in 1823.

"He is not here: for he is risen, as he said."[aa] Afterward the resurrected Lord showed Himself to many[bb] during the forty days' interval between His resurrection and ascension.[cc] Subsequent to the ascension He manifested Himself to the Nephites on the western hemisphere, as already noted in another connection.[dd] The apostles, as we shall see, ceased not to testify of the genuineness of their Lord's resurrection, nor did they fail to proclaim the resurrections of the future.

Christ, "the firstfruits of them that slept,"[ee] "the firstborn from the dead" and "the first begotten of the dead" was the first among men to come forth from the grave in an immortalized body; but soon after His resurrection many of the saints were brought from their tombs: "And the graves were opened; and many bodies of the saints which slept arose, And came out of the graves after his resurrection, and went into the holy city, and appeared unto many."[ff]

Alma, the Nephite prophet, whose writings antedate by many decades the birth of Christ, clearly understood that there would be no resurrection prior to that of the Redeemer, for he said: "Behold, I say unto you, that there is no resurrection—or, I would say, in other words, that this mortal does not put on immortality, this corruption does not put on incorruption—until after the coming of Christ." Furthermore, Alma foresaw a general resurrection in connection with Christ's coming forth from the dead, as the context of the foregoing quotation shows.[gg] Inspired men among the Nephites spoke of the death and resurrection of Christ[hh] even during the time of His actual ministry in the flesh; and their teachings were speedily confirmed by the appearance of the risen Lord among them,[ii] as had been foretold by earlier prophets.[jj]

In the latter days the Lord has again manifested Himself, declaring the facts of His death and resurrection: "For, behold, the Lord your Redeemer suffered death in the flesh; wherefore he suffered the pain of all men, that all men might repent and come unto him. And he hath risen again from the dead, that he might bring all men unto him, on conditions of repentance."[kk]

Resurrection at the Time of Christ's Second Coming—Soon after the bodily departure of Christ from earth, the apostles, upon whom then devolved the direct responsibilities of the Church, were found preaching the doctrine of a future and universal resurrection. This teaching appears to have formed a very prominent feature of their instructions; for it was made a cause of complaint by the Sadducees, who assailed the apostles, even within the sacred confines of the Temple, the accusers "being grieved that they [the apostles] taught the people, and preached through Jesus the resurrection from the dead."[ll] Paul gave offense by the zeal with which he preached the resurrection, as witness his contention with certain philosophers of the Epicureans and of the Stoics; in the course of which some said: "What will this babbler say? Other some, He seemeth to be a setter forth of strange gods: because he preached unto them Jesus, and the resurrection."[mm] The discussion was continued on Mars' Hill, where

---

aa Matt. 28:6; see Jesus the Christ, chap. 37.

bb See Matt. 28:9, 16; Mark 16:14; Luke 24:13–31, 34; John 20:14–17, 19, 26; 21:1–4; 1 Cor. 15:5–8.

cc See Luke 24:49–51; Acts 1:1–11.

dd See 3 Nephi, chaps. 11-26; Ether, chap. 3.

ee 1 Cor. 15:20, 23; see also Acts 26:23; Col. 1:18; Rev. 1:5; see *Vitality of "Mormonism,"* pp. 288–294.

ff Matt. 27:52–53.

gg Alma 40:2, 16.

hh See 3 Nephi 6:20.

ii See 3 Nephi, chap. 11.

jj See 1 Nephi 12:6; 2 Nephi 26:1, 9; Alma 16:20; 3 Nephi 11:12.

kk D&C 18:11, 12.

ll Acts 4:2; see also Matt. 22:23, 31, 32, and Acts 23:8.

mm Acts 17:18.

Paul preached the Gospel of the true and living God, including the tenets of the resurrection: "And when they heard of the resurrection of the dead, some mocked; and others said, We will hear thee again of this matter."[nn] He declared the same truth to Felix, governor of Judea;[oo] and when brought in bonds before Agrippa, the king, he asked, as if dealing with one of the principal accusations against him: "Why should it be thought a thing incredible with you, that God should raise the dead?"[pp]

The resurrection was a favorite theme with Paul; in his epistles to the saints, he gave it frequent and prominent attention.[qq] From him also we learn that an order of precedence is to be observed in the resurrection: "But now is Christ risen from the dead, and become the firstfruits of them that slept. For since by man came death, by man came also the resurrection of the dead. For as in Adam all die, even so in Christ shall all be made alive. But every man in his own order: Christ the firstfruits; afterward they that are Christ's at his coming."[rr]

It is expressly asserted that many graves shall yield up their dead at the time of Christ's advent in glory, and the just who have slept, together with many who have not died, will be caught up to meet the Lord. Paul thus wrote to the saints in Thessalonica: "Even so them also which sleep in Jesus will God bring with him. * * * For the Lord himself shall descend from heaven with a shout, with the voice of the archangel, and with the trump of God: and the dead in Christ shall rise first. Then we which are alive and remain shall be caught up together with them in the clouds to meet the Lord in the air."[ss]

To the three Nephite disciples, who had asked the blessing of John the beloved apostle, Christ promised: "And ye shall never endure the pains of death; but when I shall come in my glory, ye shall be changed in the twinkling of an eye from mortality to immortality."[tt]

Through the medium of latter-day revelation the Lord has said: "Behold, I will come; and they shall see me in the clouds of heaven, clothed with power and great glory, with all the holy angels; and he that watches not for me shall be cut off. But before the arm of the Lord shall fall, an angel shall sound his trump, and the saints that have slept shall come forth to meet me in the cloud."[uu] Of the many signs and wonders which shall attend the Lord's glorious coming we have this partial description: "And the face of the Lord shall be unveiled; And the saints that are upon the earth, who are alive, shall be quickened and be caught up to meet him. And they who have slept in their graves shall come forth, for their graves shall be opened; and they also shall be caught up to meet him in the midst of the pillar of heaven—They are Christ's, the firstfruits; they who shall descend with him first, and they who are on the earth and in their graves, who are first caught up to meet him."[vv]

Such are some of the glories to attend the resurrection of the just. And the company of the righteous will include all who have lived faithfully according to the laws of God as made known to them; children who have died in their innocence; and even the just among the heathen nations who have lived in comparative darkness while groping for light, and who have died in ignorance. This doctrine is made plain by modern revelation: "And then shall the heathen nations be redeemed, and they that knew no law shall have part in the first resurrection."[ww] The Millennium

[nn] Acts 17:32.
[oo] See Acts 24:15.
[pp] Acts 26:8.
[qq] See Rom. 6:5; 8:11; 1 Cor., chap. 15; 2 Cor. 4:14; Philip. 3:21; Col. 3:4; 1 Thess. 4:14; Heb. 6:2.
[rr] 1 Cor. 15:20–23; the entire chapter should be studied.
[ss] 1 Thess. 4:14–17.
[tt] 3 Nephi 28:8.
[uu] D&C 45:44, 45.
[vv] D&C 88:95-98.
[ww] D&C 45:54; see also Ezek. 36:23, 24; 37:28; 39:7, 21, 23; see Appendix 21:4.

then is to be inaugurated by a glorious deliverance of the just from the power of death; and of this company of the redeemed it is written: "Blessed and holy is he that hath part in the first resurrection: on such the second death hath no power, but they shall be priests of God and of Christ, and shall reign with him a thousand years."[xx]

The Final Resurrection—"But the rest of the dead lived not again until the thousand years were finished."[yy] So testified the Revelator after having described the glorious blessings of the righteous, who are given part in the first resurrection. The unworthy will be called to the judgment of condemnation, when the regenerated world is ready to be presented to the Father.[zz]

The contrast between those whose part in the first resurrection is assured, and those whose doom it is to wait until the time of final judgment, is a strong one, and in no case do the scriptures lighten it. We are told that it is right for us to weep over bereavement by death, "and more especially for those that have not hope of a glorious resurrection."[aaa] In the present day, the voice of Jesus Christ is heard in solemn warning: "Hearken ye, for, behold, the great day of the Lord is nigh at hand. For the day cometh that the Lord shall utter his voice out of heaven; the heavens shall shake and the earth shall tremble, and the trump of God shall sound both long and loud, and shall say to the sleeping nations: Ye saints arise and live; ye sinners stay and sleep until I shall call again."[bbb]

The vision of the final scene is thus described by John: "And I saw the dead, small and great, stand before God; and the books were opened: and another book was opened, which is the book of life: and the dead were judged out of those things which were written in the books, according to their works. And the sea gave up the dead which were in it; and death and hell delivered up the dead which were in them: and they were judged every man according to their works."[ccc] As the scriptures conclusively prove, the resurrection is to be universal. While it is true that the dead shall be brought forth in order, each as he is prepared for the first or a later stage, yet everyone who has tabernacled in the flesh shall again assume his body; and, with spirit and body reunited, he shall be judged.

The Book of Mormon is definite in the description of the literal and universal resurrection: "Now, there is a death which is called a temporal death; and the death of Christ shall loose the bands of this temporal death, that all shall be raised from this temporal death; The spirit and the body shall be reunited again in its perfect form; both limb and joint shall be restored to its proper frame, even as we now are at this time; and we shall be brought to stand before God, knowing even as we know now, and have a bright recollection of all our guilt. Now, this restoration shall come to all, both old and young, both bond and free, both male and female, both the wicked and the righteous; and even there shall not so much as a hair of their heads be lost; but every thing shall be restored to its perfect frame, as it is now, or in the body, and shall be brought and be arraigned before the bar of Christ the Son, and God the Father, and the Holy Spirit, which is one eternal God, to be judged according to their works, whether they be good or whether they be evil. Now, behold, I have spoken unto you concerning the death of the mortal body, and also concerning the resurrection of the mortal body. I say unto you that this mortal body is raised to an immortal body, that is from death, even from the first death unto life."[ddd]

[xx] Rev. 20:6.
[yy] Rev. 20:5.
[zz] See Appendix 21:5.
[aaa] D&C 42:45.
[bbb] D&C 43:17, 18.
[ccc] Rev. 20:12, 13.
[ddd] Alma 11:42–45.

Intelligence attained to in this life will rise with us in the resurrection—D&C 130:18.

Only contracts and relationships entered into by sealing for eternity shall be valid after the resurrection—D&C 132:7.

All to be resurrected but every man in his own order—1 Cor. 15:22, 23; read verses 22–44.

State of the soul between death and the resurrection—Alma, chap. 40.

RELIGIOUS LIBERTY AND TOLERATION

ARTICLE 11

E CLAIM the privilege of worshiping Almighty God according to the dictates of our own conscience, and allow all men the same privilege, let them worship how, where, or what they may.

Man's Right to Freedom in Worship—The Latter-day Saints proclaim their unqualified allegiance to the principles of religious liberty and toleration. Freedom to worship Almighty God as the conscience may dictate, they affirm to be one of the inherent and inalienable rights of humanity. The inspired framers of our charter of national independence proclaimed to the world, as a self-evident truth, that the common birthright of humanity gives to every man a claim to life, liberty, and the pursuit of happiness. Happiness is foreign, liberty but a name, and life a disappointment, to him who is denied the freedom to worship as he may desire. No person possessing a regard for Deity can be content if restricted in the performance of the highest duty of his existence. Could one be happy, though he were housed in a palace, surrounded with all material comforts and provided with every facility for intellectual enjoyment, if he were cut off from communion with the being whom he loved the most?

What is Worship—The derivation of the term suggests an answer. It comes to us as the lineal descendant of a pair of Anglo-

Saxon words, *weorth,* meaning worthy, and *scipe,* the old form of *ship,* signifying condition or state, and connotes the thought of *worthy-ship.* The worship of which one is capable depends upon his comprehension of the worthiness characterizing the object of his reverence. Man's capacity for worship is a measure of his comprehension of God. The fuller the acquaintance and the closer the communion between the worshiper and Deity, the more thorough and sincere will be his homage. When we say of one that he is a worshiper of the good, the beautiful, the true, we mean that he possesses a deeper conception of worth in the object of his adoration, than does another whose perception does not lead him to reverence those ennobling qualities.

Man, then, will worship according to his conception of the divine attributes and powers, and this conception approaches the correct one in proportion to the spiritual light that has come to him. True worship cannot exist where there is no reverence or love for the object. This reverence may be ill-founded; the adoration may be a species of idolatry; the object may be in fact unworthy; yet of the devotee it must be said that he worships if his conscience clothe the idol with the attribute of worthy-ship. We have spoken of "true worship"; the expression is a pleonasm. Worship, as has been affirmed, is the heart-felt adoration that is rendered as a result of a sincere conception of worthiness on the part of the object; any manifestation of reverence prompted by a conviction inferior to this is but a counterfeit of worship. Call such false worship if you choose, but let it be remembered that worship is necessarily true, the word requires no adjective to extend its meaning nor attest its genuineness. Worship is not a matter of form any more than is prayer. It consists not in posture, in gesture, in ritual or in creed. Worship most profound may be rendered with none of the artificial accessories of ritualistic service; for altar, the stone in the desert may serve; the peaks of the everlasting hills are as temple spires; the vault of heaven is of all the grandest cathedral dome.

Man is at heart an expression in part of that which he worships. The savage, who knows no triumph greater than that of bloody victory over his enemy, who regards prowess and physical strength as the most desirable qualities of his race and looks upon revenge and vindictiveness as the gratifications of life, ascribes such attributes to his deity, and offers his profoundest reverence in sacrifices of blood. The revolting practises of idolatry are traceable to perverted conceptions of human excellence, and these are reflected in the hideous creations of man-made, devil-inspired deities. On the other hand, the man whose enlightened soul has received the impress of love, pure and undefiled, will ascribe to his God the attributes of gentleness and affection, and will say in his heart "God is love." Knowledge, therefore, is essential to worship; man cannot adequately serve God in ignorance; and the greater his knowledge of the divine personality, the fuller and truer will be his adoration. He may learn to know the Father, and the Son who was sent; and such knowledge is man's guaranty to eternal life.

Worship is the voluntary homage of the soul. Under compulsion, or for purposes of display, one may insincerely perform all the outward ceremonies of an established style of adoration; he may voice words of prescribed prayers; his lips may profess a creed; yet his effort is but a mockery of worship and its indulgence a sin. God asks no reluctant homage nor unwilling praise. Formalism in worship is acceptable only so far as it is accompanied by an intelligent devoutness; and it is genuine only as it is an aid to the spiritual devotion that leads to communion with Deity. The spoken prayer is but empty sound if it be anything less than an index to the volume of the soul's righteous desire. Communications addressed to the Throne of Grace must bear the stamp of sincerity if they are to reach their high destination. The most acceptable form of worship is that which rests on an unreserved compliance with the laws of God as the worshiper has learned their purport.

Religious Intolerance—The Church holds that the right to worship according to the dictates of conscience has been conferred upon man by authority higher than any of earth; and that, in consequence, no worldly power can justly interfere with its exercise. The Latter-day Saints accept as inspired the constitutional provision by which religious liberty within our own nation is professedly guarded, that no law shall ever be made "respecting an establishment of religion, or prohibiting the free exercise thereof;"[a] and they confidently believe that with the spread of enlightenment throughout the world a similar guaranty will be acquired by every nation. Intolerance has been the greatest hindrance to progress in every period of time; yet under the sable cloak of perverted zeal for religion, nations, while boasting of their civilization, and professed ministers of the Gospel of Christ, have stained the pages of the world's history with the record of such unholy deeds of persecution as to make the heavens weep. In this respect, so-called Christianity ought to bow its head in shame before the record of pagan toleration. Rome, while arrogantly though none the less effectively posing as the mistress of the world, granted to her vanquished subjects the rights of freedom in worship, requiring of them only that they refrain from molesting others or one another in the exercise of such freedom.

The people of Israel, while yet in fact Jehovah-worshipers, flourished, but soon became intolerant, counting themselves sure of an exalted station, and looking upon all who were not of the covenant race as unworthy. Christ, in His ministry among them, saw with compassionate sorrow the spiritual and intellectual bondage of the times, and declared unto them the saving word: "The truth shall make you free." At this, some self-righteous aggressors became angry, and boastfully answered: "We be Abraham's seed, and were never in bondage to any man: how sayest thou, Ye shall be made free?" Then the Master reproved them for their bigotry: "I know that ye are Abraham's seed; but ye seek to kill me, because my word hath no place in you."[b]

There is little cause for wonder in the fact that the early Christians, zealous for the new faith unto which they had been baptized, and newly converted from idolatry and pagan superstitions, should consider themselves superior to the rest of humanity still sitting in darkness and ignorance. Even John, traditionally known as the Apostle of Love, but surnamed by the Christ, he and his brother James, Boanerges, or Sons of Thunder,[c] was intolerant and resentful toward those who followed not his path; and more than once had to be rebuked by his Master. Note this incident: "And John answered him, saying, Master, we saw one casting out devils in thy name, and he followeth not us: and we forbad him because he followeth not us. But Jesus said, Forbid him not: for there is no man which shall do a miracle in my name, that can lightly speak evil of me. For he that is not against us is on our part. For whosoever shall give you a cup of water to drink in my name, because ye belong to Christ, verily I say unto you, he shall not lose his reward."[d] And again, while traveling with their Lord through Samaria, the apostles James and John were incensed at the Samaritans' lack of respect toward the Master, and craved permission to call fire from heaven to consume the unbelievers; but their revengeful desire was promptly rebuked by the Lord, who said: "Ye know not what manner of spirit ye are of. For the Son of Man is not come to destroy men's lives, but to save them."[e]

---

[a] Constitution of the United States, First Amendment.

[b] John 8:32–45; see also Matt. 3:9; see *Jesus the Christ,* p. 408.

[c] See Mark 3:17.

[d] Mark 9:38–41; see also Luke 9:49, 50, and compare Num. 11:27–29.

[e] Luke 9:51–56; see also John 3:17, and 12:47; see Appendix 22:1.

Intolerance is Unscriptural—The teachings of our Lord breathe the spirit of forbearance and love even to enemies. He tolerated, though he could not approve, the practises of the heathen in their idolatry, the Samaritans with their degenerate customs of worship, the luxury-loving Sadducees, and the law-bound Pharisees. Hatred was not countenanced even toward foes. His instructions were: "Love your enemies, bless them that curse you, do good to them that hate you, and pray for them which despitefully use you, and persecute you; that ye may be the children of your father which is in heaven: for he maketh his sun to rise on the evil and on the good, and sendeth rain on the just and on the unjust."[f] The Twelve were commanded to salute with their blessing every house at which they applied for hospitality. True, if the people rejected them and their message, retribution was to follow; but this visitation of cursing was to be reserved as a divine prerogative. In the Parable of the Tares, Christ taught the same lesson of forbearance; the hasty servants wanted to pluck out the weeds straightway, but were forbidden lest they root up the wheat also, and were assured that a separation would be effected in the time of harvest.[g]

In spite of the prevailing spirit of toleration and love pervading the teachings of the Savior and the apostles, attempts have been made to draw from the scriptures justification for intolerance and persecution.[h] Paul's stinging words addressed to the Galatians have been given a meaning wholly foreign to the spirit that prompted them. Warning the saints of false teachers, he said: "As we said before, so say I now again, If any man preach any other gospel unto you than that ye have received, let him be accursed." On the strength of this forceful admonition combined with denunciation, some have sought to justify persecution on account of differences in religion; but such misconstruction must be charged to shallow reading and evil prejudice. Was it not—is it not—rational to say that any man or coterie of men, any sect, denomination or church that would preach its own conceptions as the authentic Gospel of Jesus Christ, is guilty of blasphemy and deserving of the curse of God? Paul leaves us not in doubt as to the character of the Gospel he so forcefully defended, as his later words show: "But I certify you, brethren, that the gospel which was preached of me is not after man. For I neither received it of man, neither was I taught it, but by the revelation of Jesus Christ."[i] Let it be remembered that vengeance and recompense belong to the Lord.[j]

The intent of John's words of counsel to the elect lady has been perverted, and his teachings have been made a cover of refuge for persecutors and bigots. Warning her of the ministers of Antichrist who were industriously disseminating their heresies, the apostle wrote: "If there come any unto you, and bring not this doctrine, receive him not into your house, neither bid him God speed: For he that biddeth him God speed is partaker of his evil deeds."[k] By no rightful interpretation can these words be made to sanction intolerance, persecution, and hatred.

The apostle's true meaning has been set forth with clearness and force by a renowned Christian writer of the current day, who, after deploring the "narrow intolerance of an ignorant dogmatism," says: "The Apostle of Love would have belied all that is best in his own teaching if he had consciously given an absolution, nay, an incentive, to furious intolerance. * * * Meanwhile, this incidental expression of St. John's brief letter will not lend itself to these gross perversions. What St. John really says and really means, is something wholly different. False teachers were rife,

[f] Matt. 5:44, 45.
[g] See Matt. 13:24–30.
[h] See Appendix 22:1.
[i] Gal. 1:8–12; see *Vitality of "Mormonism,"* p. 182.
[j] See Deut. 32:35; see also Ps. 94:1; Rom. 12:19, Heb. 10:30.
[k] 2 John 10, 11.

who, professing to be Christians, robbed the nature of Christ of all which gave its efficacy to the atonement, and its significance to the incarnation. These teachers, like other Christian missionaries, traveled from city to city, and in the absence of public inns were received into the houses of Christian converts. The Christian lady to whom St. John writes is warned that if she offers her hospitality to these dangerous emissaries, who were subverting the central truths of Christianity, she is expressing a public sanction of them; and by doing this, and offering them her best wishes, she is taking a direct share in the harm they do. This is common sense, nor is there anything uncharitable in it. No one is bound to help forward the dissemination of teaching what he regards as erroneous respecting the most essential doctrines of his own faith. Still less would it have been right to do this in the days when Christian communities were so small and weak. But, to interpret this as it has in all ages been practically interpreted—to pervert it into a sort of command to exaggerate the minor variations between religious opinions, and to persecute those whose views differ from our own—to make our own opinions the conclusive test of heresy, and to say with Cornelius-a-Lapide, that this verse reprobates 'all conversations, all intercourse, all dealings with heretics'—is to interpret scripture by the glare of partisanship and spiritual self-satisfaction, not to read it under the light of holy love."[l]

Toleration is not Acceptance—The human frailty of running to extremes in thought and action finds few more glaring examples than are presented in man's dealings with his fellows on religious matters. On the one hand, he is prone to regard the faith of others as not merely inferior to his own but as utterly unworthy of respect; or, on the other, he brings himself to believe that all sects are equally justified in their professions and practises, and that therefore there is no distinctively true order of religion. It is in no wise inconsistent for Latter-day Saints to boldly proclaim the conviction that their Church is the accepted one, the only one entitled to the designation "Church of Jesus Christ" and the sole earthly repository of the eternal Priesthood in the present age, and yet to willingly accord kind treatment and a recognition of sincerity of purpose to every soul or sect honestly professing Christ, or merely showing a respect for truth and manifesting a sincere desire to walk according to the light received. My allegiance to the Church of my choice is based on a conviction of the validity and genuineness of its high claim—as the one and only Church possessing a God-given charter of authority—nevertheless, I count the sects as sincere until they demonstrate that they are otherwise and am ready to defend them in their rights.

Joseph Smith, the first prophet of the current dispensation, while reproving certain of his brethren for intolerance toward the cherished beliefs of other men, taught that even idolators ought to be protected in their worship; that, while it would be the strict duty of any Christian to direct his efforts toward enlightening such benighted minds, he would not be justified in forcibly depriving even the heathen of their liberty in worship. In the sight of God, idolatry is most heinous; yet He is tolerant of those who, knowing Him not, yield to their inherited instinct for worship by rendering homage even to stocks and stones. Deadly as is the sin of idolatrous worship on the part of him to whom light has come, it may represent in the savage the sincerest adoration of which he is capable. The voice of the Lord has declared that the heathen who have known no law shall have part in the first resurrection.[m]

Man is Accountable for His Acts—The unbounded liberality and tolerance with which The Church of Jesus Christ of Latter-day Saints regards other religious denominations, and the teachings

[l] Canon Farrar, *The Early Days of Christianity,* pp. 587, 588.
[m] See chap. 3 herein under "Sin."

of the Church respecting the assurance of final redemption for all men except the few who have fallen so far as to have committed the unpardonable sin, thereby becoming sons of Perdition, may suggest the erroneous conclusion that we believe that all so redeemed shall be admitted to equal powers, privileges, and glories in the kingdom of heaven. Far from this, the Church proclaims the doctrine of many and varied degrees of glory, which the redeemed will inherit in accordance with their merits. We believe in no general plan of universal forgiveness or reward, by which sinners of high and low degree shall be exempted from the effects of their deeds, while the righteous are ushered into heaven as a dwelling place in common, all glorified in the same measure. As stated, the heathen whose sins are those of ignorance are to come forth with the just in the first resurrection; but this does not imply that those children of the lower races are to inherit the glory provided for the able, the valiant and the true in the cause of God on earth.

Our condition in the world to come will be strictly a result of the life we lead in this probation, as, by the light of revealed truth regarding the preexistent state, we perceive our present condition to be determined by the fidelity with which we kept our first estate.[n] The scriptures declare that man shall reap the natural harvest of his works in life, be such good or evil; in the effective language with which the Father encourages and warns his frail children, every one will be rewarded or punished according to his works.[o] In eternity, man will enjoy or loathe the "fruit of his doing."

Graded Glories—That the privileges and glories of heaven are graded to suit the various capacities of the blessed, is indicated in Christ's teachings. To the apostles He said: "In my Father's house are many mansions: if it were not so, I would have told you. I go to prepare a place for you. And if I go and prepare a place for you, I will come again, and receive you unto myself; that where I am, there ye may be also."[p]

This utterance is supplemented by that of Paul, who speaks of graded conditions in the resurrection as follows: "There are also celestial bodies, and bodies terrestrial: but the glory of the celestial is one, and the glory of the terrestrial is another. There is one glory of the sun, and another glory of the moon, and another glory of the stars: for one star differeth from another star in glory. So also is the resurrection of the dead."[q]

A fuller knowledge of this subject has been imparted in the present dispensation. From a revelation given in 1832[r] we learn that three great kingdoms or degrees of glory are established, known as the Celestial, the Terrestrial, and the Telestial. Far below the last and least of these, is the state of eternal punishment prepared for the sons of Perdition.

The Celestial Glory is provided for those who merit the highest honors of heaven. In the revelation referred to, we read of them: "They are they who received the testimony of Jesus, and believed on his name and were baptized after the manner of his burial, being buried in the water in his name, and this according to the commandment which he has given—That by keeping the commandments they might be washed and cleansed from all their sins, and receive the Holy Spirit by the laying on of the hands of him who is ordained and sealed unto this power; And who overcome by faith, and are sealed by the Holy Spirit of promise, which the Father sheds forth upon all those who are just and true. They are they who are the church of the Firstborn. They are they into whose hands the Father has given all things—They are they who are priests and kings, who

[n] P.of G.P., Abraham 3:22-26; see also "Man's Accountability" in chap. 3 and "Salvation and Exaltation" in chap. 4 herein.
[o] See Job 34:11; Ps. 62:12; Jer. 17:10; 32:19; Rom. 2:6-12; 14:12; 1 Cor 3:8; 2 Cor. 5:10; Rev. 2:33; 20:12; 22:12.
[p] John 14:1–3.
[q] 1 Cor. 15:40–42.
[r] See D&C, sec. 76.

have received of his fulness, and of his glory; And are priests of the Most High, after the order of Melchizedek, which was after the order of Enoch, which was after the order of the Only Begotten Son. Wherefore, as it is written, they are gods, even the sons of God—Wherefore, all things are theirs, whether life or death, or things present, or things to come, all are theirs and they are Christ's, and Christ is God's. * * * These shall dwell in the presence of God and his Christ forever and ever. These are they whom he shall bring with him, when he shall come in the clouds of heaven to reign on the earth over his people. These are they who shall have part in the first resurrection. These are they who shall come forth in the resurrection of the just. * * * These are they who are just men made perfect through Jesus the mediator of the new covenant, who wrought out this perfect atonement through the shedding of his own blood. These are they whose bodies are celestial, whose glory is that of the sun, even the glory of God, the highest of all, whose glory the sun of the firmament is written of as being typical."

The Terrestrial Glory—This, the next lowest degree, will be attained by many whose works do not merit the highest reward. We read of them: "These are they who are of the terrestrial, whose glory differs from that of the church of the Firstborn who have received the fulness of the Father, even as that of the moon differs from the sun in the firmament. Behold, these are they who died without law; And also they who are the spirits of men kept in prison, whom the Son visited, and preached the gospel unto them, that they might be judged according to men in the flesh; Who received not the testimony of Jesus in the flesh, but afterwards received it. These are they who are honorable men of the earth, who were blinded by the craftiness of men. These are they who receive of his glory, but not of his fulness. These are they who receive of the presence of the Son, but not of the fulness of the Father. Wherefore they are bodies terrestrial, and not bodies celestial, and differ in glory as the moon differs from the sun. These are they who are not valiant in the testimony of Jesus; wherefore, they obtain not the crown over the kingdom of our God."

The Telestial Glory—The revelation continues: "And again, we saw the glory of the telestial,[s] which glory is that of the lesser, even as the glory of the stars differs from that of the glory of the moon in the firmament. These are they who received not the gospel of Christ, neither the testimony of Jesus. These are they who deny not the Holy Spirit. These are they who are thrust down to hell. These are they who shall not be redeemed from the devil until the last resurrection, until the Lord, even Christ the Lamb, shall have finished his work." We learn further that the inhabitants of this kingdom are to be graded among themselves, comprising as they do the unenlightened among the varied opposing sects and divisions of men, and sinners of many types, whose offenses are not those of utter perdition: "For as one star differs from another star in glory, even so differs one from another in glory in the telestial world; For these are they who are of Paul, and of Apollos, and of Cephas. These are they who say they are some of one and some of another—some of Christ, and some of John, and some of Moses, and some of Elias, and some of Esaias, and some of Isaiah, and some of Enoch; But received not the gospel, neither the testimony of Jesus, neither the prophets, neither the everlasting covenant."[t] Evidently a considerable part of the human family will fail of all glory beyond that of the telestial kingdom, for we are told: "But behold, and lo, we saw the glory and the inhabitants of the telestial world, that they were as innumerable as the stars in the firmament of heaven, or as the sand upon the seashore." They are thus not wholly rejected; their every merit will be respected. "For they shall be judged according to

[s] See Appendix 22:2.
[t] D&C, sec. 76.

their works, and every man shall receive according to his own works, his own dominion, in the mansions which are prepared; And they shall be servants of the Most High, but where God and Christ dwell they cannot come, worlds without end."

That every soul shall find his place in the hereafter, that he shall be judged and assigned according to what he is, is no less truly scriptural than reasonable. He shall inherit according to his capacity to receive, enjoy, and utilize. This is made sublimely plain by revelation given in 1832, in which we read: "For he who is not able to abide the law of a celestial kingdom cannot abide a celestial glory. And he who cannot abide the law of a terrestrial kingdom cannot abide a terrestrial glory. And he who cannot abide the law of a telestial kingdom cannot abide a telestial glory; therefore he is not meet for a kingdom of glory. Therefore he must abide a kingdom which is not a kingdom of glory."[u]

The Kingdoms with Respect to One Another—The three kingdoms of widely differing glories are severally organized on a plan of gradation. The Telestial kingdom comprises subdivisions; this also is the case, we are told, with the Celestial;[v] and, by analogy, we conclude that a similar condition prevails in the Terrestrial. Thus the innumerable degrees of merit amongst mankind are provided for in an infinity of graded glories. The Celestial kingdom is supremely honored by the personal ministrations of the Father and the Son. The Terrestrial kingdom will be administered through the higher, without a fulness of glory. The Telestial is governed through the ministrations of the Terrestrial, by "angels who are appointed to minister for them."[w]

It is reasonable to believe, in the absence of direct revelation by which alone absolute knowledge of the matter could be acquired, that, in accordance with God's plan of eternal progression, advancement within each of the three specified kingdoms will be provided for; though as to possible progress from one kingdom to another the scriptures make no positive affirmation. Eternal advancement along different lines is conceivable. We may conclude that degrees and grades will ever characterize the kingdoms of our God. Eternity is progressive; perfection is relative; the essential feature of God's living purpose is its associated power of eternal increase.

The Sons of Perdition—We learn of another class of souls whose sins are such as to place them beyond the present possibility of repentance and salvation. These are called sons of Perdition, children of the fallen angel who was once a Son of the Morning, Lucifer, now Satan, or Perdition.[x] These are they who have violated truth in the light of knowledge; who, having received the testimony of Christ, and having been endowed by the Holy Spirit, then deny the same and defy the power of God, crucifying the Lord afresh and putting Him to an open shame. This, the unpardonable sin, can be committed by those only who have received knowledge and conviction of the truth, against which they then rebel. Their sin is comparable to the treason of Lucifer, by which he sought to usurp the power and glory of his God. Concerning them and their dreadful fate, the Lord has said: "They are they who are the sons of perdition, of whom I say that it had been better for them never to have been born; For they are vessels of wrath, doomed to suffer the wrath of God, with the devil and his angels in eternity; Concerning whom I have said there is no forgiveness in this world nor in the world to come—* * * And the only ones on whom the second death shall have any power; * * * they shall go away into everlasting punishment, which is

[u] D&C 88:22–24.
[v] See D&C 131:1; see also 2 Cor. 12:1–4.
[w] See D&C 76:86–88.
[x] See D&C 76:25–27.

endless punishment, which is eternal punishment, to reign with the devil and his angels in eternity, where their worm dieth not, and the fire is not quenched, which is their torment—And the end thereof, neither the place thereof, nor their torment, no man knows; Neither was it revealed, neither is, neither will be revealed unto man, except to them who are made partakers thereof; Nevertheless I, the Lord, show it by vision unto many, but straightway shut it up again; Wherefore, the end, the width, the height, the depth, and the misery thereof, they understand not, neither any man except those who are ordained unto this condemnation."[y]

The doctrines of the Church are explicit in defining the relationship between the mortal probation and the future state, and in teaching individual accountability and the free agency of man. The Church affirms that in view of the responsibility under which every man rests, as the director of his own course, he must be and is free to choose in all things, from the life that leads to the celestial home to the career that is but the introduction to the miseries of perdition. Freedom to worship, or to refuse to worship, is a God-given right, and every soul must abide the result of his choice.[z]

REFERENCES

Worship of the True and Living God Required—For scriptures relating to man's freedom in worship, his capacity to obey or disobey the divine commandments, with the assurance that he must abide by the consequences of his choice, see references under Free Agency, following chapter 3.

Thou shalt have no other gods before me—Exodus 20:3; read verses 1–6; see also 34:14.
The Lord commanded Moses and others to come up and worship—Ex. 24:1.
If the Israelites served other gods they would surely perish—Deut. 8:19.
Thou shalt set it before the Lord thy God, and worship before the Lord thy God—Deut. 26:10.
The Lord shall ye fear, and him shall ye worship, and to him shall ye do sacrifice—2 Kings 17:36.
Give unto the Lord the glory due unto his name; worship the Lord in the beauty of holiness—1 Chr. 16:29; see also Ps. 45:11.
There shall no strange god be in thee; neither shalt thou worship any strange god—Ps. 81:9.
Exalt ye the Lord our God, and worship at his footstool; for he is holy—Ps. 99:5; see also verse 9.
All flesh shall come to worship before me, saith the Lord—Isa. 66:23.
Christ said to Satan: For it is written, Thou shalt worship the Lord thy God, and him only shalt thou serve—Matt. 4:10.
So worship I the God of my fathers—Acts 24:14.
They that worship him must worship him in spirit and in truth—John 4:24.
John the Revelator saw in vision elders before the throne who did worship him that liveth forever and ever—Rev. 4:10; compare 5:14; 7:11; 11:16; 19:4.
Worship God: for the testimony of Jesus is the spirit of prophecy—Rev. 19:10.
Alma instructed the poor that could not enter the synagogues that worship would be acceptable wherever offered, if genuine—Alma, chap. 32; 33:2; 34:38.
The Nephites made sacrifices that they might worship God according to their desires—Alma 43:9–11.

[y] D&C 76:31-48; see also Heb. 6:46; Alma 39:6. For treatment of the "Second Death," see the author's *Vitality of "Mormonism,"* p. 301.
[z] See Appendix 22:3.

The Nephites and the converted Lamanites fought to maintain their rights, and the privileges of their church and of their worship, and their freedom and their liberty—3 Nephi 2:12.

The Nephite multitude worshiped the resurrected Christ—3 Nephi 17:10; see also 11:17.

The holy prophets worshiped the Father in the name of Christ, as did also the Nephites—Jacob 4:4, 5.

And you shall fall down and worship the Father in my name—D&C 18:40.

All men must worship the Father in the name of the Son—D&C 20:29.

That you may understand and know how to worship, and know what you worship, that you may come unto the Father in my name—D&C 93:19.

Worship him that made heaven, and earth, and the sea, and the fountains of waters—D&C 133:39; Rev. 14:7.

Moses refused to worship Satan and declared that God had said unto him: Worship God, for him only shalt thou serve—Moses 1:15; read verses 12–20.

Abraham worshiped the living God, though his kindred had turned to idols—Abraham 1:5.

For scriptures relating to the worship of idols see references under *Idolatry,* following chapter 2 herein.

As relating to graded conditions in the hereafter see references under *Salvation,* following Chapter 4 herein.

23

SUBMISSION TO SECULAR AUTHORITY

ARTICLE 12

E BELIEVE in being subject to kings, presidents, rulers, and magistrates, in obeying, honoring, and sustaining the law.

Introductory—It is but reasonable to expect of a people professing the Gospel of Jesus Christ, and claiming membership in the one accepted and divinely invested Church, that they manifest in practise the virtues that their precepts inculcate. True, we may look in vain for perfection among those even who make the fullest claims to a religious life; but we have a right to expect in their creed ample requirements concerning the most approved course of action, and in their lives, sincere and earnest effort toward the practical realization of their professions. Religion, to be of service and worthy of acceptance, must be of wholesome influence in the individual lives and temporal affairs of its adherents. Among other virtues the Church in its teachings should impress the duty of a law-abiding course; and the people should show forth the effect of such precepts in their probity as citizens of the nation and the community of which they are part.

The Church of Jesus Christ of Latter-day Saints makes emphatic declaration of its belief and precepts regarding the duty of its members toward the laws of the land, and sustains its position by the authority of specific revelation in ancient as in present times.

Moreover, the people are confident that when the true story of their rise and progress as an established body of religious worshipers is fully known, the loyalty of the Church and the patriotic devotion of its members will be vindicated and extolled by the world in general, as now by the few unprejudiced investigators who have studied with honest purpose the history of this remarkable organization.

Obedience to Authority Enjoined by Scripture—During the patriarchal period, when the head of the family possessed virtually the power of judge and king over his household, the authority of the ruler and the rights of the family were respected. Consider the instance of Hagar, the "plural" wife of Abram and the handmaid of Sarai. Jealousy and ill-feeling had arisen between Hagar and her mistress, the senior wife of the patriarch. Abram listened to the complaint of Sarai, and, recognizing her authority over Hagar, who, though his wife, was still the servant of Sarai, said: "Behold, thy maid is in thy hand; do to her as it pleaseth thee." Then, as the mistress dealt harshly with her servant, Hagar fled into the wilderness; there she was visited by an angel of the Lord, who addressed her thus: "Hagar, Sarai's maid, whence camest thou, and whither wilt thou go? And she said, I flee from the face of my mistress Sarai. And the angel of the Lord said unto her, Return to thy mistress, and submit thyself under her hands."[a] Observe that the heavenly messenger recognized the authority of the mistress over the bond-woman, even though the latter had been given the rank of wifehood in the family.

The filial submission of Isaac to the will of his father, even to the extent of readiness to yield his life[b] on the altar of sacrifice, is evidence of the sanctity with which the authority of the family ruler was regarded. It may appear, as indeed it has been claimed, that the requirement made of Abraham by the Lord, as a test of faith in the matter of demanding his son's life as a sacrifice, was a violation of law and therefore opposed to righteous government. The claim is poorly placed in view of the fact that the patriarchal head was possessed of full authority over the members of his household, with power extending even to judgment of life or death.[c]

In the days of the exodus, when the people of Israel were ruled by a theocracy, the Lord gave divers laws and commandments for the government of the nation; among them we read: "Thou shalt not revile the gods, nor curse the ruler of thy people."[d] Judges were appointed by divine direction. Moses, in reiterating the Lord's commands, charged the people to this effect: "Judges and officers shalt thou make thee in all thy gates, which the Lord thy God giveth thee, throughout thy tribes: and they shall judge the people with just judgment."[e] It is significant that the judges were so highly regarded as to be called gods, to which fact Jesus referred when threatened with stoning because He had said He was the Son of God.

When the people wearied of God's direct administration and clamored for a king, Jehovah yielded to their desire and gave the new ruler authority by a holy anointing.[f] David, even though he had been anointed to succeed Saul as king recognized the sanctity of the king's person, and bitterly reproached himself because on one occasion he had mutilated the robe of the monarch. Saul at that time was seeking David's life, and the latter sought only a means of showing that he had no intent to slay his royal enemy; yet we are told: "That David's heart smote him, because he had cut off Saul's skirt. And he said unto his men, The Lord forbid that I

---

[a] Gen. 16:1–9; see *Jesus the Christ,* p. 397, Note 6.
[b] See Gen.22:1–10.
[c] See Gen. 38:24.
[d] Ex. 22:28. The word "gods" in this passage is rendered by some translators "judges." (See marginal reference, Bible.)
[e] Deut. 16:18; see also 1:16; 1 Chr. 23:4; 26:29. See further Ps. 82:1, 6; John 10:34–36; and *Jesus the Christ,* pp. 489, 501.
[f] See 1 Sam.8:6, 7, 22; 9:15, 16; 10:1.

should do this thing unto my master, the Lord's anointed, to stretch forth mine hand against him, seeing he is the anointed of the Lord."[g]

Note, further, the following scriptural adjurations as recorded in the Old Testament: "My son, fear thou the Lord, and the king."[h] "I counsel thee to keep the king's commandment, and that in regard of the oath of God."[i] "Curse not the king, no not in thy thought."[j]

Examples Set by Christ and His Apostles—Our Savior's work on earth was marked throughout by His acknowledgment of the existing powers of the land, both Jewish and Roman, even though the latter had been won by cruel conquest, and were exercised unjustly. When the tax collector called for the tribute money demanded by the hierarchy, Christ, though not admitting the justice of the claim, directed that the tax be paid, and even invoked a miraculous circumstance whereby the money could be provided. Of Peter he asked: "What thinkest thou, Simon? Of whom do the kings of the earth take custom or tribute? Of their own children, or of strangers? Peter saith unto him, Of strangers. Jesus saith unto him, Then are the children free. Notwithstanding, lest we should offend them, go thou to the sea, and cast an hook, and take up the fish that first cometh up; and when thou hast opened his mouth, thou shall find a piece of money: that take, and give unto them for me and thee."[k]

At the instigation of certain wicked Pharisees, a treacherous plot was laid to make Christ appear as an offender against the ruling powers. They sought to catch Him by the casuistical question—"What thinkest thou? Is it lawful to give tribute unto Cæsar or not?" His rejoinder was an unequivocal endorsement of submission to the laws. "Shew me the tribute money" He said; "And they brought unto him a penny. And he saith unto them, Whose is this image and superscription? They say unto him, Cæsar's. Then saith he unto them, Render therefore unto Cæsar the things which are Cæsar's; and unto God the things that are God's."[l]

Throughout the tragic circumstances of His trial and condemnation, Christ maintained a submissive demeanor even toward the chief priests and council who were plotting His death. These officers, however unworthy of their priestly power, were nevertheless in authority and had a certain measure of jurisdiction in secular as in ecclesiastical affairs. When He stood before Caiaphas, laden with insult and accused by false witnesses, He maintained a dignified silence. To the high priest's question, "Answereth thou nothing? What is it which these witness against thee?" He deigned no reply. Then the high priest added: "I adjure thee by the living God, that thou tell us whether thou be the Christ, the Son of God."[m] To this solemn adjuration, spoken with official authority, the Savior gave an immediate answer, thus acknowledging the office of the high priest, however unworthy the man.

A somewhat analogous mark of respect for the high priest's office was shown by Paul while a prisoner before the ecclesiastical tribunal. His remarks displeased the high priest, who gave immediate command to those who stood near Paul to smite him on the mouth.[n] This angered the apostle, and he cried out: "God shall smite thee, thou whited wall: for sittest thou to judge me after

[g] 1 Sam. 24:5, 6, 10; see also 26:9–12, 16.
[h] Prov. 24:21.
[i] Eccl. 8:2.
[j] Eccl. 10:20; see Appendix 23:5.
[k] Matt. 17:24–27. The payment exacted in this instance may have been the temple tax or "atonement money." See *Jesus the Christ,* p. 382.
[l] Matt. 22:15–21; see also Mark 12:13–17; Luke 20:20–25.
[m] Matt. 26:57–64; Mark 14:55-62; see *Jesus the Christ,* p. 625.
[n] See Appendix 23:1.

the law, and commandest me to be smitten contrary to the law? And they that stood by said, Revilest thou God's high priest? Then said Paul, I wist not, brethren, that he was the high priest: for it is written, Thou shalt not speak evil of the ruler of thy people."[o]

Teachings of the Apostles—Paul, writing to Titus, who had been left in charge of the Church among the Cretans, warned him of the weaknesses of his flock, and urged him to teach them to be orderly and law-abiding: "Put them in mind to be subject to principalities and powers, to obey magistrates, to be ready to every good work."[p] In another place, Paul is emphatic in declaring the duty of the saints toward the civil power, such authority being ordained of God. He points out the necessity of secular government, and the need of officers in authority, whose power is to be feared by evildoers only. He designates the civil authorities as ministers of God; and justifies taxation by the state, with an admonition that the saints fail not in their dues.

These are his words addressed to the Church at Rome: "Let every soul be subject unto the higher powers. For there is no power but of God: the powers that be are ordained of God. Whosoever therefore resisteth the power, resisteth the ordinance of God: and they that resist shall receive to themselves damnation. For rulers are not a terror to good works, but to the evil. Wilt thou then not be afraid of the power? Do that which is good, and thou shalt have praise of the same: For he is the minister of God to thee for good. But if thou do that which is evil, be afraid; for he beareth not the sword in vain: for he is the minister of God, a revenger to execute wrath upon him that doeth evil. Wherefore ye must needs be subject, not only for wrath, but also for conscience sake. For for this cause pay ye tribute also: for they are God's ministers, attending continually upon this very thing. Render therefore to all their dues: tribute to whom tribute is due; custom to whom custom; fear to whom fear; honor to whom honor."[q]

In a letter to Timothy, Paul teaches that in the prayers of the saints, kings and all in authority should be remembered, adding that such remembrance is pleasing in the sight of God: "I exhort therefore, that, first of all, supplications, prayers, intercessions, and giving of thanks, be made for all men; For kings, and for all that are in authority; that we may lead a quiet and peaceable life in all godliness and honesty. For this is good and acceptable in the sight of God our Savior."[r]

The duty of willing submission to authority is elaborated in the epistles to the Ephesians and the Colossians; and illustrations are applied to the relations of social and domestic life. Wives are taught to be submissive to their husbands—"For the husband is the head of the wife, even as Christ is the head of the church"; but this duty within the family is reciprocal, and therefore husbands are instructed as to the manner in which authority ought to be exercised. Children are to obey their parents; yet the parents are cautioned against provoking or otherwise unjustly offending their little ones. Servants are told to render willing and earnest service to their masters, recognizing in all things the superior authority; and masters are instructed in their duty toward their servants, being counseled to avoid threatening and other harsh treatment, remembering that they also will have to answer to a Master greater than themselves.[s]

Peter was not less emphatic in teaching the sanctity with which the civil power should be regarded;[t] he admonished the saints in this wise: "Submit yourselves to every ordinance of man

[o] Acts 23:1–5.
[p] Titus 3:1.
[q] Rom. 13:1–7.
[r] 1 Tim. 2:1–3.
[s] See Eph. 5:22, 23; 6:1-9; Col. 5:18–22; 4:1.
[t] See Appendix 23:2.

for the Lord's sake: whether it be to the king, as supreme; Or unto governors, as unto them that are sent by him for the punishment of evildoers, and for the praise of them that do well. For so is the will of God, that with well doing ye may put to silence the ignorance of foolish men: As free, and not using your liberty for a cloak of maliciousness, but as the servants of God. Honor all men. Love the brotherhood. Fear God. Honor the king."[u]

These rules relating to submission to authority he applied, as did Paul similarly, to the conditions of domestic life. Servants are to be obedient, even though their masters be harsh and severe: "For this is thankworthy, if a man for conscience toward God endure grief, suffering wrongfully. For what glory is it, if, when ye be buffeted for your faults, ye shall take it patiently? But if, when you do well, and suffer for it, ye take it patiently, this is acceptable with God."[v] Wives also, even though their husbands be not of their faith, are not to vaunt themselves and defy authority, but to be submissive, and to rely upon gentler and more effective means of influencing those whose name they bear.[w] He gives assurance of the judgment that shall overtake evildoers, and specifies as fit subjects for condemnation "chiefly them that walk after the flesh in the lust of uncleanness, and despise government. Presumptuous are they, self-willed, they are not afraid to speak evil of dignities."[x]

Doubtless there existed excellent reason for these explicit and repeated counsels, against the spirit of revolt, with which the apostles of old sought to lead and strengthen the Church. The saints rejoiced in their testimony of the truth that had found place in their hearts—the truth that was to make them free—and it would have been easy for them to regard all others as inferior to themselves, and to rebel against all authority of man in favor of their allegiance to a higher power. There was constant danger that their zeal would lead them to acts of indiscretion, and thus furnish excuse, if not reason, for the assaults of persecutors, who would have denounced them as lawbreakers and workers of sedition. Even half-hearted submission to the civil powers would have been unwise at least, in view of the disfavor with which the Church had come to be regarded by pagan contemporaries. The voice of inspired leaders was heard, therefore, in timely counsel for humility and submission. But there were then, as ever have there been, weightier reasons than such as rest on motives of policy requiring submission to the established powers. Such is no less the law of God than of man. Governments are essential to human existence; they are recognized, given indeed, of the Lord; and His people are in duty bound to sustain them.

Book of Mormon Teachings concerning the duty of the people as subjects of the law of the land are abundant throughout the volume. However, as the civil and the ecclesiastical powers were usually vested together, the king or chief judge generally being also the high priest, there are comparatively few admonitions of allegiance to the civil authority as distinct from that of the Priesthood. From the time of Nephi, son of Lehi, to that of the death of Mosiah, a period of nearly five hundred years, the Nephites were ruled by a succession of kings; during the remaining time of their recorded history, more than five hundred years, they were subject to judges of their own choosing. Under each of these forms of government, the secular laws were rigidly enforced, the power of the state being supplemented and strengthened by that of the Church. The sanctity with which the laws were regarded is illustrated in the judgment pronounced by Alma upon Nehor, a

[u] 1 Peter 2:13–17.
[v] Same, verses 19, 20.
[w] See 1 Peter 3:1–7.
[x] 2 Peter 2:10.

murderer, and a promoter of sedition and priestcraft. "Therefore thou art condemned to die," said the judge, "according to the law which has been given us by Mosiah, our last king; and it has been acknowledged by this people; therefore this people must abide by the law."[y]

Latter-day Revelation requires of the saints in the present dispensation strict allegiance to the civil laws. In a communication dated August 1, 1831, the Lord said to the Church: "Let no man break the laws of the land, for he that keepeth the laws of God hath no need to break the laws of the land. Wherefore, be subject to the powers that be, until he reigns whose right it is to reign, and subdues all enemies under his feet."[z] At a later date, August 6, 1833, the voice of the Lord was heard again on this matter, saying: "And now, verily I say unto you concerning the laws of the land, it is my will that my people should observe to do all things whatsoever I command them. And that law of the land which is constitutional, supporting that principle of freedom in maintaining rights and privileges, belongs to all mankind, and is justifiable before me. Therefore, I, the Lord, justify you, and your brethren of my church, in befriending that law which is the constitutional law of the land."[aa]

A question has many times been asked of the Church and of its individual members, to this effect: In the case of a conflict between the requirements made by the revealed word of God, and those imposed by the secular law, which of these authorities would the members of the Church be bound to obey? In answer, the words of Christ may be applied—it is the duty of the people to render unto Cæsar the things that are Cæsar's, and unto God the things that are God's. At the present time the kingdom of heaven as an earthly power, with a reigning King exercising direct and personal authority in temporal matters, has not been established upon the earth. The branches of the Church as such, and the members composing the same, are subjects of the several governments within whose separate realms the Church organizations exist. In this day of comparative enlightenment and freedom there is small cause for expecting any direct interference with the rights of private worship and individual devotion; in all civilized nations the people are accorded the right to pray, and this right is assured by what may be properly called a common law of humankind. No earnest soul is cut off from communion with his God; and with such an open channel of communication, relief from burdensome laws and redress for grievances may be sought from the power that holds control of nations.

Pending the overruling by Providence in favor of religious liberty, it is the duty of the saints to submit themselves to the laws of their country. Nevertheless, they should use every proper method, as citizens or subjects of their several governments, to secure for themselves and for all men the boon of freedom in religious service. It is not required of them to suffer without protest imposition by lawless persecutors, or through the operation of unjust laws; but their protests should be offered in legal and proper order. The saints have practically demonstrated their acceptance of the doctrine that it is better to suffer evil than to do wrong by purely human opposition to unjust authority. And if by thus submitting themselves to the laws of the land, in the event of such laws being unjust and subversive of human freedom, the people be prevented from doing the work appointed them of God, they are not to be held accountable for the failure to act under the higher law. The word of the Lord has defined the position and duty of the people in such a contingency: "Verily, verily, I say unto you, that when I give a commandment to any of the sons of men

[y] Alma 1:14.
[z] D&C 58:21, 22.
[aa] D&C 98:4–6.

to do a work unto my name, and those sons of men go with all their might and with all they have to perform that work, and cease not their diligence, and their enemies come upon them and hinder them from performing that work, behold, it behooveth me to require that work no more at the hands of those sons of men, but to accept of their offerings. And the iniquity and transgression of my holy laws and commandments I will visit upon the heads of those who hindered my work, unto the third and fourth generation, so long as they repent not, and hate me, saith the Lord God."[bb]

An Illustration of such suspension of divine law is found in the action of the Church regarding the matter of plural marriage. This practise was established as a result of direct revelation,[cc] and many of those who followed the same felt that they were divinely commanded so to do. For ten years after plural marriage had been introduced into Utah as a Church observance, no law was enacted in opposition to the practise. Beginning with 1862, however, Federal statutes were framed declaring the practise unlawful and providing penalties therefore. The Church claimed that these enactments were unconstitutional, and therefore void, inasmuch as they violated the provision in the national Constitution forbidding the government making laws respecting any establishment of religion or prohibiting the free exercise thereof.[dd] Many appeals were taken to the national court of final resort, and at last a decision was rendered sustaining the laws as constitutional and therefore binding. The Church, through its President, thereupon discontinued the practise of plural marriage, and announced its action to the world, solemnly placing the responsibility for the change upon the nation by whose laws the renunciation had been forced. This action has been approved and confirmed by the official vote of the Church in conference assembled.[ee]

Teachings of the Church—Perhaps there can be presented herein no better summary of the teachings of The Church of Jesus Christ of Latter-day Saints regarding its relation to the civil power, and the respect due to the laws of the land, than the official declaration issued by the Prophet Joseph Smith, and which has been incorporated in the Doctrine and Covenants—one of the standard works of the Church, adopted by vote of the Church as one of the accepted guides in faith, doctrine, and practise.[ff] It reads as follows:

A DECLARATION OF BELIEF REGARDING GOVERNMENTS AND LAWS IN GENERAL

1. We believe that governments were instituted of God for the benefit of man; and that he holds men accountable for their acts in relation to them, both in making laws and administering them, for the good and safety of society.
2. We believe that no government can exist in peace, except such laws are framed and held inviolate as will secure to each individual the free exercise of conscience, the right and control of property, and the protection of life.
3. We believe that all governments necessarily require civil officers and magistrates to enforce the laws of the same; and that such as will administer the law in equity and justice should be sought for and upheld by the voice of the people if a republic, or the will of the sovereign.
4. We believe that religion is instituted of God; and that men are amenable to him, and to him only, for the exercise of it, unless their religious opinions prompt them to infringe upon the

[bb] D&C 124:49, 50; see Appendix 23:3.
[cc] See D&C, sec. 132.
[dd] See Article I, of the Amendments to the Constitution of the United States.
[ee] See Appendix 23:4.
[ff] See D&C, sec. 134.

rights and liberties of others; but we do not believe that human law has a right to interfere in prescribing rules of worship to bind the consciences of men, nor dictate forms for public or private devotion; that the civil magistrate should restrain crime, but never control conscience; should punish guilt, but never suppress the freedom of the soul.

5. We believe that all men are bound to sustain and uphold hold the respective governments in which they reside, while protected in their inherent and inalienable rights by the laws of such governments; and that sedition and rebellion are unbecoming every citizen thus protected, and should be punished accordingly; and that all governments have a right to enact such laws as in their own judgments are best calculated to secure the public interest; at the same time, however, holding sacred the freedom of conscience.

6. We believe that every man should be honored in his station, rulers and magistrates as such, being placed for the protection of the innocent and the punishment of the guilty; and that to the laws all men owe respect and deference, as without them peace and harmony would be supplanted by anarchy and terror; human laws being instituted for the express purpose of regulating our interests as individuals and nations, between man and man; and divine laws given of heaven, prescribing rules on spiritual concerns, for faith and worship, both to be answered by man to his Maker.

7. We believe that rulers, states, and governments have a right, and are bound to enact laws for the protection of all citizens in the free exercise of their religious belief; but we do not believe that they have a right in justice to deprive citizens of this privilege, or proscribe them in their opinions, so long as a regard and reverence are shown to the laws and such religious opinions do not justify sedition nor conspiracy.

8. We believe that the commission of crime should be punished according to the nature of the offense; that murder, treason, robbery, theft, and the breach of the general peace, in all respects, should be punished according to their criminality and their tendency to evil among men, by the laws of that government in which the offense is committed; and for the public peace and tranquillity all men should step forward and use their ability in bringing offenders against good laws to punishment.

9. We do not believe it just to mingle religious influence with civil government, whereby one religious society is fostered and another proscribed in its spiritual privileges, and the individual rights of its members, as citizens, denied.

10. We believe that all religious societies have a right to deal with their members for disorderly conduct, according to the rules and regulations of such societies; provided that such dealings be for fellowship and good standing; but we do not believe that any religious society has authority to try men on the right of property or life, to take from them this world's goods, or to put them in jeopardy of either life or limb, or to inflict any physical punishment upon them. They can only excommunicate them from their society, and withdraw from them their fellowship.

11. We believe that men should appeal to the civil law for redress of all wrongs and grievances, where personal abuse is inflicted or the right of property or character infringed, where such laws exist as will protect the same; but we believe that all men are justified in defending themselves, their friends, and property, and the government, from the unlawful assaults and encroachments of all persons in times of exigency, where immediate appeal cannot be made to the laws, and relief afforded.

12. We believe it just to preach the Gospel to the nations of the earth, and warn the righteous to save themselves from the corruption of the world; but we do not believe it right to interfere with bondservants, neither preach the Gospel to, nor baptize them contrary to the will and wish of their masters, nor to meddle with or influence them in the least to cause them to be dissatisfied with their situations in this life, thereby jeopardizing the lives of men; such interference we believe to be unlawful and unjust, and dangerous to the peace of every government allowing human beings to be held in servitude.

REFERENCES

Secular Government Necessary; Divinely Recognized

God showed Pharaoh what he was about to do—Gen. 41:25–57.

Training schools were established by direction of King Nebuchadnezzar—Dan. 1:3–5.

Public instruction fostered under kingly rule—2 Chr. 17:7–9.

Moses foresaw that the Israelites would establish kings to rule over them, and gave instructions that a copy of the record known as the Law of Moses should be provided for the guidance of the kings—Deut. 17:14–20. When David was crowned King of Israel he entered into a league, somewhat in the nature of a constitutional guaranty—2 Sam. 5:3. Zedekiah, King of Judah, made a covenant with the people, proclaiming liberty unto them— Jer. 34:8; read verses 8–11. See mention of the law of the Medes and Persians "which altereth not"—Dan. 6:8, 12; Esther 1:19.

Christ recognized and observed the payment of taxes—Matt. 22:17–22.

Paul taught obedience to the secular powers and required members of the church to pay their tributes and dues—Rom. 13:1–7.

The Lord requires of his people in this dispensation that if any violate the secular law they be dealt with by the laws of the land—D&C 42:79, 85, 86.

Church organization to be formed according to the laws of man—D&C 44:4.

And thus all things shall be made sure, according to the laws of the land—D&C 51:6.

Let no man break the laws of the land—D&C 58:21. Note that in the 23rd verse the Lord says: Behold, the laws which ye have received from my hand are the laws of the church, and in this light ye shall hold them forth.

Constitutional law, supporting that principle of freedom in maintaining rights and privileges, is justifiable before the Lord—D&C 98:5.

According to the laws and constitution of the people, which I have suffered to be established—D&C 101:77.

Declaration of Belief regarding Government and Laws in general—D&C, sec. 134.

24

PRACTICAL RELIGION

ARTICLE 13

E BELIEVE in being honest, true, chaste, benevolent, virtuous, and in doing good to all men; indeed, we may say that we follow the admonition of Paul—We believe all things, we hope all things, we have endured many things, and hope to be able to endure all things. If there is anything virtuous, lovely, or of good report or praiseworthy, we seek after these things.

Religion of Daily Life—In this article of their faith, the Latter-day Saints declare their acceptance of a practical religion; a religion that shall consist, not alone of professions in spiritual matters, and belief as to the conditions of the hereafter, of the doctrine of original sin and the actuality of a future heaven and hell, but also, and more particularly, of present and everyday duties, in which proper respect for self, love for fellow men, and devotion to God are the guiding principles. Religion without morality, professions of godliness without charity, church-membership without adequate responsibility as to individual conduct in daily life, are but as sounding brass and tinkling cymbals—noise without music, the words without the spirit of prayer. "Pure religion and undefiled before God and the Father is this, To visit the fatherless and widows in their affliction, and to keep himself unspotted from the world."[a] Honesty of purpose, integrity of soul, individual purity, freedom of conscience, willingness to do

---

[a] James 1:27.

good to all men even enemies, pure benevolence—these are some of the fruits by which the religion of Christ may be known, far exceeding in importance and value the promulgation of dogmas and the enunciation of theories. Yet a knowledge of things more than temporal, doctrines of spiritual matters, founded on revelation and not resting on the sands of man's frail hypotheses, are likewise characteristic of the true Church.

The Comprehensiveness of Our Faith must appeal to every earnest investigator of the principles taught by the Church, and still more to the unprejudiced observer of the results as manifested in the course of life characteristic of the Latter-day Saints. Within the pale of the Church there is a place for all truth—for everything that is praiseworthy, virtuous, lovely, or of good report. The liberality with which the Church regards other religious denominations; the earnestness of its teaching that God is no respecter of persons, but that He will judge all men according to their deeds; the breadth and depth of its precepts concerning the state of immortality, and the gradations of eternal glory awaiting the honest in heart of all nations, kindred, and churches, civilized and heathen, enlightened and benighted, have already been set forth. We have seen further that the belief of this people carries them forward, even beyond the bounds of knowledge thus far revealed, and teaches them to look with unwavering confidence for other revelation, truths yet to be added, glories grander than have yet been made known, eternities of powers, dominions, and progress, beyond the mind of man to conceive or the soul to contain. We believe in a God who is Himself progressive, whose majesty is intelligence; whose perfection consists in eternal advancement[b]—a Being who has attained His exalted state by a path which now His children are permitted to follow, whose glory it is their heritage to share. In spite of the opposition of the sects, in the face of direct charges of blasphemy, the Church proclaims the eternal truth: *"As man is, God once was; as God is, man may be."* With such a future, well may man open his heart to the stream of revelation, past, present, and to come; and truthfully should we be able to say of every enlightened child of God, that he "beareth all things, believeth all things, hopeth all things, endureth all things."[c] As being incidental to the declaration of belief embodied in this Article, many topics relating to the organization, precepts, and practise of the Church suggest themselves. Of these the following may claim attention.

Benevolence—Benevolence is founded on love for fellow men; it embraces, though it far exceeds charity, in the ordinary sense in which the latter word is used. By the Christ it was placed as second only to love for God. On one occasion certain Pharisees came to Christ, tempting Him with questions on doctrine in the hope that they could entangle Him and so make Him an offender against the law. Their spokesman was a lawyer; note his question and the Savior's answer: "Master, which is the great commandment in the law? Jesus said unto him, Thou shalt love the Lord thy God with all thy heart, and with all thy soul, and with all thy mind. This is the first and great commandment. And the second is like unto it, Thou shalt love thy neighbor as thyself. On these two commandments hang all the law and the prophets."[d] The two commandments, here spoken of as first and second, are so closely related as to be virtually one, and that one: "Thou shalt love." He who abideth one of the two will abide both; for without love for our fellows, it is impossible to please God. Hence wrote John, the Apostle of Love, "Beloved, let us love one another: for love is of God; and every one that loveth is born of God, and knoweth God. He that loveth not knoweth not God; for God is

---

[b] "The Glory of God is Intelligence"; see D&C 93:36.

[c] 1 Cor. 13:7.

[d] Matt. 22:36–40; see also Luke 10:25–27.

love. * * * If a man say, I love God, and hateth his brother, he is a liar: for he that loveth not his brother whom he hath seen, how can he love God whom he hath not seen? And this commandment have we from him, That he who loveth God love his brother also."[e]

But perhaps the grandest and most sublime of the apostolic utterances concerning the love that saves, is found in the epistle of Paul to the saints at Corinth.[f] In our current English translation of the Bible, the virtue that the apostle declares to be superior to all miraculous gifts, and which is to continue after all the rest have passed away, is designated as *charity*; but the original word meant *love*; and Paul had in mind something more than mere almsgiving, as is evident from his expression: "And though I bestow all my goods to feed the poor, * * * and have not charity, it profiteth me nothing." Though a man speak with the tongue of angels; though he possess the power of prophecy, the greatest of the ordinary gifts; though he be versed in knowledge and understand all mysteries; though his faith enable him to move mountains; and though he give his all, including even his life—yet without love is he nothing. Charity, or almsgiving, even though it be associated with the sincerest of motives, devoid of all desire for praise or hope of return, is but a feeble manifestation of the love that is to make one's neighbor as dear to him as himself; the love that suffers long; that envies not others; that vaunts not itself; that knows no pride; that subdues selfishness; that rejoices in the truth. When "that which is perfect" is come, the gifts theretofore bestowed in part only will be superseded. "Perfection will then swallow up imperfection; the healing power will then be done away, for no sickness will be there; tongues and interpretations will then cease, for one pure language alone will be spoken; the casting out of devils and power against deadly poisons will not then be needed, for in heaven circumstances will render them unnecessary. But charity, which is the pure love of God, never faileth; it will sit enthroned in the midst of the glorified throng, clothed in all the glory and splendor of its native heaven."[g] If man would win eternal life, he cannot afford to neglect the duty of love to his fellow, for "Love is the fulfilling of the law."[h]

Benevolent Works of the Church—The Church of the present day can point to a stupendous labor of benevolence already accomplished and still in progress. One of the most glorious monuments of its work is seen in the missionary labor which has ever been a characteristic feature of its activities. Actuated by no other motives than pure love for humanity and a desire to fulfil the commands of God respecting mankind, the Church sends out every year hundreds of missionaries to proclaim the Gospel of eternal life to the world, and that too without money or price. Multitudes of these devoted servants have suffered contumely and insult at the hands of those whom they sought to benefit; and not a few have given their lives with the seal of the martyr upon their testimony and work.

The charity that manifests itself in material giving is not neglected in the Church; indeed this form of benevolence is impressed as a sacred duty upon every Latter-day Saint. While each one is urged to impart of his substance to the needy, in his individual capacity, a system of orderly giving has been developed within the Church; and of this some features are worthy of special consideration.

Freewill Offerings—It has ever been characteristic of the Church and people of God, that they take upon themselves the care of the poor, if any such exist among them. To subserve this purpose,

---

[e] 1 John 4:7, 8, 20, 21.

[f] See 1 Cor., chap. 13; see also Alma 34:28, 29; Mosiah 4:16–24; also Appendix 24:1, 2.

[g] Orson Pratt, *Divine Authenticity of the Book of Mormon*, 1:15, 16.

[h] Rom. 13:10; see also Gal. 5:14; 1 Peter 4:8.

as also to foster a spirit of liberality, kindness, and benevolence, voluntary gifts and free-will offerings have been asked of those who profess to be living according to the law of God. In the Church today a systematic plan of giving for the poor is in operation. Thus, in almost every ward or branch, an organization of women, known as the Relief Society, is in operation. Its purpose is in part to gather from the society, and from the members of the Church in general, contributions of money and other property, particularly the commodities of life, and to distribute such to the deserving and needy under the direction of the local officers in the Priesthood. But the Relief Society operates also on a plan of systematic visitation to the houses of the afflicted, extending aid in nursing, administering comfort in bereavement, and seeking in every possible way to relieve distress. The good work of this organization has won the admiration of many who profess no connection with the Church; its methods have been followed by other benevolent associations, and the society has been accorded a national status in the United States.

Fast Offerings represent a still more general system of donation. The Church teaches the efficacy of continual prayer and of periodical fasting, as a means of acquiring humility meet for divine approval; and a monthly fast-day has been appointed for observance throughout the Church. The first Sunday in each month is so designated. The saints are asked to manifest their sincerity in fasting by making an offering on that day for the benefit of the poor; and, by common consent, the giving of at least an equivalent of the meals omitted by the fasting of the family is expected. These offerings may be made in money, food, or other usable commodity; they are received by the bishopric, and by the same authority are distributed to the worthy poor of the ward or branch. Special fasts are called by the presiding authorities, as occasion may require, as in times of widespread illness, war conditions or other exigency as a feature of these seasons of supplication. In these and in numerous other ways do the Latter-day Saints contribute of their substance to the needy, realizing that the poor among them may be the "Lord's poor"; and that, irrespective of worthiness on the part of the recipient, want and distress must be alleviated. The people believe that the harmony of their prayers will become a discord if the cry of the poor accompany their supplications to the throne of Grace.

Tithing—The Church today follows the doctrine of tithe-paying, similar in all of its general provisions to that taught and practised of old. Before considering the present authorized procedure in this matter, it may be instructive to study the ancient practise of tithe-paying. Strictly speaking, a tithe is a tenth, and such proportion of individual possessions appears to have been formerly regarded as the Lord's due.[i] The institution of tithing antedates even the Mosaic dispensation, for we find both Abraham and Jacob paying tithes. Abraham, returning from a victorious battle, met Melchizedek king of Salem and "priest of the most high God"; and, recognizing his priestly authority, "gave him tithes of all."[j] Jacob made a voluntary vow with the Lord to render a tenth of all that should come into his possession.[k]

The Mosaic statutes were explicit in requiring tithes: "And all the tithe of the land, whether of the seed of the land, or of the fruit of the tree, is the Lord's: it is holy unto the Lord. * * * And concerning the tithe of the herd, or of the flock, even of whatsoever passeth under the rod, the tenth shall be holy unto the Lord."[l] The tenth was to be paid as it came, without search for good

[i] See *The Law of the Tithe* by the author, *Deseret News,* Jan. 31, 1914, republished as a pamphlet by the Presiding Bishopric, Salt Lake City; also a later version entitled *The Lord's Tenth.*
[j] See Gen. 14:18–20; see also Heb. 7:1–3, 5, and Alma 13:13–16.
[k] See Gen. 28:22.
[l] Lev. 27:30–34.

or bad; under some conditions, however, a man could redeem the tithe by paying its value in some other way, but in such a case he had to add a fifth of the tithe. The tenth of all the property in Israel was to be paid to the Levites, as an inheritance given in acknowledgment of their service; and they in turn were to pay tithing on what they received, and this tithe of the tithe was to go to the priests.[m] A second tithe was demanded of Israel to be used for the appointed festivals; and a third tithe payable once in three years was devoted to the support and entertainment of the needy, the widows and fatherless and the Levites.[n]

It is evident, that while no specific penalty for neglect of the law of tithing is recorded, the proper observance of the requirement was regarded as a sacred duty. In the course of the reformation by Hezekiah, the people manifested their repentance by an immediate payment of tithes;[o] and so liberally did they give that a great surplus accumulated, observing which, Hezekiah inquired as to the source of such plenty: "And Azariah the chief priest of the house of Zadok answered him, and said, Since the people began to bring the offerings into the house of the Lord, we have had enough to eat, and have left plenty: for the Lord hath blessed his people; and that which is left is this great store." Nehemiah took care to regulate the procedure in tithe-paying;[p] and both Amos[q] and Malachi[r] admonished the people because of their neglect of this duty. Through the prophet last named, the Lord charged the people with having robbed Him; but promised them blessings beyond their capacity to receive if they would return to their allegiance: "Will a man rob God? Yet ye have robbed me. But ye say, Wherein have we robbed thee? In tithes and offerings. Ye are cursed with a curse: for ye have robbed me, even this whole nation. Bring ye all the tithes into the storehouse, that there may be meat in mine house, and prove me now herewith, saith the Lord of hosts, if I will not open you the windows of heaven, and pour you out a blessing, that there shall not be room enough to receive it."[s] In visiting the Nephites after His resurrection, the Savior told them of these sayings of Malachi, repeating the words of the Jewish prophet.[t] The Pharisees, at the time of Christ's ministry, were particularly scrupulous in the matter of tithe paying, even to the neglect of the "weightier matters of the law," and for this inconsistency they were rebuked by the Master.[u]

In the present dispensation the law of tithing has been given a place of great importance, and particular blessings have been promised for its faithful observance. This day has been called by the Lord "a day of sacrifice, and a day for the tithing of my people; for he that is tithed shall not be burned."[v] In a revelation, given through the Prophet Joseph Smith, July 8, 1838, the Lord has explicitly set forth His requirement of the people in this matter.[w]

Consecration and Stewardship—The law of tithing, as observed by the Church today, is after all but a lesser law, given by the Lord in consequence of human weaknesses, selfishness, covetousness, and greed, which prevented the saints from accepting the higher principles, according

[m] See Num. 18:21–28.

[n] See Deut. 12:5–17; 14:22, 23.

[o] See 2 Chr. 31:5, 6.

[p] See Neh. 10:37; 12:44.

[q] See Amos 4:4.

[r] See Mal. 3:7–10.

[s] Mal. 3:7–10; see also 3 Nephi 24:7–12.

[t] See 3 Nephi 24:7–10.

[u] See Matt. 23:23; Luke 11:42; see *Jesus the Christ*, p. 556.

[v] D&C 64:23, 24; see also 85:3.

[w] See D&C, sec. 119; see also Appendix 24:3.

to which the Lord would have them live. Specific requirements regarding the payment of tithes were made through revelation in 1838; but, seven years prior to that time, the voice of the Lord had been heard on the subject of consecration,[x] or the dedication of all one's property, together with his time, and talents, to the service of God, to be used as occasion may require. This again is not new; to the present dispensation the law of consecration is given as a reenactment; it was recognized and observed with profit in olden times.[y] Even in the apostolic period the doctrine of consecration of property and common ownership was old, for thirty-four centuries before that time the same principle had been practised by the patriarch Enoch and his people, and with such success that "the Lord came and dwelt with his people; * * * And the Lord called his people Zion, because they were of one heart and one mind, and dwelt in righteousness; and there was no poor among them."[z] In each of the instances cited—that of the people of Enoch, and that of the saints in the early part of the Christian era—we learn of the unity of purpose and consequent power acquired by the people who lived in this social order; they were "of one heart and one mind." Through the spiritual strength so attained the apostles were able to perform many mighty works;[aa] and of Enoch and his followers we read that the Lord took them unto Himself.

The people of whom the Book of Mormon gives us record also attained to the blessed state of equality, and with corresponding results. The disciples, whom Christ had personally commissioned, taught with power and "they had all things common among them, every man dealing justly, one with another."[bb] Further, we read of a general conversion by which the people came to a condition of ideal peace; "there were no contentions and disputations among them. * * * And they had all things common among them; therefore they were not rich and poor, bond and free, but they were all made free, and partakers of the heavenly gift."[cc] They were so blessed, that of them the prophet said: "Surely there could not be a happier people among all the people who had been created by the hand of God."[dd] But after nearly two centuries of this blessed condition the people gave way to pride; some of them yielded to a passion for costly apparel; they refused to longer have their goods in common; and straightway many classes came into existence; dissenting sects were established; and then began a rapid course of disruption, which led to the extinction of the Nephite nation.[ee]

Stewardship in the Church—A system of unity in temporal matters has been revealed to the Church in this day; such is currently known as the Order of Enoch,[ff] or the United Order,[gg] and is founded on the law of consecration. As already stated, in the early days of the latter-day Church the people demonstrated their inability to abide this law in its fulness, and, in consequence, the lesser law of tithing was given; but the saints confidently await the day in which they will devote not merely a tithe of their substance but all that they have and all that they are, to the service of their God; a day in which no man will speak of mine and thine, but all things shall

---

[x] See D&C 42:71.
[y] See Acts 4:32, 34, 35; see also 2:44–46.
[z] P.of G.P., Moses 7:16–18.
[aa] See Acts 2:43.
[bb] 3 Nephi 26:19.
[cc] 4 Nephi 2, 3.
[dd] Same, verse 16.
[ee] See same, verse 24, etc.; see Jesus the Christ, p. 741.
[ff] See D&C sec. 78.
[gg] See D&C 104:48.

be the Lord's and theirs.

In this expectation they indulge no vague dream of communism, encouraging individual irresponsibility and giving the idler an excuse for hoping to live at the expense of the thrifty; but rather, a calm trust that in the promised social order, such as God can approve, every man will be a steward in the full enjoyment of liberty to do as he will with the talents committed to his care; but with the sure knowledge that an account of his stewardship shall be required at his hands. As far as the plan of this prospective organization has been revealed, it provides that a person entering the order shall consecrate to the Lord all that he has, be it little or much, giving to the Church a deed of his property sealed with a covenant that cannot be broken.[hh] The person thus having given his all is to be made a steward over a part of the property of the Church, according to his ability to use it.

The varying grades of occupation will still exist; there will be laborers, whose qualifications fit them best for unskilled toil; and managers who have proved their ability to lead and direct; some who can serve the cause of God best with the pen, others with the plow; there will be engineers and mechanics, artizans and artists, farmers and scholars; teachers, professors, and authors—every one laboring as far as practicable in the sphere of his choice, but each required to work, and to work where and how he can be of the greatest service. His stewardship is to be assured him by written deed, and as long as he is faithful to his charge, no man can take it from him.[ii] Of the proceeds of his labors, every man may use as he requires for the support of himself and his family; the surplus is to be rendered to the Church for public and general works, and for the assistance of those who are justifiably deficient.[jj] As further illustrative of the uses to which the surplus is to be devoted, we read: "All children have claim upon their parents for their maintenance until they are of age. And after that, they have claim upon the church, or in other words, upon the Lord's storehouse, if their parents have not wherewith to give them inheritances. And the storehouse shall be kept by the consecrations of the church; and widows and orphans shall be provided for, as also the poor."[kk] Any faithful steward, requiring additional capital for the improvement of his work, has a claim for such upon the custodians of the general fund, they in turn being held accountable for their management, which constitutes their stewardship.[ll]

Equal rights are to be secured to all. The Lord said: "And you are to be equal, or, in other words, you are to have equal claims on the properties, for the benefit of managing the concerns of your stewardships, every man according to his wants and his needs, inasmuch as his wants are just—And all this for the benefit of the church of the living God, that every man may improve upon his talent, that every man may gain other talents, yea, even an hundred fold, to be cast into the Lord's storehouse, to become the common property of the whole church."[mm]

Freedom of agency is to be secured to every individual; if he be unfaithful he will be dealt with according to the prescribed rules of church discipline. A corresponding power of self-government will be exercised by the several stakes or other divisions of the Church, each having independent jurisdiction over its own storehouses and its affairs of administration,[nn] all being subject to the

[hh] See D&C 42:30.
[ii] See D&C 51:4, 5.
[jj] See D&C 42:32–35.
[kk] D&C 83:4–6.
[ll] See D&C 104:70–77.
[mm] D&C 82:17, 18.
[nn] See D&C 51:10–13, 18.

General Authorities of the Church. Only the idler would suffer in such an order as is here outlined. Against him the edict of the Almighty has gone forth: "Thou shalt not be idle; for he that is idle shall not eat the bread nor wear the garments of the laborer."[oo] "The idler shall not have place in the church, except he repents and mends his ways."[pp] "And the inhabitants of Zion also shall remember their labors, inasmuch as they are appointed to labor, in all faithfulness; for the idler shall be had in remembrance before the Lord."[qq]

Social Order of the Saints—In view of the prevailing conditions of social unrest, of the loud protest against existing systems whereby the distribution of wealth is becoming more and more unequal—the rich growing richer from the increasing poverty of the poor, the hand of oppression resting more and more heavily upon the masses, the consequent dissatisfaction with governments, and the half-smothered fires of anarchy discernible in almost every nation—may we not take comfort in the promise of a better plan, a plan that seeks without force or violence to establish a stable equality, to aid the lowly and the poor,[rr] and to give every man an opportunity to live and labor in the sphere to which he is adapted? From the tyranny of misused wealth, as from every other form of oppression, the truth will make men free. To be partakers of such freedom mankind must subdue selfishness, which is one of the most potent enemies of godliness.

The Church teaches the necessity of proper organization, in harmony with the laws of the land; the sanctity of the institution and covenant of marriage as essential to the stability of society; the fulfilment of the divine law with respect to the perpetuation of the human family; and the importance of strict personal purity.

Marriage—The teachings of the scriptures concerning the necessity of marriage are numerous and explicit. "The Lord God said, It is not good that the man should be alone;"[ss] this comprehensive declaration was made concerning Adam, immediately after his establishment in Eden. Eve was given unto him, and the man recognized the necessity of a continued association of the sexes in marriage, and said: "Therefore shall a man leave his father and his mother, and shall cleave unto his wife: and they shall be one flesh."[tt] Neither of the sexes is complete in itself as a counterpart of Deity. We are expressly told that God is the Father of spirits,[uu] and to apprehend the literalness of this solemn truth we must know that a mother of spirits is an existent personality.[vv] Of the creation of humankind we read: "So God created man in his own image, in the image of God created he him; male and female created he them."[ww] The purpose of this dual creation is set forth in the next verse of the sacred narrative: "And God blessed them, and God said unto them, Be fruitful, and multiply, and replenish the earth."[xx] Such a command would have been meaningless and void if addressed to either of the sexes alone; and without the power of perpetuating his kind, the glory and majesty of man would be insignificant; for small indeed are the attainments of any individual life in mortality.

Grand as may seem the achievements of a man who is truly great, the culmination of his glo-

[oo] D&C 42:42; see also 60:13; 75:3.
[pp] D&C 75:29.
[qq] D&C 68:30; see also 88:124.
[rr] See D&C 42:39.
[ss] Gen. 2:18.
[tt] Gen. 2:24.
[uu] See Num. 16:22; see also Heb. 12:9.
[vv] See Appendix 2:11, "The Father and the Son," concluding paragraph; and Appendix 24:4.
[ww] Gen. 1:27; 5:2.
[xx] Gen. 1:28; 9:1, 7; Lev. 26:9.

rious career lies in his leaving posterity to continue, and enhance the triumphs of their sire. And if such be true of mortals with respect to the things of earth, transcendently greater is the power of eternal increase, as viewed in the light of revealed truth concerning the unending progression of the future state. Truly the apostle was wise when he said: "Neither is the man without the woman, neither the woman without the man, in the Lord."[yy]

The Latter-day Saints accept the doctrine that marriage is honorable,[zz] and apply it as a requirement to all who are not prevented by physical or other disability from assuming the sacred responsibilities of the wedded state. They consider, as part of the birthright of every worthy man, the privilege and duty to stand as the head of a household, the father of a posterity, which by the blessing of God may never become extinct; and equally strong is the right of every worthy woman to be wife and mother in the family of mankind. Notwithstanding the simplicity, reasonableness, and naturalness of these teachings, false teachers have arisen among men declaring the pernicious doctrine that the married state is but a carnal necessity, inherited by man as an incident of his degraded nature; and that celibacy is a mark of a higher state, more acceptable in the sight of God. Concerning such the Lord has spoken in this day: "Whoso forbiddeth to marry is not ordained of God, for marriage is ordained of God unto man * * * that the earth might answer the end of its creation; And that it might be filled with the measure of man, according to his creation before the world was made."[aaa]

Celestial Marriage—Marriage, as regarded by the Latter-day Saints, is ordained of God and designed to be an eternal relationship of the sexes. With this people it is not merely a temporal contract to be of effect on earth during the mortal existence of the parties, but a solemn agreement which is to extend beyond the grave. In the complete ordinance of marriage, the man and the woman are placed under covenant of mutual fidelity, not "until death doth you part," but "for time and for all eternity." A contract as far reaching as this, extending not only throughout time but into the domain of the hereafter, requires for its validation an authority superior to that of earth; and such an authority is found in the Holy Priesthood, which, given of God, is eternal. Any power less than this, while of effect in this life, is void as to the state of the human soul beyond the grave.

The Lord has said: "All covenants, contracts, bonds, obligations, oaths, vows, performances, connections, associations, or expectations, that are not made and entered into and sealed by the Holy Spirit of promise, of him who is anointed, both as well for time and for all eternity, and that too most holy, by revelation and commandment, through the medium of mine anointed, whom I have appointed on the earth to hold this power, * * * are of no efficacy, virtue, or force in and after the resurrection from the dead; for all contracts that are not made unto this end have an end when men are dead."[bbb]

As touching the application of the principle of earthly authority for things of earth, and eternal authority for things beyond the grave, to the sacred contract of marriage, the revelation continues: "Therefore, if a man marry him a wife in the world, and he marry her not by me nor by my word, and he covenant with her so long as he is in the world and she with him, their covenant and marriage are not of force when they are dead, and when they are out of the world; therefore, they are not bound by any law when they are out of the world. Therefore, when they are out of the world they neither marry nor are given in marriage; but are appointed angels in heaven; which angels are

---

[yy] 1 Cor. 11:11.
[zz] See Heb. 13:4.
[aaa] D&C 49:15–17.
[bbb] D&C 132:7.

ministering servants, to minister for those who are worthy of a far more, and an exceeding, and an eternal weight of glory. For these angels did not abide my law; therefore, they cannot be enlarged, but remain separately and singly, without exaltation, in their saved condition, to all eternity; and from henceforth are not gods, but are angels of God forever and ever."ᶜᶜᶜ

This system of holy matrimony, involving covenants as to time and eternity, is known distinctively as Celestial Marriage—the order of marriage that exists in the celestial worlds. The ordinance of celestial marriage is permitted to those members of the Church only who are adjudged worthy of participation in the special blessings of the House of the Lord; for this ordinance, together with others of eternal validity, is to be administered in Temples reared and dedicated for such holy service.ᵈᵈᵈ Children who are born of parents thus married are natural heirs to the Priesthood; "children of the covenant" they are called; they require no rite of adoption or sealing to insure them place in the posterity of promise. But the Church sanctions marriages for earthly time only, and bestows upon such the seal of the Priesthood, among those who are not admitted to the Temples of the Lord, or who voluntarily prefer the lesser and temporal order of matrimony. No living person can be married under the ordinances of The Church of Jesus Christ of Latter-day Saints unless every requirement of the secular law applicable to marriage has been fully complied with.

Unlawful Associations of the Sexes have been designated by the Lord as among the most heinous of sins; and the Church today regards individual purity in the sexual relation as an indispensable condition of membership. The teachings of the Nephite prophet, Alma, concerning the enormity of offenses against virtue and chastity are accepted by the Latter-day Saints without modification; and such are to the effect: "That these things are an abomination in the sight of the Lord; yea, most abominable above all sins save it be the shedding of innocent blood or denying the Holy Ghost."ᵉᵉᵉ The command: "Thou shalt not commit adultery," once written by the finger of God amidst the thunders and lightnings of Sinai, has been renewed as a specific injunction in these last days; and the penalty of excommunication has been prescribed for the offender.ᶠᶠᶠ Moreover, the Lord regards any approach to sexual sin as inconsistent with the professions of those who have received the Holy Spirit, for He has declared that "he that looketh on a woman to lust after her, or if any shall commit adultery in their hearts, they shall not have the Spirit, but shall deny the faith."ᵍᵍᵍ

Sanctity of the Body—The Church teaches that everyone should regard his body as "the temple of God";ʰʰʰ and that he maintain its purity and sanctity as such. He is taught that the Spirit of the Lord dwells not in unclean tabernacles; and that therefore he is required to live according to the laws of health, which constitute part of the law of God. For the special guidance of His saints, the Lord has revealed the following:ⁱⁱⁱ

1. A WORD OF WISDOM, for the benefit of the council of high priests, assembled in Kirtland, and the church, and also the saints in Zion—
2. To be sent greeting; not by commandment or constraint, but by revelation and the word of wisdom, showing forth the order and will of God in the temporal salvation of all saints in the

---

ᶜᶜᶜ D&C 132:15–17; see *The House of the Lord,* p. 101.
ᵈᵈᵈ See D&C 124:30–40.
ᵉᵉᵉ Alma 39:5.
ᶠᶠᶠ See D&C 42:24, 80-83; 63:16, 17.
ᵍᵍᵍ D&C 63:16; see also 42:23; Matt. 5:28.
ʰʰʰ 1 Cor. 3:16; see also 6:19; 2 Cor. 6:16; D&C 93:35.
ⁱⁱⁱ D&C, sec. 89.

last days—

3. Given for a principle with promise, adapted to the capacity of the weak and the weakest of all saints, who are or can be called saints.

4. Behold, verily, thus saith the Lord unto you: In consequence of evils and designs which do and will exist in the hearts of conspiring men in the last days, I have warned you, and forewarn you, by giving unto you this word of wisdom by revelation—

5. That inasmuch as any man drinketh wine or strong drink among you, behold it is not good, neither meet in the sight of your Father, only in assembling yourselves together to offer up your sacraments before him.

6. And, behold, this should be wine, yea, pure wine of the grape of the vine, of your own make.

7. And, again, strong drinks are not for the belly, but for the washing of your bodies.

8. And again, tobacco is not for the body, neither for the belly, and is not good for man, but is an herb for bruises and all sick cattle, to be used with judgment and skill.

9. And again, hot drinks are not for the body or belly.

10. And again, verily I say unto you, all wholesome herbs God hath ordained for the constitution, nature, and use of man—

11. Every herb in the season thereof, and every fruit in the season thereof; all these to be used with prudence and thanksgiving.

12. Yea, flesh also of beasts and of the fowls of the air, I, the Lord, have ordained for the use of man with thanksgiving; nevertheless they are to be used sparingly;

13. And it is pleasing unto me that they should not be used, only in times of winter, or of cold, or famine.

14. All grain is ordained for the use of man and of beasts, to be the staff of life, not only for man but for the beasts of the field, and the fowls of heaven, and all wild animals that run or creep on the earth;

15. And these hath God made for the use of man only in times of famine and excess of hunger.

16. All grain is good for the food of man; as also the fruit of the vine; that which yieldeth fruit, whether in the ground or above the ground—

17. Nevertheless, wheat for man, and corn for the ox, and oats for the horse, and rye for the fowls and for swine, and for all beasts of the field, and barley for all useful animals, and for mild drinks, as also other grain.

18. And all saints who remember to keep and do these sayings, walking in obedience to the commandments, shall receive health in their navel and marrow to their bones;

19. And shall find wisdom and great treasures of knowledge, even hidden treasures;

20. And shall run and not be weary, and shall walk and not faint.

21. And I, the Lord, give unto them a promise, that the destroying angel shall pass by them, as the children of Israel, and not slay them. Amen.[jjj]

The Sabbath Day[kkk]—The Church accepts Sunday as the Christian Sabbath and proclaims the sanctity of the day. We admit without argument that under the Mosaic law the seventh day of the week, Saturday, was designated and observed as the holy day, and that the change from Saturday

[jjj] See Ex. 12:23.
[kkk] This treatment of the subject appears in the author's *Vitality of "Mormonism,"* pp. 330-333. See also *Jesus the Christ,* chap. 15, and p. 690. See further a pamphlet *The Lord's Day,* by Elder Brigham H. Roberts, of the First Council of Seventy, Salt Lake City.

charity, etc.—D&C 12:8.

And if you have not faith, hope, and charity, you can do nothing—D&C 18:19.

And above all things, clothe yourself with the bond of charity, as with a mantle—D&C 88:125.

Be full of charity towards all men, and to the household of faith, and let virtue garnish your thoughts unceasingly—D&C 121:45.

What ye do to the poor ye do to the Lord—D&C 42:38; read also verse 29; 44:6; 52:40.

Wo unto you rich men, that will not give your substance to the poor—D&C 56:16. Wo unto you poor men, whose hearts are not broken, etc.—verse 17.

Search to be made for the poor that their wants may be administered to—D&C 84:112.

The order of the Church for the benefit of the poor—D&C, sec. 104.

He who imparts not of his portion to the poor shall lift up his eyes in hell—D&C 104:18.

Displeasure of the Lord on account of those who would not impart of their substance to the poor and afflicted—D&C 105:3.

Tithes and Offerings

Abraham paid tithes to Melchizedek—Gen. 14:20.

Jacob covenanted to pay tithes to the Lord—Gen. 28:22.

All the tithe of the land was holy unto the Lord—Lev. 27:30; see also verse 32.

Disposition of the tithes of the children of Israel—Num. 18:24.

Thither shall ye bring your sacrifices and your tithes—Deut. 12:6.

Thou shalt truly tithe all the increase of thy seed—Deut. 14:22, 23.

Men commissioned to care for the tithes—Neh. 13:11–13.

In the days of Malachi the people had robbed God in the matter of tithes and offerings—Mal. 3:8; see also verses 9–12.

The frequent mention of offerings as distinct from tithes in Exodus, Leviticus, Numbers, and Deuteronomy.

See mention of tithes in Book of Mormon, Alma 13:15; 3 Nephi 24:8–10. For mention of offerings see 1 Nephi 5:9; 7:22; 2:7.

Tithing as required in the present dispensation—D&C, sec. 119.

Verily it is a day of sacrifice, and a day for the tithing of my people—D&C 64:23.

House of the Lord to be built by the tithing of the people—D&C 97:11, 12.

Note that the Nephites were strict observers of the law of Moses until that law was superseded by direction of the resurrected Lord, Jesus Christ, who ministered unto them in person, and declared that the law had been given by him. As shown by Biblical references herein, tithes and offerings figure conspicuously in the requirements of the Mosaic law. In proof that the Nephites did observe the requirements of the law of Moses see the following: Mosiah 3:14, 15; 12:28–37; 13:27–33; Helaman 15:5; 3 Nephi 15:2–10.

The Sabbath

Tomorrow is the rest of the holy sabbath unto the Lord—Ex. 16:23.

Remember the sabbath day to keep it holy—Ex. 20:8–11. Note in verse 11 that the institution of the sabbath was prefigured in the events of creation: And God blessed the seventh day and sanctified it—Gen. 2:2, 3; also Moses 3:2; Abraham 5:1–3.

Six days in which to do work and the seventh on which man and animals should rest—Ex. 23:12.

The keeping of the sabbath was made a sign between Jehovah and his people Israel—Ex. 31:13–17; Ezek. 20:12.

The seventh day to be one of rest even in earing time and in harvest—Ex. 34:21; see also 35:2; Lev. 23:3.

Special offerings were to be made on the sabbath—Num. 28:9, 10.

The Israelites in the wilderness were commanded to gather an extra quantity of manna on the sixth day and none on the seventh—Ex. 16:16–31; see also verses 4 and 5.

Blessings on the man who kept the sabbath—Isa. 56:2; see also 58:13, 14.

Under the law of Moses the punishment for sabbath violation was death—Ex. 35:2; Num. 15:32–36; compare Jer. 17:27.

Christ's teachings regarding the sabbath, his actions thereon, and accusations brought against him as a sabbath-breaker—Matt. 12:1–8; also verses 10–14; compare Luke 6:1–11, and Mark 2:23–28. See instance of the woman healed on the sabbath day—Luke 13:11–17. A man suffering from the dropsy was healed on the sabbath—Luke 14:1–6. See other instances—John 5:5–18; 7:21–24.

Therefore the Son of Man is Lord also of the sabbath—Mark 2:28; see also Matt. 12:8.

The sabbath was made for man, and not man for the sabbath—Mark 2:27.

Paul reasoned in the synagogue every sabbath—Acts 18:4; see also 17:2. Observe that on the first day of the week, not the seventh, the disciples are said to have come together to break bread—Acts 20:7.

Sunday, the first day of the week, was the day on which Christ was resurrected—Matt. 28:1; Mark 16:9.

The first day of the week came to be observed instead of the seventh day as the sabbath—1 Cor. 16:2. I was in the Spirit on the Lord's day—Rev. 1:10.

Let no man judge you of the sabbath days—Colos. 2:16.

The Nephites observed to keep the sabbath day holy unto the Lord—Jarom 5; see also Mosiah 13:16–19.

Alma commanded the people that they should observe the sabbath day, and keep it holy—Mosiah 18:23.

Note that the observance of the sabbath was an important feature of the law of Moses; and furthermore, observe that the Nephites were strict observers of the law of Moses until the law was superseded by the gospel left to them by the resurrected Christ, who was he who had given the law—2 Nephi 5:10; 25:24–30; Jarom 5; Mosiah 2:3; Alma 30:3; 3 Nephi 1:24.

Go to the house of prayer and offer up thy sacraments upon my holy day—D&C 59:9, 10.

Remember that on this, the Lord's day, thou shalt offer thine oblations and thy sacraments unto the Most High—verses 12–14.

And the inhabitants of Zion shall also observe the sabbath day to keep it holy—D&C 68:29.

25

APPENDIX

OMPRISING NOTES TO THE
FOREGOING CHAPTERS

APPENDIX 1—Notes Relating to Chapter 1

1. The Articles of Faith date from March 1, 1841. The Articles were published in the History of Joseph Smith, *Millennial Star,* vol. 19, p. 120; also *Times and Seasons,* vol. 3, p. 709. As stated elsewhere, the Articles have been formally adopted by the Church as an authorized summary of its principal doctrines.

2. The Standard Works of the Church—The *Bible* and the *Book of Mormon*—the first two of the standard works of the Church—are treated in chapters 13, 14 and 15 herein. The *Doctrine and Covenants* is a compilation of modern revelations as given to the Church in the present dispensation. The *Pearl of Great Price* comprises the visions and writings of Moses as revealed to Joseph Smith, the Book of Abraham—a translation by Joseph Smith from certain ancient papyri—and some of the writings of Joseph Smith. These books have been adopted by the members of the Church, in conference officially assembled, as their Standard Works.

3. Tribute to Joseph Smith—While few people outside the Church have had much to say in commendation of this modern prophet, it is interesting to note that there are some honorable exceptions to the rule. Josiah Quincy, a prominent American, made the acquaintance of Joseph Smith a short time before the latter's martyrdom; and after the tragic event he wrote: "It is by no means improbable that some future text-book, for the use of generations yet unborn, will contain a question something like this: What historical American of the nineteenth century has exerted the most powerful influence upon the destinies of his countrymen? And it is by no means impossible that the answer to that interrogatory may be thus written: *Joseph Smith, the Mormon Prophet.* And the reply, absurd as it doubtless seems to most men now living, may be an obvious commonplace to their descendants. History deals in surprises and paradoxes quite as startling as this. The man who established a religion in this age of free debate, who was and is today accepted by hundreds of thousands as a direct emissary from the Most High—such a rare human being is not to be disposed of by pelting his memory with unsavory epithets. * * * The most vital questions Americans are asking each other today have to do with this man and what he has left us. * * * Burning questions they are, which must give a prominent place in the history of the country to that sturdy self-asserter whom I visited at Nauvoo. Joseph Smith, claiming to be an inspired teacher, faced adversity such as few men have been called to meet, enjoyed a brief season of prosperity such as few men have ever attained, and finally, forty-three days after I saw him, went cheerfully to a martyr's death. When he surrendered his person to Governor Ford, in order to prevent the shedding of blood, the prophet had a presentiment of what was before him. 'I am going like a lamb to the slaughter,' he is reported to have said; 'but I am as calm as a summer's morning. I have a conscience void of offense, and shall die innocent.'" *Figures of the Past* by Josiah Quincy, p. 376.

4. **Joseph Smith's Descent**—"Joseph Smith was of humble birth. His parents and their progenitors were toilers; but their characters were godly and their names unstained. Near the middle of the seventeenth century, Robert Smith, a sturdy yeoman of England, emigrated to the New World, the land of promise. With his wife, Mary, he settled in Essex, Massachusetts. The numerous descendants of these worthy people intermarried with many of the staunchest and most industrious families of New England. Samuel, the son of Robert and Mary, born January 26th, 1666, wedded Rebecca Curtis, January 25th, 1707. Their son, the second Samuel, was born January 26th, 1714; he married Priscilla Gould, and was the father of Asael, born March 1st, 1744. Asael Smith took to wife Mary Duty, and their son Joseph was born July 12th, 1771. On the 24th of January, 1796, Joseph married Lucy Mack, at Tunbridge, in the State of Vermont. She was born July 8th, 1776, and was the daughter of Solomon and Lydia Mack and was the granddaughter of Ebenezer Mack."—*The Life of Joseph Smith, the Prophet,* by George Q. Cannon, chapter 1. Joseph the Prophet was the third son and fourth child of Joseph and Lucy (Mack) Smith; he was born at Sharon, Vermont, December 23d, 1805.

5. **Joseph Smith's Early Persecution**—The Prophet wrote as follows concerning the persecution of his boyhood days, which dated from the time of his first mention of his vision of the Father and the Son: "It caused me serious reflection then, and often has since, how very strange it was that an obscure boy, of a little over fourteen years of age, and one, too, who was doomed to the necessity of obtaining a scanty maintenance by his daily labor, should be thought a character of sufficient importance to attract the attention of the great ones of the most popular sects of the day, and in a manner to create in them a spirit of the most bitter persecution and reviling. But strange or not, so it was, and it was often the cause of great sorrow to myself. However, it was nevertheless a fact that I had beheld a vision. I have thought since, that I felt much like Paul, when he made his

defense before King Agrippa, and related the account of the vision he had when he saw a light, and heard a voice; but still there were but few who believed him; some said he was dishonest, others said he was mad; and he was ridiculed and reviled. But all this did not destroy the reality of his vision. He had seen a vision, he knew he had, and all the persecution under heaven could not make it otherwise; and though they should persecute him unto death, yet he knew, and would know to his latest breath, that he had both seen a light, and heard a voice speaking unto him, and all the world could not make him think or believe otherwise. So it was with me. I had actually seen a light, and in the midst of that light I saw two Personages, and they did in reality speak to me; and though I was hated and persecuted for saying that I had seen a vision, yet it was true; and while they were persecuting me, reviling me, and speaking all manner of evil against me falsely for so saying, I was led to say in my heart, Why persecute me for telling the truth? I have actually seen a vision, and who am I that I can withstand God?" P.of G.P., p. 50, 51; HC, vol. 1, p. 7.

6. Joseph Smith; and the Restored Church—See *The Life of Joseph Smith, the Prophet,* by George Q. Cannon. See also *Divine Authority, or the question, Was Joseph Smith Sent of God?* a pamphlet by Apostle Orson Pratt; *Joseph Smith's Prophetic Calling; Millennial Star,* vol. 42, pp. 164, 187, 195, 227. *A New Witness for God,* vol. 1, by B. H. Roberts. *Essentials of Church History,* by Joseph Fielding Smith; *A Brief History of the Church* of *Jesus Christ of Latter-day Saints,* by Edward H. Anderson.

7. The Seal of Martyrdom—"The highest evidence of sincerity that a man can give his fellow-men—the highest proof that he has spoken the truth in any given case—is that he perseveres in it unto death, and seals his testimony with his blood. * * * So important did such a testimony become in the estimation of Paul that he said: 'Where a testament is, there must also of necessity be the death of the testator. For a testament is of force after men are dead: otherwise it is of no strength at all while the testator liveth.' (Heb. 9:16–17.) In the light of this principle, and when the importance of the great testimony which he bore to the world is taken into account, it is not to be wondered at that Joseph Smith was called upon to affix the broad seal of martyrdom to his life's work. Something of incompleteness in his work would likely have been complained of had this been lacking; but now, not so; his character of prophet was rounded out to complete fulness by his falling a martyr under the murderous fire of a mob at Carthage, in the State of Illinois."— B. H. Roberts, in *A New Witness for God*, pp. 477–478.

8. Joseph Smith a True Prophet—The man of whom we speak, Joseph Smith, the prophet of the Gospel of Christ in the latter days, the man through whom was opened the latest dispensation in the work of the Lord—a dispensation called new, though characterized by the restoration of the authority and powers of all preceding epochs—this man is one whom men cannot forget or ignore, try as they may. His place in history is secure; his work is recognized as that of a mission delegated to him alone. * * * A prophet or revelator truly sent of God will bear power and authority to instruct and administer in the ordinances of the Gospel of Christ. No envoy from the courts of Heaven, no ambassador from the throne of the Great King, will be sent out unprovided with the credentials by which his appointment is authenticated; nor will such a messenger present himself and assert his claims among men unequipped with the insignia of his office. In the effective discharge of his duties, the true prophet will not only testify in words as to his authoritative appointment and ordination, but will manifest his actual possession of spiritual gifts and specific powers pertaining to the prophetic office, by duly exercising the same as conditions require. * * * We affirm that by the foregoing, and by all other tests involving the characteristics essential to and distinctive of the exalted calling and office of the prophet, *Joseph Smith was a Prophet of the Living God.*—From an article by the present author in *Improvement Era,* vol. 9, p. 155, which see.

9. Restoration of the Gospel—Plainly the vision-prophecy of John (Rev. 14:6, 7), relating to the restoration of the Gospel to earth, could not refer to the Gospel record preserved in the Holy Bible, for that record has remained in the possession of mankind. As stated in the text a partial fulfilment is found in the visitation of Moroni and the restoration of the *Book of Mormon,* which is to us of modern times a new scripture, and one containing a fuller record of "the everlasting Gospel." However, a record of the Gospel is not the Gospel itself. Authority to administer in the saving ordinances of the Gospel is essential to the effective preaching and administration thereof; this was restored through John the Baptist, who brought the Aaronic Priesthood, and through Peter, James, and John, who brought again to earth the Melchizedek Priesthood. For commentary on Rev. 14:6, 7, see *The Great Apostasy,* p. 168, by the present author.

APPENDIX 2—Notes Relating to Chapter 2

1. Natural to Believe in God—"The great and primary truth 'that there is a God' has obtained among men almost universally and in all ages; so that the holy scriptures, which speak of God in every page, and which advert to the sentiments of mankind for the period of about four thousand years, always assume this truth as admitted. In the early ages of the world, indeed, there is no positive evidence that speculative theism had any advocates; and if, at a subsequent period, the 'fool said in his heart, There is no God,' the sentiment appears more prominent in his affections than in his judgment; and, withal, had so feeble an influence over the minds of men, that the sacred writers never deemed it necessary to combat the error, either by formal arguments, or by an appeal to miraculous operations. Polytheism, not atheism, was the prevailing sin; and therefore the aim of inspired men was not so much to prove the existence of one God, as the non-existence of others—to maintain His authority, to enforce His laws, to the exclusion of all rival pretenders."—*Cassell's Bible Dictionary;* article "God."

2. Importance of Belief in God—"The existence of a Supreme Being is, without doubt, the sublimest conception that can enter the human mind, and, even as a scientific question, can have no equal, for it assumes to furnish the cause of causes, the great ultimate fact in philosophy, the last and sublimest generalization of scientific truth. Yet this is the lowest demand it presents for our study; for it lies at the very foundation of morality, virtue, and religion; it supports the social fabric, and gives cohesion to all its parts; it involves the momentous question of man's immortality and responsibility to supreme authority, and is inseparably connected with his brightest hopes and highest enjoyments. It is, indeed, not only a fundamental truth, but the grand central truth of all other truths. All other truths in science, ethics, and religion radiate from this. It is the source from which they all flow, the center to which they all converge, and the one sublime proposition to which they all bear witness. It has, therefore, no parallel in its solemn grandeur and momentous issues." *Cassell's Bible Dictionary,* article "God."

3. Belief in God, Natural and Necessary—Dr. Joseph Le Conte, late Professor of Geology and Natural History in the University of California, has written as follows: *"Theism,* or a belief in

God or in gods, or in a supernatural agency of some kind, controlling the phenomena around us, is the fundamental basis and condition of all religion, and is therefore universal, necessary, and intuitive. I will not, therefore, attempt to bring forward any proof of that which lies back of all proof, and is already more certain than anything can be made by any process of reasoning. The ground of this belief lies in the very nature of man; it is the very foundation and groundwork of reason. It is this and this only which gives significance to nature; without it, neither religion nor science, nor indeed human life, would be possible. For, observe what is the characteristic of man in his relation to external nature. To the brute, the phenomena of nature are nothing but sensuous phenomena; but man, just in proportion as he uses his human faculties, instinctively ascends from the phenomena to their cause. This is inevitable by a law of our nature, but the process of ascent is different for the cultured and uncultured races. The uncultured man, when a phenomenon occurs, the cause of which is not immediately perceived, passes by one step from the sensuous phenomenon to the first cause; while the cultured, and especially the scientific man, passes from the sensuous phenomena through a chain of secondary causes to the first cause. The region of second causes, and this only, is the domain of science. Science may, in fact, be defined, as the *study of the modes of operation of the first cause.* It is evident, therefore, that the recognition of second causes cannot preclude the idea of the existence of God. * * * Thus, Theism is necessary, intuitive, and therefore universal. We cannot get rid of it if we would. Push it out, as many do, at the front door, and it comes in again, perhaps unrecognized, at the back door. Turn it out in its *nobler forms* as revealed in Scripture, and it comes in again in its *ignoble forms,* it may be as magnetism, electricity, or gravity, or some other supposed efficient agent controlling nature. In some form, noble or ignoble, it will become a guest in the human heart. I therefore repeat, *Theism neither requires nor admits of proof.* But in these latter times, there is a strong tendency for Theism to take the form of *Pantheism,* and thereby religious belief is robbed of all its power over the human heart. It becomes necessary, therefore, for me to attempt to show, not the existence indeed, but the *personality of Deity.* * * * Among a certain class of cultivated minds, and especially among scientific men, there is a growing sentiment, sometimes openly expressed, sometimes only vaguely felt, that what we call God is only a universal, all-pervading principle animating nature—a general principle of evolution—an unconscious, impersonal life—force under which the whole cosmos slowly develops. Now, this form of Theism may possibly satisfy the demands of a purely speculative philosophy, but cannot satisfy the cravings of the human heart. * * * The argument for the personality of Deity is derived from the evidences of intelligent contrivance and design in nature, or in the adjustment of parts for a definite and an intelligent purpose. It is usually called '*the argument from design.*' The force of this argument is felt at once intuitively by all minds, and its effect is irresistible and overwhelming to every plain, honest mind, unplagued by metaphysical subtleties."—Prof. Joseph Le Conte, in *Religion and Science,* pp. 12–14.

4. **God in Nature**—Sir Isaac Newton, in writing to his friend Dr. Bentley in 1692, said in reference to the natural universe: "To make such a system, with all its motions, required a Cause which understood and compared together the quantities of matter in the several bodies of the sun and planets, and the gravitating powers resulting from them, the several distances of the primary planets from the sun, and of the secondary ones from Saturn, Jupiter, and the earth; and the velocities with which these planets could revolve about those quantities of matter in the central bodies; and to compare and adjust all these things together in so great a variety of bodies argues the Cause to be not blind and fortuitous, but very well skilled in mechanics and geometry."

5. Natural Indications of God's Existence—"It may not be, it is not likely, that God can be found with microscope and scalpel, with test-tube or flask, with goniometer or telescope; but with such tools, the student, earnestly working, cannot fail to recognize a power beyond his vision, yet a power of which the pulses and the motions are unmistakable. The extent of our solar system once seemed to man more limited than it does at present; and the discovery of the most distant of the planetary family was due to a recognition of an attractive force inexplicable except on the supposition of the existence of another planet. The astronomer, tracing known bodies along their orbital paths, could feel the pull, could see the wire that drew them from a narrower course; he saw not Neptune as he piled calculations sheet on sheet; but the existence of that orb was clearly indicated, and by heeding such indications he sought for it, and it was found. Theory alone could never have revealed it, though theory was incomplete, unsatisfactory without it; but the practical search, instigated by theory, led to the great demonstration. And what is all science but theory compared to the practical influence of prayerful reliance on the assistance of an omnipotent, omniscient power? Disregard not the indications of your science work—the trembling of the needle that reveals the magnetic influence; the instinct within that speaks of a life and a Life-Giver, far beyond human power of explanation or comprehension. As you sit beneath the canopied vault, pondering in the silence of night over the perturbations, the yearnings which the soul cannot ignore, turn in the direction indicated by those impulses, and with the penetrating, space-annihilating, time-annulling glass of prayer and faith, seek the source of that pervading force."—The Author in Baccalaureate Sermon, *Utah University Quarterly*, Sept., 1895.

6. Theism; Atheism, etc.—According to current usage, *Theism* signifies a belief in God—the acceptance of one living and eternal Being who has revealed Himself to man. *Deism* implies a professed belief in God, but denies to Deity the power to reveal Himself, and asserts a disbelief in Christianity; the term is used in different senses, prominent among which are:—(1) belief in God as an intelligent and eternal Being, with a denial of all providential care: (2) belief in God, with denial of a future state of the soul; (3) as advocated by Kant, denial of a personal God, while asserting belief in an infinite force, inseparably associated with matter, and operating as the first great cause. *Pantheism* regards matter and mind as one, embracing everything finite and infinite, and calls this universal existence God. In its philosophical aspect, pantheism "has three generic forms with variations: (1) *one-substance pantheism* which ascribes to the universal being the attributes of both mind and matter, thought and extension, as in Spinoza's system; (2) *materialistic pantheism* which ascribes to it only the attributes of matter, as in the system of Strauss; (3) *idealistic pantheism* which ascribes to it only the existence of mind as in Hegel's system." In its doctrinal aspect, pantheism comprises "the worship of nature and humanity founded on the doctrine that the entire phenomenal universe, including man and nature, is the ever-changing manifestation of God." *Polytheism* is the doctrine of a plurality of gods, who are usually regarded as personifications of forces or phenomena of nature. *Monotheism* is the doctrine that there is but one God. *Atheism* signifies disbelief in God, or the denial of God's existence; *dogmatic atheism* denies, while *negative atheism* ignores, the existence of a God. *Infidelity* is sometimes used as synonymous with atheism, though specifically the term signifies a milder form of unbelief, manifesting itself in skepticism on matters religious, a disbelief in the religion of the Bible, and of course a rejection of the doctrines of Christianity. *Agnosticism* holds that God is unknown and unknowable; that His existence can neither be proved nor disproved; it neither affirms nor denies the existence of a personal God; it is the doctrine of "We do not know."—See *Standard Dictionary*.

7. Idolatrous Practises in General—The soul of man, once abandoned to depravity, is strongly prone to depart from God and His institutions. "Hence," says Burder, "have arisen the altars and demons of heathen antiquity, their extravagant fictions, and abominable orgies. Hence we find among the Babylonians and Arabians, the adoration of the heavenly bodies, the earliest forms of idolatry; among the Canaanites and Syrians, the worship of Baal, Tammuz, Magog, and Astarte; among the Phoenicians, the immolation of children to Moloch; among the Egyptians, divine honors bestowed on animals, birds, insects, leeks, and onions; among the Persians, religious reverence offered to fire; and among the polished Greeks, the recognition in their system of faith of thirty thousand gods. Hence, moreover, we find at the present time, among most Pagan tribes, the deadliest superstitions, the most cruel and bloody rites, and the most shocking licentiousness and vice practised under the name of religion."—*History of All Religions,* p. 12.

8. Examples of Atrocious Idolatry—The worship of Moloch is generally cited as an example of the cruelest and most abhorrent idolatry known to man. Moloch, called also Molech, Malcham, Milcom, Baal-melech, etc., was an Ammonite idol: it is mentioned in scripture in connection with its cruel rites (Lev. 18:21; 20:2–5; see also 1 Kings 11:5, 7, 33; 2 Kings 23:10, 13; Amos 5:26; Zeph. 1:5; Jer. 32:35). Keil and Delitzsch describe the idol as being "represented by a brazen statue which was hollow, and capable of being heated, and formed with a bull's head, and with arms stretched out to receive the children to be sacrificed." While the worship of this idol did not invariably include human sacrifice, it is certain that such hideous rites were characteristic of this abominable shrine. The authors last quoted say: "From the time of Ahaz, children were slain at Jerusalem in the valley of Ben-Hinnom, and then sacrificed by being laid in the heated arms and burned" (2 Kings 23:10; 16:3; 17:17; 21:6; Jer. 32:35; Ezek. 16:20, 21; 20:31; compare Ps. 106:37, 38). Many authorities state that the sacrifice of children to this hideous monster long antedated the time of Ahaz. "The offering of living victims was probably the climax of enormity in connection with this system, and it is said that Tophet, where it was to be witnessed, was so named from the beating of drums to drown the shrieks and groans of those who were burned to death. The same place was called the Valley of Hinnom, and the horrible associations connected with it led to both Tophet and Gehenna ('valley of Hinnom') being adopted as names and symbols of future torment." For foregoing facts, and others, see *The Pentateuch* by Keil and Delitzsch, and *Cassell's Bible Dictionary.*

Scarcely less horrible were the practises of voluntary suicide under the car of the idol juggernaut, and the drowning of children in the sacred Ganges as found among the Hindoos. The practises of Druidism among the ancient Britons furnish another example of degradation in religion through the absence of authoritative guidance and the light of revelation. The Druids professed a veneration for the oak, and performed most of their distinctive ceremonies in sacred groves. Human sacrifices were offered as a feature of their system. Of their temples, some, e.g. Stonehenge on Salisbury Plain, Wiltshire, and others in Kent, still remain. These circular enclosures which were open to the sky, were called *doom-rings:* near the center of each was an altar *(dolmen)* on which victims were sacrificed. The horrible ceremonies included on special occasions the burning alive of large numbers of human beings, enclosed in immense cages of wicker-work.

9. Immaterialists and Atheists—"There are two classes of atheists in the world. One class denies the existence of God in the most positive language; the other denies his existence in duration or space. One says 'There is no God;' the other says 'God is not *here* or *there,* any more than he exists *now* and *then.*' The infidel says 'God does not exist anywhere.' The immaterialist says

'He exists *nowhere.*' The infidel says 'There is no such substance as God.' The immaterialist says 'There is such a substance as God, but it is *without parts.* The atheist says, 'There is no such substance as *spirit.*' The immaterialist says 'A spirit, though he lives and acts, occupies no room, and fills no space in the same way and in the same manner as matter, not even so much as does the minutest grain of sand.' The atheist does not seek to hide his infidelity; but the immaterialist, whose declared belief amounts to the same things as the atheist's, endeavors to hide his infidelity under the shallow covering of a few words. * * * The immaterialist is a religious atheist; he only differs from the other class of atheists by clothing an indivisible unextending *nothing* with the powers of a God. One class believes in no God; the other believes that *Nothing* is god and worships it as such."—Orson Pratt, in pamphlet *Absurdities of Immaterialism, p. 11.*

10. Atheism, a Fatal Belief—"During the Reign of Terror, the French were declared by the National Assembly to be a nation of atheists; but a brief experience convinced them that a nation of atheists could not long exist. Robespierre then 'proclaimed in the convention, that belief in the existence of God was necessary to those principles of virtue and morality upon which the republic was founded; and on the 7th of May [1794], the national representatives, who had so lately prostrated themselves before the Goddess of Reason, voted by acclamation that the French people acknowledged the existence of the Supreme Being, and the immortality of the soul.' —*Students' France,* 27, 6.

11. The Father and The Son—In the treatment of the "Personality of Each Member of the Godhead" and "Divine Attributes" no attempt has been made to segregate the references made to The Father and The Son. It is to be remembered that the Personage most generally designated in the Old Testament as God or the Lord, is He who in the mortal state was known as Jesus Christ, and in the antemortal state as Jehovah. See the author's work, *Jesus the Christ,* chap. 4. That Jesus Christ or Jehovah is designated in certain scriptures as the Father in no wise justifies an assumption of identity between Him and His Father, Elohim. This matter has been explained by the presiding authorities of the Church in a special publication as follows:

The Father and The Son: A Doctrinal Exposition by The First Presidency and The Twelve—The scriptures plainly and repeatedly affirm that God is the Creator of the earth and the heavens and all things that in them are. In the sense so expressed, the Creator is an Organizer. God created the earth as an organized sphere; but He certainly did not create, in the sense of bringing into primal existence, the ultimate elements of the materials of which the earth consists, for "the elements are eternal" (D&C 93:33).

So also life is eternal, and not created; but life, or the vital force, may be infused into organized matter, though the details of the process have not been revealed unto man. For illustrative instances see Genesis 2:7; Moses 3:7; and Abraham 5:7. Each of these scriptures states that God breathed into the body of man the breath of life. See further Moses 3:19, for the statement that God breathed the breath of life into the bodies of the beasts and birds. God showed unto Abraham "the intelligences that were organized before the world was"; and by "intelligences" we are to understand personal "spirits" (Abraham 3:22, 23); nevertheless, we are expressly told that "Intelligence" that is, "the light of truth, was not created or made, neither indeed can be" (D&C 93:29).

The term "Father" as applied to Deity occurs in sacred writ with plainly different meanings. Each of the four significations specified in the following treatment should be carefully segregated.

1. *"Father" as Literal Parent*—Scriptures embodying the ordinary signification—literally that of Parent—are too numerous and specific to require citation. The purport of these scriptures is to the effect that God the Eternal Father, whom we designate by the exalted name-title "Elohim," is the literal Parent of our Lord and Savior Jesus Christ, and of the spirits of the human race. Elohim is the Father in every sense in which Jesus Christ is so designated, and distinctively He is the Father of spirits. Thus we read in the Epistle to the Hebrews: "Furthermore we have had fathers of our flesh which corrected us, and we gave them reverence: shall we not much rather be in subjection unto the Father of spirits, and live?" (Hebrews 12:9). In view of this fact we are taught by Jesus Christ to pray: "Our Father which art in heaven, Hallowed be thy name."

Jesus Christ applies to Himself both titles, "Son" and "Father." Indeed, He specifically said to the brother of Jared: "Behold, I am Jesus Christ. I am the Father and the Son" (Ether 3:14). Jesus Christ is the Son of Elohim both as spiritual and bodily offspring; that is to say, Elohim is literally the Father of the spirit of Jesus Christ and also of the body in which Jesus Christ performed His mission in the flesh, and which body died on the cross and was afterward taken up by the process of resurrection, and is now the immortalized tabernacle of the eternal spirit of our Lord and Savior. No extended explanation of the title "Son of God" as applied to Jesus Christ appears necessary.

2. *"Father" as Creator*—A second scriptural meaning of "Father" is that of Creator, e.g. in passages referring to any one of the Godhead as "The Father of the heavens and of the earth and all things that in them are" (Ether 4:7; see also Alma 11:38, 39 and Mosiah 15:4).

God is not the Father of the earth as one of the worlds in space, nor of the heavenly bodies in whole or in part, nor of the inanimate objects and the plants and the animals upon the earth, in the literal sense in which He is the Father of the spirits of mankind. Therefore, scriptures that refer to God in any way as the Father of the heavens and the earth are to be understood as signifying that God is the Maker, the Organizer, the Creator of the heavens and the earth.

With this meaning, as the context shows in every case, Jehovah who is Jesus Christ the Son of Elohim, is called "the Father," and even "the very eternal Father of heaven and of earth" (see passages before cited, and also Mosiah 16:15). With analogous meaning Jesus Christ is called "The Everlasting Father" (Isaiah 9:6; compare 2 Nephi 19:6). The descriptive titles "Everlasting" and "Eternal" in the foregoing texts are synonymous.

That Jesus Christ, whom we also know as Jehovah, was the executive of the Father, Elohim, in the work of creation is set forth in the book *Jesus the Christ,* chapter 4. Jesus Christ, being the Creator, is consistently called the Father of heaven and earth in the sense explained above; and since His creations are of eternal quality He is very properly called the Eternal Father of heaven and earth.

3. *Jesus Christ the "Father" of Those Who Abide in His Gospel*—A third sense in which Jesus Christ is regarded as the "Father" has reference to the relationship between Him and those who accept His Gospel and thereby become heirs of eternal life. Following are a few of the scriptures illustrating this meaning.

In the fervent prayer offered just prior to His entrance into Gethsemane, Jesus Christ supplicated His Father in behalf of those whom the Father had given unto Him, specifically the apostles, and more generally, all who would accept and abide in the Gospel through the ministry of the apostles. Read in our Lord's own words the solemn affirmation that those for whom He particularly prayed were His own, and that His Father had given them unto Him: "I have manifested thy name unto the men which thou gavest me out of the world: thine they were, and thou gavest them me; and they have kept thy word. Now they have known that all things whatsoever thou hast given me are of thee. For I have given unto them the words which thou gavest me; and they have received them, and have known surely that I came out from thee, and they have believed that thou didst send me. I pray for them: I pray not for the world, but for them which thou hast given me; for they are thine. And all mine are thine, and thine are mine; and I am glorified in them. And now I am no more in the world, but these are in the world, and I come to thee. Holy Father, keep through thine own name those whom thou hast given me, that they may be one as we are. While I was with them in the world, I kept them in thy name: those that thou gavest me I have kept, and none of them is lost, but the son of perdition; that the scripture might be filled" (John 17:6–12).

And further: "Neither pray I for these alone, but for them also which shall believe on me through their word; That they all may be one; as thou, Father, art in me, and I in thee, that they also may be one in us: that the world may believe that thou hast sent me. And the glory which thou gavest me I have given them; that they may be one, even as we are one: I in them, and thou in me, that they may be made perfect in one; and that the world may know that thou hast sent me, and hast loved them, as thou hast loved me. Father, I will that they also, whom thou hast given me, be with me where I am; that they may behold my glory, which thou hast given me: for thou lovedst me before the foundation of the world" (John 17:20–24).

To His faithful servants in the present dispensation the Lord has said: "Fear not, little children, for you are mine, and I have overcome the world, and you are of them that my Father hath given me" (D&C 50:41).

Salvation is attainable only through compliance with the laws and ordinances of the Gospel; and all who are thus saved become sons and daughters unto God in a distinctive sense. In a revelation given through Joseph the Prophet to Emma Smith the Lord Jesus addressed the woman as "My daughter," and said: "for verily I say unto you, all those who receive my gospel are sons and daughters in my kingdom" (D&C 25:1). In many instances the Lord has addressed men as His sons (e.g. D&C 9:1; 34:3; 121:7).

That by obedience to the Gospel men may become sons of God, both as sons of Jesus Christ, and, through Him, as sons of His Father, is set forth in many revelations given in the current dispensation. Thus we read in an utterance of the Lord Jesus Christ to Hyrum Smith in 1829: "Behold, I am Jesus Christ, the Son of God. I am the life and the light of the world. I am the same who came unto mine own and mine own received me not; But verily, verily, I say unto you, that as many as receive me, to them will I give power to become the sons of God, even to them that believe on my name. Amen." (D&C 11:28–30). To Orson Pratt the Lord spoke through Joseph the Seer, in 1830: "My son Orson, hearken and hear and behold what I, the Lord God, shall say unto you, even Jesus Christ your Redeemer; The light and the life of the world; a light which shineth in darkness and the darkness comprehendeth it not; Who so loved the world that he gave his own life, that as many as would believe might become the sons of God. Wherefore you are my son" (D&C 34:1–3). In 1830 the Lord thus addressed Joseph Smith and Sidney Rigdon: "Listen to the voice of the Lord your God, even Alpha and Omega, the beginning and the end, whose course is one eternal round, the same today as yesterday, and forever. I am Jesus Christ, the Son of God, who was crucified for the sins of the world, even as many as will believe on my name, that they may become the sons of God, even one in me as I am one in the Father, as the Father is one in me, that we may be one" (D&C 35:1–2). Consider also the following given in 1831: "Hearken and listen to the voice of him who is from all eternity to all eternity, the Great I AM, even Jesus Christ—The light and the life of the world; a light which shineth in darkness and the darkness comprehendeth it not; The same which came in the meridian of time unto mine own, and mine own received me not; But to as many as received me, gave I power to become my sons; and even so will I give unto as many as will receive me, power to become my sons" (D&C 39:1–4). In a revelation given through Joseph Smith in March, 1831, we read: "For verily I say unto you that I am Alpha and Omega, the beginning and the end, the light and the life of the world—a light that shineth in darkness and the darkness comprehendeth it not. I came unto mine own, and mine own received me not; but unto as many as received me, gave I power to do many miracles, and to become the sons of God, and even unto them that believed on my name gave I power to obtain eternal life" (D&C 45:7–8).

A forceful exposition of this relationship between Jesus Christ as the Father and those who comply with the requirements of the Gospel as His children was given by Abinadi, centuries before our Lord's birth in the flesh: "And now I say unto you, who shall declare his generation? Behold, I say unto you, that when his soul has been made an offering for sin, he shall see his seed. And now what say ye? And who shall be his seed? Behold I say unto you, that whosoever has heard the words of the prophets, yea, all the holy prophets who have prophesied concerning the coming of the Lord—I say unto you, that all those who have hearkened unto their words, and believed that the Lord would redeem his people, and have looked forward to that day for a remission of their sins, I say unto you, that these are his seed, or they are the heirs of the kingdom of God. For these are they whose sins he has borne; these are they for whom he has died to redeem them from their transgressions. And now, are they not his seed? Yea, and are not the prophets, every one that has opened his mouth to prophesy, that has not fallen into transgression, I mean all the holy prophets ever since the world began? I say unto you that they are his seed" (Mosiah 15:10–13).

In tragic contrast with the blessed state of those who become children of God through obedience to the Gospel of Jesus Christ is that of the unregenerate, who are specifically called the children of the devil. Note the words of Christ, while in the flesh, to certain wicked Jews who boasted of their Abrahamic lineage: "If ye were Abraham's children, ye would do the works of Abraham. * * * Ye do the deeds of your father * * * If God were your Father, ye would love me. * * * Ye are of your father the devil, and the lusts of your father ye will do" (John 8:39, 41, 42, 44). Thus Satan is designated as the father of the wicked, though we cannot assume any personal relationship of parent and children as existing between him and them. A combined illustration showing that the righteous are the children of God and the wicked the children of the devil appears in the parable of the Tares: "The good seed are the children of the kingdom; but the tares are the children of the wicked one" (Matt. 13:38).

Men may become children of Jesus Christ by being born anew—born of God, as the inspired word states: "He that committeth sin is of the devil; for the devil sinneth from the beginning. For this purpose the Son of God was manifested, that he might destroy the works of the devil. Whosoever is born of God doth not commit sin; for his seed remaineth in him: and he cannot sin, because he is born of God. In this the children of God are manifest, and the children of the devil: whosoever doeth not righteousness is not of God, neither he that loveth not his brother" (1 John 3:8–10).

Those who have been born unto God through obedience to the Gospel may by valiant devotion to righteousness obtain exaltation and even reach the status of godhood. Of such we read: "Wherefore, as it is written, they are gods, even the sons of God" (D&C 76:58; compare 132:20, and contrast paragraph 17 in same section; see also paragraph 37). Yet, though they be gods they are still subject to Jesus Christ as their Father in this exalted relationship; and so we read in the paragraph following the above quotation: "and they are Christ's, and Christ is God's" (76:59).

By the new birth—that of water and the Spirit—mankind may become children of Jesus Christ, being through the means by Him provided "begotten sons and daughters unto God" (D&C 76:24). This solemn truth is further emphasized in the words of the Lord Jesus Christ given through Joseph Smith in 1833: "And now, verily I say unto you, I was in the beginning with the Father, and am the Firstborn; And all those who are begotten through me are partakers of the glory of the same, and are the church of the Firstborn" (D&C 93:21, 22). For such figurative use of the term "begotten" in application to those who are born unto God see Paul's explanation: "for in Christ Jesus I have begotten you through the gospel" (1 Cor. 4:15). An analogous instance of sonship attained by righteous service is found in the revelation relating to the order and functions of Priesthood, given in 1832: "For whoso is faithful unto the obtaining of these two priesthoods of which I have spoken, and the magnifying their calling, are sanctified by the Spirit unto the renewing of their bodies. They become the sons of Moses and of Aaron and the seed of Abraham, and the church and kingdom, and the elect of God" (D&C 84:33, 34).

If it be proper to speak of those who accept and abide in the Gospel as Christ's sons and daughters—and upon this matter the scriptures are explicit and cannot be gainsaid nor denied—it is consistently proper to speak of Jesus Christ as the Father of the righteous, they having become His children and He having been made their Father through the second birth—the baptismal regeneration.

4. *Jesus Christ the "Father" by Divine Investiture of Authority*—A fourth reason for applying the title "Father" to Jesus Christ is found in the fact that in all His dealings with the human family Jesus the Son has represented and yet represents Elohim His Father in power and authority. This is true of Christ in His preexistent, antemortal, or unembodied state, in the which He was known as Jehovah; also during His embodiment in the flesh; and during His labors as a disembodied spirit in the realm of the dead; and since that period in His resurrected state. To the Jews He said: "I and my Father are one" (John 10:30; see also 17:11, 22); yet He declared "My Father is greater than I" (John 14:28); and further, "I am come in my Father's name" (John 5:43; see also 10:25). The same truth was declared by Christ Himself to the Nephites (see 3 Nephi 20:35 and 28:10), and has been reaffirmed by revelation in the present dispensation (D&C 50:43). Thus the Father placed His name upon the Son; and Jesus Christ spoke and ministered in and through the Father's name; and so far as power, authority, and Godship are concerned His words and acts were and are those of the Father.

We read, by way of analogy, that God placed His name upon or in the Angel who was assigned to special ministry unto the people of Israel during the exodus. Of that Angel the Lord said: "Beware of him, and obey his voice, provoke him not; for he will not pardon your transgressions: for my name is in him" (Exodus 23:21).

The ancient apostle, John, was visited by an angel who ministered and spoke in the name of Jesus Christ. As we read: "The Revelation of Jesus Christ, which God gave unto him, to shew unto his servants things which must shortly come to pass; and he sent and signified it by his angel unto his servant John" (Revelation 1:1). John was about to worship the angelic being who spoke in the name of the Lord Jesus Christ, but was forbidden: "And I John saw these things, and heard them. And when I had heard and seen, I fell down to worship before the feet of the angel which shewed me these things. Then saith he unto me, See thou do it not: for I am thy fellowservant, and of thy brethren the prophets, and of them which keep the sayings of this book: worship God" (Rev. 22:8, 9). And then the angel continued to speak as though he were the Lord Himself: "And, behold, I come quickly; and my reward is with me, to give every man according as his work shall be. I am Alpha and Omega, the beginning and the end, the first and the last" (verses 12, 13). The resurrected Lord, Jesus Christ, who had been exalted to the right hand of God His Father, had placed His name upon the angel sent to John, and the angel spoke in the first person, saying "I come quickly," "I am Alpha and Omega," though he meant that Jesus Christ would come, and that Jesus Christ was Alpha and Omega.

None of these considerations, however, can change in the least degree the solemn fact of the literal relationship of Father and Son between Elohim and Jesus Christ. Among the spirit children of Elohim the firstborn was and is Jehovah or Jesus Christ to whom all others are juniors. Following are affirmative scriptures bearing upon this great truth. Paul, writing to the Colossians, says of Jesus Christ: "Who is the image of the invisible God, the firstborn of every creature: For by him were all things created, that are in heaven, and that are in earth, visible and invisible, whether they be thrones, or dominions, or principalities, or powers; all things were created by him, and for him: And he is before all things, and by him all things consist. And he is the head of the body, the church: who is the beginning, the firstborn from the dead; that in all things he might have the preeminence. For it pleased the Father that in him should all fulness dwell" (Colossians 1:15–19). From this scripture we learn that Jesus Christ was "the firstborn of every creature" and it is evident that the seniority here expressed must be with respect to ante-mortal existence, for Christ was not the senior of all mortals in the flesh. He is further designated as "the firstborn from the dead," this having reference to Him as the first to be resurrected from the dead, or as elsewhere written "the firstfruits of them that slept" (1 Corinthians 15:20, see also verse 23); and "the first begotten of the dead" (Revelation 1:5; compare Acts 26:23). The writer of the Epistle to the Hebrews affirms the status of Jesus Christ as the firstborn of the spirit children of His Father, and extols the preeminence of the Christ when tabernacled in flesh: "And again, when he bringeth in the firstbegotten into the world, he saith, And let all the angels of God worship him" (Hebrews 1:6; read the preceding verses). That the spirits who were juniors to Christ were predestined to be born in the image of their Elder Brother is thus attested by Paul: "And we know that all things work together for good to them that love God, to them who are the called according to his purpose. For whom he did foreknow, he also did predestinate to be conformed to the image of his Son, that he might be the firstborn among many brethren" (Romans 8:28, 29). John the Revelator was commanded to write to the head of the Laodicean church, as the words of the Lord Jesus Christ: "These things saith the Amen, the faithful and true witness, the beginning of the creation of God" (Revelation 3:14). In the course of a revelation given through Joseph Smith in May, 1833, the Lord Jesus Christ said as before cited: "And now, verily I say unto you, I was in the beginning with the Father, and am the Firstborn" (D&C 93:21). A later verse makes plain the fact that human beings generally were similarly existent in spirit state prior to their embodiment in the flesh: "Ye were also in the beginning with the Father; that which is Spirit, even the Spirit of truth" (verse 23).

There is no impropriety, therefore, in speaking of Jesus Christ as the Elder Brother of the rest of human kind. That He is by spiritual birth Brother to the rest of us is indicated in Hebrews: "Wherefore in all things it behoved him to be made like unto his brethren, that he might be a merciful and faithful high priest in things pertaining to God, to make reconciliation for the sins of the people" (Hebrews 2:17). Let it not be forgotten, however, that He is essentially greater than any and all others, by reason (1) of His seniority as the oldest or firstborn; (2) of His unique status in the flesh as the offspring of a mortal mother and of an immortal, or resurrected and glorified, Father; (3) of His selection and foreordination as the one and only Redeemer and Savior of the race; and (4) of His transcendent sinlessness.

Jesus Christ is not the Father of the spirits who have taken or yet shall take bodies upon this earth, for He is one of them. He is The Son, as they are sons or daughters of Elohim. So far as the stages of eternal progression and attainment have been made known through divine revelation, we are to understand that only resurrected and glorified beings can become parents of spirit offspring. Only such exalted souls have reached maturity in the appointed course of eternal life; and the spirits born to them in the eternal worlds will pass in due sequence through the several stages or estates by which the glorified parents have attained exaltation.

THE FIRST PRESIDENCY AND THE COUNCIL
OF THE TWELVE APOSTLES OF THE CHURCH
OF JESUS CHRIST OF LATTER-DAY SAINTS
SALT LAKE CITY, UTAH, JUNE 30, 1916.

APPENDIX 3—Notes Relating to Chapter 3

1. Man's Agency is God-given—The following is an extract from a discourse delivered by President Brigham Young, July 5, 1855 (see Journal of Discourses of that date, and *Millennial Star*, vol. 20, p. 43). "What is the foundation of the rights of man? The Lord Almighty has organized man for the express purpose of becoming an independent being like unto Himself, and has given him his individual agency. Man is made in the likeness of his Creator, the great archetype of the human species, who bestowed upon him the principles of eternity, planting immortality within him, and leaving him at liberty to act in the way that seemeth good unto him—to choose or refuse for himself, to be a Latter-day Saint or a Wesleyan Methodist, to belong to the Church of England, the oldest daughter of the Mother Church, to the old Mother herself, to her sister the Greek Church, or to be an infidel and belong to no church. When the kingdom of God is fully set up and established on the face of the earth, and takes the preeminence over all other nations and kingdoms, it will protect the people in the enjoyment of all their rights, no matter what they believe, what they profess, or what they worship."

2. The Nature of Sin—The English word sin represents a variety of terms occurring in the original languages, the literal translation of which bear to one another a great similarity. Thus, in the Old Testament, the following Hebrew terms among others occur:—*setim* (referred to in Psalms 101:3), signifying "to deviate from the way;" *shegagah* (Lev. 4:2; Num. 15:27), "to err in the way;" *avon*, "the crooked, or perverted;" *avel*, "to turn aside." In the New Testament we find among the Greek originals, *hamartia*, "the missing of a mark;" *parabasis*, "the transgressing of a line;" *parakoe*, "disobedience to a voice;" *paraptoma*, "falling from uprightness;" *agnoema*, "unjustifiable ignorance;" *hettema*, "giving only partial measure;" *anomia*, "non-observance of law;" *plemmeleia*, "a discord." The above illustrations are taken mainly from M̦ller and French. In all these expressions, the predominant idea is that of departure from the way of God, of separation from His companionship by opposition to the divine requirements. Sin was introduced into the world from without; it was not a natural product of earth. The seed of disobedience was planted in the mind of Eve by Satan; that seed took root; and much fruit, of the nature that we, with unguarded words, call calamity, is the result. From these thorns and thistles of mortality, a Savior has been prepared to deliver us.

3. Eden—In the Hebrew tongue, from which our word Eden is taken, this term signifies something particularly delightful—a place of pleasantness; the place is also called "the garden of the Lord." One particular spot in the land of Eden was prepared by the Lord as a garden; this was situated eastward in Eden. From the garden, the parents of the race were expelled after the fall, though it is reasonable to suppose that they still dwelt in the land or region of Eden. We read that at a later date, Cain, the first murderer, "went out from the presence of the Lord, and dwelt in the land of Nod, on the east of Eden" (Gen. 4:16). Though there is no uniform belief among Christian scholars as to the geographical location of Eden, the majority claim that it was in Persia. The Latter-day Saints have more exact knowledge on the matter, a revelation having been given through Joseph Smith, at Spring Hill, Mo., May 19, 1838, in which that place is named by the Lord "Adam-ondi-Ahman, because, said he, it is the place where Adam shall come to visit his people, or the Ancient of Days shall sit, as spoken of by Daniel the prophet" (D&C sec. 116). From another revelation we learn (D&C 107:52, 53) that three years before his death, Adam called together in the valley of Adam-ondi-Ahman those of his sons who had been made high priests, together with the rest of his righteous posterity, and there bestowed upon them his patriarchal blessings, the event being marked by special manifestations from the Lord (see also D&C 117:8). There is no authentic record of the human race having inhabited the eastern hemisphere until after the flood. The western continent, called now the New World, comprises indeed the oldest inhabited regions of earth. The West not the East is the "cradle of nations."

4. "Original Sin"—Our first parents disobeyed the command of God by indulging in food unsuited to their condition; and, as a natural consequence, they suffered physical degeneracy, whereby bodily weakness, disease, and death came into the world. Their posterity have inherited the resultant ills, to all of which we now say flesh is heir; and it is true that these human imperfections came through disobedience, and are therefore the fruits of sin. But as to accountability for Adam's transgression, in all justice, Adam alone must answer. The present fallen status of mankind, as expressed in our mortal condition, was inaugurated by Adam and Eve; but divine justice forbids that we be accounted sinners solely because our parents transgressed. Though the privations, the vicissitudes, and the unrelenting toil enforced by the state of mortal existence be part of our heritage from Adam, we are enriched thereby; for in just such conditions do we find opportunity to develop the powers of soul that shall enable us to overcome evil, to choose the good, and to win salvation and exaltation in the mansions of our Father.—*Vitality of "Mormonism,"* by the present author, p. 45, article "Original Sin."

5. Mortality a Boon—Man in his mortal state is the union of a preexistent spirit with a body composed of earthly elements. This union of spirit and body marks progress from the unembodied to the embodied condition, and is an inestimable advancement in the soul's onward course. The penalty incurred by proud Lucifer and his rebel hordes for their attempt to thwart the divine purpose in the matter of man's agency was the doom of being denied bodies of flesh. Mortal birth is a boon to which only those spirits who kept their first estate are eligible (see Jude 6). Expressive of the awful state of the utterly unregenerate among men, of those who have sunk to such depths in sin as to become "sons of perdition" the Lord has applied the extreme malediction that for such it were better never to have been born (see Matt. 26:24; D&C 76:32). The blessedness of advancement to the mortal state lies in the possibilities of achievement therein. Mortality is the preparatory school for eternity. Its curriculum is comprehensive and exacting. In its laboratories we pupils meet the experiences that test and try to conclusive demonstration the individual effect of precept and profession. For the founding and maintenance of this school the earth was created.—See *Vitality of "Mormonism,"* by the present author, pp. 236–239, articles "We Lived Before We Were Born" and "Man Is Eternal."

6. Beneficent Results of the Fall—"Honor thy father and thy mother." This was one of the ten special commandments given to Israel, during a grand display of God's power and glory on Mount Sinai. In the past centuries of darkness it appears to have lost its significance with the Christian world. They do not appear to realize that honor is due to the first parents of the human race. They have been long taught that Adam and Eve were great transgressors, and have mourned over the fact that they partook of the forbidden fruit and brought death into the world. There is no possibility that the fall of man was an accident or chance, any more than was his creation. If an accident, then why was Christ prepared from before the foundation of the world as a propitiation for sin, and to open up the way for man to immortality? Christ's mediation was a sequence of the fall" (see Acts 5:31). "Without the fall there would have been no broken law, and therefore nothing to repent of; and there could be no forgiveness of sin without the atonement of Christ. The Book of Mormon makes this subject very plain: `And now, behold, if Adam had not transgressed he would not have fallen, but he would have remained in the garden of Eden. And all things which were created must have remained in the same state in which they were after they were created; and they must have remained forever, and had no end. And they would have had no children; wherefore they would have remained in a state of innocence, having no joy, for they knew no misery; doing no good, for they knew no sin' (2 Nephi 2:22, 23). * * * We, the children of Adam, have no right to bring accusations against the patriarch of the race. But rather, we should rejoice with them, that through their fall and the atonement of Jesus Christ, the way of eternal life has been opened up to us."—*A Compendium of the Doctrines of the Gospel,* F. D. Richards and J. A. Little.

7. The Fall Foreknown—"Mormonism" accepts the doctrine of the fall, and the account of the transgression of Eden, as set forth in Genesis; but it affirms that none save Adam shall ever have to account for Adam's disobedience; that mankind in general are absolutely absolved from the responsibility for that ?original sin,' and that each shall answer for his own transgressions alone; that the fall was foreknown of God—that it was the accepted means by which the necessary condition of mortality should be inaugurated; and that a Redeemer was provided before the world was. That general salvation, in the sense of redemption from the effects of the fall, comes to all without their seeking it; but that individual salvation or rescue from the effects of personal sins is to be acquired by each for himself, by faith and good works through the redemption wrought by Jesus Christ."—*The Philosophy of "Mormonism,"* by the present author.

8. The Fall a Process of Physical Degeneracy—For a concise treatment of this topic see *Jesus the Christ,* by the present author, pp. 19 and 29.

APPENDIX 4—Notes Relating to Chapter 4

1. The Atonement in Accordance with Divine Law—We have learned but little of the eternal laws operative in the heavens; but that God's purposes are accomplished through and by law is beyond question. There can be no irregularity, inconsistency, arbitrariness or caprice in His doings, for such would mean injustice. Therefore, the atonement must have been effected in accordance with law. The self-sacrificing life, the indescribable agony, and the voluntary death of One who had life in Himself with power to halt His torturers at any stage, and whom none could slay until He permitted, must have constituted compliance with the eternal law of justice, propitiation and expiation by which victory over sin and death could be and has been achieved. Through the mortal life and sacrificial death of our Lord Jesus Christ the demands of justice have been fully met, and the way is opened for the lawful ministration of mercy so far as the effects of the fall are concerned. Sin, followed by death, came into the world through the transgression of one man. The entailment of mortality upon that man's posterity, with all its elements of a fallen state, is natural, we say, because we think we know something about heredity. Is it any more truly natural that one man's transgression should be of universal effect than that the redeeming and saving achievement of One, fully empowered and qualified for the work of atonement, should be of universal blessing? The ancient apostles were explicit in answer. Thus spake Paul: "Therefore as by the offense of one judgment came upon all men to condemnation; even so by the righteousness of one the free gift came upon all men unto justification of life" (Rom. 5:18). And further: "For there is one God, and one mediator between God and men, the man Christ Jesus; Who gave himself a ransom for all" (1 Tim. 2:5, 6).—From the author's *Vitality of "Mormonism,"* article "Philosophy of the Atonement," p. 58, which see.

2. Redemption from the Fall Universal and Unconditional—"We believe that through the sufferings, death, and atonement of Jesus Christ all mankind, without one exception, are to be completely and fully redeemed, both body and spirit, from the endless, banishment and curse to which they were consigned by Adam's transgression; and that this universal salvation and redemption of the whole human family from the endless penalty of the original sin, is effected without any conditions whatever on their part; that is, they are not required to believe or repent, or be baptized, or do anything else, in order to be redeemed from that penalty; for whether they believe or disbelieve, whether they repent or remain impenitent, whether they are baptized or unbaptized, whether they keep the commandments or break them, whether they are righteous or unrighteous, it will make no difference in relation to their redemption, both soul and body, from the penalty of Adam's transgression. The most righteous man that ever lived on the earth, and the most wicked wretch of the whole human family, were both placed under the same curse without any transgression or agency of their own, and they both alike will be redeemed from that curse, without any agency or conditions on their part."—Apostle Orson Pratt in *Remarkable Visions.*

3. Christ the Author of Our Salvation—President John Taylor speaks of the death of Christ as an expiatory sacrifice, and adds: "The Savior thus becomes master of the situation—the debt is paid, the redemption made, the covenant fulfilled, justice satisfied, the will of God done, and all power is now given into the hands of the Son of God—the power of the resurrection, the power of the redemption, the power of salvation, the power to enact laws for the carrying out and accomplishment of this design. * * * The plan, the arrangement, the agreement, the covenant was made, entered into and accepted, before the foundation of the world; it was prefigured by sacrifices, and was carried out and consummated on the cross. Hence, being the Mediator between God and man, He becomes by right the dictator and director on earth and in heaven for the living and for the dead, for the past, the present, and the future, pertaining to man as associated with this earth or the heavens, in time or eternity, the captain of our salvation, the apostle and high priest of our profession, the Lord and Giver of *life.*"—*Mediation and Atonement,* John Taylor, p. 171.

4. The Atonement Inaugurated by Christ—"The Apostle Paul quite comprehensively sums up the results of Christ's death and resurrection: 'But now is Christ risen from the dead, and become the firstfruits of them that slept. For since by man came death, by man came also the resurrection of the dead. For as in Adam all die, even so in Christ shall all be made alive' (1 Cor. 15:20–22). That is, death having come on all men through the disobedience of Adam, so must all be raised to immortality and eternal life through the death and resurrection of Christ. Paul also asserted that 'the last enemy that shall be destroyed is death' (verse 26). John the Revelator declares that he saw death and hell cast into the lake of fire (Rev. 20:14). The atonement, as wrought out by Jesus Christ, further signifies that He has opened up the way for man's redemption from his own sins, through faith in Christ's sufferings, death, and resurrection. The Apostle Paul well expresses this: 'For all have sinned, and come short of the glory of God; being justified freely by his grace through the redemption that is in Christ Jesus: whom God hath set forth to be a propitiation through faith in his blood, to declare his righteousness for the remission of sins that are past, through the forbearance of God' (Romans 3:23–26). These passages evidence that redemption from death, through the sufferings of Christ, is for all men, both the righteous and the wicked; for this earth, and for all things created upon it. The whole tenor of the scriptures assures us that, while they may be sure of resurrection from death, regardless of their personal acts, yet they will be rewarded for their works, whether they be good or evil, and that redemption from personal sins can only be obtained through obedience to the requirements of the gospel, and a life of good works. The transgression of Adam being infinite in its consequences, those consequences cannot be averted, except through an infinite atonement."—*Compendium,* F. D. Richards & J. A. Little, pp. 8,9.

5. The Atonement Necessary—"In the economy of God and the plan proposed by the Almighty, it was provided that man was to be placed under a law apparently simple in itself, yet the test of that law was fraught with the gravest consequences. The observance of that law would secure eternal life, and the penalty for the violation of that law was death. * * * If the law had not been broken, man would have lived; but would man thus living have been capable of perpetuating his species, and of thus fulfilling the designs of God in preparing tabernacles for the spirits which had been created in the spirit world? And further, could they have had the need of a mediator, who was to act as a propitiation for the violation of this law, which it would appear from the circumstances was destined to be broken; or could the eternal increase and perpetuity of man have been continued, and his high exaltation to the Godhead been accomplished, without the propitiatory atonement and sacrifice of the Son of God?"—*Mediation and Atonement,* John Taylor, pp. 128, 129.

6. The Need of a Redeemer—For special treatment see *Jesus the Christ,* by the present author, pp. 17–31.

APPENDIX 5—Notes Relating to Chapter 5

1. Usage of the Term Faith—"In the New Testament the Greek word *pistis* has been translated 'faith' 235 times, and 'belief' once (2 Thess. 2:13), but there is no apparent reason why it should not have been rendered 'faith' in this text also. We have no English verb for faith, but use 'believe,' which by derivation means *to live by (Systematic Theology,* by Dr. Charles Hodge, vol. 3, pp. 42, 43). In our language 'to believe' certainly admits of degrees of assurance from the slightest perception of truth, or error, to the fullest assurance. But that is not the way it is used in the Bible by the original authors. In their vocabulary 'belief' is full assurance and 'to believe' is *to live* accordingly. The Greek word is *pistevo,* from which we have *pistis.* It occurs at least 211 times and every time it means to have *faith.* There is, however, another word, *peithomai,* which has been translated 'believe' in Acts 17:4; 27:11; and 28:24. It means 'to be persuaded' without having actually accepted the 'faith' *(pistis).* In five places *pistevo* ('to believe') might well be translated 'to be steadfast.'

"But the word 'faith' *(pistis)* frequently has another meaning in the New Testament than 'trust,' 'confidence,' or 'assurance.' It stands for 'creed' or rather for the gospel of Christ in contrast to the law of Moses—the new dispensation that took the place of the old (see Acts 6:7; 13:8; 14:22, 27; Rom. 1:5; 3:27; 10:8; Gal. 1:23; 2:16, 20; 3:2, 5; Eph. 2:8; 1 Tim. 1:2; 4:1, and many other passages). In all these 'faith' is almost synonymous with 'the gospel.' it is frequently used in that sense in English. Confusion and needless discussion have arisen from the fact that this obvious, though secondary, meaning of 'faith' has not received due attention in the study of the scriptures."—From note to the author by Elder J. M. Sjodahl.

2. The Sectarian Dogma of Justification by Faith Alone has exercised an influence for evil. The idea upon which this pernicious doctrine was founded was at first associated with that of an absolute predestination, by which man was foredoomed to destruction, or to an undeserved salvation. Thus, Luther taught as follows: "The excellent, infallible, and sole preparation for grace is the eternal election and predestination of God." "Since the fall of man, free will is but an idle word." "A man who imagines to arrive at grace by doing all that he is able to do, adds sin to sin, and is doubly guilty." "That man is not justified who performs many works; but he who without works has much faith in Christ." (For these and other doctrines of the so-called "Reformation," see D'Aubigne's *History of the Reformation,* vol. 1, pp. 82, 83, 119, 122.) In Miller's *Church History* (vol. 4, p. 514) we read: "The point which the reformer [Luther] had most at heart in all his labors, contests, and dangers, was the justification by faith alone." Melanchthon voices the doctrine of Luther in these words: "Man's justification before God proceeds from faith alone. This faith enters man's heart by the grace of God alone;" and further, "As all things which happen, happen necessarily according to the divine predestination, there is no such thing as liberty in our wills" (D'Aubigne, vol. 3, p. 340). It is true that Luther strongly denounced and vehemently disclaimed responsibility for the excesses to which this teaching gave rise, yet he was not less vigorous in proclaiming the doctrine. Note his words: "I, Doctor Martin Luther, unworthy herald of the gospel of our Lord Jesus Christ, confess this article, that faith alone without works justifies before God; and I declare that it shall stand and remain forever in despite of the emperor of the Romans, the emperor of the Turks, the emperor of the Persians—in spite of the pope and all the cardinals, with the bishops, priests, monks, and nuns—in spite of kings, princes, and nobles, and in spite of all the world and of the devils themselves; and that if they endeavor to fight against this truth they will draw the fires of hell upon their heads. This is the true and holy gospel, and the declaration of me, Doctor Luther, according to the teachings of the Holy Ghost" (D'Aubigne, vol. 1, p. 70). It should be remembered, however, that Luther, and even the most pronounced contenders for the doctrine of justification by faith, affirmed the necessity of sanctification as well as justification. Fletcher, *End of Religious Controversy,* p. 90, illustrates the vicious extreme to which this evil doctrine led, by accusing one of its adherents with having said: "Even adultery and murder do not hurt the pleasant children, but rather work for their good. God sees no sin in believers, whatever sin they may commit. * * * It is a most pernicious error of the schoolmen to distinguish sins according to the fact, and not according to the person. Though I blame those who say, let us sin that grace may abound, yet adultery, incest, and murder, shall upon the whole, make me holier on earth, and merrier in heaven."

A summary of the mediaeval controversy regarding the means of grace, including the doctrines of Luther and others, is presented in Roberts' *Outlines of Ecclesiastical History,* part 3, section 2, to which the student is referred. The quotations given above are incorporated therein.

3. Faith Includes Works—By isolating certain passages of scripture and regarding them as though they are complete in themselves some readers have assumed inconsistency if not contradiction to exist. Paul has been misrepresented as a proponent of the sufficiency of faith without works, and James has been cited in opposition. Compare Rom. 4:25; 9:11; Gal. 2:16; 2 Tim. 1:9; Titus 3:5, with James 1:22, 23; 2:14–26. Paul specifies the outward forms and ceremonies of the Mosaic law, which had been superseded by the higher requirements of the Gospel, as unessential works. James speaks of actual effort and effective deeds as the works that result from true faith in.God and His requirements. But after all, the apparent differences lie in the words and not in the spirit or the fact. The following note by Elder J. M. Sjodahl of the Church Historian's Office is instructive and in point: "If we comprehend fully the meaning in which the authors of the scriptures use the word 'faith' we shall see that there is no difference in meaning between true faith and works of faith. In the Bible the two terms mean the same thing. James does not contradict Paul. For, to 'believe' is to *live by* the laws of the gospel. The verbs *credere* and *vivere* are synonymous, since faith without works is dead. That is the teaching of James, and Paul certainly does not teach salvation by means of *dead* faith."

4. Forgiveness Not Always Immediate—"On account of the magnitude of sins committed, repentance is not always followed by forgiveness and restoration. For instance, when Peter was preaching to the Jews who had slain Jesus and taken His blood on themselves and their children he did not say, Repent and be baptized for the remission of sins; but, 'Repent ye therefore, and be converted, that your sins may be blotted out, when the times of refreshing shall come from the presence of the Lord. And [when] he shall send Jesus Christ, which before was preached unto you; Whom the heaven must receive until the times of restitution of all things' (Acts 3:19–21). That is, repent now, and believe in Jesus Christ, that you may be forgiven when He whom you have slain shall come again in the days of the restitution of all things, and prescribe to you the terms on which you may be saved."—*Compendium,* p. 28.

5. Sin and the Sinner—"For I the Lord cannot look upon sin with the least degree of allowance; Nevertheless, he that repents and does the commandments of the Lord shall be forgiven" (D&C 1:31, 32; see also Alma 45:16). In this forceful epigram a clear distinction is made between sin and the sinner. Many find it difficult to entirely segregate the one from the other, to apprehend sin as an abstract conception apart from personal guilt. Can there be theft without a thief, falsehood without a falsifier, murder with no slayer?

Men may be potential liars, robbers or murderers, but lacking opportunity to become criminals in fact, or restraining their evil impulses through considerations of policy or personal advantage, they may maintain outward signs of probity. The wearing of a sheep's fleece by a ravening wolf is no modern camouflage. But in all such dissemblings, the fact of wicked purpose exists; and the evil purpose, thought or desire is of itself essentially sin; and such a case, therefore, presents no phenomenon of abstract guilt, but actual and individual offense; for the thinker of evil is a sinner.

Who of us can regard tuberculosis, smallpox or the insidious and deadly influenza with other feelings than repugnance and fear? Yet we treat the afflicted person with effort to bring about his recovery; and if we loved him while well, we do not hate him because he has become ill; but, to the contrary, we become the more solicitous in his behalf. Health officers and the medical fraternity look not upon disease with compromise, toleration or allowance. They are the marshalled assailants of physical malady, whatever its disguise; and their best means of waging war on disease is that of ministering to each afflicted one, while taking all measures possible to protect the well against infection.

The germs of disease exist, whether they find lodgment in human bodies or not; and, by analogy, we may say that the spirit of or incentive to thievery, adultery, or murder is alive, as the definite contagion of evil, though men may or may not be actually overcome thereby. Now, in the case of physical affliction, definite treatment is invoked; and compliance with prescribed conditions is enforced so far as the patient will submit.

In fine and purposeful irony, the Divine Healer met the casuistry of certain self-righteous Scribes and Pharisees with the declaration: "They that are whole have no need of the physician, but they that are sick: I came not to call the righteous, but sinners to repentance" (Mark 2:17).

But as the scriptures abundantly affirm, and as experience demonstrates, there are none of us entirely free from sin; to the contrary, every one is in need of the Great Physician's healing ministrations. "Sin is the transgression of the law" (1 John 3:4); furthermore: "There is none righteous, no, not one" (Rom. 3:10); and again: "If we say that we have no sin, we deceive ourselves, and the truth is not in us" (1 John 1:8).

The treatment for sin-infected mortals is that prescribed in the Gospel of Jesus Christ, by compliance with which the ravages of soul-destroying contagion may be arrested, and relative immunity against later attacks be secured through the developed powers of resistance. The prescription is simple; the means are easily accessible; they are the same today as they were of old, and as they shall remain while there is sin in the world. These are obedience to the laws and ordinances of the Gospel.

Do these things, continuing in righteous living, and, though the mephitic atmosphere of sin be ever so foul about you, you shall be preserved to the attainment of eternal life, which of all God's gifts to man is the greatest.—From article by the present author, entitled "Sin and the Sinner," Series C-10.

APPENDIX 6—Notes Relating to Chapter 6

1. Preparation for Baptism—The doctrine that baptism, to be acceptable, must be preceded by efficient preparation, was generally taught and understood in the days of Christ, as also in the so-called apostolic period and the time immediately following. But this belief gradually declined, and baptism came to be regarded as an outward form, the application of which depended little, if at all, on the candidate's appreciation or conception of its purpose; and, as stated in the text, the Lord has reannounced the doctrine in the present dispensation. Concerning the former belief a few evidences are here given:

"In the first ages of Christianity, men and women were baptized on a profession of faith in the Lord Jesus *Christ.*"—*Canon Farrar.*

"But as Christ enjoins them (Mark 16:15, 16) to teach before baptizing, and desires that none but believers shall be admitted to baptism, it would appear that baptism is not properly administered unless when it is preceded by faith. * * * In the apostolic age no one is found to have been admitted to baptism without a previous profession of faith and repentance."—*Calvin.*

"You are not first baptized and then begin to receive the faith, and have a desire; but when you are to be baptized you make known your will to the teacher, and make a full confession of your faith with your own mouth." *Ar nobius* (a rhetorician who wrote in the latter half of the third century).

"In the primitive church, instruction preceded baptism, agreeable to the order of Jesus Christ 'Go, teach all nations, baptizing them,' etc."—*Saurin* (a French Protestant; 1677–1730).

"In the first two centuries no one was baptized, except, being instructed in the faith and acquainted with the doctrine of Christ, he was able to profess himself a believer; because of those words, 'He that believeth and is baptized.'"—*Salmasius* (a French author; 1588–1653.)

2. Historical Notes on Infant Baptism—"The baptism of infants, in the first two centuries after Christ, was altogether unknown. * * * The custom of baptizing infants did not begin before the third age after Christ was born. In the former ages no trace of it appears; and it was introduced without the command of Christ."—*Curcellaeus.*

"It is certain that Christ did not ordain infant baptism. * * * We cannot prove that the apostles ordained infant baptism. From those places where baptism of a whole family is mentioned (as in Acts 16:33; 1 Cor. 1:16) we can draw no such conclusion, because the inquiry is still to be made, whether there were any children in the families of such an age that they were not capable of any intelligent reception of Christianity; for this is the only point on which the case turns. * * * As baptism was closely united with a conscious entrance on Christian communion, faith and baptism were always connected with one another; and thus it is in the highest degree probable that baptism was performed only in instances where both could meet together, and that the practise of infant baptism was unknown at this (the apostolic) period. * * * That not till so late a period as (at least certainly not earlier than) Irenaeus, a trace of infant baptism appears; and that it first became recognized as an apostolic tradition in the course of the third century, is evidence rather against than for the admission of its apostolic origin."—Johann *Neander* (a German theologian who flourished in the first half of the present century).

"Let them therefore come when they are grown up—when they can understand—when they are taught whither they are to come. Let them become Christians when they can know Christ."—*Tertullian* (one of the Latin "Christian Fathers"; he lived from 150 to 220 A.D.). Tertullian's almost violent opposition to the practise of pedobaptism is cited by Neander as "a proof that it was not usually considered an apostolic ordinance; for in that case he would hardly have ventured to speak so strongly against it."

Martin Luther, writing in the early part of the sixteenth century, declared: "It cannot be proven by the sacred scriptures that infant baptism was instituted by Christ, or begun by the first Christians after the apostles."

"By *tekna* the apostle understands, not infants, but posterity; in which signification the word occurs in many places of the New Testament (see among others John 8:39); whence it appears that the argument which is very commonly taken from this passage for the baptism of infants, is of no force, and good for nothing."—*Limborch* (a native of Holland, and a theologian of repute; he lived 1633–1712).

APPENDIX 7—Notes Relating to Chapter 7

1. Usage of the Term "Baptize" in Ancient Times—The following instances show the ordinary meaning attached to the Greek term from which our word "baptize" is derived. In all, the idea of immersion is plainly intended (For these and other examples, see *Millennial Star,* vol. 21, pp. 687, 688.)

Polybius, a writer of history, who flourished during the second century before Christ, uses the following expressions. In describing a naval conflict between the Carthaginian and Roman fleets off the shores of Sicily he says: "If any were hard pressed by the enemy they withdrew safely back, on account of their fast sailing, into the open sea, and then turning around and falling on those of their pursuers who were in advance, they gave them frequent blows and baptized many of their vessels."—Book 1, ch. 51.

The same writer thus refers to the passage of the Roman soldiers through the river Trebia: "When the passage of the river Trebia came on, which had risen above its usual current, on account of the rain which had fallen, the infantry with difficulty crossed over, being baptized up to the chest."—Book 3, ch. 72.

Describing a catastrophe which befell the Roman ships at Syracuse, Polybius states: "Some were upset, but the greater number, their prow being thrown down from a height, were baptized and became full of sea."

Strabo, who lived during the time of Christ, used the term "baptized" in the same sense. He thus describes an instrument used in fishing: "And if it fall into the sea it is not lost: for it is compacted of oak and pine wood; so that even if the oak is baptized by its weight, the remaining part floats and is easily recovered."

Strabo refers to the buoyancy of certain saline waters thus: "These have the taste of salt water, but a different nature, for even persons who cannot swim are not liable to be baptized in them, but float like logs on the surface."

Referring to a salt spring in Tatta, the same writer says: "So easily does the water form a crust round everything baptized into it that if persons let down a circlet of rushes they will draw up wreaths of salt."

Speaking of a species of pitch from the lake Sirbonis, Strabo says: "It will float on the surface owing to the nature of the water, which, as we said, is such as to render swimming unnecessary, and such that one who walks upon it is not baptized."

Dio Cassius, speaking of the effects of a severe storm near Rome says: "The vessels which were in the Tiber, which were lying at anchor near the city, and to the river's mouth, were baptized."

The same author thus alludes to the fate of some of Curio's soldiers while fleeing before the forces of Juba: "Not a few of these fugitives perished, some being knocked down in their attempts to get on board the vessels, and others, even when in the boats, being baptized through their weight."

Alluding to the fate of the Byzantians who endeavored to escape the siege by taking to the sea, he says: "Some of those, from the extreme violence of the wind, were baptized."

2. Baptism Among the Greeks—"The native Greeks must understand their own language better than foreigners, and they have always understood the word baptism to signify dipping; and therefore from their first embracing of Christianity to this day they have always baptized, and do yet baptize, by immersion."—Robinson.

3. Early Form of Christian Baptism—History furnishes ample proof that in the first century after the death of Christ, baptism was administered solely by immersion. Tertullian thus refers to the immersion ceremony common in his day: "There is no difference whether one is washed in a sea or in a pool, in a river or in a fountain, in a lake or in a channel. * * * We are immersed in the water."

The following are but a few of the instances on record (see *Millennial Star,* vol. 21, pp. 769, 770):

Justin Martyr describes the ceremony as practised by himself. First describing the preparatory examination of the candidate, he proceeds: "After that they are led by us to where there is water, and are born again in that kind of new birth by which we ourselves were born again. For upon the name God, the Father and Lord of all, and of Jesus Christ, our Savior, and of the Holy Spirit, the immersion in water is performed, because the Christ hath also said, 'Except a man be born again, he cannot enter into the kingdom of heaven.'"

Bishop Bennett says concerning the practises of the early Christians: "They led them into the water and laid them down in the water as a man is laid in a grave; and then they said these words, 'I baptize (or wash) thee in the name of the Father, Son, and Holy Ghost'; then they raised them up again, and clean garments were put on them; from whence came the phrases of being baptized into Christ's death, of being buried with Him by baptism into death, of our being risen with Christ, and of our putting on the Lord Jesus Christ, of putting off the old man, and putting on the new."

"That the apostles immersed whom they baptized there is no doubt. And that the ancient church followed their example is very clearly evinced by innumerable testimonies of the fathers."—*Vossius.*

"Burying as it were the person baptized in the water, and raising him out again, without question was anciently the more usual method."—*Archbishop Secker.*

"'Immerson' was the usual method in which baptism was administered in the early Church. * * * Immersion was undoubtedly a common mode of administering baptism, and was not discontinued when infant baptism prevailed.

* * * Sprinkling gradually took the place of immersion without any formal renunciation of the latter."—*Canon Farrar.*

4. The Fathers and the Children—"The revelation in our day of the doctrine of baptism for the dead may be said to have constituted a new epoch in the history of our race. At the time the Prophet Joseph received that revelation, the belief was general in Christendom that at death the destiny of the soul was fixed irrevocably and for all eternity. If not rewarded with endless happiness, then endless torment was its doom, beyond all possibility of redemption or change. The horrible and monstrous doctrine, so much at variance with every element of divine justice, was generally believed, that the heathen nations who had died without a knowledge of the true God, and the redemption wrought out by His Son Jesus Christ, would all be eternally consigned to hell. The belief upon this point is illustrated by the reply of a certain bishop to the inquiry of the king of the Franks, when the king was about to submit to baptism at the hands of the bishop. The king was a heathen, but had concluded to accept the form of religion then called Christianity. The thought occurred to him that if baptism were necessary for his salvation, what had become of his dear ancestors who had died heathens? This thought framed itself into an inquiry which he addressed to the bishop. The prelate, less politic than many of his sect, bluntly told him they had gone to hell. 'Then, by Thor, I will go there with them,' said the king, and thereupon refused to accept baptism or become a Christian."—Geo. Q. Cannon's *Life of Joseph Smith,* p. 510.

5. Temples and Sacred Places—"When the Lord brought Israel out of Egypt, determined to make that people a nation to himself, as soon as they had arrived at a safe distance from surrounding peoples, he required them to build a tabernacle, which is sometimes called the temple, wherein he could institute certain ordinances and regulations for their guidance and worship. This, at the commencement of their pilgrimage in the wilderness, was made portable, and of the costliest and best material within their reach; and one of the tribes was set apart to have charge of it and its appurtenances. Such has ever been the purpose of the Lord. This served them through their journey and in the promised Canaan, until suitable wealth enabled Solomon to erect a magnificent Temple on Mount Moriah, since called the Hill of Zion, to which all Israel came annually to worship or attend conference. The Lord has informed us (D&C 124:39) that his people are always commanded to build temples, or holy houses, unto his holy name. This accounts for our reading in the *Book of Mormon* of so many temples having been erected on this continent. It also explains why the Prophet Joseph so early taught the commencement of a temple in every important location of the saints."—*Compendium,* F. D. Richards and J. A. Little, pp. 283–288. Consult: Exo., chaps. 25–28; 1 Kings, chaps. 6–8; Ezra, chap. 6; 2 Nephi 5:16; and compare Jacob 1:17; 2:2–11; Mosiah 1:18; 2:6, 7; Alma 16:13; 23:2; 26:29; Helaman 3:9; 10:8; D&C 84:3, 5, 31; 97:10; 124:29–51, 55. See *Temples,* J. M. Sjodahl, Salt Lake City, 1892. See *The House of the Lord, a Study of Holy Sanctuaries, Ancient and Modern,* by James E. Talmage, Salt Lake City, 1912.

APPENDIX 8—Notes Relating to Chapter 8

1. Effect of the Holy Ghost on the Individual—"An intelligent being, in the image of God, possesses every organ, attribute, sense, sympathy, affection, of will, wisdom, love, power and gift, which is possessed by God himself. But these are possessed by man in his rudimental state in a subordinate sense of the word. Or, in other words, these attributes are in embryo, and are to be gradually developed. They resemble a bud, a germ, which gradually develops into bloom, and then, by progress, produces the mature fruit after its own kind. The gift of the Holy Spirit adapts itself to all these organs or attributes. It quickens all the intellectual faculties, increases, enlarges, expands, and purifies all the natural passions and affections, and adapts them by the gift of wisdom to their lawful use. It inspires, develops, cultivates, and matures all the fine-toned sympathies, joys, tastes, kindred feelings, and affections of our nature. It inspires virtue, kindness, goodness, tenderness, gentleness, and charity. It develops beauty of person, form and features. It tends to health, vigor, animation, and social feeling. It develops and invigorates all the faculties of the physical and intellectual man. It strengthens, invigorates, and gives tone to the nerves. In short, it is, as it were, marrow to the bone, joy to the heart, light to the eyes, music to the ears, and life to the whole being."—Parley P. Pratt, *Key to Theology,* pp. 96, 97 (4th ed.).

2. The Laying on of Hands—From the scriptures cited it is plain that the usual mode of bestowing the gift of the Holy Ghost consisted in part in the imposition of hands by those in authority (Acts 8:17; 9:17; 19:2–6; Alma 31:36; 3 Nephi 18:36, 37; D&C 20:41). The same outward sign has marked other authoritative acts; for example, ordination to the Priesthood, and administration to the afflicted. It is probable that Paul had reference to Timothy's ordination when he exhorted him thus: "Neglect not the gift that is in thee, which was given thee by prophecy, with the laying on of the hands of the presbytery" (1 Tim. 4:14). And again, "Stir up the gift of God, which is in thee by the putting on of my hands" (2 Tim. 1:6). The first ordination to the Priesthood in latter times was done by the imposition of hands by John the Baptist (D&C sec. 13). That Christ in healing the sick sometimes laid His hands upon the afflicted ones is certain (Mark 6:5); and He left with the apostles a promise that healing should follow the authoritative laying on of hands (Mark 16:15, 18). The same promise has been repeated in this day (D&C 42:43, 44). Yet, notwithstanding the importance given to this sign of authority, the laying on of hands is but exceptional among the practises of the many sects professing Christianity today.

3. Operation of the Holy Ghost—The means through which the Holy Ghost operates are no more truly the Holy Ghost in person than the light and heat and actinic energy of the sun are the sun itself. The influence, spirit, or power of the Holy Ghost is that of enlightenment and progression, and this is given unto men in proportion to their receptiveness and worthiness; but the right to the special ministrations of the third member of the Godhead is obtainable only through compliance with the preliminary requirements of the Gospel—faith, repentance, and baptism. The terms "Spirit" and "Ghost" occur in the scriptures frequently without differentiation. The Holy Ghost is an individual personage, the third member of the Godhead; the Holy Spirit, in a distinctive sense, is the "divine essence" by means of which the Godhead operates upon man and in nature.—See *Jesus the Christ,* p. 720.

4. Mode of Conferring the Holy Ghost—Questions may arise as to the mode of confirmation and bestowal of the Holy Ghost, particularly as to the propriety of saying: *Receive the Holy Ghost;* or *Receive the gift of the Holy Ghost.* Since the companionship of the Holy Ghost embraces all the spiritual graces and gifts in so far as such are deserved by and appropriate to the person, the Church teaches that officiating elders in confirming baptized candidates should use the form: *Receive the Holy Ghost.*

In explaining the reception of the Holy Ghost by the apostles of old, the First Presidency of the Church issued an instructive statement Feb. 5, 1916—See *Deseret News* of that date, and *Improvement Era,* March, 1916; and for excerpt from same see *Jesus the Christ,* p. 720.

APPENDIX 9—Notes Relating to Chapter 9

1. The Term "Sacrament" is used with both general and specific meanings. According to derivation it signifies a sacred thing or holy ordinance, and with this meaning it is applied by different sects to several ceremonies of their churches. Thus, the Protestants speak of two sacraments—

baptism and the Lord's Supper; the Roman and Greek Catholics recognize seven sacraments—the two named above, and also confirmation, matrimony, the bestowal of church orders, penance, and extreme unction. Some sections of the Greek church are said to exclude confirmation and extreme unction from among the seven sacraments. Specifically, however, the word denotes the Lord's Supper. Eucharist and Holy Communion are terms employed in certain churches as synonymous with the Sacrament of the Lord's Supper. From the custom of regarding the ceremony of communion, that is, the partaking of the sacrament, as an evidence of standing in any church, and from the rule which withholds this privilege from those who are judged to be unworthy of fellowship, comes the term *excommunicate,* as applied to deprivation of church fellowship, meaning literally to cast out from communion.

2. The Lord's Supper—As stated, this designation of the sacrament occurs but once in the Bible. The "Lord's Supper" is referred to by Paul in his first epistle to the Corinthians. In all probability this name was used because the rite was first administered at the time of the evening meal. However, the *deipnon* or evening supper among the Jews was the principal meal of the day, and really corresponded to our dinner.

3. The Passover and the Sacrament—The Feast of the Passover was the chief of the annual ceremonials of the Jews, and derived its name from the circumstances of its origin. In setting His hand to deliver Israel from the bondage of Egypt the Lord wrought many miracles and wonders before Pharaoh and his idolatrous house; and, as the last of the ten plagues to which the Egyptians were subjected, the first-born of every household was smitten with death during a single night. By previous command, the Israelites had marked the posts and lintels of their doorways with the blood of a lamb slain for the occasion, the blood having been sprinkled from a bunch of hyssop. Death passed over the houses so marked (Exo. 12:12, 13); while in all the Egyptian homes the fatal stroke fell. Hence arises the name Passover, from *pasach,* to pass by. The flesh of the paschal lamb was eaten amid the haste of departure. To commemorate their deliverance from bondage, the Lord required of the Israelites an annual celebration of this event, the occasion being known as the Feast of the Passover, also as the Feast of Unleavened Bread, the latter name arising from the Lord's command that during the specified time of the observance no leaven should be found in the houses of the people (Exo. 12:15); and the occasion of the feast was to be taken advantage of for instructing the children concerning the merciful dealings of God with their forefathers (Exo. 12:26, 27). But aside from its commemorative purpose, the Passover became to the people a type of the sacrifice on Calvary. Paul says, "Christ our passover is sacrificed for us" (1 Cor. 5:7). As being typical of the future atoning death of Christ the Passover lost part of its significance by the crucifixion, and was superseded by the sacrament. There is perhaps no closer relation between the two than this. Surely the sacrament was not designed to fully supplant the Passover, for the latter was established as a perpetually recurring feast: "And this day shall be unto you for a memorial; and ye shall keep it a feast to the Lord throughout your generations; ye shall keep it a feast by an ordinance forever" (Exo. 12:14).

4. Errors Concerning the Sacrament, and its signification, and the manner of administering it, grew rapidly during the early centuries of the Christian era. As soon as the power of the Priesthood had departed much disputation arose in matters of ordinance, and the observance of the sacrament became distorted. Theological teachers strove to foster the idea that there was much mystery attending this naturally simple and most impressive rite; that all who were not in full communion with the Church should be excluded, not only from participation in the ordinance, which was justifiable, but from the privilege of witnessing the service, lest they profane the mystic rite by their unhallowed presence. Then arose the heresy of transubstantiation—which held that the sacramental emblems by the ceremony of consecration lost their natural character of simple bread and wine, and became in reality flesh and blood—actually parts of the crucified body of Christ. Argument against such dogmas is unnecessary. Then followed the veneration of the emblems by the people, the bread and wine, regarded as part of Christ's body, being elevated in the mass for the adoration of the people; and later, the custom of suppressing half of the sacrament was introduced. By the innovation last mentioned, only the bread was administered, the dogmatic assertion being that both the body and the blood were represented in some mystical way in one of the "elements." Certain it is, that Christ required his disciples to both eat and drink in remembrance of Him. See *The Great Apostasy,* pp. 119, 128.

APPENDIX 10—Notes Relating to Chapter 10

1. Authority Given of God—"The most comprehensive evidence that Joseph Smith received the authority and power of the Holy Priesthood, is that the works of John the Baptist, of Jesus and His apostles, are being again done on the earth by his administration. To receive the powers of this priesthood, it is necessary that men should obey the laws and ordinances of the gospel. The Lord has personally appeared to some men, and covenanted with them as He did with Abraham (see Gen. 12:1–3; 13:14–17). The Lord also personally called and authorized His twelve Jewish apostles. So fully were they authorized to labor for Him, and act in His name, that He said to them: 'He that receiveth you receiveth me, and he that receiveth me receiveth him that sent me' (Matt. 10:40). More generally, it is from the prophets and apostles of Christ that men receive the priesthood. Many received it under the hands of the apostles of the first gospel dispensation. Those who have received it in this latter-day dispensation, have received it from Joseph Smith and Oliver Cowdery; and, in doing so, have received it through a legitimate channel from God the Father and His Son Jesus Christ. Those who have received this priesthood have covenanted with God the Father, and He with them. This is evidently the view taken of the subject in the above passage quoted from Matthew. The doctrine is more fully illustrated: 'All they who receive this priesthood receive me, saith the Lord; For he that receiveth my servants receiveth me; And he that receiveth me receiveth my Father; And he that receiveth my Father receiveth my Father's kingdom; therefore all that my Father hath shall be given unto him. And this is according to the oath and covenant which belongeth to the priesthood" (D&C 84: 35–39).—*Compendium,* F. D. Richards and J. A. Little, p. 66, 67.

2. Foreordination and Foreknowledge—In a note to the author, Elder J. M. Sjodahl of the Church Historian's Office, says: "The doctrine of foreordination, or election as it is also called, appears to me to be set forth in scripture for the purpose of showing us that God acts independently of human advice to bring about His objects and carry out His plans for the benefit of all. It gives us to understand that the success of the kingdom of Christ is absolutely secured, notwithstanding the unbelief and actual enmity of all adversaries. Foreordination takes into consideration repentance, faith, and obedience on the part of man, although unbelief and disobedience cannot prevent, but only retard, the divine plan. God is sovereign in His kingdom; that is the great truth taught as the doctrine of foreordination.

"The true relationship of foreknowledge to foreordination is difficult to explain. God fore-tells, through His prophets, for instance, the division of the kingdom of Solomon, the captivity of Israel, and the very place of the exile. Human reason would naturally conclude that if God saw that these things were to happen, then they *had* to happen, no matter what man would do. But history shows that they came about through the sins of the rulers and the people, and that the Lord warned them incessantly against these sins, as if anxious to prevent the predictions from coming true. The very disobedience to the warnings became the immediate justification for the punishment predicted. Could the people have repented and averted the calamities predicted and foreseen? If so, how could they have been foreseen, except conditionally? Perhaps the history of Jonah and Nineveh, by showing that repentance averts disaster even when predicted, offers the only satisfactory answer to that question."

3. Spiritual Creations—The preexistent condition is not characteristic of human souls alone; all things of earth have a spiritual being of which the temporal structure forms but the counter-part. We read of the creation of "every plant of the field before it was in the earth, and every herb of the field before it grew" (Gen. 2:5). This is set forth with greater fulness in another revelation to Moses: "These are the generations of the heaven and of the earth, when they were created, in the day that I, the Lord God, made the heaven and the earth; And every plant of the field before it was in the earth, and every herb of the field before it grew. For I, the Lord God, created all things of which I have spoken, spiritually before they were naturally upon the face of the earth. * * * And I, the Lord God, had created all the children of men, and not yet a man to till the ground; for in heaven created I them; and there was not yet flesh upon the earth, neither in the water, neither in the air; But I, the Lord God, spake, and there went up a mist from the earth, and watered the whole face of the ground. And I, the Lord God, formed man from the dust of the ground, and breathed into his nostrils the breath of life; and man became a living soul, the first flesh upon the earth, the first man also; nevertheless, all things were before created, but spir-itually were they created and made according to my word."—P.of G.P., Moses 3:4–7.

APPENDIX 11—Notes Relating to Chapter 11

1. Degeneracy of Worship Incident to the Apostasy—That, as the Priesthood disappeared from the earth after the apostolic period, the forms of worship were perverted, while many pagan influences and practices crept in, may be reasonably inferred from the records of history. Mosheim, an authority of note in ecclesiastical history, has this to say regarding pagan innovations during the fourth century: "The Christian bishops introduced, with but slight alterations, into the Christian worship, those rites and institutions by which, formerly, the Greeks and Romans and other nations had manifested their piety and reverence towards their imaginary deities; sup-posing that the people would more readily embrace Christianity if they saw that the rites handed down to them from their fathers still existed unchanged among the Christians, and perceived that Christ and the martyrs were worshiped in the same manner as formerly their gods were. There was, of course, little difference, in these times, between the public worship of the Christians and that of the Greeks and Romans. In both alike, there were splendid robes, mitres, tiaras, wax tapers, crosiers, processions, illustrations, images, golden and silver vases, and numberless other things."

Of the form of professedly Christian worship in the fifth century, the same authority says: "Public worship everywhere assumed a form more calculated for show and for the gratification of the eye. Various ornaments were added to the sacerdotal garments, in order to increase the veneration of the people for the clerical order. * * * In some places it was appointed that the praises of God should be sung perpetually night and day, the singers succeeding each other without interruption: as if the Supreme Being took pleasure in clamor and noise, and in the flatteries of men. The magnificence of the temples knew no bounds. Splendid images were placed in them; * * * the image of the Virgin Mary holding her infant in her arms occupied the most conspicuous place."

2. Early Beginning of the Apostasy—Orson Pratt, an apostle of the present age, has written as follows concerning the early falling away from the authorized practises of the Church: "The great apostasy of the Christian church commenced in the first century, while there were yet inspired apostles and prophets in their midst; hence Paul, just previous to his martyrdom, enumerates a great number who had 'made shipwreck of their faith,' and 'turned aside into vain jangling,' teaching 'that the resurrection was already past;' giving 'heed to fables and endless genealogies;' 'doubting about questions and strifes of words whereof come envyings, railings, evil surmisings, perverse disputings of men of corrupt minds, and destitute of the truth, supposing that gain is godliness.' This apostasy had become so general that Paul declares to Timothy 'that all they which are in Asia be turned away from me;' and again he says 'at my first answer, no man stood with me, but all men forsook me;' he further states that 'there are many unruly, and vain talkers, deceivers,' 'teaching things which they ought not, for filthy lucre's sake.' These apostates, no doubt, pretended to be very righteous, 'for,' says the apostle, 'they profess that they know God, but in works they deny him, being abominable and disobedient, and unto every good work reprobate.'"

3. The Rule of the Priesthood—That the power of the Priesthood is to be exercised in the spirit of patience and love, and not in opposition to individual free agency, is apparent from many scriptures, among which is the following: "Behold, there are many called, but few are chosen. And why are they not chosen? Because their hearts are set so much upon the things of this world, and aspire to the honors of men, that they do not learn this one lesson—That the rights of the priesthood are inseparably connected with the powers of heaven, and that the powers of heaven cannot be controlled nor handled only upon the principles of righteousness. That they may be conferred upon us, it is true; but when we undertake to cover our sins, or to gratify our pride, our vain ambition, or to exercise control or dominion or compulsion upon the souls of the children of men, in any degree of unrighteousness, behold, the heavens withdraw themselves; the Spirit of the Lord is grieved; and when it is withdrawn, Amen to the priesthood or the authority of that man. Behold, ere he is aware, he is left unto himself, to kick against the pricks; to persecute the saints; and to fight against God. We have learned by sad experience that it is the nature and disposition of almost all men, as soon as they get a little authority, as they suppose, they will immediately begin to exercise unrighteous dominion. Hence many are called, but few are chosen. No power or influence can or ought to be maintained by virtue of the priesthood, only by persuasion, by longsuffering, by gentleness and meekness, and by love unfeigned; By kindness, and pure knowledge, which shall greatly enlarge the soul without hypocrisy and without guile—Reproving betimes with sharpness, when moved upon by the Holy Ghost; and then showing forth afterwards an increase of love toward him whom thou hast reproved, lest he esteem thee to be his enemy; That he may know that thy faithfulness is stronger than the cords of death. Let thy bowels also be full of charity towards all men, and to the household of faith, and let virtue garnish thy thoughts unceasingly; then shall thy confidence wax strong in the presence of God; and the doctrine of the priesthood shall distil upon thy soul as the dews from heaven. The Holy Ghost shall be thy constant companion, and thy scepter an unchanging scepter of righteousness and truth; and thy dominion shall be an everlasting dominion, and without compulsory means it shall flow unto thee forever and ever."—D&C 121:34–46.

APPENDIX 12—Notes Relating to Chapter 12

1. A Seeming Miracle—It is stated that Herr Werner Siemens, a German scientist of note, visited the pyramid of Gizeh, and accompanied by a couple of Arab guides, climbed to the top. He observed that the atmospheric conditions were very favorable to electric manifestations. Fastening a large brass button to an empty water-gourd in the hands of one of the Arabs, and then placing his knuckle within a short distance from the button, he drew therefrom a succession of brilliant sparks, accompanied of course by the crackling noises characteristic of electric discharges. The guides viewed this exhibition of supernatural powers with amazement and terror, which reached a climax when their master stretched his staff above his head, and the stick was surmounted by a beautiful St. Elmo's flame. This spectacle was more than the superstitious Bedouins could bear, they trembled before an enchanter who could play with lightning and fire as with a toy, and who carried miniature thunder in his coat pocket; so they fled down the steps with dangerous precipitation, and soon disappeared in the desert.

2. The Term "Prophet" appears in the English Bible as the translation of a number of ancient terms, the most usual of which is *nabhi* (Hebrew), signifying "to bubble forth like a fountain." Another of the original words is *rheo* (Greek), meaning "to flow," and by derivation, "to speak forth," "to utter," "to declare." A prophet then, is one from whom flow forth the words of a higher authority. Aaron is spoken of as a prophet or spokesman to Moses (Exo. 7:1); but in the usual sense, the prophet is the representative of God. Closely allied with the calling of the prophet is that of the seer; indeed, at a time prior to that of Samuel, the common designation of the oracle of God was seer: "for he that is now called a Prophet was beforetime called a Seer" (1 Sam. 9:9). The seer was permitted to behold the visions of God, the prophet to declare the truths so learned; the two callings were usually united in the same person. Unto the prophet and seer the Lord usually communicated in visions and dreams; but exceptions to this order were made as in the case of Moses, who was so faithful in all things good that the Lord communed with him face to face (Num. 12:6–8).

3. Prophets Organized—The prophet's office existed among men in the earliest periods of history. Adam was a prophet (D&C 107:53–56); as also were Enoch (Jude 14; P.of G.P., Moses 6:26), Noah (Gen., chaps. 6, 7; P.of G.P., Moses 8:19; 2 Peter 2:5), Abraham (Gen. 20:7), Moses (Deut. 34:10), and a multitude of others who ministered at intermediate and subsequent times. Samuel, who was established in the eyes of all Israel as a prophet of the Lord (1 Sam. 3:19, 20), organized the prophets into a society for common instruction and edification. He established schools for the prophets, where men were trained in things pertaining to holy offices; the students were generally called "sons of the prophets" (1 Kings 20:35; 2 Kings 2:3, 5, 7; 4:1, 38; 9:1). Such schools were established at Ramah (1 Sam. 19:19, 20), Bethel (2 Kings 2:3), Jericho (2 Kings 2:5), Gilgal (2 Kings 4:38). The members seem to have lived together as a society (2 Kings 6:1–4). In the present dispensation, a similar organization was effected under the direction of the prophet Joseph Smith; this also received the name of the School of the Prophets.

4. The Decline of Spiritual Gifts in Former Days is admitted by many authorities on ecclesiastical history and Christian doctrine. As an instance of this kind of testimony to the departure of the spiritual graces from the apostate church, the following words of John Wesley may be applied: "It does not appear that these extraordinary gifts of the Holy Spirit were common in the church for more than two or three centuries. We seldom hear of them after that fatal period when the emperor Constantine called himself a Christian, and from a vain imagination of promoting the Christian cause thereby, heaped riches and power and honor upon Christians in general, but in particular upon the Christian clergy. From this time they almost totally ceased; very few instances of the kind were found. The cause of this was not as has been supposed because there was no more occasion for them—because all the world was become Christians. This is a miserable mistake; not a twentieth part of it was then nominally Christian. The real cause of it was the love of many, almost all Christians, so called, was waxed cold. The Christians had no more of the Spirit of Christ than the other heathens. The Son of Man, when he came to examine His Church, could hardly find faith upon the earth. This was the real cause why the extraordinary gifts of the Holy Ghost were no longer to be found in the Christian Church—because the Christians were turned heathens again, and only had a dead form left."—*Wesley's Works,* vol. 7, 89:26, 27.

5. Sectarian Views Concerning Continuance or Decline of Spiritual Gifts—"Protestant writers insist that the age of miracles closed with the fourth or fifth century, and that after that the extraordinary gifts of the Holy Ghost must not be looked for. Catholic writers, on the other hand, insist that the power to perform miracles has always continued in the Church; yet those spiritual manifestations which they describe after the fourth and fifth centuries savor of invention on the part of the priests, and childish incredulity on the part of the people; or else, what is claimed to be miraculous falls far short of the power and dignity of those spiritual manifestations which the primitive church was wont to witness. The virtues and prodigies, ascribed to the bones and other relics of the martyrs and saints, are puerile in comparison with the healings by the anointing with oil and the laying on of hands, speaking in tongues, interpretations, prophecies, revelations, casting out devils in the name of Jesus Christ; to say nothing of the gifts of faith, wisdom, knowledge, discernment of spirits, etc.—common in the Church in the days of the apostles (1 Cor. 12:8–10). Nor is there anything in the scriptures or in reason that would lead one to believe that they were to be discontinued. Still this plea is made by modern Christians—explaining the absence of these spiritual powers among them—that the extraordinary gifts of the Holy Ghost were only intended to accompany the proclamation of the gospel during the first few centuries, until the Church was able to make its way without them, and they were to be done away. It is sufficient to remark upon this, that it is assumption pure and simple, and stands without warrant either of scripture or right reason; and proves that men had so far changed the religion of Jesus Christ that it became a form of godliness without the power thereof."—Elder B. H. Roberts, *Outlines of Ecclesiastical History,* part 2, sec. 5:6–8.

6. Miracles an Aid to Spiritual Growth—Apostle Orson Pratt, commenting on the utterances of Paul concerning the passing away of certain spiritual gifts (1 Cor, chap. 13), writes in part as follows: "The Church in its militant and imperfect state, compared with its triumphant, immortal, and perfect state, is (in the 11th verse) represented by the two very different states of childhood and manhood. 'When,' says St. Paul, 'I was a child, I spake as a child, I understood as a child, I thought as a child: but when I became a man, I put away childish things.' In the various stages of education from childhood to manhood, certain indispensable rules, and diagrams, and scientific instruments are employed for the use and benefit of the pupil, that he may acquire a correct knowledge of the sciences, and be perfected in his studies. When the principles have been once acquired, and the student has been perfected in every branch of education, he can dispense with many of his maps, charts, globes, books, diagrams, etc.; as being, like childish things, no longer necessary; they were useful before his education was perfected, in imparting the desired knowledge, but having fulfilled their purposes, he no longer needs their assistance. * * * So it is with the Church in relation to spiritual gifts. While in this state of existence it is represented as a child: prophecy, revelations, tongues, and other spiritual gifts are the instruments of education. The child, or Church, can no more be perfected in its education without the aid of these gifts as instruments, than the chemist could in his researches if he were deprived of the necessary apparatus for experiments. As the chemist needs his laboratory for experiments, as long as there remains any undiscovered truths in relation to the elements and compounds of our globe, so does the Church need the great laboratory of spiritual knowledge—namely, revelation and prophecy— as long as it knows only in part. * * * As a human being, when a child, speaks as a child, understands as a child, and thinks as a child, so does the Church in this state of existence know only in part; but as the child, when it becomes a man, puts away childish things, so will the Church put away such childish things as 'prophesy in part,' 'knowledge in part,' and 'seeing in part,' when it grows up, through the aid of these things, to a perfect man in Christ Jesus; that which is in part will be done away or merged into the greater fulness of knowledge which there reigns."—*Divine Authenticity of the Book of Mormon,* 1:15.

But none of these gifts will be done away as long as the occasion for their exercise continues. That this was the conviction of Apostle Orson Pratt, whose words are quoted above, is evident from the following utterances by the same authority: "The affliction of devils, the confusion of tongues, deadly poisons and sickness, are all curses which have been introduced into the world by the wickedness of man. The blessings of the gospel are bestowed to counteract these curses. Therefore, as long as these curses exist, the promised signs [Mark 16:16–18; D&C 84:65–72] are needed to counteract their evil consequences. If Jesus had not intended that the blessings should be as extensive and unlimited in point of time as the curses, He would have intimated something to that effect in His word. But when He makes a universal promise of certain powers, to enable every believer in the gospel throughout the world to overcome certain curses, entailed upon man because of wickedness, it would be the rankest kind of infidelity not to believe the promised blessing necessary, as long as the curses abound among men."

7. **Modern Manifestations**—The official and incidental publications of the Church abound in instances of miraculous manifestations during the current dispensation. A number of authenticated accounts with many cases are to be found as follows: Orson Pratt's *Divine Authenticity of the Book of Mormon,* chap. 5; B. H. Roberts' *A New Witness for God,* chap. 18.

For a brief treatment of "The Attitude of Science towards Miracles," see *Jesus the Christ,* p. 151. Note 7—summary of an article published by the Victoria Institute or Philosophical Society of Great Britain.

APPENDIX 13—Notes Relating to Chapter 13

1. **John Chrysostom,** one of the Greek "Christian Fathers," flourished during the latter half of the fourth century; he was patriarch of Constantinople, but was deposed and exiled some time

before his death, which occurred in 407. His use of the term *biblia* to designate the scriptural canon is among the earliest applications yet found. He entreated his people to avail themselves of the riches of inspired works in this wise: "Hear, I exhort, all yet in secular life, and purchase *biblia,* the medicine of the soul." Speaking of the Jewish Christians, he says: "They have the *biblia,* but we have the treasures of the *biblia;* they have the letters, we have the letters and the understanding."

As to the errors of translation or mistakes due to other causes, Bengel, a German Lutheran theologian, who died in 1752, is quoted as having written: "Eat the scripture bread in simplicity, just as you have it; and do not be disturbed if here and there you find a grain of sand, which the mill-stone may have suffered to pass. If the Holy Scriptures, which have been so often copied, were absolutely without variations, this would be so great a miracle that faith in them would be no longer faith."

2. The Samaritan Copy of the Pentateuch—In his valuable course of lectures on Bible subjects, Elder David McKenzie presented the following, with references to the writings of Horne: "Nine hundred and seventy years before Christ, the nation of Israel was divided into two kingdoms. Both retained the same book of the law. Rivalry prevented either of them from altering or adding to the law. After Israel was carried into Assyria, other nations occupied Samaria. These received the Pentateuch (2 Kings 17:26–28). The language being Hebrew or Phoenician, whereas the Jewish copy was changed into Chaldee, corruption or alteration was thus made impracticable, yet the texts remain almost identical."

3. Versions of the Bible or of Parts Thereof—*The Septuagint:* "Various opinions have been put forth to explain its appellation of *Septuagint;* some say that Ptolemy Philadelphus requested of Eleazar the High Priest a copy of the Hebrew scriptures, and six learned Jews from each tribe (together seventy-two), competent to translate it into Greek; these were shut up in the isle of Pharos, and in seventy-two days they completed their task; as they dictated it, Demetrius Phalereus, the king's chief librarian, transcribed it; but this is now considered a fable. Others say that these same interpreters, having been shut up in separate cells, wrote each one a translation; and so extraordinarily did they all coincide together in words as well as sentiment, that evidence was thus afforded of their inspiration by the Holy Spirit; this opinion has also been set aside as too extravagant. It is very possible that seventy-two writers were employed in the translation; but it is more probable that it acquired the name of *Septuagint* from having received the approbation of the Jewish Sanhedrin, which consisted of seventy-two persons. Some affirm it to have been executed at different times; and Horne says it is most probable that this version was made during the joint reigns of Ptolemy Lagus and his son Philadelphus, about 285 or 286 B.C."

The Vulgate: "There was a very ancient version of the Bible translated from the Septuagint into Latin, but by whom and when is unknown. It was in general use in the time of Jerome, and was called the *Itala* or *Italic Version.* About the close of the fourth century, Jerome began a new translation into Latin from the Hebrew text, which he gradually completed. It at last gained the approbation of Pope Gregory I, and has been used ever since the seventh century. The present Vulgate, declared authentic by the Council of Trent in the sixteenth century, is the ancient Italic version, revised and improved by the corrections of Jerome and others; and is the only one allowed by the Church of Rome."

The Authorized Version: "Certain objections having been made to the *Bishops' Bible* at the Hampton Court conference in A.D. 1603, King James I directed a new translation to be made. Forty-seven persons, eminent for their piety and biblical learning, were chosen to this end; they were divided into six committees, two to sit at Oxford, two at Cambridge, and two at Westminster; and each committee had a certain portion of the scriptures assigned to it. They began their task in A.D. 1607, and the whole was completed and in print in A.D. 1611. This is called the *Authorized English Version* and is the one now in use."—From *Analysis of Scripture History*, by Pinnock; pp. 3, 5; (6th ed.).

4. The Prophetical Books of the Old Testament are arranged with little or no regard to their chronological order, the extent of the contained matter placing the larger works first. The chronological arrangement would probably be Jonah, Joel, Amos, Hosea, Isaiah, Micah, Nahum, Zephaniah:—all of these prophesied previous to the captivity; then follow Jeremiah, Habakkuk, Ezekiel, and Daniel, who wrote during the captivity; then Haggai, Zechariah, and Malachi, after the return of the Jews from captivity.

5. Manuscript Copies of the New Testament—Three manuscripts of the New Testament writings now in existence are regarded as authentic. These are known as the *Vatican* (now in Rome), the *Alexandrian* (now in London), and the *Sinaitic* (placed in the St. Petersburg library). The last named or Sinaitic is considered to be the oldest copy of the New Testament in existence. The manuscript was discovered in 1859 among the archives of a monastery on Mount Sinai, hence its name. It was found by Tischendorf, and was in the imperial library at St. Petersburg, now Petrograd, Russia.

6. Concerning the Genuineness of Parts of the New Testament—In answer to objections that have been urged by critics in the matter of genuineness or authenticity of certain books of the New Testament, the following array of testimony may be considered. The items are presented here as collated by Elder David McKenzie, and as used by him in his lectures on the Bible.

(1) *The Four Gospels—1. Matthew.* Papias, Bishop of Hierapolis, was a hearer of the Apostle John. With respect to St. Matthew's Gospel, Eusebius quotes him as saying: "Matthew composed the Oracles in the Hebrew tongue, and each one interpreted them as he could."— (Eusebius, *Eccl. Hist.* 3:39.)

2. Mark. Of Mark's writing, Papias also says: "Mark having become the interpreter of Peter, wrote down accurately everything that he remembered, without, however, recording in order what was either said or done by Christ. For neither did he hear the Lord, nor follow Him, but afterward attended Peter, who adapted his instructions to the needs of his hearers, but had no design of giving a connected account of the Lord's oracles (or discourses)."(Bishop Lightfoot's translations, in *Contemporary Review*, August, 1875.)

3. Luke. Internal evidence shows that Luke's Gospel and the Acts of the Apostles were composed by the same author. St. Paul speaks of Luke as a physician; and Dr. Hobart, in 1882, published at London a treatise on *The Medical Language of St. Luke,* and points out the frequent use of medical terms in Luke's writings, permeating the entire extent of the third Gospel, and the Acts of the Apostles. Even M. Renan makes a similar admission. He says: "One point which is beyond question is that the Acts are by the same author as the third Gospel, and are a continuation of that Gospel. One need not stop to prove this proposition, which has never been seriously contested. The prefaces at the commencement of each work, the dedication of each to Theophilus, the perfect resemblance of style and of ideas, furnish on this point abundant demonstrations." "A second proposition is that the author of the Acts is a disciple of Paul, who accompanied him for a considerable part of his travels."—(M. Renan, *The Apostles;* see preface.)

4. John. Irenaeus, Bishop of Lyons, about 177 A.D., a pupil of Polycarp who was martyred in 155 or 156, relates in a letter to a fellow pupil his recollections of what he had heard Polycarp say about his intercourse with John, and with the rest who had seen the Lord; and about the Lord, and about His miracles, and about His teaching. All these he would relate altogether in accordance with *the Scriptures* (Eusebius, Eccl. Hist. 5:20). That Irenaeus meant by "the Scriptures," Matthew, Mark, Luke, and John, is evident from the text. Besides, he urges, "not only that four gospels alone have been handed down from the beginning, but that in the nature of things there could not be more nor less than four. There are four regions in the world, and four principal winds, and the Church, therefore, as destined to be conterminous with the world, must be supported by four gospels as four pillars.—*(Contemporary Review,* August, 1876, p. 413.) [The forced analogy assumed by Irenaeus between the *four* Gospels and the *four* winds, etc., is of course without foundation, and its use appears absurd; nevertheless the fact that he noted it furnishes evidence of the acceptance of the four Gospels in his day.—J. E. T.]

(2) *The Pauline Epistles*—The following extracts from the testimony of the Tubingen critics on four of Paul's epistles, are instructive.

De Wette says, in his introduction to the *Books of the New Testament* (123 a.): "The letters of Paul bear the marks of his powerful genius. The most important of them are raised above all contradiction as to their authenticity; they form the solid kernel of the book of the New Testament.

Baur says, in his *Apostle Paul* (1:8): "Not only has no suspicion of the authenticity of these epistles even arisen, but they bear so incontestably the seal of the originality of Paul that one cannot comprehend for what reason critics could raise any objection to them."

Weizsaeker writes (*Apost. Zeitalter,* 1866, p. 190): "The letters to the Galatians and the Corinthians are, without doubt, from the hand of the Apostle; from his hand also came incontestably the epistle to the Romans."

Holtzmann says (*Einleitein's N. T.,* p. 224): "These four epistles are the Pauline Homologoumena (books universally received) in the modern acceptation of the word. We can realize, with respect to them, the proof of authenticity undertaken by Paley against the freethinkers of his time."

M. Renan in *The Gospels* (pp. 40, 41), thus expresses himself: "The epistles of Paul have an unequaled advantage in this history—that is, their absolute authenticity." Of the Epistles to the Corinthians, the Galatians, and the Romans, Renan speaks as "indisputable and undisputed;" and adds, "The most severe critics, such as Christian Baur, accept them without objection."

7. Archeological Evidence Confirming the Bible—Prof. A. H. Sayce, M. A., sums up his learned treatise on the testimony of the ancient monuments, thus: "The critical objections to the truth of the Old Testament, once drawn from the armory of Greek and Latin writers, can never be urged again; they have been met and overthrown once for all. The answers to them have come from papyrus and clay and stone, from the tombs of ancient Egypt, from the mounds of Babylonia, and from the ruined palaces of the Assyrian kings."

8. Missing Scripture—Those who oppose the doctrine of continual revelation between God and His Church, on the ground that the Bible is complete as a collection of sacred scriptures, and that alleged revelation not found therein must therefore be spurious, may profitably take note of the many books not included in the Bible, yet mentioned therein, generally in such a way as to leave no doubt that they were once regarded as authentic. Among these extra-biblical scriptures, the following may be named; some of them are in existence today, and are classed with the

Apocrypha; but the greater number are unknown. We read of the Book of the Covenant (Exo. *24:7);* Book of the Wars of the Lord (Num. 21:14); Book of Jasher Josh. 10:13); Book of the Statutes (1 Sam. 10:25); Book of Enoch (Jude 14); Book of the Acts of Solomon (1 Kings 11:41); Book of Nathan the Prophet, and that of Gad the Seer (1 Chron. 29:29); Book of Ahijah the Shilonite, and visions of Iddo, the Seer *(2 Chron. 9:29);* Book of Shemaiah *(2 Chron. 12:15);* Story of the Prophet Iddo (2 Chron. 13:22); Book of Jehu (2 Chron. 20:34); the Acts of Uzziah, by Isaiah, the son of Amoz (2 Chron. 26:22); Sayings of the Seers (2 Chron. 33:19); a missing Epistle of Paul to the Corinthians (1 Cor. 5:9); a missing Epistle to the Ephesians (Eph. 3:3); missing Epistle to the Colossians, written from Laodicea (Col. 4:16); a missing Epistle of Jude Jude 3); a declaration of belief mentioned by Luke (1:1).

APPENDIX 14—Notes Relating to Chapter 14

1. Book of Mormon Title Page—"I wish to mention here that the title page of the *Book of Mormon is* a literal translation, taken from the very last leaf on the left hand side of the collection or book of plates, which contained the record which has been translated, the language of the whole running the same as all Hebrew writing in general; and that said title page is not by any means a modern composition, either of mine or any other man who has lived or does live in this generation."—Joseph Smith, HC, vol. 1, p. 71.

2. Theories Concerning the Origin of the Book of Mormon. The Spaulding Story—The true account of the origin of the *Book of Mormon* was rejected by the public in general, who thus assumed the responsibility of explaining in some plausible way the source of the record. Many vague theories, based on the incredible assumption that the book was the work of a single author, were put forward; of these the most famous, and indeed, the only one that lived long enough in public favor to be discussed, is the so-called "Spaulding story." Solomon Spaulding, a clergyman of Amity, Pa., wrote a romance to which no title other than *Manuscript Story* was prefixed. Twenty years after the author's death, a Mr. Hurlburt, an apostate from the Church of Jesus Christ of Latte-day Saints, announced a resemblance between the story and the *Book of Mormon,* and expressed as his opinion that the work presented to the world by Joseph Smith was nothing but Spaulding's romance revised and amplified. The manuscript was lost for a time, and, in the absence of proof to the contrary, stories of the parallelism between the two works multiplied. But, in 1884, President James H. Fairchild of Oberlin College, Ohio, and a literary friend, a Mr. Rice, in examining a heterogeneous collection of old papers that had been purchased by the latter, found the original story. The gentlemen made a careful comparison of the manuscript and the *Book of Mormon,* and, with the sole desire of subserving the purposes of truth, made public their results. President Fairchild published an article in the *New York Observer,* Feb. 5, 1885, in which he said: "The theory of the origin of the *Book of Mormon* in the traditional manuscript of Solomon Spaulding will probably have to be relinquished. * * * Mr. Rice, myself and others compared it [the Spaulding manuscript] with the *Book of Mormon* and could detect no resemblance between the two. * * * Some other explanation of the *Book of Mormon* must be found, if any explanation is re quired."

The manuscript was deposited in the library of Oberlin College, Ohio, where it now reposes. Still, the theory of the *Manuscript Found,* as Spaulding's story has come to be known, is occasionally pressed into service in the cause of anti-"Mormon" zeal, by some whom we will charitably believe to be ignorant of the facts set forth by President Fairchild. A letter of more recent date, written by that gentleman in reply to an inquiring correspondent, was published in the *Millennial Star,* Liverpool, Nov. 3, 1898, and is as follows:

OBERLIN COLLEGE OHIO
October 17, 1895.

J. R. Hindley, Esq.,
DEAR SIR:—We have in our College Library an original manuscript of Solomon Spaulding—unquestionably genuine.

I found it in 1884 in the hands of Hon. L. L. Rice of Honolulu, Hawaiian Islands. He was formerly State Printer at Columbus, O., and before that, publisher of a paper in Painesville, whose preceding publisher had visited Mrs. Spaulding and obtained the manuscript from her. It had lain among his old papers forty years or more, and was brought out by my asking him to look up anti-slavery documents among his papers.

The manuscript has upon it the signatures of several men of Conneaut, O., who had heard Spaulding read it and knew it to be his. No one can see it and question its genuineness. The manuscript has been printed twice at least—once by the Mormons of Salt Lake City, and once by the Josephite Mormons of Iowa. The Utah Mormons obtained the copy of Mr. Rice at Honolulu, and the Josephites got it of me after it came into my possession.

This manuscript is not the original of the Book of Mormon.
Yours very truly,
JAS. H. FAIRCHILD.

Printed copies of the *Manuscript Found* are obtainable, and any inquirer may examine for himself. For further information, see *The Myth of the Manuscript Found,* by Elder George Reynolds, Salt Lake City; Whitney's *History of Utah,* vol. 1, pp. 46–56; Elder George Reynolds' preface to the story as issued by the Deseret News Company, Salt Lake City, 1886; and the story itself. See also three articles by Pres. Joseph F. Smith in *Improvement Era,* vol. 3, pp. 241, 377, 451. See critical treatment in *The Real Mormonism,* chap. 3, by Robert C. Webb, New York, 1916.

3. The Three Witnesses—Oliver Cowdery—Born at Wells, Rutland Co., Vermont, October, 1805; baptized May 15, 1829; died at Richmond, Mo., March 3, 1850.

David Whitmer—Born near Harrisburg, Pa., January 7, 1805; baptized June, 1829; excommunicated from the Church, April 13, 1838; died at Richmond, Mo., January 25, 1888.

Martin Harris—Born at Easttown, Saratoga Co., New York, May 18, 1783; baptized 1830; removed to Utah, August, 1870, and died at Clarkston, Cache Co., Utah, July 10, 1875.

4. The Eight Witnesses—Christian Whitmer—Born January 18, 1798; baptized April 11, 1830; died in full fellowship in the Church, Clay County, Missouri, November 27, 1835. He was the eldest son of Peter Whitmer.

Jacob Whitmer—Second son of Peter Whitmer; born in Pennsylvania, January 27, 1800; baptized April 11, 1830; died April 21, 1856, having previously withdrawn from the Church.

Peter Whitmer, Jr.—Born September 27,1809; fifth son of Peter Whitmer; baptized June, 1829; died a faithful member of the Church, at or near Liberty, Clay Co., Missouri, September 22, 1836.

John Whitmer—Third son of Peter Whitmer; born August 27, 1802; baptized June, 1829; excommunicated from the Church March 10, 1838; died at Far West, Missouri, July 11, 1878.

Hiram Page—Born in Vermont 1800; baptized April 11, 1830; withdrew from the Church, 1838; died in Ray Co., Missouri, August 12, 1852.

Joseph Smith, Sr.—The Prophet Joseph's father; born at Topsfield, Essex Co., Mass., July 12, 1771; baptized April 6, 1830; ordained Patriarch to the Church, December 18, 1833; died in full fellowship in the Church at Nauvoo, Ill., Sept. 14, 1840.

Hyrum Smith—Second son of Joseph Smith, Sr., born at Tunbridge, Vt., February 9, 1800; baptized June, 1829; appointed one of the First Presidency of the Church November 7, 1837; Patriarch to the Church January 19, 1841; martyred with his brother, the Prophet, at Carthage, Ill., June 27, 1844.

Samuel Harrison Smith—Born Tunbridge, Vt., March 13, 1808; fourth son of Joseph Smith, Sr., baptized May 15, 1829; died July 30, 1844.

5. Consistency of the Book of Mormon—"If the historical parts of the *Book of Mormon* be compared with what little is known from other sources, concerning the history of ancient America, there will be found much evidence to substantiate its truth; but there cannot be found one truth among all the gleanings of antiquity that clashes with the historical truths of the *Book of Mormon*. If the prophetical part of this wonderful book be compared with the prophetical declarations of the Bible, there will be found much evidence in the latter to establish the truth of the former. But though there are many predictions in the *Book of Mormon,* relating to the great events of the last days, which the Bible gives us no information about, yet there is nothing in the predictions of the Bible that contradicts in the least, the predictions of the *Book of Mormon.* If the doctrinal part of the *Book of Mormon* be compared with the doctrines of the Bible, there will be found the same perfect harmony which we find on the comparison of the prophetical parts of the two books. Although there are many points of the doctrine of Christ that are far more plain and definite in the *Book of Mormon* than in the Bible, and many things revealed in relation to doctrine that never could be fully learned from the Bible, yet there are not any items of doctrine in the two sacred books that contradict each other or clash in the least. If the various books which enter into the collection called the *Book of Mormon* be carefully compared with each other, there will be found nothing contradictory in history, in prophecy, or in doctrine. * * * If we compare the historical, prophetical, and doctrinal parts of the *Book of Mormon* with the great truths of science and nature, we find no contradictions—no absurdities—nothing unreasonable. The most perfect harmony therefore exists between the great truths revealed in the *Book of Mormon* and all other known truths, whether religious, historical, or scientific."—Apostle Orson Pratt in *Divine Authenticity of the Book of Mormon,* p. 56.

APPENDIX 15—Notes Relating to Chapter 15

1. Ishmael an Ephraimite—"The Prophet Joseph Smith informed us that the record of Lehi was contained on the one hundred sixteen pages that were first translated and subsequently stolen, and of which an abridgment is given us in the First Book of Nephi, which is the record of Nephi individually, he himself being of the lineage of Manasseh; but that Ishmael was of the lineage of Ephraim, and that his sons married into Lehi's family, and Lehi's sons married Ishmael's daughters, thus fulfilling the words of Jacob upon Ephraim and Manasseh in the 48th chapter of Genesis [verse 16] which says: 'And let my name be named on them, and the name of my fathers Abraham and Isaac; and let them grow into a multitude in the midst of the earth.' Thus these descendants of Manasseh and Ephraim grew together upon this American continent, with a sprinkling from the house of Judah, from Mulek descended, who left Jerusalem eleven years after Lehi, and founded the colony afterwards known as Zarahemla and found by Mosiah—thus making a combination, an intermixture of Ephraim and Manasseh with the remnants of Judah, and for aught we know, the remnants of some other tribes that might have accompanied Mulek. And such have grown up upon the American continent."—From "Discourse by Apostle Erastus Snow," at Logan, Utah, May 6, 1882; see *Journal of Discourses,* vol. 23, pp. 184, 185.

2. Diversity of Literary Style in the Book of Mormon—"There is a marked difference in the literary style of Nephi and some of the other earlier prophets from that of Mormon and Moroni. Mormon and his son are more direct and take fewer words to express their ideas than did the earlier writers; at least their manner is, to most readers, the more pleasing. Amos, the son of Jacob, has also a style peculiar to himself. There is another noticeable fact that when original records or discourses, such as the record of Limhi, the sermons of Alma, Amulek, etc., the epistles of Helaman, and others, are introduced into Mormon's abridgment, words and expressions are used that appear nowhere else in the *Book of Mormon.* This diversity of style, expression, and wording is a very pleasing incidental testimony to the truth of the claim made for the *Book of Mormon*—that it is a compilation of the work of many writers."—From *Lectures on the Book of Mormon,* by Elder George Reynolds.

3. Mexican Date of the Deluge—In speaking of the time of the Deluge as given by the Mexican author, Ixtilxochitl, Elder George Reynolds says: "There is a remarkable agreement between this writer's statements and the Book of Genesis. The time from the fall to the flood only differs sixty, possibly only five years, if the following statement in the *Book of Doctrine and Covenants* (107:49) regarding Enoch lengthens the chronology: 'And he saw the Lord, and he walked with him, and was before his face continually; and he walked with God three hundred and sixty-five years, making him four hundred and thirty years old when he was translated." The same statement is made in the *Pearl of Great Price* (Moses 7:68).—"External Evidences of the Book of Mormon," by Elder George Reynolds in *Contributor,* vol. 17, p. 274.

4. Ancient Civilization in America—"That a civilization once flourished in these regions [Central America and Mexico] much higher than any the Spanish conquerors found upon their arrival, there can be no doubt. By far the most important work that has been done among the remains of the old Maya civilization has been carried on by the Peabody Museum of Harvard College, through a series of expeditions it has sent to the buried city now called Copan, in Spanish Honduras. In a beautiful valley near the borderland of Guatemala, surrounded by steep mountains and watered by a winding river, the hoary city lies wrapped in the sleep of ages. The ruins at Copan, although in a more advanced state of destruction than those of the Maya cities of Yucatan, have a general similarity to the latter in the design of the buildings, and in the sculptures, while the characters in the inscriptions are essentially the same. It would seem, therefore, that Copan was a city of the Mayas; but if so it must have been one of their most ancient settlements, fallen into decay long before the cities of Yucatan reached their prime. The Maya civilization was totally distinct from the Aztec or Mexican; it was an older and also a much higher civilization. Henry C. Walsh, in article, "Copan—a City of the Dead," *Harper's Weekly,* September, 1897.

The following statements are derived from Bradford's "Conclusions," p. 431, in his *American Antiquities,* published in 1841, relating to the ancient inhabitants of America:

"That they were all of the same origin, branches of the same race, and possessed of similar customs and institutions.

"That they were populous, and occupied a great extent of territory.

"That they had arrived at a considerable degree of civilization, were associated in large communities, and lived in extensive cities.

"That they possessed the use of many of the metals, such as lead, copper, gold, and silver, and probably the art of working in them.

"That they sculptured in stone, and sometimes used that material in the construction of their edifices.

"That they had the knowledge of the arch of receding steps; of the art of pottery, producing urns and utensils formed with taste, and constructed upon the principles of chemical composition; and the art of brick-making.

"That they worked the salt springs, and manufactured salt.

"That they were an agricultural people, living under the influence and protection of regular forms of governments.

"That they possessed a decided system of religion, and a mythology connected with astronomy, which, with its sister science, geometry, was in the hands of the priesthood.

"That they were skilled in the art of fortification.

"That the epoch of their original settlement in the United States is of great antiquity; and that the only indications of their origin to be gathered from the locality of their ruined monuments, point toward Mexico."

5. American Traditions Concerning the Deluge—"Don Francisco Munoz de la Vega, the Bishop of that diocese (Chiapas), certifies in the prologue to his *Diocesan Constitutions,* declaring that an ancient manuscript of the primitive Indians of that province, who had learned the art of writing, was in his record office, who retained the constant tradition that the father and founder of their nation was named Teponahuale, which signifies lord of the hollow piece of wood; and that he was present at the building of the Great Wall, for so they named the Tower of Babel; and beheld with his own eyes the confusion of language; after which event, God, the Creator, commanded him to come to these extensive regions, and to divide them amongst mankind."—Lord Kingsborough, *Mexican Antiquities,* vol. 8, p. 25.

"It is found in the histories of the Toltecs that this age and first world, as they call it, lasted 1,716 years: that men were destroyed by tremendous rains and lightnings from the sky, and even all the land, without the exception of anything, and the highest mountains, were covered up and submerged in water fifteen cubits (caxtolmolatli); and here they added other fables of how men came to multiply from the few who escaped from this destruction in a 'toptlipetlocali'; that this word nearly signifies a close chest; and how, after men had multiplied, they erected a very high 'zacuali,' which is today a tower of great height, in order to take refuge in it should the second world (age) be destroyed. Presently their languages were confused, and, not being able to understand each other, they went to different parts of the earth."—The same, vol. 9, p. 321.

"The most important among the American traditions are the Mexican, for they appear to have been definitely fixed by symbolic and mnemonic paintings before any contact with Europeans. According to these documents, the Noah of the Mexican cataclysm was Coxcox, called by certain people Teocipactli or Tezpi. He had saved himself, together with his wife Xochiquetzal, in a bark, or, according to other traditions, on a raft made of cypress wood (*Cypressus disticha*). Paintings retracing the deluge of Coxcox have been discovered among the Aztecs, Miztecs, Zapotecs, Tlascaltecs, and Mechoacaneses. The tradition of the latter is still more strikingly in conformity with the story as we have it in Genesis, and in Chaldean sources. It tells how Tezpi embarked in a spacious vessel with his wife, his children, and several animals, and grain, whose preservation was essential to the subsistence of the human race. When the great god Tezcatlipoca decreed that the waters should retire, Tezpi sent a vulture from the bark. The bird, feeding on the carcasses with which the earth was laden, did not return. Tezpi sent out other birds, of which the humming bird only came back, with a leafy branch in its beak. Then Tezpi, seeing that the country began to vegetate, left his bark on the mountain of Colhuacan."—Donnelly's *Atlantis,* p. 99.

The tradition of a Deluge "was the received notion, under some form or other, of the most civilized people in the Old World, and of the barbarians of the New. The Aztecs combined with this some particular circumstances of a more arbitrary character, resembling the accounts of the east. They believed that two persons survived the deluge, a man named Coxcox and his wife. Their heads are represented in ancient painting, together with a boat floating on the waters at the foot of a mountain. A dove is also depicted, with a hieroglyphical emblem of language in his mouth, which he is distributing to the children of Coxcox, who were born dumb. The neighboring people of Michoacan, inhabiting the same high plains of the Andes, had a still further tradition, that the boat in which Tezpi, their Noah, escaped, was filled with various kinds of animals and birds. After some time a vulture was sent out from it, but remained feeding on the dead bodies of the giants which had been left on the earth as the waters subsided. The little humming bird, *huitzitzilin,* was then sent forth, and returned with a twig in his mouth. The coincidence of both these accounts with the Hebrew and Chaldean narratives is obvious."—Prescott, *Conquest of Mexico,* Appendix, part 1, p. 386.

6. Survival of the Hebrew Language Among American Tribes—"It is claimed that such survivals are numerous in the religious songs and ceremonies of many of the tribes. A number of writers who visited or resided among the tribes of the northern continent, assert that the words Yehovah, Yah, Ale, and Hallelujah, could be distinctly heard in these exercises. Laet and Escarbotus assure us that they often heard the South American Indians repeat the sacred word Hallelujah."—Elder George Reynolds, "The Language of the Book of Mormon," *Contributor,* Salt Lake City, vol. 17, p. 236.

7. "The Origin of the Pre-Columbian Civilization of America"—Under this title an instructive article by G. Elliot Smith appeared in *Science,* vol. 44, pp. 190–195 (August 11, 1916). As to the interest accorded to the subject, the author says: "In the whole range of ethnological discussion perhaps no theme has evoked livelier controversies and excited more widespread interest than the problems involved in the mysteries of the wonderful civilization that revealed itself to the astonished Spaniards on their first arrival in America.

"During the last century, which can be regarded as covering the whole period of scientific investigation in anthropology, the opinions of those who have devoted attention to such inquiries have undergone the strangest fluctuations. If one delves into the anthropological journals of forty or fifty years ago they will be found to abound in careful studies on the part of many of the leading ethnologists of the time, demonstrating, apparently in a convincing and unquestionable manner, the spread of curious customs or beliefs from the Old World, to the New." The writer decries the fallacy of assuming that similarities in customs and culture of widely separated peoples can be explained on any other basis than that of a common origin, and proceeds as follows: "Why then, it will be asked, in the face of the overwhelming mass of definite and well-authenticated evidence clearly pointing to the sources in the Old World from which American civilization sprung, do so many ethnologists refuse to accept the clear and obvious meaning of the facts and resort to such childish subterfuges as I have mentioned? Putting aside the influence of Darwin's work, the misunderstanding of which, as Huxley remarked, 'led shallow persons to talk nonsense in the name of anthropological science,' the main factor in blinding so many investigators to appreciate the significance of the data they themselves so laboriously collect results from a defect incidental to the nature of their researches. * * * The failure to recognize the fact, recently demonstrated so convincingly by Dr. Rivers, that useful arts are often lost is another, and perhaps the chief, difficulty that has stood in the way of an adequate appreciation of the history of the spread of civilization." Dr. Smith presents an impressive array of evidence pointing to the Old World and specifically to Egypt, as the source of many of the customs by which the American aborigines are distinguished. The article is accompanied by a map showing probable routes of travel from the Old World to the New, and two landing places on the west coast, one in Mexico and another near the boundary common to Peru and Chile, from which place the immigrants spread.

APPENDIX 16—Notes Relating to Chapter 16

1. Freedom Under Inspiration—Faussett has this to say of man's agency under the influence of inspiration: "Inspiration does not divest the writers of their several individualities of style, just as the inspired teachers in the early Church were not passive machines in prophesying (1 Cor. 14:32). 'Where the Spirit of the Lord is, there is liberty' (2 Cor. 3:17). Their will became one with God's will; His Spirit acted on their spirit, so that their individuality had full play in the sphere of His inspiration. As to religious truths, the collective Scriptures have unity of authorship; as to other matters, their authorship is palpably as manifold as the writers. The variety is human, the unity divine. If the four evangelists were mere machines, narrating the same events in the same order and words, they would cease to be independent witnesses. Their very discrepancies (only *seeming* ones) disprove collusion. * * * The slight variations in the decalogue between Exo. 20 and its repetition Deut. 5, and in Ps. 18 compared with 2 Sam. 22, in Ps. 14 compared with Ps. 53, and in New Testament quotations of Old Testament (sometimes from the Septuagint, which varies from the Hebrew, sometimes from neither in every word), all prove the spiritproduced independence of the sacred writers, who, under divine guidance and sanction, presented on different occasions the same substantial truths under different aspects, the one complementing the other."—*Bible Cyclopedia,* A. R. Faussett, p. 308.

2. The Doctrine of No Further Revelation, New and False—"The History of the people of God, from the earliest ages, shows that *continued revelation* was the only way by which they could possibly learn all their duties or God's will concerning them. They never once thought that the revelations given to previous generations were sufficient to guide them into every duty. A doctrine which rejects new revelation is a new doctrine, invented by the devil and his agents during the second century after Christ; it is a doctrine in direct opposition to the one believed in and enjoyed by the saints in all ages. Now, to subvert and do away a doctrine four thousand years old, and introduce a new one in its stead can only be done by divine authority. * * * As the doctrine, then, of continued revelation is one that was always believed by the saints, it ought not to be required of any man to prove the necessity of the continuation of such a doctrine. If it were a new doctrine, never before introduced into the world, it would become necessary to establish its divine origin; but inasmuch as it is only the continuation of an old doctrine, established thousands of years ago, and which has never ceased to be believed and enjoyed by the saints, it would be the greatest presumption to call it in question at this late period; and hence it would seem almost superfluous to undertake to prove the necessity of its continuance. Instead of being required to do this, all people have the right to call upon the new-revelation deniers of the last seventeen centuries to bring forward their strong reasonings and testimonies for breaking in upon the long-established order of heaven, and introducing a new doctrine so entirely different from the old. If they wish their new doctrine to be believed, let them demonstrate it to be of divine origin, or else all people will be justified in rejecting it and clinging to the old."—Orson Pratt, *Divine Authenticity of the Book of Mormon*, I (2) 15, 16.

3. Inspiration—"Inspiration has been defined to be the 'actuating energy of the Holy Spirit, in whatever degree or manner it may have been exercised, guided by which the human agents chosen by God have officially proclaimed his will by word of mouth or have committed to writing the several portions of the Bible.' *By plenary inspiration* we mean that this energy was so fully and perfectly exercised as to make the teaching of the sacred writers to be, in the most literal sense of the words, God's teaching, as proceeding from Him, truly expressing His mind, and bearing with it the sanction of His authority. *By verbal inspiration* we mean that this energy was not exhausted in suggesting to the writers the matter of Scripture, and then leaving them to themselves to convey, in their own manner and after an exclusively human sort, what had been supernaturally suggested; but that they were assisted and guided in the conveyance of the truth received. * * * When the doctrine of plenary and verbal inspiration is thus disentangled from the misapprehensions which have been entertained of it, it presents in no point of view any just ground of objection. It is consistent with all the conclusions relative to the Word which modern scholarship has succeeded in establishing; for the dreams of the 'higher criticism' are little more than the vagaries of arbitrary caprice; and it is much to be regretted that they have been honored with a deference wholly undeserved, and have been rashly placed side by side with the valuable and precious results of genuine criticism. These results, in many respects, point decisively in the direction of plenary inspiration, when the doctrine itself is rightly understood, as supplying the only consistent and logical ground on which the authority of the canonical writings can be safely based."—Cassell's *Bible Dictionary*, pp. 559, 561. Observe that the distinction here specified between *plenary* and *verbal* inspiration, expresses the essential element of difference between *inspiration* and *revelation*.

4. Rational to Believe in Continued Revelation—"Is it unreasonable, is it unphilosophical, thus to look for additional light and knowledge? Shall religion be the one department of human thought and effort in which progression is impossible? What would we say of the chemist, the astronomer, the physicist, or the geologist, who would proclaim that no further discovery or revelation of scientific truth is possible, or who would declare that the only occupation open to students of science is to con the books of bygone times and to apply the principles long ago made known, and that none others shall ever be discovered? The chief motive impelling to research and investigation is the conviction that to knowledge and wisdom there is no end. We affirm that all wisdom is of God, that the halo of His glory is intelligence, and that man has not yet learned all there is to learn of Him and His ways. We hold that the doctrine of continued revelation from God is not less philosophical and scientific than scriptural."—"The Philosophy of 'Mormonism'" by the author, in *The Story and Philosophy of "Mormonism,"* p. 116; Salt Lake City, 1914.

APPENDIX 17—Notes Relating to Chapter 17

1. Hebrews—Shem is called "the father of all the children of Eber," as Ham is called father of Canaan. The Hebrews and Canaanites were often brought into contact, and exhibited the respective characteristics of the Shemites and the Hamites. The term "Hebrews" thus is derived from "Eber" (Gen. 10:21; compare Num. 24:24). *Bible Cyclopedia,* by Faussett.

The writer of the article "Hebrew" in Cassell's *Bible Dictionary* questions the evidence on which the derivation of "Hebrew" from "Eber" or "Heber" is asserted, and says: "All that can be confidently affirmed is that the term is employed of Abraham, and of the descendants of Jacob in general. The interest attaching to the word, coupled with its obscure origin, suffices to account for the many speculations in regard to it. It may be added that some scholars have found the name 'Hebrews,' a little changed, on the monuments of Egypt. If this interpretation is verified, it will be of value, as showing that when the Egyptians called Joseph a Hebrew, they employed the designation which was accepted among them."

2. Jews—The term properly signifies "a man of Judah, or a descendant of Judah, but the word came to be applied to all those who were otherwise designated 'Hebrews.' It does not appear to have come into use until long after the revolt of Jeroboam and the ten tribes, and so long as the kingdom stood it was naturally employed of the citizens of the kingdom of Judah (2 Kings 16:6; 25:25); but it rarely occurs in this sense. After the exile it took the extension of meaning which it has to the present day. It was adopted by the remnants of all the tribes, and was the one name by which the descendants of Jacob were known throughout the ancient world; certainly it was far more common than 'Hebrew.' It occurs in the books of Ezra, Nehemiah, Esther, Daniel, etc., is found in the Apocrypha; and is common in Josephus, and in the New Testament."—Cassell's *Bible Dictionary.*

"Under the theocracy they were known as Hebrews, under the monarchy as Israelites, and during foreign domination as Jews. The modern representatives of this stock call themselves Hebrews in race and language, and Israelites in religion, but Jews in both senses."—*Standard Dictionary.*

3. Zenos—"A Hebrew prophet, often quoted by the Nephite servants of God. All we are told of his personal history is that he was slain because he testified boldly of what God revealed to him. That he was a man greatly blessed of the Lord with the spirit of prophecy is shown by that wonderful and almost incomparable parable of the Vineyard, given at length by Jacob (Jacob, chap. 5). His prophecies are also quoted by Nephi (1 Nephi 19:10, 12, 16), Alma (Alma 33:3, 13, 15), Amulek, Alma (34:7), Samuel the Lamanite (Helaman 15:11), and Mormon (3 Nephi 10:16)."— *Dictionary of the Book of Mormon,* by Elder George Reynolds.

4. The Journeyings of the Lost Tribes—Esdras, whose books, as stated in the next, are classed among the Apocrypha, describes a vision, in the course of which the ten tribes are noticed in this way: "Those are the tribes which were carried away captives out of their own land in the time of Oseas [Hosea] the king, whom Shalmanezer, the king of the Assyrians, took captive, and crossed them beyond the river; so were they brought into another land. But they took counsel to themselves, that they would leave the multitude of the heathen, and go forth into a further country where never man dwelt, that they there might keep their statutes, which they never kept in their own land. And they entered in at the narrow passage of the river Euphrates. For the Most High then showed them signs, and stayed the springs of the flood till they were passed over. For through the country there was a great journey, even of a year and a half, and the same region is called Arsareth (or Ararah). Then dwelt they there until the latter time, and when they come forth again, the Most High shall hold still the springs of the river again, that they may go through."—2 Esdras 13.

Concerning the journeyings of the tribes toward the north, Elder George Reynolds, in his little work *Are We of Israel?* says: "They determined to go to a country 'where never man dwelt,' that they might be free from all contaminating influences. That country could only be found in the north. Southern Asia was already the seat of a comparatively ancient civilization; Egypt flourished in northern Africa; and southern Europe was rapidly filling with the future rulers of the world. They had therefore no choice but to turn their faces northward. The first portion of their journey was not however north; according to the account of Esdras, they appear to have at first moved in the direction of their old home; and it is possible that they originally started with the intention of returning thereto; or probably, in order to deceive the Assyrians, they started as if to return to Canaan, and when they crossed the Euphrates and were out of danger from the hosts of Medes and Persians, then they turned their journeying feet toward the polar star. Esdras states that they entered in at the narrow passage of the river Euphrates, the Lord staying the springs of the flood until they were passed over. The point on the river Euphrates at which they crossed would necessarily be in its upper portion, as lower down would be too far south for their purpose. The upper course of the Euphrates lies among lofty mountains; near the village of Pastash it plunges through a gorge formed by precipices more than a thousand feet in height, and so narrow that it is bridged at the top; it shortly afterward enters the plain of Mesopotamia. How accurately this portion of the river answers to the description of Esdras of the 'Narrows' where the Israelites crossed!"

"The tribes shall come; they are not lost unto the Lord; they shall be brought forth as hath been predicted; and I say unto you there are those now living—aye, some here present—who shall live to read the records of the Lost Tribes of Israel, which shall be made one with the record of the Jews, or the Holy Bible, and the record of the Nephites, or the Book of Mormon, even as the Lord hath predicted; and those records, which the tribes lost to man but yet to be found again shall bring, shall tell of the visit of the resurrected Christ to them, after He had manifested Himself to the Nephites upon this continent."—From address by the author, October 8, *1916*, see Proceedings of 87th Semi-annual Conference of the Church.

APPENDIX 18—Notes Relating to Chapter 18

1. Gathering Now in Progress—The Latter-day Saints "are building up stakes of Zion in the Rocky Mountain valleys, and in this way are fulfilling predictions of the ancient prophets. Isaiah hath it written, 'And it shall come to pass in the last days, that the mountain of the Lord's house shall be established in the top of the mountains, and shall be exalted above the hills; and all nations shall flow unto it. And many people shall go and say, Come ye, and let us go up to the mountain of the Lord, to the house of the God of Jacob; and he will teach us of his ways, and we will walk in his paths; for out of Zion shall go forth the law, and the word of the Lord from Jerusalem' (Isaiah 2:2, 3). It is remarkable how minutely the Latter-day Saints are fulfilling the terms of this prophecy: 1. They are building the temples of God in the tops of the mountains, so that the house of the Lord is truly where Isaiah saw it would be. 2. The saints engaged in this work are people gathered from nearly all the nations under heaven, so that all nations are flowing unto the house of the Lord in the top of the mountains. 3. The people who receive the gospel in foreign lands joyfully say to their relatives and friends: Come ye, and let us go up to the house of the Lord, and he will teach us of his ways and we will walk in his paths.”—Roberts' *Outlines of Ecclesiastical History*, p. 409.

2. Israel a Chosen People—“The promise to Abram that he should become a great nation, has been fulfilled in his chosen seed occupying the land of Palestine, as such, for fifteen hundred years. It will again be fulfilled when they become a nation on that land forever. The history of the eastern hemisphere for the two thousand years which intervened between the calling of Abraham and the destruction of Jerusalem by the Romans, witnesses that every nation that fought against Israel, or in any way oppressed them, passed away. Time will show the same general result from the destruction of Jerusalem to the millennium. The Prophet Isaiah, speaking of the time when the Lord should favor Israel, said, 'All they that were incensed against thee shall be ashamed and confounded: they shall be as nothing; and they that strive with thee shall perish' (41:11). 'I will feed them that oppress thee with their own flesh; and they shall be drunken with their own blood' (49:26). 'I have taken out of thine hand the cup of trembling, even the dregs of the cup of my fury; thou shalt no more drink it again: but I will put it into the hand of them that afflict thee; which have said to thy soul, Bow down, that we may go over.”—*A Compendium of the Doctrines of the Gospel,* by Elders Franklin D. Richards and James A. Little, pp. 228, 229.

3. Israel Among the Nations—“When we reflect that it is thirty-two centuries since the enemies of Israel began to oppress them in the land of Canaan, that about one-third of the time they were a people in that land they were more or less in bondage to their enemies; that seven hundred years before the coming of Christ the ten tribes were scattered throughout western Asia; that we have no record that any have as yet returned to the land of their inheritance; that nearly six hundred years before Christ, the Babylonish captivity took place, and that, according to the Book of Esther, only a part of the Jews ever returned, but were scattered through the one hundred twenty-seven provinces of the Persian empire; that Asia was the hive from which swarmed the nomadic tribes who over-ran Europe; that at the destruction of Jerusalem by the Romans the Jews were scattered over the known world; we may well ask the question, Does not Israel today constitute a large proportion of the human family?”—*Compendium,* by Elders F. D. Richards and James A. Little, p. 89.

APPENDIX 19—Notes Relating to Chapter 19

1. Jerusalem—“The city has, in different ages, borne a variety of names, and even in the Bible it has several designations. Salem, mentioned in Gen. 14:18, was perhaps its name in the time of Melchizedek, and it is certainly so called in Psa. 76:2. Isaiah (29:1, 7) calls it Ariel. Jebus, or Jebusi, the city of the Jebusites, was its name in the days of Joshua and the Judges Josh. 15:8;

18:16, 28; Judges 19:10, 11), and this name continued in use till David's time (1 Chron. 11:4, 5). Some have thought that Jerusalem is itself a corruption of Jebus-Salem, but it is a theory unsupported by facts. Jerusalem is also termed 'the city of David,' 'the city of Judah,' 'the holy city,' 'the city of God' (2 Kings 14:20; 2 Chron. 25:28; Neh. 11:18; Psa. 87:3). To this day it is called el-Kuds, or 'the holy,' in most countries of the East. No city in the world has received more honorable appellations; our Savior himself called it 'the city of the great King.'"—Cassell's *Bible Dictionary*, p. 600.

The following note to the author by Elder J. M. Sjodahl is instructive: "In 1 Kings, chap. 14, there is a brief mention of a military expedition of Shishak, the king of Egypt, into Palestine during the fifth year of King Rehoboam. The Egyptian carried away the treasures of the palace and the temple, including, presumably, the 300 shields of beaten gold made by Solomon and valued in modern coin at about $1,054,880 (see Clarke's *Commentary* on 1 Kings 10:17). This expedition was placed on record in Egypt on the southern wall of the court of the temple of Amon at Karnak. One hundred and fifty-six places are there enumerated as having been looted by the Egyptians. One of these places is called *Yuteh Mark* (Smith's *Bible Dictionary* under Shishak). The Hebrew transliteration of this name is *Judah Malech,* which Champollion translates 'kingdom of Judah,' but which Dr. Birch, more correctly, recognizes as the name, or one name, of the City of Jerusalem; literally, '[The City of] the King of Judah'—Malech being the word for royalty (Comp. a paper by Prof. George Frederick Wright, Oberlin College, in *Fundamentals,* vol. 2, p. 11). In the Book of Mormon we are told that the fugitives who escaped the fate of Zedekiah and came to the western world called their first settlement here *Mulek,* which is a word identical with the *Mark* on the temple wall at Karnak in Egypt, or the Hebrew, *Malech.* The full meaning of *Mulek* is, therefore, according to the testimony of scholarship, '[The City of] the King of Judah,' already known in the records of Egypt. The fact that *Mark* and *Malech* and *Mulek* are only slight variants of one and the same word should be noted. For the word occurs in one form or another in American aboriginal languages, especially in Central and South American dialects, and they are all, in my judgment, derived from the Book of Mormon *Mulek.*"

2. **The Founding of Zion in Missouri**—" * * * A company of Saints known as the Colesville Branch—from their having lived at Colesville, Broome County, New York—had arrived in Missouri, and having received instructions to purchase the lands in the regions around about Zion, they secured a tract of land in a fertile prairie some ten or twelve miles west of Independence, in Kaw township, not far from the present location of Kansas City. On the 2nd of August [1831]—the day preceding the dedication of the temple site—in the settlement of the Colesville Saints, the first log was laid for a house as the foundation of Zion. The log was carried by twelve men, in honor of the Twelve Tribes of Israel; and Elder Sidney Rigdon consecrated and dedicated the land of Zion for the gathering of the saints."—*Outlines of Ecclesiastical History,* by Elder B. H. Roberts, p. 352.

3. **Temple Site, Independence, Jackson County, Missouri**—"Taking the road running west from the Court House for a scant half mile, you come to the summit of a crowning hill, the slope of which to the south and west is quite abrupt, but very gradual toward the north and east. * * * This is the temple site. It was upon this spot on the third day of August, 1831, that Joseph Smith, Sidney Rigdon, Edward Partridge, W. W. Phelps, Oliver Cowdery, Martin Harris, and Joseph Coe, and another person whose name I cannot learn, for there were eight in all—men in whom the Lord was well pleased, assembled to dedicate this place as the temple site in Zion. The eighty-

seventh psalm was read. Joseph [the prophet] then dedicated the spot, where is to be built a temple on which the glory of God shall rest. Yea, the great God hath so decreed it, saying: 'For, verily this generation shall not pass away until an house shall be built unto the Lord, and a cloud shall rest upon it, which cloud shall be even the glory of the Lord, which shall fill the house. * * * For the sons of Moses and also the sons of Aaron shall offer an acceptable offering and sacrifice in the house of the Lord, which house shall be built unto the Lord in this generation, upon the consecrated spot as I have appointed.'—(D&C, sec. 84:5, 31.)"—Elder B. H. Roberts, *Missouri Persecutions.* See *The House of the Lord,* by James E. Talmage, chapter 5.

APPENDIX 20—Notes Relating to Chapter 20

1. "The Anointed One"—"Christ, the official name of the Redeemer of mankind, as Jesus, or in the Hebrew, *Joshua,* 'Savior,' was His natural name. Christ means 'anointed,' from *chrio,* 'to anoint.' Under the Old Testament dispensation, high priests, kings, and prophets were appointed to their office by the pouring of the sacred oil upon their heads. The rite was performed by the recognized officer of Jehovah, and was an outward testimony that their appointment proceeded direct from God himself, as the source of all authority, and as being under the ancient covenant, in a peculiar way, the governor of his people. The oil used in the consecration of priests, and the anointing of the tabernacle and sacred vessels, was a special preparation of myrrh, cinnamon, calamus, and cassia (Exo. 30:23–25), which the Jews were forbidden to apply to the body, or to copy under pain of death. It was no doubt intended to typify the gifts and graces of the Holy Spirit." —Cassell's *Bible Dictionary,* p. 257.

2. Millennial Peace—"The wolf also shall dwell with the lamb, and the leopard shall lie down with the kid; and the calf and the young lion and the fatling together; and a little child shall lead them. And the cow and the bear shall feed; their young ones shall lie down together: and the lion shall eat straw like the ox. And the sucking child shall play on the hole of the asp, and the weaned child shall put his hand on the cockatrice' den. They shall not hurt nor destroy in all my holy mountain: for the earth shall be full of the knowledge of the Lord, as the waters cover the sea."— Isa. 11:6–9; see also 65:25.

"Through the lurid gloom of smoke and fire in which the nations have been enshrouded, amidst the awful stench of blood that has sickened the world, mankind has had reason to rejoice in the enlightening beams of comforting assurance that an era of peace is to be established. And this shall be a peace that cannot be broken, for righteousness shall rule, and man's birthright to liberty shall be inviolate. Of necessity this blessed state shall be attained only after due preparation; for in the economy of God it would be as incongruous to force upon mankind an unappreciated and undesired boon as to arbitrarily afflict with an undeserved curse."— *Vitality of "Mormonism,"* p. 176.

3. The Earth Before, During, and After the Millennium—"There are three conditions of the earth spoken of in the inspired writings,—the present, in which everything pertaining to it must go through a change which we call death; the millennial condition, in which it will be sanctified for the residence of purer intelligences, some mortal and some immortal; and the celestial condition, spoken of in the twenty-first and twenty-second chapters of Revelation, which will be one of immortality and eternal life."—*Compendium,* by Elders F. D. Richards and James A. Little, p. 186.

APPENDIX 21—Notes Relating to Chapter 21

1. Natural Phenomena Related to Human Agency—As the present author has written elsewhere: We learn from scripture that Adam's transgression brought about a fallen condition, not of mankind alone, but likewise of the earth itself. In this and in numerous other epochal events, wherein the direct interposition of divine action is affirmed, nature is seen to be in intimate relation with man.

Thus the sins of mankind may produce calamity in the form of destructive phenomena, which we may properly call natural because deserved; and human righteousness may invoke peaceful and beneficent cooperation of the elements.

"Cursed is the ground for thy sake" was the divine fiat to the first man. In contrast, note the assurance given to Israel that by faithfulness the seasons should be made propitious, that nurturing rains should come, bringing such harvests that the people would lack room to store their products (See Mal. 3: 8–12).

Abject apostasy from the laws of God in Noah's time brought about the deluge, in which "were all the fountains of the great deep broken up, and the windows [more properly flood-gates] of heaven were opened."

Enoch, who lived before Noah, was sent to proclaim repentance to the degenerate race, and so great was the power and authority vested in him that "he spake the word of the Lord, and the earth trembled, and the mountains fled, even according to his command: and the rivers of water were turned out of their course." He foresaw the coming of the Noachian flood, and the events of history, including the Savior's ministry, down to the days of the Lord's second advent, when "the heavens shall be darkened, and a veil of darkness shall cover the earth; and the heavens shall shake, and also the earth" (P.of G.P., Moses 7:61).

As a fit setting for the tragedy on Calvary, a pall of darkness fell about the place, and, when the crucified Lord expired, "the earth did quake, and the rocks rent" (Matt. 27:51).

On the western continent, widespread disruption signalized the Savior's death; and destruction befell the wicked who had flouted prophetic warnings and inspired admonitions to repentance. Many of the Nephites had forgotten the signs and wonders by which the fact of the Lord's birth had been made known, and had fallen into abominable wickedness. Then, at the time of the crucifixion, great and terrible tempests broke over the land, with thunderings, lightnings, and both elevations and depressions of the earth's crust, so that mountains were sundered, and many cities were destroyed by earthquake, fire, and the inrush of the sea. For three hours the unprecedented holocaust continued; and then thick darkness fell, in which it was found impossible to kindle a fire. The awful gloom was like unto the darkness of Egypt in that its clammy vapors could be felt. This condition lasted until the third day, so that a night a day and a night were as one unbroken night; and the impenetrable blackness was rendered the more terrible by the wailing of the people, whose heartrending refrain was everywhere the same: "O that we had repented before this great and terrible day!" Then, piercing the darkness, a Voice was heard, proclaiming that destruction had befallen the people because of wickedness, and that those who had lived to hear were the more righteous of the inhabitants, to whom hope was offered on condition of more thorough repentance and reformation (3 Nephi, chaps. 8–10).

Calamitous phenomena, before which the wicked shall fall, are definitely predicted as accompaniments of the second advent of our Lord. This is the prediction made through the prophet Joseph Smith in these days; and the fulfilment is nigh: "For not many days hence and the earth shall tremble and reel to and fro as a drunken man, and the sun shall hide his face, and shall refuse to give light; and the moon shall be bathed in blood, and the stars shall become exceedingly angry, and shall cast themselves down as a fig that falleth from off a fig-tree. And after your testimony cometh wrath and indignation upon the people. For after your testimony cometh the testimony of earthquakes, that shall cause groanings in the midst of her, and men shall fall upon the ground and shall not be able to stand. And also cometh the testimony of the voice of thunderings, and the voice of lightnings, and the voice of tempests, and the voice of the waves of the sea heaving themselves beyond their bounds. And all things shall be in commotion; and surely, men's hearts shall fail them; for fear shall come upon all people" (D&C 88:87–91).

It may be argued that the storms, earthquakes, and other destructive occurrences heretofore cited, are not natural but supernatural phenomena, specially inflicted by divine intent. Say rather that these happenings are divinely directed, following naturally and inevitably the sins of mankind and the unregenerate state of the race.

"The earth also is defiled under the inhabitants thereof; because they have transgressed the laws, changed the ordinance, broken the everlasting covenant" (Isa. 24:5).

2. Pagan Ignorance Concerning the Resurrection—In connection with the statement that human knowledge of the resurrection is based on revelation, the following is of interest: "Whatever heathen philosophers may have *guessed* as to the immortality of the soul, even admitting that this was really the result of their own speculations, and not at all due to the relics of tradition, it is certain that they never reached so far as the doctrine of a bodily resurrection. Pliny, when enumerating the things which it was not even in the power of God to do, specified these two—the endowment of mortals with an eternal existence, and the recalling of the departed from the grave (2, 100, 7). A similar opinion is enunciated by Δschylus in the 'Eumenides' (647, 648). The utmost to which they attained in their ethical speculations was a conception of the possible continuance of life, in some new forms and conditions, beyond the grave; but this was all. A resurrection in the scripture sense of the word they never imagined."—Cassell's *Bible Dictionary*, p. 936.

3. The Sadducees, when mentioned in the New Testament, are usually represented as being in opposition to the Pharisees, the two classes constituting the most influential of the sects existing among the Jews at the time of Christ. The two differed on many fundamental matters of belief and practise, including preexistence of spirits; the reality of spiritual punishment and future retribution for sin; the necessity of self-denial in individual life; the immortality of the soul; and the resurrection from the dead; in all of which the Pharisees stood for the affirmative while the Sadducees denied. Josephus says: "The doctrine of the Sadducees is that the soul and body perish together; the law is all that they are concerned to observe" (Ant. 18:1, 4). The sect consisted mainly of members of the aristocracy. Special mention of the Sadducees here is suggested by their determined opposition to the doctrine of the resurrection, which they sought to assail by arrogant assumption or to belittle by ridicule.

4. Heathen in the First Resurrection—The statement that the heathen dead will have place in the first resurrection is sustained by the word of scripture, and by a consideration of the principles of true justice according to which humanity is to be judged. Man will be accounted blameless or guilty, according to his deeds as interpreted in the light of the law under which he is required to live. It is inconsistent with our conception of a just God, to believe Him capable of inflicting condemnation upon any one for noncompliance with a requirement of which the person had no knowledge. Nevertheless, the laws of the Church will not be suspended even in the case of those who have sinned in darkness and ignorance; but it is reasonable to believe that the plan of redemption will afford such benighted ones an opportunity of learning the laws of God; and surely, as fast as they so learn, will obedience be required on pain of the penalty. Note the following passages in addition to the citations in the text:

"And if there was no law given, if men sinned what could justice do, or mercy either, for they would have no claim upon the creature?"—Alma 42:21.

"Wherefore he has given a law; and where there is no law given there is no punishment; and where there is no punishment there is no condemnation; and where there is no condemnation the mercies of the Holy One of Israel have claim upon them, because of the atonement; for they are delivered by the power of him."—2 Nephi 9:25.

"And moreover, I say unto you, that the time shall come when the knowledge of a Savior shall spread throughout every nation, kindred, tongue, and people. And behold, when that time cometh, none shall be found blameless before God, except it be little children, only through repentance and faith on the name of the Lord God Omnipotent."—Mosiah 3:20, 21. See also Helaman 15:14, 15.

5. The Intermediate State of the Soul; Paradise—The condition of the spirits of men between death and the resurrection is a subject of great interest, and one concerning which much dispute has arisen. The scriptures prove, that at the time of man's final judgment he will stand before the bar of God, clothed in his resurrected body, and this, irrespective of his condition of purity or guilt. While awaiting the time of their coming forth, disembodied spirits exist in an intermediate state, of happiness and rest or of suffering and suspense, according to their works in mortality. The prophet Alma said: "Now, concerning the state of the soul between death and the resurrection—Behold, it has been made known unto me by an angel, that the spirits of all men, as soon as they are departed from this mortal body, yea, the spirits of all men, whether they be good or evil, are taken home to that God who gave them life. And then shall it come to pass, that the spirits of those who are righteous are received into a state of happiness, which is called paradise, a state of rest, a state of peace, where they shall rest from all their troubles and from all care, and sorrow. And then shall it come to pass, that the spirits of the wicked, yea, who are evil—for behold, they have no part nor portion of the Spirit of the Lord; for behold, they chose evil works rather than good; therefore the spirit of the devil did enter into them, and take possession of their house—and these shall be cast out into outer darkness; there shall be weeping, and wailing, and gnashing of teeth, and this because of their own iniquity, being led captive by the will of the devil. Now, this is the state of the souls of the wicked; yea, in darkness, and a state of awful, fearful looking for the fiery indignation of the wrath of God upon them; thus they remain in this state, as well as the righteous in paradise, until the time of their resurrection."—Alma 40:11–14.

Reference to paradise, as a place prepared for righteous spirits while awaiting the resurrection, is made also by the first Nephi (2 Nephi 9:13), by a later prophet of the same name (4 Nephi, 14), and by Moroni (Moroni 10:34). New Testament mention supports the same (Luke 23:43; 2 Cor. 12:4; Rev. 2:7). Paradise, then, is not the place of final glory; for such the thief who died with Christ was assuredly not prepared, yet we cannot doubt the fulfilment of our Lord's promise that the penitent malefactor should be with Him in paradise that day; and, moreover, the declaration of the risen Savior to Mary Magdalene, three days later, that He had not at that time ascended to His Father, is proof of His having spent the intermediate time in paradise.

The word "paradise," by its derivation through the Greek from the Persian, signifies a pleasure ground.

APPENDIX 22—Notes Relating to Chapter 22

1. Intolerance among Christian Sects—"It must be said—though I say it with the deepest sorrow—that the cold exclusiveness of the Pharisee, the bitter ignorance of the self-styled theologian, the usurped infallibility of the half-educated religionist, have been ever the curse of Christianity. They have imposed 'the senses of men upon the words of God, the special senses of men on the general words of God;' and have tried to enforce them on all men's consciences with all kinds of burnings and anathemas under equal threats of death and damnation. And thus they incurred the terrible responsibility of presenting religion to mankind in a false and repellent guise. Is theological hatred still to be a proverb for the world's just contempt? Is such hatred—hatred in its bitterest and most ruthless form—to be regarded as the legitimate and normal outcome of the religion of love? Is the spirit of peace never to be brought to bear on religious opinions? Are such questions always to excite the most intense animosities, and the most terrible divisions? * * * Is the world to be forever confirmed in its opinion that theological partisans are less truthful, less candid, less high-minded, less honorable even than the partisans of political and social causes, who make no profession as to the duty of love? Are the so-called 'religious' champions to be forever as they now are, the most unscrupulously bitter, the most conspicuously unfair? Alas! they might be so with far less danger to the cause of religion if they would forego the luxury of 'quoting scripture for their purpose.'"—Canon Farrar, *The Early Days of Christianity*, pp. 584–585.

2. "Telestial"—The adjective "telestial" has not become current in the language; its use is at present confined to the theology of The Church of Jesus Christ of Latter-day Saints. It is applied as a distinguishing term to the lowest of the three kingdoms of glory provided for the redeemed. The only English word approaching it in form is the adjective "telestic," which is defined thus: "tending toward the end or final accomplishment; tending to accomplish a purpose."

In this connection the following note, from Elder J. M. Sjodahl to the author, may be profitably studied: "Paul speaking of the several times of resurrection (1 Cor. 15:22–25) says of the last: 'Then cometh the end, when he shall have delivered up the kingdom to God,' etc. The word translated *end* is *telos,* and the glory of those who are resurrected last may therefore properly be called *telestial,* as related to *telos.* Their resurrection is the end, the finish, the completion, of the resurrection series."

3. Toleration—"'Mormonism' offers no modified or conditional claims as to the necessity of compliance with the laws and ordinances of the gospel by every independent inhabitant of earth unto whom salvation shall come. It distinguishes not between enlightened and heathen nations, nor between men of high or low intelligence; nor even between the living and the dead. No human being who has attained years of accountability in the flesh, may hope for salvation in the kingdom of God until he has rendered obedience to the requirements of Christ, the Redeemer of the world. But while thus decisive, 'Mormonism' is not exclusive. It does not claim that all who have failed to accept and obey the gospel of eternal life shall be eternally and forever damned. While boldly asserting that The Church of Jesus Christ of Latter-day Saints is the sole repository of the Holy Priesthood as now restored to earth, it teaches and demands the fullest toleration for all individuals, and organizations of individuals, professing righteousness; and holds that each shall be rewarded for the measure of good he has wrought, to be adjudged in accordance with the spiritual knowledge he has gained. And for such high claims combined with such professions of tolerance, the Church has been accused of inconsistency. Let it not be forgotten, however, that toleration is not acceptance. * * * The bounds to the liberty of an individual are such as mark the liberty of another, or the rights of the community. God Himself treats as sacred, and therefore inviolable, the freedom of the human soul. * * * 'Mormonism' contends that no man or nation possesses the right to forcibly deprive even the heathen of his right to worship his deity. Though idolatry has been marked from the earliest ages with the seal of divine disfavor, it may represent in the benighted mind the sincerest reverence of which the person is capable. He should be taught better, but never compelled. There is no claim of universal forgiveness; no unwarranted glorification of Mercy to the degrading or neglect of justice; no thought that a single sin of omission or of commission shall fail to leave its wound or scar. In the great future there shall be found a place for every soul, whatever his grade of spiritual intelligence may be."—The author, in *The Story and Philosophy of "Mormonism,"* Salt Lake City, 1914.

APPENDIX 23—Notes Relating to Chapter 23

1. Insults to Paul and to Christ—See Acts 23:1–5. "Scarcely had the apostle uttered the first sentence of his defense, when, with disgraceful illegality, Ananias ordered the officers of the court to smite him on the mouth. Stung by an insult so flagrant, an outrage so undeserved, the naturally choleric temperament of Paul flamed into that sudden sense of anger which ought to be controlled, but which can hardly be wanting in a truly noble character. No character can be perfect which does not cherish in itself a deeply seated, though perfectly generous and forbearing, indignation against intolerable wrong. Smarting from the blow, 'God shall smite thee,' he exclaimed, 'thou whitewashed wall! What! Dost thou sit there judging me according to the law, and in violation of law biddest me to be smitten?' The language has been censured as unbecoming in its violence, and has been unfavorably compared with the meekness of Christ before the tribunal of his enemies. [See John 18:19–23.] 'Where,' asks St. Jerome, 'is that patience of the Savior, who—as a lamb led to the slaughter opens not his mouth—so gently asks the smiter, "If I have spoken evil, bear witness to the evil; but if well, why smitest thou me?" We are not detracting from the apostle, but declaring the glory of God, who, suffering in the flesh, reigns above the wrong and frailty of the flesh.' Yet we need not remind the reader that not once or twice only did Christ give the rein to righteous anger, and blight hypocrisy and insolence with a flash of holy wrath. The bystanders seemed to have been startled by the boldness of St. Paul's rebuke, for they said to him, 'Dost thou revile the high priest of God?' The apostle's anger had expended itself in that one outburst, and he instantly apologized with exquisite urbanity and self-control. 'I did not know,' he said, 'brethren, that he is the high priest'; adding that, had he known this, he would not have addressed to him the opprobrious name of 'whited wall,' because he reverenced and acted upon the rule of scripture, 'Thou shalt not speak ill of a ruler of thy people.—Farrar, *The Life and Work of St. Paul,* pp. 539–540.

2. Peter's Teachings Regarding Submission to Law—A special "duty of Christians in those days was due respect in all things lawful, to the civil government. * * * Occasions there are—and none knew this better than an apostle who had himself set an example of splendid disobedience to unwarranted commands [Acts 4:18, 31; 5:28–32; 40–42]—when 'we must obey God rather than men.' But those occasions are exceptional to the common rule of life. Normally, and as a whole, human law is on the side of divine order, and, by whomsoever administered, has a just claim to obedience and respect. It was a lesson so deeply needed by the Christians of the day that it is taught as emphatically by St. John and by St. Peter, as by St. Paul himself. It was more than ever needed at a time when dangerous revolts were gathering to a head in Judea; when the hearts of Jews throughout the world were burning with a fierce flame of hatred against the abominations of a tyrannous idolatry; when Christians were being charged with 'turning the world upside-down' [Acts 17:6]; when some poor Christian slave, led to martyrdom or put to the torture, might easily relieve the tension of his soul by bursting into apocalyptic denunciations of sudden doom against the crimes of the mystic Babylon; when the heathen, in their impatient contempt, might wilfully interpret a prophecy of the final conflagration as though it were a revolutionary and incendiary threat; and when Christians at Rome were, on this very account, already suffering the agonies of the Neronian persecution. Submission, therefore, was at this time a primary duty of all who wished to win over the heathen, and to save the Church from being overwhelmed in some outburst of indignation which would be justified even to reasonable and tolerant pagans as a political necessity. * * * 'Submit, therefore,' the apostle says, 'to every human ordinance, for the Lord's sake, whether to the emperor as supreme [the name "king" was freely used of the emperor in the provinces], or to governors, as missioned by him for punishment of malefactors and praise to well-doers; for this is the will of God, that by your well-doing ye should gag the stolid ignorance of foolish persons; as free, yet not using your freedom for a cloak of baseness, but as slaves of God. 'Honor all men' as a principle; and as your habitual practice, 'love the brotherhood. Fear God. Honor the King." [See 1 Peter 2:13–17.]—Farrar, *Early Days of Christianity*, pp. 89, 90.

3. Obedience to Secular Law—"Religion is essentially a matter of everyday life. It has as much to do with the adjustment of the individual to his material environment as with his abstract belief in matters spiritual. A man's religion should be a concrete demonstration of his conceptions concerning God and the divine purposes respecting himself and his fellows. Anything less lacks both the form of godliness and the power thereof.

"The Master associated love for God with love for fellowman; and surely love comprises duty, and duty means effort and action. See Matt. 22:35–40. A very large part of the course of education provided in the school of mortality is attained through association with our kind and the righteous observance of duty in community life. We are not here to be recluses nor to hold ourselves aloof from public service, but to live in a state of mutual helpfulness and effective cooperation.

"It is a fundamental necessity that laws shall be established among men for general governance; and obedience to law is the obvious duty of every member of organized society. Violation of the law, therefore, is not only a secular offense, but a transgression of the principles of true religion. This world would be a happier one if men carried more religion into their daily affairs—into business, politics, and statesmanship. Mark you, I say *religion*, not *church*. Under existing conditions it is imperative that State and Church be kept separate; and this segregation must be maintained until the inauguration of Christ's personal reign.

"Loyal citizenship is at once a characteristic and a test of a man's religion; and as to the incumbent duties of citizenship, the voice of the people, as expressed through the established channels of government, must determine."—The author, in *Vitality of "Mormonism,"* p. 186.

4. Discontinuance of Plural Marriage—The official act terminating the practise of plural marriage among the Latter-day Saints was the adoption by the Church, in conference assembled, of a manifesto proclaimed by the President of the Church. The language of the document illustrates the law-abiding character of the people and the Church, as is shown by the following clause: "Inasmuch as laws have been enacted by Congress forbidding plural marriages, which laws have been pronounced constitutional by the court of last resort, I [President Wilford Woodruff) hereby declare my intention to submit to those laws, and to use my influence with the members of the Church over which I preside to have them do likewise." In the course of a sermon immediately following the proclaiming of the manifesto, President Woodruff said regarding the action taken: "I have done my duty, and the nation of which we form a part must be responsible for that which has been done in relation to that principle" (i.e., plural marriage). See D&C, pp. 256, 257.

5. A Striking Instance of Submission to Secular Authority—"Governments are instituted of God, sometimes by his direct interposition, sometimes by His permission. When the Jews had been brought into subjection by Nebuchadnezzar, king of Babylon, the Lord commanded through the prophet Jeremiah (27:4–8) that the people render obedience to their conqueror, whom He called His servant; for verily the Lord had used the pagan king to chastise the recreant and unfaithful children of the covenant. The obedience so enjoined included the payment of taxes and extended to complete submission." See *Jesus the Christ*, p. 564, Note 2.

APPENDIX 24—Notes Relating to Chapter 24

1. Love, the Fulfilling of the Law—"Peter says, 'Above all things have fervent love [charity] among yourselves' [1 Peter 4:8]. *Above all things.* And John goes farther, 'God is love' [1 John 4:8]. And you remember the profound remark which Paul makes elsewhere, 'Love is the fulfilling of the law' [Rom. 13:10; Gal. 5:14]. Did you ever think what he meant by that? In those days men were working their passage to heaven by keeping the ten commandments, and the hundred and ten other commandments which they had manufactured out of them. Christ said, I will show you a more simple way. If you do one thing, you will do these hundred and ten things without ever thinking about them. If you love, you will unconsciously fulfil the whole law. * * * Take any of the commandments, 'Thou shalt have no other gods before me.' If a man love God you will not require to tell him that. Love is the fulfilling of that law. 'Take not his name in vain.' Would he ever dream of taking his name in vain if he loved him? 'Remember the Sabbath day to keep it holy.' Would he not be too glad to have one day in seven to dedicate more exclusively to the object of his affection? Love would fulfil all these laws regarding God. And so if he loved man, you would never think of telling him to honor his father and mother. He could never do anything else. It would be preposterous to tell him not to kill. You could only insult him if you suggested that he should not steal,—how could he steal from those he loved? It would be superfluous to beg him not to bear false witness against his neighbor. If he loved him it would be the last thing he would do. And you would never dream of urging him not to covet what his neighbors had. He would rather they possessed it than himself. In this way 'Love is the fulfilling of the law.'"—Drummond: *The Greatest Thing in the World.*

2. Charity and Love "According to the etymology and original usage, *beneficence* is the doing well, *benevolence* the wishing or willing well to others; but *benevolence* has come to include *benef-*

icence and to displace it. * * * *Charity*, which originally meant the purest love for God and man (as in 1 Cor., chap. 13), is now almost universally applied to some form of *alms-giving* and is much more limited in meaning than *benevolence.*"—*Standard Dictionary*.

Charity means "properly, love, and hence acts of kindness. The word never occurs in the Old Testament; in the New Testament it is always, with one exception, synonymous with love, and in every case the love of man toward his fellow man, and to that which is good (see especially 1 Cor., chap. 13). The 'feasts of charity' in Jude 12, are commonly understood to be the *agapæ*, or 'love-feasts,' which were prevalent in the early church, and which consisted in a simple fraternal meeting for worship, and an equally simple social repast." *Bible Dictionary*, Cassell.

3. The Lord's Tenth—As of old, so in this day, the tithe is the Lord's and therefore is holy. Tithing funds or properties of any kind paid as tithes are not to be administered by unappointed hands. The priests of ancient Israel were charged with this sacred duty; and in the present dispensation the same order prevails. Responsibility for the handling of the tithes is placed upon the bishops today, and they, thus officiating, act in their capacity as presiding officers over the Aaronic Priesthood. Again, as of old, so now, the tithes are to be paid at the places appointed and to the duly ordained and commissioned receivers. Today the Bishop of the Church, who is known as the Presiding Bishop, is assisted by many ward bishops, and to these as representatives of and assistants to the Presiding Bishop, the tithing is to be paid and is to be by them forwarded to the office of the Presiding Bishop. The order of the Church as at present constituted provides that the several bishops may convert into cash the produce paid as tithing in kind, and deliver the proceeds to the Presiding Bishop.

It is an interesting fact that during recent years, particularly during the two decades last past, attempts have been made by many sects and denominations to revive the ancient practise of the tithe. Churches are organizing from among their members societies or clubs of "tithers," who voluntarily pledge themselves to pay to their respective churches a tenth of their individual incomes. Among some of these societies the tithers are permitted to indicate the purpose to which their contributions shall be applied. The great difficulty which our sectarian friends find in reestablishing the practise of the tithe amongst their numerous sects is—and they realize it in part—that they have no priests nor Levites amongst them authorized to receive the tithe and administer it strictly in accordance with divine command. The authority of the Holy Priesthood is essential to the regulation of the tithing system of the Lord. Tithing is the Lord's revenue system, and He requires it of the people, not because He is lacking in gold or silver, but because they need to pay it.

Tithe-paying must be a voluntary, free-will sacrifice, not to be exacted by secular power, nor enforced by infliction of fine or other material penalties. While in one sense the obligation is self-assumed, it is nevertheless one to be observed with full purpose of heart by the earner who claims standing in the Church and who professes to abide by the revealed word given for the spiritual development of its members.

It is essential that men learn to give. Without provision for this training the curriculum in the school of mortality would be seriously defective. Human wisdom has failed to devise a more equitable means of individual contribution for community needs than the simple plan of the tithe. Every one is to give in the amount proportionate to his income, and to so give regularly and systematically. The spirit of giving makes the tithe holy; and it is by means thus sanctified that the material activities of the Church are carried on. Blessings, specific and choice, are placed within the reach of all. In the Lord's work, the widow's penny is as acceptable as the gold piece of the millionaire.

The Latter-day Saints believe that the tithing system has been divinely appointed for their observance; and they esteem themselves blessed with thus being permitted to have part in the furtherance of God's purposes. Under this system the people have prospered severally and as an organized body. It is the simple and effective revenue law of the Church; and its operation has been a success from the time of its establishment. Amongst us it obviates the necessity of taking up collections in religious assemblies, and makes possible the promulgation of the Church's message through the printed and spoken word, the building and maintenance of Temples for the benefit of both the living and the dead, and phases of service to mankind too numerous to mention.

There is an important distinction between tithes and other offerings. While the observance of the tithing law must be willing and voluntary, tithe-paying is nevertheless required, demanded in fact, by the Lord of those who, by their own free will, have become His covenant children by baptism.

A great and all too common mistake is that we consider the paying of tithes as the giving of a gift unto the Lord. This does not express the whole truth. Provision is made for free-will offerings as any man may choose to make; and if he offers with pure purpose of heart and is himself an approved giver, his gift shall be accepted and be counted unto him for righteousness; but such is not the tithe; the tithe is rather a debt than a gift.

As the matter presents itself to my mind, it is as though there had been a contract made between myself and the Lord, and that in effect He had said to me—You have need of many things in this world—food, clothing, and shelter for your family and yourself, the common comforts of life, and the things that shall be conducive to refinement, to development, to righteous enjoyment. You desire material possessions to use for the assistance of others, and thereby gain greater blessings for yourself and yours. Now, you shall have the means of acquiring these things; but remember they are mine, and I require of you the payment of a rental upon that which I give into your hands. However, your life will not be one of uniform increase in substance and possessions; you will have your losses, as well as your gains; you will have your periods of trouble as well as your times of peace. Some years will be years of plenty unto you, and others will be years of scarcity. And now, instead of doing as mortal landlords do—require you to contract with them to pay in advance, whatever your fortunes or your prospects may be—you shall pay me not in advance, but when you have received; and you shall pay me in accordance with what you receive. If it so be that in one year your income is abundant, then you can afford to pay me a little more; and if it be so that the next year is one of distress and your income is not what it was, then you shall pay me less; and should it be that you are reduced to the utmost penury so that you have nothing coming in you will pay me nothing.

Have you ever found a landlord of earth who was willing to make that kind of a contract with you? When I consider the liberality of it all, and the consideration that my Lord has had for me, I feel in my heart that I could scarcely raise my countenance to His heaven above if I tried to defraud Him out of that just rental.

Consider further how therein and thereby He has provided that even the humblest may receive abundantly of the blessings of His house. The wealth of heaven is not reserved for the rich people of earth; even the poorest may be a stockholder in the great corporation of our God, organized for the carrying on of His purposes, in spreading the Gospel, in the building of Temples and other houses of worship to His name, and in doing good to all mankind. * * *

After all, the prime or great purpose behind the establishment of the law of the tithe is the development of the soul of the tithe-payer, rather than the providing of revenue. The latter is an all-important purpose, for so far as money is needed for the carrying on of the work of the Church the Lord requires money that is sanctified by the faith of the giver; but blessings beyond estimate, as gaged by the coin of the realm, are assured unto him who strictly conforms to the law of the tithe because the Lord hath so commanded.—From *The Lord's Tenth*, by the author, published by Presiding Bishopric, Salt Lake City, 1923.

4. Man's Relationship to God—"'Mormonism' claims an actual and literal relationship of parent and child between the Creator and man—not in the figurative sense in which the engine may be called the child of its builder; not the relationship of a thing mechanically made to the maker thereof; but the connection between father and offspring. In short it is bold enough to declare that man's spirit being the offspring of Deity, and man's body though of earthy components yet being in the very image and likeness of God, man even in his present degraded—aye, fallen condition—still possesses, if only in a latent state, inherited traits, tendencies and powers that tell of his more than royal descent; and that these may be developed so as to make him, even while mortal, in a measure Godlike.

"But 'Mormonism' is bolder yet. It asserts that in accordance with the inviolable law of organic nature—that like shall beget like, and that multiplication of numbers and perpetuation of species shall be in compliance with the condition 'each after his kind,' the child may achieve the former status of the parent, and that in his mortal condition man is a God in embryo. However far in the future it may be, what ages may elapse, what eternities may pass before any individual now a mortal being may attain the rank and sanctity of godship, nevertheless man carries in his soul the possibilities of such achievement; even as the crawling caterpillar or the corpse-like chrysalis holds the latent possibility, nay, barring destruction in an earlier stage, the certainty indeed, of the winged imago in all the glory of maturity.

"'Mormonism' claims that all nature, both on earth and in heaven, operates on a plan of advancement; that the very Eternal Father is a progressive Being; that his perfection, while so complete as to be incomprehensible by man, possesses this essential quality of true perfection—the capacity of eternal increase. That therefore, in the far future, beyond the horizon of eternities perchance, man may attain the status of a God. Yet this does not mean that he shall be then the equal of the Deity we worship, nor that he shall ever overtake those intelligences that are already beyond him in advancement; for to assert such would be to argue that there is no progression beyond a certain stage of attainment, and that advancement is a characteristic of low organization and inferior purpose alone. We believe that there was more than the sounding of brass or the tinkling of wordy cymbals in the fervent admonition of the Christ to his followers—'Be ye therefore perfect, even as your Father which is in heaven is perfect.'"—*The Philosophy of "Mormonism,"* pp. 108–110; the author, in *The Story and Philosophy of "Mormonism,"* Salt Lake City, 1920.

ARTWORK

INDEX

Elias, appearance to Joseph Smith and Oliver Cowdery 12; committing the dispensation of the gospel of Abraham to Joseph and Oliver 12

Elijah the Prophet, appearing to Joseph Smith and Oliver Cowdery 9

Evangelist, see Patriarch

Eve, knowledge of God 18; tempted by Satan 38

exaltation, different from salvation 54

existence, eternal nature of 20

Ezekiel, prophesy concerning the Book of Mormon 10

Faith, compared to works 65; conditions of 64; definition of 59–61; different than belief or knowledge 59–61; examples of 21, 22, 63; foundation of 61; importance of 64, 65; nature of 59; necessity of 60; power of 62, 63

Fall of Adam, inevitability of 39; necessity of 39; result of 39

family, importance of 94, 95

fast offerings, definition of 284

First Presidency, duties of 135

foreordination, definition of 121

gifts (spiritual), defined 14; Holy Ghost 99, 105; imitations of 149; importance of 141; list of 144, 145–48; modern-day 149, 150; nature of 142; purpose of 143

God, appearances of 21, 22; attributes of 24, 25, 34; corporal nature of 22; defined by the Church of England 27; existence of 17; existence proven by nature 19; historical record of 18; knowledge of 18; not the same as nature 20; punishment of 35, 36

Godhead, attributes of 24–26; definition of 22; Holy Ghost a member of 100; personality of each member 23; sectarian view of 26; unity of 23

Gold Plates, description of 169; see also Book of Mormon

Gospel, comprehensive nature of 282; daily living 281, 282; preached to the dead 92, 93; withheld from many 91

Great Apostasy, see Church, apostasy

healing, definition of the gift of 145

High Priest, duties of 134

Holy Ghost, attributes of 100, 101; bestowed after baptism 103; confusion concerning 101; evidences of 100; gift of 99, 102, 104; gift of God 99, 105; Godhead, member of 100; method of bestowal 104; mission of 102, 105; necessity of 99; other names of 100; power of 100; promise of 99; requirements to receive 102, 103

idolatry, prevalence of 25

infant baptism, an abomination 78, 79

inspiration, definition of 191, 192

Israel, Biblical prophecies of 205, 206, 214, 215; Book of Mormon prophecies concerning 206, 207, 215–17; covenant people 219; definition of 203, 204; dispersion, prophecies of 204, 205; gathering of 10, 213, 218; latter-day revelation concerning 217, 218; prophecies of already fulfilled 207–09; Ten Tribes 209, 219, 220

Jaredites, history of 168, 169

Jerusalem (New), site of Zion 226, 227

John the Baptist, ordaining Joseph Smith and Oliver Cowdery 11

John the Revelator, Book of Mormon prophecy concerning 9

judgment of God 33

kingdoms of glory, differences between 266; see also Celestial Glory, Terrestrial Glory, Telestial Glory

knowledge, different than faith 59–61; importance of 38; not sufficient for salvation 60–61

Lost Tribes of Israel 209

Man, accountability of 263, 264; creation of 37

marriage, necessity of 288, 289

Melchizedek Priesthood, naming of 133; see also Priesthood

Millennium, death, end of 247; description of 239–41

Miracles, definition of 143; examples of 143, 144; nature of 142; testimony of 148, 149

Moroni: appearing to Joseph Smith 7, 165, 166

Moses, appearing to Joseph Smith and Oliver Cowdery 10; authority over the gathering of Israel 10, 218; God appearing to 19, 21

Mutual Improvement Association, definition of 137

Nephi, prophecies of the Book of Mormon 10; prophecies of Christ 50

New Jerusalem 10

New Testament, authenticity of 158; origin of 158; parts of 159; see also Bible, Old Testament

Nicene Creed, description of 26, 27

Noah, knowledge of God 18

obedience, necessity of 53; see also civil law, examles of obedience to